Lonely Planet Publications
Melbourne | Oakland | London | Paris

KT-558-871

Mara Vorhees

Washington DC

The Top Five

1 Smithsonian Institution
There's a museum here to suit everyone (p47)

2 Capitol
A spectacular symbol of democracy (p63)

3 Georgetown
A neighborhood with antebellum architecture and ambience (p72)

4 Rock Creek Park
Hiking and biking in a woodsy setting in the city (p94)

5 Supreme Court
See justice (and the justices) at work (p65)

Contents

Published by Lonely Planet Publications Pty Ltd
ABN 36 005 607 983

Australia Head Office, Locked Bag 1, Footscray,
Victoria 3011, ☎ 03 8379 8000, fax 03 8379 8111,
talk2us@lonelyplanet.com.au

USA 150 Linden St, Oakland, CA 94607,
☎ 510 893 8555, toll free 800 275 8555,
fax 510 893 8572, info@lonelyplanet.com

UK 72–82 Rosebery Ave, Clerkenwell, London,
EC1R 4RW, ☎ 020 7841 9000, fax 020 7841 9001,
go@lonelyplanet.co.uk

France 1 rue du Dahomey, 75011 Paris,
☎ 01 55 25 33 00, fax 01 55 25 33 01,
bip@lonelyplanet.fr, www.lonelyplanet.fr

The Authors

MARA VORHEES

Born and raised in St Clair Shores, Michigan, Mara set out for the big city at the age of 18. But not just any old big city – the nation's capital, where she could do good deeds to her heart's delight. At Jesuit Georgetown University, she gave up Catholicism, became a socialist, learned Russian, had an affair with her professor and graduated with a degree from the acclaimed School of Foreign Service.

Thus armed, Mara entered the field of international development, committed to making the world a better place. She spent two years chasing contracts for a Beltway bandit. Frustrated by her inability to change the world from the basement of a Georgetown row house, she took an assignment in the field. But not just any field – Mother Russia, where she could finally do a good deed. In a gritty Urals town, she fought a losing battle with the tax police and gave up socialism.

The pen-wielding traveler has since resorted to seeing and saving the world by other means, working on a variety of Lonely Planet titles before returning to Washington DC for this book. When not cruising capital cities, she resides in Somerville, Massachusetts with her professor and her cat.

CONTRIBUTORS
MARK H FURSTENBERG

Before turning a life-long baking hobby into a profession, Mark H Furstenberg worked as a writer for ABC News and the *Washington Post*. He began his career working in the Kennedy White House on the War on Poverty. In July 1990, Furstenberg introduced high-quality traditional breads to Washington when he opened his first bakery, Marvelous Market. In 1997, he opened the BreadLine, a fast-food restaurant that makes bread-based foods traditional in many cultures. The BreadLine has been one of the *Washington Post*'s 50 favorite restaurants and one of America's top restaurants, according to the Zagat guide. Mark wrote the boxed text 'State of the Kitchen,' (p14).

PHOTOGRAPHER
DAN HERRICK

Dan Herrick got his start in photography on a six-month trip through Europe before attending university. Since then he's covered the spectrum of stories, from the Chiapas uprising in Mexico to movie premieres at home in New York City. In Washington DC he interacted with great people. Climbers at Carderock offered him a hand. An old taxi driver gave an informal tour of Shaw. Jazz musicians shared the lowdown on their favorite clubs and venues. The ethnic food eateries in Adams-Morgan were top notch.

Introducing Washington DC

Equality. Justice. Life, Liberty and the pursuit of Happiness. A more perfect Union. These are the ideals on which Washington DC was built. And although it is a relatively new city – just over 200 years old – the ideals are timeless, harkening back to republican Rome and ancient Greece.

Washington DC hits you in the face with it: the scale and grandeur of the National Mall is the architectural embodiment of Liberty and Justice for All. The Washington Monument, proud and straight, towers over the city like the stoic first president himself. The glistening US Capitol dome is capped by the statue Freedom. (By federal law, no new structure can rise above Freedom.) The Declaration of Independence and the Constitution – guarantors of the Blessings of Liberty – are enshrined in the temple-like National Archives building. At the opposite end of the Mall, the marble-columned Lincoln Memorial venerates the preserver of the Union. The moving war memorials and the solemn Arlington National Cemetery honor the men and women who made the ultimate sacrifice.

These are the symbols of a national ideology, the iconography of America. And like pilgrims on the hajj, Americans journey to the capital to pay tribute – to the war dead, to the founding fathers and to the ideals that inspired them.

The actual implementation of democracy is less inspirational. It requires selling ideas, fighting for rights and making deals. The capital serves as the national soapbox, battleground and negotiation table. As such, Washington DC is the capital of the free world – and free lunch, if you're a member of Congress. Indeed, the city beats to the pulse of politics, attracting power brokers and favor seekers, lawyers and lobbyists, good deed–doers and good dry-cleaners. (Somebody has to clean all those suits.) It is a city of people who want to make a difference, from the student intern stuffing envelopes to the PhD expert dispensing policy advice.

With all the comedy and tragedy that politics entails, it's easy to forget the other side of DC, where the federal government and its machinery are merely backdrops to life, not the main-stage drama. This is the city where people – ordinary and extraordinary – live, work and play.

Sixty percent of them are black. Formerly a capital of the slave trade, and later a beacon to freed slaves heading north, today's Washington DC is a hub of African American culture. Trends of the 1920s – like New

---

Essential DC

Dumbarton Oaks (p74) Gorgeous gardens and a curious collection of art.

Eastern Market (p64) Crab-cake sandwiches, Mongolian artwork, refinished antiques, cut flowers.

National Zoological Park (p85) From big cats to hanging bats.

Politics & Prose Bookstore (p187) Browsing the books and sipping cappuccinos.

Rock Creek Park (p94) Bike riding on the weekend, when cars are taboo.

Lowdown

Population 572,000.

Time zone Eastern Standard Time (GMT - 5 hours).

3-star room Around $100.

Coffee $3.

Essential drink Martini ($6).

Metro fare $1.20.

Negro and Black Broadway – are being revived in tantalizing, new forms in the streets around Howard University. Music is in the air. But the echoes of the injustices of the past can still be heard in the present, when 20% of the population lives below the poverty line. Those handsome brownstones on U St still have bars on their windows.

DC is – at heart – a Southern town. These roots are revealed in spring, when the city is awash in the fragrance of dogwood and honeysuckle. April and May are standout times to visit DC, especially if your visit coincides with the blooming of the cherry blossoms. It is an active town, where bureaucrats spend their lunch hours jogging along the Potomac. It is an international town, where world music wafts from open windows. It is a trendy town, where sidewalks are paved with decaf latte and low-fat biscotti.

It is a town of contrasts, where the poignancy of Calder's mobiles dangling in the atrium of the National Gallery of Art is matched only by that of somebody's basketball shoes dangling from a telephone wire in Anacostia. It is an educational town, a living civics lesson, and arguably the best field trip in America. But most of all, Washington DC is a patriotic town where people come to play their part – whether as petitioner or protester or president.

MARA'S TOP DC DAY

It's Saturday and I wake up in **Georgetown** (p72). I start the day with a bike ride along the Potomac and a loop around the **Lincoln Memorial** (p45). I'm starting to feel hunger pangs, so instead of heading home, I ride up Independence Ave to **Eastern Market** (p64) for some famous blue-bucks (blueberry-buckwheat pancakes) and a large coffee. After breakfast, I wander around Eastern Market examining the arty merchandise, and look across the street for a bargain at the flea market. Sampling the juicy fruits along the way, I pick out a few items of fresh produce for dinner and toss them in my backpack. Then I ride back down Independence Ave toward the **Capitol** (p63), and cut across the Mall to the **National Gallery of Art** (p49) to check out Georgia O'Keeffe's 'jack-in-the-pulpit'series. I'm far too tired to ride home, so I catch the Metro to Dupont Circle, arriving just in time for a late-afternoon snack and an extended browse at **Kramerbooks** (p182). I ride home to recuperate, before heading back out on the town in **Adams-Morgan** (p79). I meet friends at **Tryst** (p153) for an aperitif, then head to **Habana Village** (p164) for a night of salsa and merengue.

City Life

City Life

WASHINGTON DC TODAY

Washington DC is discovering that there is more to this city than the federal government. Downtown – once a network of desolate streets and edgy clubs set in empty warehouses – becomes the target of a localized revitalization program. Shaw – once devastated by racial tension and riots – is a destination for African heritage tours. Even Brookland – an Upper Northeast 'hood until recently unknown to many DC residents – is suddenly the city's hottest real-estate market. Neighborhoods from downtown to Georgetown are enjoying the fruits of revitalization efforts that celebrate their quirky characters.

Revitalization means hip restaurants and clubs and valuable community services. It means renovatio of buildings and influx of new residents. It means increasing property values and rising rents. And inevitably, it means forcing out less affluent, longtime residents who can no longer afford to stay. In DC, this conflict invariably comes down to race: well-to-do whites are scooping up property in places like Shaw and Logan Circle, while poorer blacks are moving out.

The good news is that these neighborhoods look terrific. Downtown, the streets are busting with restaurants, theatres and galleries, capped by the huge new convention center. Shaw is just a few years behind. Its development is unique, however: the 'New U' remembers its days as Black Broadway and is drawing on that history.

U St is hands down the hottest place to hear live music in DC today. It has long been the site of cutting-edge rock venues like the **9:30 Club** (p158) and **Black Cat** (p159). But now you can also hear jazz and the infectious local style, go-go, in the same historic clubs where Duke Ellington and Pearl Bailey played. DC's music scene is about the rediscovery and rebirth of its roots – blending blues and jazz and go-go with modern urban sounds like hip-hop and house.

DC is also feeling the effects of African, Asian and Latin influxes. Global culture is all the rage. DC can't get enough of salsa music, woven tapestries, Mediterranean meze and

Lincoln Memorial (p45)

minty *mojitos*. The immigrant community rises to the occasion, opening bistros, bodegas, spice shops, foreign bookstores and world-music clubs.

Meanwhile, back on the National Mall, the federal government has its own revitalization program underway, with the renovation of old museums (National Museum of American Art and National Portrait Gallery) and the opening of new ones (National Museum of the American Indian). The sparkling, new National World War II Memorial glorifies national unity at a time when that commodity is much in demand.

The attacks of September 11, 2001 affected the nation's capital in an infinite number of ways – ways we can't fathom, and ways that are frightening and in-your-face – like the countless ongoing construction projects to improve security and keep out the bad guys. The White House is no longer open for daily public tours, but the nearby visitors center shows a video. The US Capitol building no longer allows the public to wander freely, but soon – in 2005 – a visitors center will exhibit photographs. Weary walkers can no longer sit and rest on the grass in the shade of the Washington Monument. The phallic structure itself is still open for city views, but the vast grassy expanse around it is surrounded on all sides by cement barricades. (They have become ubiquitous in this city.) What will happen at the Washington Monument is the subject of a heated debate. Security freaks want to keep the park enclosed, allowing access to the monument through a 500ft tunnel, which would contain – you guessed it – a visitors center.

The devastation of 9-11 is deep in DC, where many residents were touched personally, and many more became suddenly aware of the danger of living in the capital. But this city is resilient. After the British attack of 1814, nearly all of the public buildings were burned to the ground, but DC recovered. After the riots of 1968, entire neighborhoods were devastated and their populations fled, but DC recovered. And so, now, DC is recovering, generating goals and growth along the way.

Hot Conversation Topics

Here is some scuttlebutt that you might overhear while sipping martinis in a DC lounge:

- Did you hear if Mei Xiang the giant panda is pregnant?
- When are they going to build a memorial to the veterans of the War of 1812?
- Will DC get a Major League baseball team again?
- Do you have a recipe for *caipirinhas* that I can serve at my tapas party?
- I live in Virginia – why should I have to pay DC taxes?
- Will the kids be allowed to fly kites next to the Washington Monument this year?
- Don't you think this town needs another martini lounge?

CITY CALENDAR

Washington DC's calendar is packed with events, highlights being the Cherry Blossom Festival and the Smithsonian Folklife Festival. DC also gets fired up for the nation's birthday, celebrating Independence Day with free concerts and fireworks.

On national holidays, banks, schools, government offices and some attractions close; transportation runs on a Sunday schedule. For additional events information, contact the Washington DC Convention & Tourism Co (☎ 202-789-7000; www.washington.org).

JANUARY

Winter is mild, with temperatures in the 30s. Every four years (or eight if the US people are forgiving), it's the ultimate social-political event: Inauguration Day.

FEBRUARY

For Black History Month the **Smithsonian** (p47) organizes an incredible educational program.

CHINESE NEW YEAR

Chinatown lights up with dancing and firecrackers. A giant dragon leads a parade through the downtown streets.

MARCH

Spring arrives (temperatures from 40° to 55° F); prepare for festival and parade season. The Cherry Blossom Festival takes place in late March or early April.

ST PATRICK'S DAY

☎ 202-637-2474; www.dcstpatsparade.com
On March 17, DC's Irish and wannabes whoop it up at a parade down Constitution Ave.

SMITHSONIAN KITE FESTIVAL
☎ 202-357-2700; www.kitefestival.org
On the last Saturday of March, the skies near the Washington Monument come alive with colors.

NATIONAL CHERRY BLOSSOM FESTIVAL
☎ 202-728-1137;
www.nationalcherryblossomfestival.org
This two-week arts and culture fest celebrates the blooming of DC's cherry trees and culminates in a parade extravaganza (p72).

CHERRY BLOSSOM 10-MILE RUN
☎ 301-320-3350; www.cherryblossom.org
Thousands of racers run around the Tidal Basin and along the Potomac for cash prizes (or just for fun).

APRIL
Weather goes from fine to fabulous (temperatures between 50° and 66° F), making April one of the loveliest months in DC. Easter Sunday usually occurs in April.

WHITE HOUSE EASTER EGG ROLL
www.whitehouse.gov/easter; 1600 Pennsylvania Ave
On the Monday after Easter, kids aged three to six are invited to the South Lawn for stories, games and colorful characters (besides your typical politicians).

SMITHSONIAN CRAFT SHOW
☎ 202-357-4000; www.si.edu/craftshow; 401 F St NW, National Building Museum
In mid-April, leading American potters, furniture makers, metalsmiths, glass, paper and textile artists, and jewelry creators display and sell their work.

SHAKESPEARE'S BIRTHDAY
☎ 202-544-4600; www.folger.edu; 201 E Capitol St
On April 23, the Folger Shakespeare Library & Theatre (p64) celebrates the Bard's birthday with jugglers and jesters, music, song and dance.

FILMFEST DC
☎ 202-724-6578; www.filmfestdc.org
Shown at venues around the city, this festival features cutting-edge films by national and international directors.

MAY
May in DC is truly delightful: temperatures range from 60° to 75° F, and tourist season swings into high gear. Memorial Day – the last Monday – honors the war dead and marks the start of summer.

GAY BLACK PRIDE
☎ 202-667-8188
The nation's largest annual Gay Black Pride celebration takes place on Memorial Day weekend and draws participants from across the country.

ROLLING THUNDER RIDE FOR FREEDOM
☎ 908-369-5439; www.rollingthunder1.com
The Harley-Davidson contingent of Vietnam Vets commemorates Memorial Day with a ride on the National Mall to draw attention to the POWs and MIAs who were left behind.

JUNE
Things heat up, as temperatures climb into the 70s and 80s. Summer tourist season is in full swing – arrive early and be prepared to stand in line.

CAPITAL PRIDE
☎ 202-797-3510; www.capitalpride.org
DC's version of the international gay pride holiday draws thousands of marchers to the Mall; many bars and clubs host special events.

SMITHSONIAN FOLKLIFE FESTIVAL
☎ 202-275-1119; www.folklife.si.edu
For 10 days before Independence Day, this extravaganza celebrates international and US cultures on the Mall lawns in front of the Smithsonian Castle (p47).

JULY & AUGUST
Hot town, summer in the city. Expect temperatures in the 80s and drippy, sweaty humidity. Congress shuts down and locals retreat to the beach.

INDEPENDENCE DAY
July 4 commemorates the adoption of the Declaration of Independence in 1776. Huge crowds gather on the National Mall to watch fireworks, listen to free concerts and picnic in the sunshine. The Declaration is read from the National Archives' steps.

SEPTEMBER

Life returns to DC after Labor Day (the first Monday in September), the unofficial end of summer. From mid-September to mid-October, cultural events occur in honor of Hispanic Heritage Month.

DC BLUES FESTIVAL
☎ 301-926-1336; www.dcblues.org
In late August or early September, the all-volunteer DC Blues Society sponsors a free, day-long festival of top local blues acts at Rock Creek Park's **Carter Barron Amphitheater** (p155).

ADAMS MORGAN FESTIVAL
www.adamsmorganday.org
DC's biggest neighborhood festival takes over 18th St NW on the weekend after Labor Day with live music, vendors and food stalls.

OCTOBER

Autumn brings colorful leaves and wonderful weather for outdoor activities. Look for temperatures ranging from 60° to 70° F and clear blue skies.

MARINE CORPS MARATHON
☎ 703-784-2225; www.marinemarathon.com
Known as the people's marathon, this popular road race starts and ends at the Iwo Jima Memorial on the last Sunday in October.

DRAG RACE
On October 31, Halloween is celebrated unofficially, including the fiercely competitive

Drag Race, when Dupont Circle's highest heels and craziest costumes race down 17th St.

NOVEMBER & DECEMBER

Holiday season swings into gear. Weather is chilly (40° to 50° F) and tourism declines (read: prices drop). DC takes on a festive air leading up to Christmas.

KENNEDY CENTER HOLIDAY CELEBRATION
☎ 202-467-4600; www.kennedy-center.org
During the month of December, the Kennedy Center sponsors free music and activities.

NATIONAL CHRISTMAS TREE & MENORAH LIGHTING
On the second Thursday in December, the president does the honors on the Ellipse.

CULTURE

IDENTITY

Washington is a company town, the company being the federal government. About a third of DC workers are employed by the government, in either federal or city bureaucracies.

Beginning in the 1960s, when there were about 764,000 Washingtonians, the city population began to flow outward into the suburbs seeking to escape the capital's increasing crime rates and failing infrastructure. Today, Washington is a relatively small city, with a population of about 572,000 people. But the metropolitan area, including the Virginia and Maryland suburbs, is home to 5.7 million people. Three-quarters of metropolitan DC's employed population now works in the suburbs. Even some of the bigger federal agencies have gone suburban – as they grew, they simply ran out of DC real estate.

Quite recently, the outflow has slowed, as good economic times have enabled Washington to revitalize downtown neighborhoods. While widely welcomed, this gentrification also increases racial tensions. Affluent, primarily white home buyers have moved into downtown, Shaw and Adams-Morgan during recent years, pushing less affluent black renters further east.

African Americans represent about 60% of the population, one of the highest percentages of blacks in the country. Other ethnic groups include growing numbers of Asians (2.7%) and Hispanics (7.9%). Despite this diverse population, DC is one of the most segregated cities in the country: the 31% of the population that is white lives almost exclusively in Northwest DC.

Since the 1970s, masses of Salvadorans and Jamaicans have transformed segments of DC into modern barrios. More recently, African and Asian immigrants have arrived in lesser numbers. These ethnic groups do not mix particularly well – not with each other and not with pre-existing black and white populations. In fact, as of 2002 Washington DC has claimed the dubious distinction of 'murder capital,' with more murders per capita than any other city in the nation. Many of these deaths are attributed to ethnic gang warfare, especially among Hispanic groups.

The city's economic boundaries are as sharp as its racial ones. Twenty percent of the population falls below the poverty line, and most of this segment is black. This percentage is eight points above the national average, which – in a city with the second highest per-capita income in the country – demonstrates a disturbing income disparity.

The racial and economic divide has defined city politics and social relations for decades. Sadly, white and black Washingtonians do not often mix socially or professionally. These tensions are exacerbated by DC's odd political situation. Congress (mostly white and conservative) controls the budget of DC (mostly black and liberal), although most Congress members don't even live in the city. (See Government & Politics, p18.)

Considering this situation, it is not surprising that DC's most revolutionary ideas have been the result of racial tension. In the early 20th century, black intellectuals in Shaw enjoyed a local version of the Harlem Renaissance. Known as the New Negro movement, it produced music, poetry and literature by great minds like Alain Locke and Langston Hughes. Later, DC was a hub for the civil rights movement. Local black churches provided gathering places and support networks for participants in the movement (just as they had served as stops on the underground railroad years before). When Martin Luther King was assassinated in 1968, the city exploded in protest and violence – a 'revolution' that DC is still recovering from.

Outside the African American community, DC is a secular town – the business of government doesn't exactly lend itself to spiritual contemplation. However, the capital is also an international town so most of the world's faiths are represented, including an influential Jewish population, Muslims, Hindus, Mormons, Buddhists and Baha'is.

LIFESTYLE

The metropolitan DC area is the home of the nation's political class. The US political system still retains the spoils of office: thousands of politically appointed positions in the civil service. Each change of administration means a turnover in these positions, bringing newcomers to town. Once out of office, these politicos tend to stick around, taking temporary refuge at think tanks and policy institutes, working their contacts and biding their time until electoral fortunes change. The political class can often be observed in the early evening at their preferred Hill hang-outs and downtown digs.

The federal government attracts one of the nation's best-educated populations. Thirty-nine percent of the population has a bachelor's degree (compared to 24% nationally) and almost 19% has an advanced degree – the highest rate in the country. Education translates into purposefulness on the job. These people are serious about their work, whatever it may be. Not as obsessed as a Wall Street banker (after all, federal employees and contractors are not likely to be getting paid for more than 40 hours of work a week), but dedicated nonetheless.

An influx of interns every summer – plus 70,000 students in town – makes for a young, active city: sport and nightlife are big in DC. With a high population of foreign-born residents (13% in 2000), international influences are ubiquitous: ethnic cuisine, world music, foreign films. Recreation varies widely, not surprising considering the prospects. Most Washingtonians recognize the vast cultural resources at their disposal, but are apt to not take regular advantage of them. Ask any local the last time they visited the Smithsonian and the answer

For the Love of Cakes

Despite the name of his bakery, **Cakelove** (p131), Warren Brown does not love cake. 'I don't have a sweet tooth,' he explains. 'But I love the response I get from people when I prepare food – especially desserts. It's nice to see people get giddy.'

So nice, that Warren Brown – after earning a dual degree in law and public health from George Washington University – and working for two years as an attorney for the Department of Health and Human Services – quit his day job so he could make people giddy all the time. Now he owns the bakery Cakelove at 15th and U Sts NW.

The legal calling is a common one – LA Law, doing good deeds, making money. But Warren says, 'It wasn't really there for me.' With friends, he would conspire about leaving it all behind to launch a business. One Friday night over drinks they decided to set up a venture: leavingthelaw-dot-com. Come Monday, Warren's colleagues had all forgotten their plan. So he made his own plan: cakelove-dot-com.

Warren got mixed responses when he decided to quit his job to bake cakes full time. Strangers thought he was crazy. Friends – who had tasted his cakes – supported him ('at least to my face,' he adds). But now strangers approach him asking, 'How did you do it? How can I do it?'

Very methodically. He ripped the appropriate page out of the *Yellow Pages* and visited every bakery in DC. He found a simple niche: making cakes better than anybody else ('the Mercedes of cakes').

The life of a chef is a far cry from the life of a lawyer, and not in the ways you might expect. As an attorney for the federal government, Warren put in his 40 hours and headed home. Now he is working 12 to 16 hours a day and there is no end in sight. 'I'm at peace with the fact that chaos is a part of the reality,' he attests. 'I really enjoy when there's a lot of stuff coming at me and I have to respond to it. Maybe that's why I like basketball.'

And for the future? 'My intention is not to be doing cakes forever. I think I'll be doing this for seven to 10 years. But my future – I want to keep it wide open.' Apparently, Warren wants to have his cake and eat it too.

will inevitably be when an out-of-town guest was visiting. Which means only that residents have their own thing going on, whether it be training for the Marine Corps Marathon or volunteering as a docent at the Octagon or singing in the St Augustine gospel choir.

FOOD

DC's culinary choices match its population, ie they represent every state in the nation and just about every country on the planet (see the boxed text 'State of the Kitchen,' p14). Downtown DC, Capitol Hill and the White House area are packed with upscale venues catering to the capital-city jet set – steakhouses, seafood and more exotic fare done up for the modern American palette. Adams-Morgan, Dupont Circle and Georgetown have their fair share of swank, as well as hole-in-the-wall eateries hawking spicy falafel and cheesy pizza until all hours of the night. This is the best place outside of East Africa to sample Ethiopian cuisine (see the boxed text 'Dinner on a Pancake,' p133). For a truly authentic international eating experience, venture into Shaw or Mount Pleasant for *rotis* with the Jamaicans or *pupusas* (corn meal pastries stuffed with meat or cheese) with the Salvadorans.

Café Milano (p126)

SPORTS

America loves its football, and in DC, that means the celebrated Washington Redskins. In recent years, the 'Skins have not lived up to their glory days of the 1980s,

State of the Kitchen *by Mark Furstenberg*

I came to Washington in 1961 to work for the Kennedy White House. In those marvelous days of elegant Francophilia, the most celebrated restaurants were the Bistro, Knife & Fork, Rive Gauche, San Souci and Place Vendome – traditional French cooking in formal, somewhat stuffy surroundings. Across Lafayette Sq from the White House, Chez Francois was offering Alsatian cassoulets, *choucroutes* and plum tarts to an eager if uninformed clientele in those pre-Julia Child days.

Elsewhere in the city, restaurants were unpolished – although we didn't know it. To us, it seemed pretty exotic to be ushered into restaurants so dark that we should have been accompanied not by those young women in tight black dresses, but by seeing-eye dogs. And there we could eat prime rib, veal Orloff, chicken Kiev and beef Stroganoff.

How we have changed. Washington is not New York or San Francisco, but as a dining city it is now as sophisticated and eclectic as any other in the country.

What do you want? Elegant French? In 1998, Michel Richard arrived from Los Angeles to take over **Citronelle** (p126) in Georgetown, perhaps the most original restaurant in America – a playful, personal cuisine filled with vivid, sometimes mysterious flavors.

How about Italian? Roberto Donna's **Laboratorio del Galileo** (p129) is one of the most personal restaurants in America, where the chef stands in a small dining room each night preparing an 11-course meal for 55 people.

What about Spanish? No restaurant in the nation is doing more with tapas than **Jaleo** (p118), two branches so far, one downtown and the other in Bethesda. And for more formal Spanish food, **Taberna del Alabadero** (p121) and **Cafe Atlantico** (p118) are available.

Seafood? The busiest restaurant in the city is **Kinkead's** (p122), whose chef/owner came from Nantucket to Washington, bringing with him a knowledge of seafood that enriched the city.

I could go on about the restaurants in Washington, and you might ask whether one wouldn't expect a world capital to offer grand cuisines. But it wasn't always so.

Washington grew and developed for two reasons. One was the arrival in 1969 of the late Jean Louis Palladin, then a young two-star chef from southwest France, who created at the Watergate a restaurant of extraordinary invention. Palladin opened up the city; his expansive, generous personality challenged others in Washington to take culinary risks and challenged diners to support that. He brought national attention to a city that previously had been ridiculed as a place where the only good cooking was done in people's homes.

The legacy of Palladin lives in Washington: each month 'the chefs' club about nothing' meets for wine, cigars and several nighttime hours of gossip. It is not pointless, however. In no other city are chefs as eager to support each other and enrich their peers with culinary ideas. And in no city are chefs quite as adept at putting down the stuffiness and egocentricity that can poison a city's restaurant community.

The other change was the arrival in Washington of ethnic diversity. Our city – which before the 1970s had been populated by upper-income whites and lower-income blacks – became home to Koreans, Burmese, Cambodians, Filipinos, Chileans, Peruvians, Salvadorans, Ethiopians, Vietnamese and Indians. In the spreading Virginia and Maryland suburbs, they found inexpensive storefronts where they could open restaurants and offer their own versions of the food they had eaten in their home countries.

The ethnic offerings are far too rich to list – look at the annual dining guide in the *Washington Post* and in 'Cheap Eats' of the *Washingtonian* magazine. When you plan your dining out, understand that having a car is helpful. But if you don't, you will find that the Metro extends your culinary reach.

So be daring. If you can afford it, go to one of Washington's great downtown restaurants. Look first for restaurants that are not branches of chains you find in every other city of America. Don't play it safe: look for restaurants that feature Washington's imaginative chefs cooking their own creations that you won't find elsewhere. And then look too for restaurants that are offering cuisines you may not be able to find where you live.

Mark Furstenberg began his career working on policy in the Kennedy White House before turning his talents to baking and opening the BreadLine in 1997 (p122).

when they won two Super Bowls. But they still inspire face-painting, beer-guzzling fans and sell out every game.

The DC National Basketball Association (NBA) team, the Washington Wizards, recently generated a lot of publicity when Michael Jordan bought into the team's ownership, then came out of retirement to play. He could not reverse the Wizards' fortunes, however, and he left DC under bad circumstances in 2003. The women's (WNBA) and college (NCAA) basketball league teams maintain loyal followings among their audiences (pre-teen girls and Georgetown students respectively), but neither the Mystic nor the Hoyas have had much success on the courts in recent years either.

The Washington Capitals – dubbed the Caps – are the National Hockey League (NHL) team that recently acquired Czech phenomenon Jaromir Jagr. DC United has enjoyed modest major-league soccer success; sadly, the Women's United Soccer League champion Washington Freedom would not have a chance to defend their title, as the league folded for lack of funding in 2003.

For information on obtaining tickets to all sports events, see Sports, Health & Fitness (p165).

Ghost of the Senators

In 2003, Washington DC was one of several places competing for the attention of major league baseball, vying for the relocation of the all-American sport to their town. The Montreal Expos were up for grabs, and DC wanted in on it. Mayor Anthony Williams was promising fancy financing schemes for a new downtown stadium. Ironically, the District was competing with its neighbor to the south, Northern Virginia, who was opting to locate the stadium in the suburbs.

And why shouldn't the nation's capital enjoy America's favorite pastime? Five-plus million people in one of the nation's richest metropolitan areas deserve a team of their own. But advocates of this plan are overlooking one point. Well, two. Washington DC has twice had a baseball team and failed to support it. Despite the pitching exploits of Hall-of-Famer Walter Johnson, the Washington Senators were chronic underachievers. Washington was – as the saying went – 'first in war, first in peace and last in the American League.' The Washington Senators No 1 (1901–60) are now the Minnesota Twins. The Washington Senators No 2 (1961–71) are now the Texas Rangers. Meanwhile, just 50 miles north of the city exists a viable baseball club, the Baltimore Orioles, of which DC fans grew tired when Cal Ripkin retired.

There is a reason that Washington DC does not have a baseball team: this city belongs to the Redskins. Washington will always be a football town. But its interest in baseball waxes and wanes with the cycles of its transient population.

MEDIA

The media in DC really means only one thing: the *Washington Post*. Widely read and widely respected, the local daily is considered among the nation's top newspapers. Its competitor, the *Washington Times*, is owned by the Unification Church and provides an unsurprising, more conservative perspective. The national newspaper *USA Today* is based across the Potomac in Arlington, Virginia. Several television programs are also based in DC, including the PBS *News Hour* with longtime host Jim Lehrer, CNN's *Larry King Live* and all of the major networks' Sunday morning news programs.

The *Post*, of course, is famed for its role in the uncovering of the Watergate scandal in the early 1970s. Budding reporters Bob Woodward and Carl Bernstein traced a break-in at the Watergate Hotel to the top ranks of the White House administration. Then editor and local legend Ben Bradlee took a risk in supporting the investigation and publishing the stories. The discoveries eventually forced the resignation of President Richard Nixon.

With the arrival of the 30th anniversary of Nixon's resignation, the attitude of the media – in DC as around the country – is surprisingly complacent. Not that they don't love a good scandal (p16). But the sex-&-drugs-&-rock-and-roll scandals have somehow distracted the media from more pertinent questions.

Washington's independent media is a refreshing exception. The weekly *City Paper* keeps an alternative but informed eye on local politics and trends. Another valuable venue for local and national events is the DC Independent Media Center (dc.indymedia.org).

LANGUAGE

Washington's English is as varied as the city itself. You'll hear plenty of accents and slang from New York, the Midwest, Southern USA and California among the residents of this most transient US city, as well as the urban dialect of its African American neighborhoods. Diplomatic and immigrant communities add pockets of multilingualism to the city – you'll

Washington's Sites of Scandal, Seduction & Skulduggery

Washington media loves a good scandal (and some argue spends too much time trying to sniff one out). We offer here only a brief primer on some of the city's best-known scandal sites.

Scandal Central: Watergate Towering over the Potomac banks, this chi-chi apartment/hotel complex has lent its name to generations of political crime. It all started when Committee to Re-Elect the President (CREEP) operatives were found here, hiding under a desk after trying to bug Democratic National Committee headquarters. Thus was launched Woodward and Bernstein's investigation, which would eventually topple Nixon.

Swimming for It: Tidal Basin In 1974, Arkansas Representative Wilbur Mills was stopped for speeding, whereupon his companion – the stripper Fanne Foxe, known as the 'Argentine Firecracker' – leapt into the Basin to escape. The 65-year-old chairman of the House Ways and Means Committee and his 38-year-old friend were both several sheets to the wind. Unfortunately for Mills' political career, a TV cameraman was there to film the fun.

What's Your Position, Congressman?: Capitol Steps John Jenrette was a little-known South Carolina representative until he embroiled himself in the bribery scandal (dubbed Abscam after Abdul Enterprises Ltd, the faux company set up by the FBI to offer money to congressmen in return for political favors). Jenrette's troubles were compounded when his ex-wife Rita revealed to *Playboy* that she and her erstwhile husband used to slip out during dull late-night congressional sessions for an alfresco quickie on the Capitol's hallowed marble steps. (And that's not all.)

Smoking Gun: Vista Hotel It was in room No 727 that former DC Mayor Marion Barry uttered his timeless sobriquet, 'Bitch set me up!' when the FBI caught him taking a friendly puff of crack in the company of ex-model (and police informant) Rasheeda Moore. The widely broadcast FBI video of his toke horrified a city lacerated by crack violence, but didn't stop it from re-electing Barry in 1994. (The Vista has since changed its name to the Wyndham Washington Hotel.)

Suicidal Tendencies: Fort Marcy Park The body of Vince Foster, Deputy Counsel to President and Hillary Clinton, was found in this remote Mclean, Virginia park in 1993. Foster was dead from a bullet shot to the head. Investigations by both the Park Police and the FBI determined that the death was a suicide, but conspiracy theories abounded in right-wing rags.

Stool Pigeon Sushi: Pentagon City Food Court It was by the sushi bar that Monica Lewinsky awaited Linda Tripp, her lunch date (and betrayer) who led Ken Starr's agents down the mall escalators to snag her up for questioning in the nearby Ritz-Carlton Hotel. Who knew a food court could provide such a media fiesta?

hear more Spanish than English in Mount Pleasant and lots of Amharic in Adams-Morgan's African restaurants; Vietnamese is the lingua franca in suburban Virginia's 'Little Saigon.'

Washington bureaucrats – who spend their days crafting acronyms, abbreviations and neologisms – make their own peculiar contributions to the language. Only in this city can you hear constructions like, 'If HR 3401 passes, everyone under GS-10 at HUD and HHS will be SOL' and phraseologies like 'non–means-tested entitlement,' 'soft money' and 'what the meaning of *is* is.'

Washingtonspeak: a Glossary

Beltway bandits Consultants who clean up on high-priced government contracts.

Camp intern The city in summer, when young students flood in for short stints on the Hill and at federal agencies and think tanks.

Cave dweller Old-money Washingtonians, many of whom can trace their ancestry in the city back to pre–Civil War days.

DC, the District What locals call the place (never 'Washington DC' – who has the time?).

Eye St I St (to avoid confusion with 1st St).

GS Government service level; a professional caste system. The higher the number (eg GS-1 vs GS-15), the higher the salary and prestige.

Hill rat Lifer congressional staffers; named for the book *Hill Rat* by John Jackley.

Langley Often synonymous with 'CIA'; Langley, Virginia is that agency's home.

Potus Secret Service shorthand for President of the United States.

'Skins! Redskins (DC's football team). Generally bellowed.

ECONOMY & COSTS

The greater Washington area is the fourth-largest regional economy in the United States, with a gross regional product of nearly $272 billion in 2002. While the federal government is the main story in DC, thriving private-sector industries include information technology, bioscience, international business, professional services and tourism. The federal government provides fuel for all of these industries In the 1990s, the high-tech industry in particular benefited from government spending, sprouting up – seemingly overnight – in northern Virginia along the Dulles corridor.

In 2002, the annual per-capita income in the greater Washington area was $35,333, second only to the Silicon Valley. The result is that Washington DC is an expensive place to live and to visit. Once in Washington, the bulk of your travel expenses will be for accommodation. Although fancy hotels in Washington can cost as much as you are willing to pay, it is possible – taking advantage of discounted Web rates – to stay in a central, four-star hotel for $100 to $120. Mid-range hotels run $80 to $100, while the hostels in DC cost $20 to $30 for a bed. Eating in DC is also not cheap. Three sit-down meals per day, including one at an upscale restaurant, will easily cost $60 per person. Forgoing drinks or grabbing a meal at a less expensive venue trims that estimate to $40.

How Much?

Bicycle rental (three hours) $20.

Cappuccino $3.50.

Concert ticket at the 9:30 Club $25.

Guinness $5.

Cab fare Downtown from Ronald Reagan Washington National Airport $15.

Movie ticket $8.50.

Museum entry Free.

One-bedroom apartment (one month) $1200.

Parking garage (one hour) $6.

Washington Post 50c.

At best, self-catering and cheap eats make it possible to eat for about $20 per day.

Keep in mind that DC offers many opportunities to save money. With free federal sites, museums, concerts and festivals, it's possible to be fully entertained – day and night – without paying a dime. See the boxed text 'Top Five Free Entertainment Options,' (p149). The Smithsonian museums are always free, while galleries like the Phillips and the Corcoran have reduced entry or free admission on certain days of the week. Happy hours (p150) offer excellent value for eating and drinking, while many upscale restaurants have prix-fixe and pre-theatre menus that are good value.

Supreme Court (p65)

GOVERNMENT & POLITICS

According to the Constitution, the nation's capital would be exclusively administered by the US Congress. More than 200 hundred years later, Congress has yet to give up this power. Despite the emergence of Washington DC as a major metropolitan center, it is an anomalous political entity that functions more like a colony than a state. The grievance of 'taxation without representation,' which sparked the American Revolution, remains unaddressed for Washington residents. In fact, it has recently reappeared as a logo on some DC license plates.

From the late 19th century, an appointed three-man commission managed city affairs and residents were denied voting rights. The call for Home Rule was first heard early in the 20th century, but it was not until 1964 that DC residents voted in a presidential election for the first time. In 1968, President Johnson replaced the commission system with a mayor and city council. Finally, the Home Rule Act went into effect in 1974, granting limited autonomy, including the right to vote for mayor.

Twenty years later, the maladministration of Mayor Marion Barry prompted Congress to reassert itself in city affairs. Barry was accused by congressional critics of fiscal mismanagement and corruption, while from the other side came charges of meddling, paternalism and racism. The city's alienated black residents sided with the mayor, and voted him in for a fourth term, despite his well-publicized run-ins with the law. The Republican Congress reacted by seizing control of city finances and placing the school system and police department into receivership. Gradually, Congress has passed the power back to Barry's successor, the less-controversial Anthony Williams.

Washingtonians are still denied representation at the federal level, despite having a larger population than Wyoming. In the 1990s, the issue of DC statehood was advanced to redress this situation. The Clinton administration supported the initiative, which was voted down by the House of Representatives. Washington is an overwhelmingly Democratic town and Republicans have little incentive to bring their votes into the political mix.

Martin Luther King Jr Memorial Library (p53)

Mall of Justice

Washington DC is not just the center of government, it is also the center of demonstration. What the Capitol is to conventional politics, the National Mall is to protest politics. In the 20th century, the Mall has provided a forum for people who feel that they or their issue has been shut out by the establishment. Peace-loving war veterans, long-skirted suffragettes, civil rights activists, shrouded white supremacists, tractor-driving farmers and million man marchers have staged political pageants on the Mall. Great moments in American protest politics include:

Bonus Army (1932) WWI veterans, left unemployed by the Great Depression, petitioned the government for an early payment of promised bonuses for their wartime service. As many as 10,000 vets settled in for an extended protest, pitching tents on the Mall and Capitol lawn. President Hoover dispatched Douglas MacArthur to evict the 'Bonus Army.' In a liberal display of force, the veterans were routed and their campsites razed.

'I Have a Dream' (1963) The Civil Rights movement was the most successful protest movement, effectively employing boycotts and demonstrations. Reverend Martin Luther King's stirring speech, delivered from the steps of the Lincoln Memorial to 200,000 supporters, remains a high point in the historic struggle for racial equality.

Anti-War Protests (1971) The Vietnam War aroused some of the most notable episodes of protest politics. In April, an estimated 500,000 Vietnam veterans and students gathered on the Mall to oppose continued hostilities. Several thousand arrests were made.

AIDS Memorial Quilt (1996) Lesbian and gay activists drew more than 300,000 supporters in a show of solidarity for equal rights under the law and to display the ever-growing AIDS quilt, which covered the entire eastern flank of the Mall from the Capitol to the Washington Monument.

Million Mom March (2000) A half-million people convened on the Mall on Mother's Day, to draw attention to hand-gun violence and to influence Congress into passing stricter gun-ownership laws.

In March 2000, a federal court panel ruled that Washingtonians have no legal right to a vote in Congress, dealing a severe setback to community leaders and home-rule activists. Mayor Williams summed up the city's disappointment: 'Over the last 200 years, residents of the District of Columbia have fought in nine wars and paid billions of dollars in federal taxes. Yet in our nation's capital – the epicenter of democracy – we lack the most fundamental right of all: the right to vote.'

Taxation remains a chronic source of tension for cash-strapped DC. Two-thirds of the income earned in DC is not taxable by DC because it is earned by suburbanites. In 2003, Mayor Williams proposed instituting a controversial commuter tax on out-of-city residents working in the DC; whether mostly suburbanite Congress will allow it remains to be seen.

ENVIRONMENT

THE LAND

DC stands at a pivotal place upon the fall line, the exact point where the coastal plain intersects with the higher, rockier piedmont plateau. Most of downtown and Southeast DC lie on the delta formed by the joining of the Potomac River and its smaller tributary, the Anacostia River. The federal city was sited here precisely because of this geographic anomaly: it is the last navigable point on the Potomac, which city founders deemed important for trade. Just north of here at Great Falls, the river tangles itself in a series of cliffs and crags, impeding the progress of ships.

In the city, the high ground defined by the fall line proved an attractive setting for the mansions of Washington's wealthy residents: it runs through Georgetown and traces the course of Kalorama Rd. The southern, monumental part of Washington around the Mall is coastal lowlands smoothed out by the seasonal flooding of the Potomac and Anacostia Rivers. To control flooding in the 19th century, developers created land fills like West Potomac Park and dredged the Washington Channel.

Washington DC is a small city with wide sidewalks and few highways, making it an ideal city for walking to many destinations.

GREEN DC

Today Washington DC is a uniquely green city. Hundreds of acres of protected parks and wetlands make a good home for urban wildlife, including small woodland creatures and aquatic animals like raccoons, turtles, salamanders, beavers, white-tailed deer, weasels, muskrats, foxes and opossums. Olmstead's 2000-acre Rock Creek Park is a particularly attractive habitat. Cardinals, pileated woodpeckers and wood thrushes also flit around here.

The mixed woodlands of DC parks are fetching in springtime, when forsythia, fruit trees – especially cherries and crab apples – and wildflowers (violets, bluebells, wild orchids, chicory and trilliums) burst into a pale-pastel rainbow of blooms. Also native to the city, sometimes in near-virgin stands, are tulip poplars, red and white oaks, sycamore, elm, willow, dogwood, beech, hickory and pine.

The waterways and wetlands surrounding the city attract waterfowl and other feathered friends. Hundreds of bald eagles and ospreys nest along the Potomac south of Washington and along the Patuxent River to the east. Kenilworth Gardens, in Northeast DC, is thick with wading great blue herons, red-winged blackbirds and bitterns. In 2000, Mayor Anthony Williams announced a major riverfront redevelopment and cleanup effort that will, hopefully, spur revitalization of the Anacostia as a natural and recreational resource.

URBAN PLANNING & DEVELOPMENT

Since the 1970s, DC's population has declined, as residents have moved up and out to burgeoning suburbia, see Identity (p11). DC's outlying areas have been among the nation's fastest growing; suburban sprawl and the accompanying automobile dependence have resulted in traffic problems and air pollution. In recent years, the local government responded with innovative transportation solutions: expanding the Metrorail, adding and enforcing designated lanes for High Occupancy Vehicles (HOVs), and allowing bicycles on trains and buses are all ways of encouraging commuters to leave their car keys at home.

The economic upswing in the 1990s sparked investment in Washington neighborhoods, especially downtown. Projects such as the MCI Center and the Convention Center are the backbone of the ongoing revitalization in the area. New additions like the National Museum of the American Indian and the National World War II Memorial promise to continue to draw visitors to the Mall. Especially since September 11, 2001, public works projects have focused on security concerns, which motivated the construction of the new Capitol visitors center (scheduled to open in 2005) and the renovation of the FBI Building.

Arts

Arts

Washington is the showcase of American arts, home to such prestigious venues as the National Gallery and the Kennedy Center. The National Symphony Orchestra and the National Theatre embody everything that their titles imply: top-notch music and theater to represent the nation. Likewise, Washington's architecture and city design are the product of founding fathers and city planners who intended to construct a capital city befitting a powerful nation. The result is that Washington's arts scene – where it is most visible and most acclaimed – is national rather than local in scope.

It is a blessing for local culture vultures, for sure. Access to the nation's (and the world's) top artists and musicians is reserved for residents of only a few cities; DC is among them because it was deemed appropriate for a political capital.

Often overlooked, however, is another arts scene – a scene representative of DC and not necessarily the USA. It is edgier, blacker, more organic and more experimental. It is colored by the experiences of the city's African American and immigrant populations, lending diversity and ethnicity. It dances around the edges of the more conservative national scene and discreetly tests its boundaries. The Arena Stage, the Corcoran Gallery and the Dance Place are examples of the innovative, experimental venues that draw on local talent and themes in their productions. Loads of smaller art galleries and community theaters around the city are the backbone of this vibrant arts scene.

ARCHITECTURE

The early architecture of Washington DC was shaped by two influences: Pierre Charles L'Enfant's 1791 city plan (p34), and the infant nation's desire to prove to European powers that its capital possessed political and artistic sophistication rivaling the ancient, majestic cities of the Continent.

The L'Enfant Plan imposed a street grid marked by diagonal avenues, roundabouts and grand vistas. He had in mind the magisterial boulevards of Europe. To highlight the primacy of the city's political buildings, he intended that no building would rise higher than the Capitol. This rule rescued DC from the windy, dark, skyscraper-filled fate of most modern American cities.

In an effort to rival European cities, Washington's early architects – many of them self-taught 'gentlemen architects' – depended heavily upon the classic revival and romantic revival styles, with their borrowed columns and marble facades (witness the **Capitol**, p63) and **Ford's Theatre** (p53). Federal-style row houses dominated contemporary domestic architecture and still line the streets of Capitol Hill and Georgetown.

Other fine examples from the Federal period are the **Sewall-Belmont house** (p65) and the uniquely shaped **Octagon Museum** (p59). The colonnaded **Treasury Building** (p60), built by Robert Mills in the mid-19th century, represented the first major divergence from the L'Enfant Plan, as it blocked the visual line between the White House and the Capitol. Mills also designed the stark, simple **Washington Monument** (p47), another architectural anomaly (and not only because it is 555ft high, taller than the Capitol). Later, other styles would soften the lines of the cityscape, with creations like the medieval **Smithsonian Castle** (p47) and the French-inspired **Renwick Gallery** (p60), both designed by James Renwick.

At the turn of the 20th century, the McMillan Plan revived many elements of the L'Enfant Plan. It restored public spaces downtown, lent formal lines to the Mall and Capitol grounds, and added more classically inspired buildings such as the beaux-arts **Union Station** (p66). During this period, John Russell Pope built the **Scottish Rite Masonic Temple** (p78), modeled after the mausoleum at Halicarnassus, as well as the **National Archives** (p54).

Classicism came to a screaming halt during and after WWII, when war workers flooded the city. Temporary offices were thrown onto the Mall and new materials developed during wartime enabled the construction of huge homogenous office blocks. Slum clearance after the war – particularly in Southwest DC – meant the wholesale loss of old neighborhoods in favor of modernist boxes, such as the monolithic government agencies that currently dominate the ironically named L'Enfant Plaza.

Washington architecture today is of uncertain identity. Many new buildings, particularly those downtown, pay homage to their classical neighbors while striving toward a sleeker, postmodern monumentalism. Check out the pillared facade of the huge **Ronald Reagan Building** (p56), an odd pairing with the soaring space-age atrium within. A handful of world-renowned architects have left examples of their work in the city: IM Pei's ethereal East Building of the

Top Five DC Beaux-Arts Buildings

McMillan's Plan would change the face of the nation's capital and it would do it in the style of beaux-arts. Here are some of the best examples of this eclectic French-inspired style that is so DC.

- **City Museum of Washington, DC** (p52) Formerly the DC Public Library.
- **Corcoran Gallery of Art** (p58) Deemed by Frank Lloyd Wright to be the best building in Washington.
- **Meridian International Center** (p80) A limestone chateau by John Russell Pope.
- **Organization of American States** (p60) A blend of North and South American styles.
- **Union Station** (p66) The classic example of beaux-arts, a monument to the age of railroads.

National Gallery of Art (p49), Mies van der Rohe's **Martin Luther King Jr Memorial Library** (p53) and Eero Saarinen's **Washington Dulles International Airport** (p222). Plans are under way for the **Corcoran Gallery of Art** (p58) to expand with a fantastic addition designed by Frank Gehry and scheduled for completion by 2006 (p59). Gehry is famed for his work on Bilbao's Guggenheim museum.

Sometimes appalling and sometimes awesome, the architecture of this unique city tells much about American political ideals and their occasionally awkward application to reality. The **National Mall** (p44) today is a perfect example. Current construction projects reflect current values: a growing concern about our security and safety (new visitors center at the **Capitol**, p63), a broadening definition of our society and culture (**National Museum of the American Indian**, p50) and a reignited need for national unity (**National World War II Memorial**, p46). The result will be a National Mall that looks quite different in 2004 than it did in 1904, or even 1994. Like the city as a whole, it is a product of city plans, federal mandates, clashing social agendas and the ever-shifting national vision of what a capital should be.

VISUAL ARTS

Visual arts in DC has three faces: the vast holdings of the **National Gallery of Art** (p49) and the **Smithsonian Institution** (p47); the private collections and special exhibits at the **Corcoran Gallery of Art** (p58) and the **Phillips Collection** (p77); and the wealth of small commercial galleries supporting local, national and international artists.

The first hardly needs an explanation. The National Gallery of Art comprises two buildings filled with paintings, sculpture, photography and decorative arts from the Middle Ages to the present. The Smithsonian Institution operates the **Freer Gallery**, the **Hirshhorn Museum & Sculpture Garden**, the **National Museum of African Art**, the **National Museum of American Art**, the **Portrait Gallery** (p55), the **Renwick Gallery** (p60) and the **Sackler Gallery** (p47) – an impressive collection to be sure. From ancient handicrafts to modern sculpture, the spectrum of the works at these national museums is truly mind-boggling.

The Corcoran and the Phillips are private museums that were built from the collections of philanthropic art lovers. The **Corcoran Gallery of Art** (p58) has a renowned collection of 20th-century American prints, photography and painting; the **Phillips Collection** (p77) holds impressionist and modern masterpieces from both Europe and America. Both museums host special exhibits to lure visitors off the National Mall and into their decked-out halls.

Less known, but no less important, DC is riddled with grassroots galleries, many owned or operated by the artists themselves. This scene has blossomed since the 1990s, fuelled by DC's reinvigorated neighborhoods and increasingly cosmopolitan population. It is no longer a given that a talented artist will flee to New York to make it big. Some artistic names to look out for on the DC scene include Colby Caldwell, Steve Cushner, Sam Gilliam, Ryan Hackett,

Top Five Dupont Circle Art Galleries

Nearly two dozen art galleries around Dupont Circle offer glimpses of contemporary artwork by local and international artists. A complete list is available in the *Guide to the Galleries of Dupont Circle,* available for free at most DC galleries. The 21-member Dupont Gallery Association holds a collective open house on the first Friday of each month, 6pm to 8pm (except August and September). See www.artgalleriesdc.com for details. Here's our take on where to go if you gotta have art.

- **Anton Gallery** (Map pp258-60; ☎ 202-328-0828; 2108 R St NW; ☺ 11am-6pm Tue-Sat) Specializes in contemporary realist and abstract canvases, with shows changing monthly.
- **Foundry Gallery** (Map pp258-60; ☎ 202-387-0203; 9 Hillyer Ct NW; ☺ 11am-5pm Tue-Sat, 1-5pm Sun) Features diverse ultracontemporary (21st-century!) art.
- **Gallery K** (Map pp258-60; ☎ 202-234-0339; 2010 R St NW; ☺ 11am-6pm Tue-Sat) A top-notch two-floor showcase for contemporary international artists' work.
- **Studio Gallery** (Map pp258-60; ☎ 202-232-8734; 2108 R St NW; ☺ 11am-5pm Wed-Sat, 1-5pm Sun) A 30-artist cooperative featuring canvases and sculpture.
- **Troyer Gallery** (Map pp258-60; ☎ 202-328-7189; 1710 Connecticut Ave NW; ☺ 11am-5pm Tue-Sat) Among DC's better-known galleries, especially for emerging artists.

Jae Ko and Nancy Sansom Reynolds. DC can boast bona fide art districts in Dupont Circle and downtown. The **Old Torpedo Factory** (p187) in Old Town Alexandria is also an incredible conglomeration of creative minds. These are the places to see the face of DC art at its most pure.

LITERATURE

Washington's literary legacy is, not surprisingly, deeply entwined with American political history. The city's best-known early literature consists of writings and books that hammered out the machinery of American democracy. From Thomas Jefferson's *Notes on the State of Virginia* to James Madison's *The Federalist Papers* and Abraham Lincoln's historic speeches and proclamations, this literature fascinates modern readers – not only because it is the cornerstone of the US political system, but because of the grace and beauty of its prose. Skill with the pen is, alas, no longer a notable characteristic of US presidents.

Apart from politicians' writings, 19th-century Washington literature was created primarily by authors and journalists who resided here only temporarily, drawn to DC by circumstance, professional obligation or wanderlust. Walt Whitman's *The Wound Dresser* and *Specimen Days* and Louisa May Alcott's *Hospital Sketches* were based upon the authors' harrowing experiences as Civil War nurses at Washington's hospitals. Mark Twain had an ill-starred (and short) career as a senator's speechwriter, memorialized in *Washington in 1868*.

Frederick Douglass (1818–95), the abolitionist, editor, memoirist and former slave, is perhaps Washington's most revered writer. His seminal antislavery works *The Life & Times of Frederick Douglass* and *My Bondage & My Freedom* were written in DC, where Douglass lived on Capitol Hill and in Anacostia.

Henry Adams (1838–1918), grandson of President John Adams, often invited DC's *literati* to salons at his mansion on Lafayette Sq, which became the literary center of the day. His brilliant *Democracy* was the forerunner of many political-scandal novels of the 20th century. His later autobiography, *The Education of Henry Adams*, provides a fascinating insider's account of Washington high society during this period.

In the early 20th century, another salon often took place across town at 15th and S Sts in Shaw. Artists and writers often gathered here, at poet Georgia Douglas Johnson's home, which became the center of the Harlem Renaissance in DC. Her guests included African American poets Langston Hughes and Paul Dunbar.

Another member of this circle was Jean Toomer, author of the subtle, sad *Cane*. Not a novel in the traditional sense, Toomer's seminal work is part poetry, part prose and part play. The book – while lacking a continuous plot or defined characters – is among the strongest representations of Harlem Renaissance literature.

In DC, the Harlem Renaissance is sometimes called the New Negro movement, named for the famous volume by Howard University professor Alain Locke. *The New Negro* – the bible of the Renaissance – is a collection of essays, poems and stories written by Locke and his colleagues. The writing is energetic and subversive; as a snapshot of the Renaissance and the African American experience it is invaluable.

Throughout the 20th century, Washington literature remains a deeply political beast, defined by works such as Carl Bernstein and Bob Woodward's *All the President's Men* and John Kennedy's *Profiles in Courage*. Perhaps the most eloquent poem about DC is Robert Lowell's *July in Washington*, written about the poet's participation in a 1968 political protest. Today, literary life is populated by journalists and speechwriters, from William Safire to George Will to David Brinkley. For fun, humor columnist Dave Barry gives his hilarious version of Civics-101 in *Hits Below the Beltway*.

But many more purely literary writers have appeared on the scene, too. The contemporary writer who is best able to capture the streets and sounds and sights of DC in his writing is Edward Jones. His National Book Award nominee *Lost in the City* is an incredible collection of 14 stories set in inner-city DC in the 1960s and 1970s. Each recounts a tale of an individual facing the complexity of city life in a strangely hopeful way. The portrayal of the city – like the characters themselves – is real and raw.

George Pelecanos is another talent whose crime novels show the hard, fast streets of DC that most visitors never see. Filled with sex, drugs and rock 'n' roll, he shows off his intimate knowledge of the city street scene and the latest pop culture. (The 'soundtracks' are among the highlights of reading the books.) Pelecanos has written 16 such novels with interwoven themes and characters, but his most recent – *Hell to Pay* and *Right to Rain* – are considered his best.

Marita Golden is a modern African American writer whose novels about contemporary African American families have attracted a loyal following. Her characters deal with betrayal, loss, growth and reconciliation, just like real people in modern America. *The Edge of Heaven* is set in DC, where an accomplished 20-year-old student confronts her confusion about reuniting with her parents upon her mother's release from four years in prison.

Paul Kafka-Gibbons addresses the touchy subject of marriage in his second novel, *Dupont Circle*. From the title (and setting), you might guess the subject is gay marriage, but the novel does not exclude anyone. Intertwining plots revolve around three couples – only one is gay but all three are untraditional – who deal with the expectations and realities of being in a relationship. Kafka-Gibbons won the Los Angeles Times Book Prize for his first novel *Love <Enter>* (which does not take place in DC), but this second novel has not been as well received.

Zenith Gallery (p177)

Top Five DC Books

- *Advise & Consent*, Allen Drury (1981) A compelling fictional account of personalities and politics in the US Senate.
- *The Dream Keeper and Other Poems*, Langston Hughes (1996) A collection of poignant poems written especially for kids.
- *Hits Below the Beltway*, Dave Barry (2002) Not exactly literature, but still a hilarious account of history and politics by one of America's best-loved columnists.
- *Lost in the City*, Edward Jones (2003) Evocative short stories about people and places in DC.
- *Narrative of the Life & Times of Frederick Douglass*, Frederick Douglass (2000) Douglass' autobiographical account of his own journey from slave to statesman.

Native Washingtonian Gore Vidal often aims his satirical pen at his hometown, that is, Federal DC. His six-volume series of historical novels about the American past includes *Washington, DC*, an insightful examination of the period from the New Deal to the McCarthy era from the perspective of the capital. *The Smithsonian Institution* is a fantastical historical account of a 13-year-old boy who travels through time to save the world. Readers who can throw all caution to the wind and follow Vidal without skepticism will enjoy the weird and wonderful ride.

Advise & Consent is Allen Drury's fictional account of Alger Hiss' nomination as Secretary of State under FDR. The novel brilliantly portrays the conflicting personal and political motivations of his characters – a real revelation of what goes in inside the US Senate.

On a less elevated note, DC has also inspired thousands of potboilers. A representative is the oeuvre of Tom Clancy, northern Virginia resident and creator of innumerable right-wing thrillers that sometimes feature Washington's apocalyptic destruction (see *Debt of Honor* and *Executive Orders* for much President-and-Congress offing).

For a fine profile of the contemporary Washington literary scene, check out David Cutler's *Literary Washington: A Complete Guide to the Literary Life in the Nation's Capital*.

MUSIC

Only in the capital can national orchestras coexist with rebellious punk, all under the rubric of the local music scene. That military marches and soulful go-go both reached their peaks under the watchful eye (and attentive ear) of DC fans is tribute to the city's electric – if eclectic – music scene.

A national orchestra of sorts is the Marine Corps Marching Band, based at the **Marine Barracks** (p66) in Southeast DC. Back in the late 19th century, military marching-band music reached its apotheosis (such as it was) in the work of John Philip Sousa, who directed the Marine Corps Marching Band for many years (and was born and buried nearby). Needless to say in this patriotic era, this genre is still alive and well: the band still performs his work today.

In the early 20th century, segregation of entertainment venues meant that black Washington had to create its own arts scene – so it created one far more vibrant than anything white Washington could boast. Jazz, big band and swing flourished at clubs and theatres around DC and particularly in the Shaw district. Greats such as Duke Ellington (p27), Pearl Bailey, Shirley Horne, Johnny Hodges and Ben Webster all got their starts in the clubs of U St NW. Today this district is reviving, as new clubs and theaters open in the historic buildings in the area. After 30 years of neglect, the renowned **Bohemian Caverns** (p159) now hosts local soul-jazz music. But other venues in the area – like the **Black Cat** (p159) and the **9:30 Club** (p158) – are now DC's premier venues for modern rock, blues and hip-hop. Shaw is not a recreation of a historical fantasy: it is an organic area, shaped not only by its history but also by modern musical movements.

The scene at these venues is varied, but not particularly unique to DC. The exception – where DC really stands out musically – is where it builds on its local roots in go-go and punk. Go-go is an infectiously rhythmic dance music combining elements of funk, rap, soul and Latin percussion, which stomped onto the city scene in the 1970s (p160). These days, go-go soul blends with hip-hop's rhythm – everybody dance now!

DC's hardcore take on punk, as embodied by such bands as Fugazi and Dag Nasty, combined super-fast punk with a socially conscious mindset and flourished at venues like the now-defunct dc space. Arlington-based Dischord Records, one of the country's most successful small labels, grew out of the punk scene and remains a fierce promoter of local bands. Check out *Banned in DC*, a photo book by Cynthia Connolly that documents the Washington punk scene of the 1970s and 1980s. While punk is no longer the musical force it once was, its influence on grunge and other modern genres is undeniable. Local bands such as Dismemberment Plan and Dog Fashion Disco are carrying the post-punk torch in DC.

Top Five DC CDs

- *Far East Suite*, Duke Ellington. An exotic collection based on the Duke's travels in Asia.
- *Go Go Swing Live*, Chuck Brown. The granddaddy of go-go goes swing, because it don't mean a thing if you ain't got it.
- *In this Land*, Sweet Honey in the Rock. Sixteen sweet voices incorporating gospel, blues and even rap styles into their a cappella arrangements.
- *Repeater*, Fugazi. Ian McKaye is energetic, honest and pure punk.
- *The Way It Is*, Bruce Hornsby. A killer keyboardist showing off his songwriting skills.

Showing off its southern roots, DC has spawned some folk and country stars of its own, too, including Emmylou Harris, Mary Chapin Carpenter and John Fahey (who named his seminal folk record label Takoma for Takoma Park, his boyhood home). Folksy keyboardist Bruce Hornsby is a native of nearby Williamsburg, Virginia.

The capital's most visible musicians are the big boys – those from the weighty cultural landmarks like the **National Symphony Orchestra** (NSO; p158) and the **Washington Opera** (p158). For the most part, they are not doing anything new. At the NSO, directed by Leonard Slatkin, classical means classical. Placido Domingo directs the Washington Opera. Repertoire and productions tend to be pretty traditional but technically sound – highlighted by special occasions when Domingo conducts or sings. Diva Denyce Graves, graduate of the local Duke Ellington School of Performing Arts, occasionally graces its stage and thrills her hometown audiences.

At the **National Museum of American History** (p49), the Music Room features a series of performances demonstrating the role of classical, jazz, popular and traditional music in the nation's cultural history. A great resource for the contemporary local music scene is the DC Music Network at www.dcmusicnet.com.

The Duke

'My road runs from Ward's Place to my grandmother's at Twentieth and R, to Seatan Street, around to 8th Street, back up to T Street, through LeDroit Park to Sherman Avenue,' wrote DC's most famous musical son, jazz immortal Edward Kennedy 'Duke' Ellington (1899–1974), describing his childhood in Washington's Shaw district. In the segregated DC of the early 20th century, Shaw hosted one of the country's finest black arts scenes – drawing famed actors, musicians and singers to perform at venues like the Howard Theatre and Bohemian Caverns – so the Duke took root in rich soil.

As a tot, Ellington purportedly first tackled the keyboard under the tutelage of a teacher by the name of Mrs Clinkscales. He honed his chops by listening to local ragtime pianists like Doc Perry, Louis Thomas and Louis Brown at Frank Holliday's T St poolroom. His first composition, written at 16, was the 'Soda Fountain Rag'; next came 'What You Gonna Do When the Bed Breaks Down?' The handsome, suave young Duke played hops and cabarets all over black Washington before decamping for New York in 1923.

There, Ellington started out as a Harlem stride pianist, performing at Barron's and the Hollywood Club; but he soon moved to the famed Cotton Club, where he matured into an innovative bandleader, composer and arranger. He collaborated with innumerable artists – including Louis Armstrong and Ella Fitzgerald – but his most celebrated collaboration was with composer/arranger Billy Strayhorn, who gave the Ellington Orchestra their theme, 'Take the "A" Train,' in 1941. Strayhorn worked with Duke throughout his life, collaborating on later works like *Such Sweet Thunder* (1957) and *The Far East Suite* (1964).

Ellington's big-band compositions, with their infectious melodies, harmonic sophistication and ever-present swing, made him one of the 20th-century's most revered American composers and his ability to craft arrangements highlighting the singular talents of his musicians made him the foremost bandleader of his time. His huge volume of work – more than 1500 pieces – is preserved in its entirety at the Smithsonian in his old hometown.

For more on the Duke, check out his witty memoir *Music Is My Mistress*, which details his DC childhood and later accomplishments.

National Gallery of Art (p49)

THEATER & COMEDY

Political comedy and theatre are certainly a fixture of the DC arts scene: the **Ford's Theatre** (p155) – site of Lincoln's assassination – holds its place in history by presenting traditional, Americana-themed productions; the capital's foremost comedy troupe, the **Capitol Steps Political Satire** (p158), cuts up exclusively with biting satire of the goings-on in the White House and on Capitol Hill. Such theatrical ventures certainly have their place in the nation's capital.

There is more, however, to theatre in DC. Most Broadway shows will eventually find their way to the **National Theatre** (p155) or the **Kennedy Center** (p156). The **Arena Stage** (p155), home to one of the country's oldest troupes, was the first theatre outside of New York to win a Tony and continues to stage diverse productions by new playwrights. Over the course of 25 years, smaller companies like **Studio Theatre** (p156) have established a strong presence. The **Source Theatre** (p156) has for almost as long hosted the Annual Washington Theatre Festival, a venue for new plays, workshops and the insanely popular 10-Minute Play Competition. The **Folger Shakespeare Library & Theatre** (p155) gives new perspective to the Bard. The edgy **Woolly Mammoth Theatre Co** (p156) and the multicultural **Gala Hispanic Theatre** (p156) have expanded into new space – both physically and theatrically.

What's really exciting on the DC theater scene is the proliferation of brand-new companies and community theatres, stepping into the empty spaces that their predecessors have left behind. Heritage-based companies, such as **Asian Stories in America** (p156) and **Theater J** (p156), are highlighting the works of various ethnic groups. The **DCAC** (District of Columbia Arts Center; p156) hosts the innovative Playback, where the audience provides stories to fuel the plot on stage. Acting guilds and theatre groups are popping up on every stage in Shaw, Dupont Circle and Capitol Hill, pressing the limits of what theatre can do.

FILM

Hollywood directors can't resist the black limousines, white marble, counterintelligence subterfuges and political scandal that official Washington embodies. But local film buffs offer up two complaints about all this attention. First, unofficial Washington – the real place where real people live – might as well be Waikiki; few films are set anywhere other than Capitol Hill and it's the rare movie character that does not live in Georgetown (unless they live in the White House). Second, even the movies about official Washington fail to capture how the personalities and politics really work. Then again, since when does Hollywood capture how anything *really* works?

Hollywood's favorite theme for a Washington movie is the political naïf who stumbles into combat with corrupt capital-veterans. Such is the story in the preeminent Washington film *Mr Smith goes to Washington,* in which Jimmy Stewart and his troop of 'Boy Rangers' defeat big, bad government and preserve democracy for the rest of the country. This theme reappears in the 1950 hit *Born Yesterday,* as well as in the less lauded but more recent *Dave* and *Legally Blonde 2,* and the best of the lot – *Being There.* Needless to say, these flicks do not go over well in Washington. (The Jimmy Stewart flick was roundly rebuffed at its Washington premiere.) But for sheer entertainment value, *Mr Smith* is a DC classic.

Another popular theme for DC-based cinema is the total destruction of the nation's capital by aliens (perhaps some wishful thinking on the part of the West Coast). The best of this genre is *The Day the Earth Stood Still,* both for its underlying pacifist message and its off-Mall DC scenes. Adaptations of this theme include the Cold War era *Earth vs Flying Saucers* and the more recent *Independence Day.*

DC is a popular setting for political thrillers: action-adventure fans might enjoy *In the Line of Fire* (Clint Eastwood as a savvy secret-service agent protecting the President); *Patriot Games* (Harrison Ford as a tough CIA agent battling Irish terrorists); and *No Way Out* (Kevin Costner as a Navy officer outracing Russian spies). All of them are pretty good for scenes of DC's famous sites.

A twist on this action-packed genre goes like this: unwitting but wise hero discovers a dangerous state secret and so must outwit intelligence forces to save the day. In *The Pelican Brief,* law student Julia Roberts discovers the conspiracy behind the death of two Supreme Court justices, resulting in a whirlwind flight from and fight against the FBI. Most of this film – based on the John Grisham novel – takes place in New Orleans, but there are a few shots of Georgetown and one classic scene at the **Florida Avenue Grill** (p135). Essentially the same storyline is played out in *Enemy of the State*, except lawyer Will Smith takes on the ultra-mysterious National Security Agency right here in the capital. Both of these entertaining films have suspense-filled plots and well-developed characters, even if the themes are trite. For a lighter look at intelligence, *The Man with One Red Shoe* is a silly, spoofy story of an unsuspecting musician (Tom Hanks) who is mistaken for a CIA mole. It's good for some laughs and some glimpses of the city.

Real-life intrigue is the subject of one classic DC film: *All the President's Men*, based on Carl Bernstein and Bob Woodward's first-hand account of their uncovering of the Watergate scandal. (Young Robert Redford and Dustin Hoffman are brilliant as the reporters.) This film's only disappointment is that it does not take the insiders' account to its completion, but concludes – anticlimactically – with the 1973 *Post* headlines recounting the end of the story.

The only movies where the politician is a good guy are those depicting the US President: *Air Force One, The American President, Primary Colors, Thirteen Days* – all entertaining but idealistic portraits of the Chief Executive facing various crises. A variation on this theme is *Wag the Dog*, a hilarious parody of presidential-election spin: a presidential advisor (Robert De Niro) hires a Hollywood producer (Dustin Hoffman) to 'produce' a war in order to distract voters from an unfolding sex scandal. This marriage of Hollywood and Washington results in the cleverest satire of national politics to date.

Arguably the best – most realistic, most captivating – Washington movie is Otto Preminger's *Advise & Consent* (p26), based on Allen Drury's novel by the same name. For its portrayal of our political system at work, complete with personalities and processes, this film is a must-see. Interesting tidbit: the DC scenes include the first in Hollywood history that were shot in a gay bar.

Top Five DC Films

- *Advise & Consent* An incredible inside-the-Capitol story of the interplay of personalities and politics.
- *All the President's Men* Robert Redford's suspenseful rendition of Woodward and Bernstein uncovering the Watergate scandal.
- *The Exorcist* All hell breaks loose in Georgetown.
- *Mr Smith Goes to Washington* Jimmy Stewart saves the day on Capitol Hill.
- *Wag the Dog* A side-busting comparison of making movies and saving elections.

Only a very few films set in Washington DC are not about politics. The horrific highlight is undoubtedly *The Exorcist*, set in Georgetown. The creepy long staircase in the movie – descending from Prospect St to M St in reality – has become known as the **Exorcist Stairs** (p75). Another Georgetown classic is the 1980s Brat Pack flick *St Elmo's Fire*. Demi Moore and Judd Nelson are supposed to be Georgetown grads, but the college campus is actually the University of Maryland in College Park (although there is the key scene shot in the popular Georgetown bar the **Third Edition**, p163). For its excellent acting and suspense-filled storyline (and not a few shots of the nation's capital at its finest), *A Few Good Men* is an excellent DC movie.

Film fans who want the lowdown on every movie ever shot in DC should read *DC Goes to the Movies* by Jean K Rosales and Michael R Jobe.

TELEVISION

Portrayals of DC on TV range from national capital to murder capital. Wildly popular *West Wing* stars Martin Sheen as the beneficent, liberal president ('The best president we've ever had', claim fans) that could never be elected in real-life, modern-day America. But he is on TV and we get to witness him confronting the crises and controversies that a president might face. The primetime drama gets high marks (including four consecutive Emmys for Outstanding Drama) for its plausible portrayal of contemporary political issues.

The District is about the other side of DC – the dangerous, crime-ridden streets that are so far (symbolically if not geographically) from the White House. Craig Nelson plays the chief of police who uses unconventional means to fight crime in the capital. The drama is inspired by the real-life experiences of New York Deputy Police Commissioner Jack Maple, who is also one of its creators.

Another show with a cult following is the *X-Files*, tales of two FBI special agents, Scully and Mulder, who try to solve mysterious or unexplained cases. The show walks the line between science fiction and drama, testing the limits of science and imagination and throwing in some old-fashioned romantic tension for fun. The two traverse the world investigating superhuman crime, but their base is FBI headquarters (p52) in DC.

History

History

THE RECENT PAST
TRANSITIONS
The turn of the 21st century brought new leadership to Washington DC at both the local and national levels. In 2001, George W Bush was sworn in as the 43rd President of the United States. Two years earlier – 25 years after DC was granted Home Rule – Anthony Williams took his oath as the fourth elected mayor of the capital city.

Williams' tenure has been marked by an upswing in the city's economic fortunes, sparked mainly by the boom of the 1990s. Rising real-estate values have prompted a renaissance for some depressed neighborhoods. Population outflow stabilized, unemployment declined and crime rates dropped. The composed technocrat Williams is in many ways the political opposite of his controversial predecessor, Marion Barry. Having previously stripped the mayoral office of its purse-string responsibility, Congress handed most city controls back to Williams shortly after his inauguration.

The celebration of President Bush's arrival in Washington was tarnished only slightly by the controversy surrounding his election. The Clintons vacated the White House for a less prominent home on Whitehaven St in Georgetown. And George and Laura Bush, along with hundreds of political appointees and hopefuls, settled into new digs in the capital. As a practical (political) joke, staff members of the Clinton White House removed the letter 'W' from all of the computer keyboards in the White House offices. But otherwise, the transition was without incident.

WASHINGTON UNDER FIRE
On September 11, 2001, 30 minutes after the attack on New York's World Trade Center, a plane departing Washington Dulles International Airport bound for Los Angeles was hijacked and redirected toward Washington. Speculation was that the hijackers' primary objective was the White House, but they opted for a more exposed target. The plane crashed into the Pentagon's west side, penetrating to the building's third ring. Sixty-six passengers and crew, as well as 125 Pentagon personnel, were killed in the suicide attack.

Top Five Books on DC History

- *The Birth of the Nation: A Portrait of the American People on the Eve of Independence*, Arthur Schlesinger (1968) A vivid portrait of colonial life.
- *On this Spot: Pinpointing the Past in Washington, DC*, Paul Dickson and Douglas Evelyn (1992) Pinpoints the spots and shows photos where historic events took place.
- *Political Terrain: Washington, DC, from Tidewater Town to Global Metropolis*, Carl Abbott (1999) Explores DC's symbolic identity, from its days as a sleepy Southern town to its present iconic status.
- *Washington Goes to War*, David Brinkley (1996) A delightfully readable book about the change that WWII wrought upon DC as thousands of newcomers flooded into town to fill government jobs.
- *Washington Odyssey: A Multicultural History of the Nation's Capital*, Francine Cary (2003) A collection of essays explores the contributions of DC's immigrants and ethnic minorities.

TIMELINE	1608	1791
	Captain John Smith sails up the Potomac and makes contact with the Piscataway Indians	The juncture of the Potomac and Anacostia Rivers is chosen as the site of the new federal capital

Like most Americans, Washingtonians had no living memory of war on their territory. The shock of terrorism registered deeply in the public psyche.

In the wake of the hijackers' exploits, prominent media and political figures received lethal doses of anthrax in the mail. Several congressional staffers were infected and two DC postal workers died. Though unsolved, the anthrax mailings were eventually attributed to a domestic source.

Over a three-week period in the autumn of 2002, area residents were once again terrorized by unseen assailants. A pair of serial snipers went on a shooting spree in the Washington suburbs; 10 people were dead and thousands badly frightened before the snipers were finally apprehended by police.

The city has been palpably changed by these tragedies. From increasing security measures to declining tourism, the effects of the terrorist attack are evident throughout the capital. Yet no matter how deep the wound that was inflicted in 2001, Washington DC has seen – and survived – worse. So the cogs of the capital continue to grind, forcing the wheels of the government to spin. The local and federal city carries on.

FROM THE BEGINNING

EARLY SETTLEMENT

Before the first European colonists sailed up from Chesapeake Bay, Native Americans, primarily the Piscataway tribe of the Algonquian language group, made their home near the confluence of the Potomac and Anacostia Rivers. The first recorded white contact with the Piscataway was in 1608 by the English Captain John Smith, who set out from Jamestown colony to explore the upper Potomac.

Relations with the peaceful Piscataway were amicable at first, but soon turned ruinous for the natives. As many as 10,000 Piscataway inhabited the region, but their numbers were reduced by half within 25 years. Vulnerable to European sicknesses, many natives succumbed to disease. In mid-century, the Piscataway suffered further losses from entanglements in the Indian Wars between the English and the more hostile Susquehannock and Powhatan tribes. By 1700, the few remaining Piscataway migrated out of the region to Iroquois territory in Pennsylvania and New York.

The first Europeans in the region were traders and fur trappers, who plied the woodlands beyond the Allegheny Mountains, often working with local Algonquin Indians. English and Scots-Irish settlers followed, turning the forests into farmland. With the founding of Maryland, soul-saving Jesuits arrived to convert the locals.

By the late 1600s, expansive agricultural estates lined both sides of the Potomac. These tidewater planters became a colonial aristocracy, dominating regional affairs. Their most lucrative crop was the precious sotweed – tobacco – which was tended by African indentured servants and slaves. The river ports of Alexandria and Georgetown became prosperous commercial centers.

FOUNDING THE NATION'S CAPITAL

Following the Revolutionary War, the fledgling US Congress launched a search for a permanent home. The Constitution, ratified in 1788, specified that a federal territory, no greater than 10 sq miles, should be established for the nation's capital. The newly inaugurated President Washington chose the site on the Potomac. It was strategically suitable for commerce and river traffic, and politically pleasing to both northern and southern concerns. Maryland and Virginia agreed to cede land to the new capital.

Over drinks at a Georgetown tavern, Washington persuaded local residents to sell their holdings to the government for $65 an acre. In March 1791 the African American mathematician Benjamin Banneker and surveyor Andrew Ellicott mapped out a diamond-shaped

1800	1814
Congress convenes in the new capital for the first time; John Adams moves into the President's House	An attack by British troops devastates the fledgling capital

African American Civil War Museum (p82)

territory that spanned the Potomac and Anacostia Rivers. Its four corners were at the cardinal points of the compass, and it embraced the river ports of Georgetown and Alexandria (the latter eventually returned to Virginia). Pierre Charles L'Enfant, a French officer in the Revolutionary War, sketched plans for a grandiose European-style capital of monumental buildings and majestic boulevards. It was named the 'Territory of Columbia' (to honor Christopher Columbus) and the 'City of Washington' (to honor George).

But L'Enfant's showcase capital went unfinished. The French major was a diva, quarrelling with city commissioners, running afoul of local politicians and knocking down people's houses while they were out of town. In 1792, Washington fired his planner. Meanwhile, land speculators grabbed prized properties and buildings sprang up haphazardly along mucky lanes. In 1793, construction began on the President's House and the Capitol, the geographic center points of the city. In 1800, John Adams became the first president to occupy the still uncompleted mansion. His wife Abigail hung the family's laundry in the East Room. The city remained a half-built, sparsely populated work in progress.

SLAVERY IN THE FEDERAL CITY

When Congress first convened in Washington in 1800, the city had about 14,000 residents. It was even then a heavily African American town: slaves and free blacks composed 29% of the population. Free blacks lived in the port of Georgetown, where a vibrant African American community emerged. They worked alongside and socialized with the city's slaves.

Since its introduction in Jamestown colony in 1619, slave labor had become an essential part of the regional tobacco economy. In 1800, more than half of the nation's 700,000 slaves

1862	1864
The District Emancipation Act outlaws slavery in the capital	The Battle of Fort Stevens – the only battle fought on capital soil – is won by the Union

lived in Maryland and Virginia. The capital of America's slave trade at that time, Washington contained slave markets and holding pens. Slavers conducted a highly profitable business buying slaves locally and selling them to Southern plantations.

The city's slave population steadily declined throughout the 19th century, while the number of free blacks rose. They migrated to the city, establishing their own churches and schools.

Washington became a front line in the intensifying conflict between north and south over slavery. The city was a strategic stop on the Underground Railroad, shuttling fugitive slaves to freedom in the northern states. The abolitionist movement fueled further racial tensions. In 1835, the Snow Riots erupted as white mobs set loose on black Washingtonians. When the rampage subsided, legislation was passed restricting the economic rights of the city's free blacks. At last, Congress outlawed the slave trade in Washington in 1850; the District Emancipation Act abolished slavery outright in 1862.

WASHINGTON IN THE AGE OF DEMOCRACY

To most visitors in the first half of the 19th century, the city was more a desolate provincial outpost than a dynamic urban center. Washington may have been the seat of federal government, but the states were the real players in political power and economic wealth. Governor Morris, a prominent New Yorker, acidly observed, 'We only need here houses, kitchens, scholarly men, amiable women and a few other trifles, to possess a perfect city.'

The city's rough-hewn appearance was, at least partially, intended. Thomas Jefferson disliked formal displays of power and privilege, and dispensed with the ceremonial pomp of the Washington and Adams presidencies. He was known to greet foreign dignitaries in his slippers. Another champion of the common man, President Andrew Jackson celebrated his inauguration with a raucous open-house party, at which inebriated guests made off with White House furnishings. This sort of official humility tempered – to some extent – the aristocratic pretensions of Washington high society.

From Slave to Statesman: Frederick Douglass

Born a slave in 1818 on a plantation on Maryland's Eastern Shore, Frederick Douglass is remembered as one of the country's most outstanding black 19th-century leaders.

When he was 21, he escaped wretched treatment at the hands of Maryland planters and established himself as a freeman in the booming whaling port of New Bedford, Massachusetts. Largely self-educated, Douglass had a natural gift of eloquence. In 1841 he won the admiration of New England abolitionists with an impromptu speech at an antislavery convention, introducing himself as 'a recent graduate from the institution of slavery, with his diploma, ie whip marks on his back.' The Massachusetts Anti-Slavery Society hired Douglass, and he traveled the free states as an energetic spokesman for abolition and the Underground Railroad.

Douglass' effectiveness so angered proslavery forces that his friends urged him to flee to England to escape seizure and punishment under the Fugitive Slave Law. But he kept lecturing in England, and admirers contributed enough money to enable him to purchase his freedom and return home in 1847.

Douglass then became the self-proclaimed 'station master and conductor' of the Underground Railroad in Rochester, New York, working with other famed abolitionists like Harriet Tubman and John Brown. In 1860, Douglass campaigned for Abraham Lincoln, and when the Civil War broke out, he helped raise two regiments of black soldiers – the Massachusetts 54th and 55th – to fight for the Union.

After the war, Douglass went to Washington to lend his support to the 13th, 14th and 15th Constitutional Amendments, which abolished slavery, granted citizenship to former slaves and guaranteed citizens the right to vote. He later became US marshal for Washington and the US minister to Haiti (the country's first black ambassador).

Douglass died at his Anacostia home, Cedar Hill, now the **Frederick Douglass National Historic Site** (p66), in 1895. His funeral was held at DC's historic Metropolitan AME Church, 1518 M St NW, where one speaker mourned him in words that illustrated what Douglass had meant to black Washington: 'Howl, fir tree, for the Cedar of Lebanon has fallen.'

1867	1900
Howard University is founded as an institute of higher education for the growing black population	The McMillan Plan transforms the face of the capital

Frederick Douglass National Historic Site (p66)

WAR OF 1812: WASHINGTON BURNS

In the early 19th century, the young nation had yet to become a formidable force in world affairs. US merchants and seamen were regularly bullied on the high seas by the British Navy. Responding to congressional hawks, President James Madison declared war in 1812. In retaliation for the razing of York (Toronto) by US troops, the British assaulted Washington. Work was barely complete on the Capitol in August 1814, when redcoats sailed up the Patuxent River and burned it to the ground. The victorious British embarked on a night of looting and arson. When it was over, most of the city's public buildings had been torched. President and Dolley Madison fled to the Virginia suburbs, with the Declaration of Independence and Constitution in hand.

Although the British were expelled and the city rebuilt, Washington was slow to recover. A congressional initiative to abandon the dispirited capital lost by just nine votes.

A HOUSE DIVIDED: WASHINGTON IN CIVIL WAR

The 1860 election of Abraham Lincoln meant that the office of president would no longer protect Southern interests in the increasingly irreconcilable rift over slavery. Rather than abide by the electoral outcome, Southern secessionists opted to exit the Union, igniting a four-year fratricidal clash. A prized target, Washington was often near the frontlines of fighting. A ring of earthwork forts was hastily erected around the city to protect it from attack. Washington saw only one battle on its soil: Confederate General Jubal Early's unsuccessful attack on Fort Stevens in northern DC, in July 1864. Washingtonians lived in constant anxiety, however, as bloody battles raged nearby at Antietam, Gettysburg and Manassas.

Washington experienced an influx of soldiers, volunteers, civil servants and ex-slaves. Within three months of hostilities, over 50,000 enlistees descended on the capital to join

1916–19	1941–44
WWI attracts thousands of people to Washington for the administration of the war	The growth of the federal government and its wartime bureaucracy causes another population explosion

the Army of the Potomac. The city served as an important rearguard position for troop encampments and supply operations.

Only five days after Confederate General Robert E Lee surrendered to Union General Ulysses S Grant at Appomattox, Lincoln was assassinated in downtown Washington at Ford's Theatre (p53).

The Civil War had a lasting impact on the city. The war strengthened the power of the federal government, marking the first efforts to conscript young men into military service and to collect income tax from private households. Warfare brought new bureaucracies, workers and buildings to the capital. Between the war's start and end, the city's population nearly doubled to more than 130,000. Howard University was founded in 1867 to educate black residents; by this time, blacks comprised nearly half the population.

The capital economy was bolstered by a postwar boom. Although in many ways a southern city, Washington was already part of the commercial networks of the north. The B&O Railroad connected the city via Baltimore to the industry of the northeast; while the Chesapeake and Ohio Canal opened a waterway to the agriculture of the Midwest. In 1871, President Ulysses Grant appointed a Board of Public Works to upgrade the urban infrastructure and improve living conditions. The board was led by Alexander Shepherd, who energetically took on the assignment. He paved streets, put in sewers, installed gas lights, planted trees, filled in swamps and carved out parklands. But he also ran over budget by $20 million or so, and was sacked by Congress, who reclaimed responsibility for city affairs. 'Boss' Shepherd was the closest thing that DC would have to self-government for 100 years.

THE AMERICAN CENTURY

As the 1900s began, the US asserted itself on the world stage, competing with Europe to extend its influence overseas. With the Spanish-American War and Theodore Roosevelt's presidency, the US had entered the Age of Empire.

In 1900, Senator James McMillan of Michigan formed an all-star city-planning commission to make over the capital, whose population now surpassed a quarter-million. The McMillan Plan effectively revived L'Enfant's vision of a resplendent city on par with Europe's best. The Plan proposed grand public buildings in the beaux-arts style (p23), which reconnected the city to its neoclassical republican roots, but with an eclectic flair. It was impressive, orderly and upper class. The plan entailed an extensive beautification project. It removed the scrubby trees and coal-fired locomotives that belched black smoke from the Mall, and created the expansive lawn and reflecting pools that exist today.

The Mall became a showcase of the symbols of American ambition and power: monumental tributes to the founding fathers; the enshrinement of the Declaration of Independence and Constitution in a Greek temple; and the majestic Memorial Bridge leading to Arlington National Cemetery, hallowed ground of the nation's fallen warriors. Washington had become the nation's civic center, infused with the spirit of history, heroes and myths. The imagery was embraced by the country's budding political class.

The Plan improved living conditions for middle-class public servants and professionals. New 'suburbs', such as Woodley Park and Mount Pleasant, offered better-off residents a respite from the hot inner city, and electric trolleys crisscrossed the streets. Of course, the daily life of many Washingtonians was less promising. Impoverished slums like Murder Bay and Swamppoodle stood near government buildings, and about 20,000 poor blacks still dwelled in dirty alleyways.

THE 20TH-CENTURY AMERICAN STATE

Two world wars and one great depression changed forever the place of Washington in American society. These events hastened a concentration of power in the federal government in general and the executive branch in particular. National security and social

1963	1968
Martin Luther King Jr leads the civil rights march on the National Mall	Martin Luther King Jr is shot in Atlanta; Washington DC erupts in riotous violence

From Jackie O to Just Say No

An exhibit on First Lady inaugural gowns has been a longtime Smithsonian favorite, but the role of First Lady has changed in recent years. First ladies are now better known for their social causes than their ceremonial costumes.

From the outset, first ladies served principally as the nation's chief hostess. America's first First Lady, Martha Washington, likened this role to a 'state prisoner.' Cultured Abigail Adams did her best to preside over formal dinners, but privately hated living in a 'wilderness.' Among the founding mothers, vivacious Dolley Madison impressed as hostess *par excellence*.

In the early 20th century, influenced by the women's movement, the role of First Lady began to move beyond reception halls. Nellie Taft was involved in the capital beautification project and suggested the planting of the cherry trees around the tidal basin. Edith Bolling Wilson secretly performed some of her husband's presidential duties when he was stricken by illness. But it was Eleanor Roosevelt who truly transformed the part. She was a tireless campaigner for her husband and a heartfelt spokesperson for the underprivileged.

Few first ladies have captivated the public as did the graceful Jackie Kennedy, who used her position to patronize the arts. Betty Ford spoke out on a number of issues once taboo for a first lady, like breast cancer and drug abuse. Rosalyn Carter participated in cabinet meetings. Nancy Reagan discouraged drug use, while Barbara Bush promoted literacy.

Hillary Clinton expanded the political role of first lady still further. A practicing lawyer, she was substantially involved in policy making, and then later successfully ran for Senate from New York. Her strong personality, however, provoked a backlash from partisan quarters. Her successor, librarian Laura Bush, has returned to the less-controversial model of her mother-in-law as reading advocate and stay-at-home mom.

---

welfare became the high-growth sectors of public administration. City life was transformed from Southern quaintness to cosmopolitan clamor.

WWI witnessed a wave of immigration. The administration of war had an unquenchable thirst for clerks, soldiers, nurses and other military support staff. By war's end, the city's population was over half a million. This phenomenon recurred in WWII, when the city's population topped a million. A burgeoning organizational infrastructure supported the new national security state. The US Army's city-based civilian employee roll grew from 7000 to 41,000 in the first year of the war. The world's largest office building, the Pentagon, was hastily built across the river to house them all.

In response to the Great Depression, Franklin Roosevelt's New Deal extended the reach of the federal government into the economy. Federal regulators acquired greater power to intervene into business and financial affairs. Dozens of relief agencies were created to administer the social guarantees of the nascent welfare state. In Washington, New Deal work projects included tree planting on the Mall and finishing public buildings, such as the Supreme Court.

The Cold War and the Great Society furthered the concentration of political power in Washington-based bureaucracies. It attracted new breeds of policy specialists – macro-economists, international experts and social engineers. They comprised a better-educated and more prosperous middle-class. This trend continued unabated until the Reagan presidency in the 1980s. Even then, the foundations of 'big government' proved too firm to undermine. Candidate Reagan vowed to abolish the Commerce Department once elected; not only did the bureaucracy survive his tenure, but constructed a fabulous new office building, ironically named for the 40th president.

SEGREGATION & THE CIVIL RIGHTS MOVEMENT

In the early 20th century, Washington adopted racial segregation policies, like the rest of the South. Its business establishments and public spaces became, in practice if not in law, 'whites only.' The 'progressive' Wilson administration reinforced discrimination by refusing to hire black federal employees and insisting on segregated government offices. In 1925, the Ku Klux Klan marched on the Mall.

1973	1976
Washington DC is granted the right to Home Rule	Metrorail opens to serve the growing suburban community

Vietnam Veterans Memorial (p47)

Nonetheless, Washington was a black cultural capital in the early 20th century. Shaw and LeDroit Park, near Howard University, sheltered a lively black-owned business district, and black theater and music flourished along U St NW. Southern blacks continued to move to the city in search of better economic opportunities. Between 1920 and 1930, Washington's black population jumped 20%. Citywide segregation eased somewhat with the New Deal (which brought new black federal workers to the capital) and WWII (which brought lots more).

In 1939, the DC-based Daughters of the American Revolution barred the black contralto Marian Anderson from singing at Constitution Hall. At Eleanor Roosevelt's insistence, Anderson instead sang at the Lincoln Memorial before a huge audience – and that iconic moment highlighted a new era of black-led demonstrations, sit-ins, boycotts and lawsuits. Parks and recreational facilities were legally desegregated in 1954; schools followed soon thereafter. President John Kennedy appointed the city's first black federal commissioner in 1961. The Home Rule Act was approved in 1973, giving the city some autonomy from its federal overseers. The 1974 popular election of Walter Washington brought the first black mayor to office. The capital became one of the most prominent African American–governed cities in the country.

1990	1994
Mayor Marion Barry is arrested for possession and use of cocaine	After serving six months in prison, Barry is re-elected to a fourth term in office

Washington hosted key events in the national civil rights struggle. In 1963, Martin Luther King Jr led the March on Washington to lobby for passage of the Civil Rights Act. His stirring speech, delivered before 200,000 people on the steps of the Lincoln Memorial, was a defining moment of the campaign. The capital was staggered by the assassination of Reverend King five years later. Racial tensions exploded in two nights of riots and arson (centered on 14th and U Sts NW in the Shaw district). Twelve people were killed and hundreds of businesses, many black-owned, were damaged. White residents began to flee the city, and downtown Washington north of the Mall – especially the Shaw district – fell into years of economic slump.

The legacy of segregation proved difficult to overcome. For the next quarter-century, white and black Washington grew further apart. By 1970, the city's population declined to 750,000, while the wealthier suburbs boomed to nearly three million. When the sleek, federally funded Metrorail system opened in 1976, it bypassed the poorer black neighborhoods and instead connected the downtown to the white suburbs.

The negative trends continued in the 1980s. Marion Barry, a veteran of the civil rights struggle, was elected mayor in 1978. Combative and charismatic, he became a racially polarizing figure in the city. Tainted by corruption, Barry's administration alienated middle-class white residents, who continued to move out to suburbia. By decade's end, the population dipped below 600,000. When Barry was reelected to a fourth term, following a stint in jail, Congress acted to reclaim financial control of the city, thus ending yet another episode in Home Rule. See Government & Politics (p18).

1999

Anthony Williams is elected as the fourth mayor of Washington DC

Neighborhoods

Neighborhoods

The neighborhoods of the US capital are almost as diverse as the country itself, from the federal heart in the center to the local communities on the outskirts, from down-and-out Southeast to up-and-coming Northeast to upscale Northwest.

We've broken the city into twelve manageable pieces, each defined by geographic factors, but also by activities and atmosphere. We start at the center of it all, the National Mall. Here the museums and monuments alone could occupy a visitor for days. Then we cruise the surrounding neighborhoods: the revitalized downtown, packed with restaurants and theaters; the stately White House area and nearby Foggy Bottom; the political heart of Capitol Hill and its poorer neighbor Southeast DC; and the bureaucratic Southwest DC. Each maintains an official feel close to the Mall, but acquires a tastier flavor as you move away.

Moving further out into the city's vast Northwest and Northeast quadrants, we reach the neighborhoods where local life is liveliest. We pilgrimage to the Catholic shrines and lush parklands of Brookland and Northeast DC; explore the unique architecture and history of Georgetown; browse the bookstores and coffee shops of cosmopolitan Dupont Circle and Kalorama; eat ethnic cuisine and bop to world beats in Adams-Morgan; and dive into DC's black heritage in Shaw. City coverage wraps up with Rock Creek Park and the residential streets of Upper Northwest DC. Finally, we head across the Potomac River to discover Arlington and Alexandria.

Capitol (p63)

ITINERARIES

One Day

Start your Washington DC express tour with breakfast at **Jimmy T's** (p124) on Capitol Hill. Then wander down to the Mall, admiring the mighty Capitol along the way. Pick a museum on the **Mall** (p44), or if the weather is fine, stay outside, enjoy the sunshine and explore the many monuments. Hop on the Orange Line to Foggy Bottom or enjoy a long stroll along the Potomac into Georgetown for lunch at **Dean & Deluca** (p126) or **Café La Ruche** (p126). Spend the afternoon exploring the shops and galleries. Don't be afraid to wander away from Wisconsin Ave – check out the still waters of the **C&O Canal** (p74) and the gorgeous gardens of **Dumbarton Oaks** (p74). When your stomach starts grumbling, hop in a cab to Adams-Morgan and choose the ethnic eatery that suits you (p132). All the nightlife you can squeeze into one evening is right here, whether you want to hear some live tunes at **Madam's Organ** (p160) or get your groove on at **Chief Ike's Mambo Room** (p164). For a complete night out, try the **Night Crawl** (p109).

Three Days

Spend a full day on the Mall, visiting a few different museums, our favorites being the **National Gallery of Art** (p49) and the **National Museum of Natural History** (p50). Take time to catch a flick at the

IMAX theater. Between museums, relax in the surreal **National Sculpture Garden** (p50), where you can lunch at the **Pavilion Café** (p118). When you grow weary of dinosaur bones and impressionist paintings, head across the street to the **National Archives** (p54) to see first-hand the documents that are the foundation of this country. Finish your day downtown – dine at one of the 'Top Five Politico-Spotting Spots' (p120) or catch a show at the **National Theatre** (p155).

Spend a Saturday morning at **Eastern Market** (p64) and find some treasures in the North Hall, as well as at the flea market across the street. Feast on a breakfast of blue-buck pancakes at **Market Lunch** (p124). Pick up some produce for a picnic. Then hop on the Orange Line to Foggy Bottom, rent a bike at **Thompson Boat Center** (p170) and pedal the **Monumental Bike Ride** (p107). In the evening, catch a cab to Adams-Morgan for a night on the town, as under One Day.

On your third day, chill out in the morning. If it's a Sunday, you may want to attend a traditional service at the **Washington National Cathedral** (p95) or the inspiring gospel service at **St Augustine Catholic Church** (p78). Afterwards, take the bus into Georgetown (No 32, 34 or 36 from the National Cathedral, D2 from Dupont Circle) for brunch at the **Peacock Café** (p127). Spend the afternoon as outlined under One Day.

One Week

Cover the three-day itinerary, adding breathing space where you feel rushed. Spend a day investigating one of DC's newest museums (see the boxed text 'Top Five New DC Additions,' p50) and exploring the surrounding 'hood. Spend a morning at **Mount Vernon** (p207) with lunch and an afternoon in **Alexandria** (p99) exploring Old Town. You may wish to head further afield to escape urbanity, either for a day at **Great Falls** (p217) or longer on the **Chesapeake Bay** (p212) or at **Shenandoah National Park** (p210).

ORGANIZED TOURS

DC has more organized tour options than hanging chads in a ballot box. From history to architecture to black heritage to spies and scandal, there are tours catering to every interest. Likewise for mode of transport: you can find someone to lead you by boat, bus or bike, or even on your good old-fashioned feet. For a complete list of organized tours of DC, see **Cultural Tourism DC** (www.culturaltouris mdc.org). Here are some of our favorites.

BIKE THE SITES Map pp246-8

☎ 202-842-BIKE; www.bikethesites.com; 1100 Pennsylvania Ave, Old Post Office Pavilion; adult/child $40/30; ⌚ 9am & 1pm; Metro: Federal Triangle

Knowledgeable guides lead tours of DC's major landmarks, as well as more specialized options, such as tours over and under Washington bridges and tours of Civil War sites. Additional tours vary with the season. The price includes bikes and all necessary equipment.

DC DUCKS

☎ 202-966-3825; www.dcducks.com; 50 Massachusetts Ave NE, Union Station; adult/child $26/13; ⌚ 10am-4pm Apr-Oct; Metro: Union Station

In a classic case of defense conversion, amphibious land/water vehicles carry tourists on a waddle around the city streets and float along the Potomac. The 90-minute tour departs from Union Station and features visits to the Mall and monuments, as well as the corniest jokes on a city tour.

DC HERITAGE

☎ 202-661-7576; www.culturaltourismdc.org

An extensive list of specialized tour options focuses on cultural heritage themes, like Duke Ellington's DC, Civil War history and Old Anacostia.

ODYSSEY CRUISES Map pp254-5

☎ 888-741-0281; www.odysseycruises.com; 6th & Water Sts, Gangplank Marina; lunch/brunch/dinner $37/49/80-90; ⌚ brunch/lunch 11am-1:30pm, dinner 7-10pm Sun-Thu, 8-11pm Fri & Sat; Metro: Waterfront

Odyssey has the only ship that is designed to fit underneath all of the Potomac's historic bridges; it cruises up past Arlington Cemetery, the Lincoln Memorial, the Kennedy Center and Georgetown.

SPIRIT CRUISES Map pp254-5

☎ 866-211-3811; www.spiritcruises.com; 6th & Water Sts, Pier 4; Metro: Waterfront

The *Spirit of Washington* is a huge ship which hosts lunch, dinner and midnight cruises that sail down the Potomac to Old Town Alexandria. *Spirit* also operates day trips and one-way trips to Mount Vernon (March to November).

TOUR DC

☎ 301-588-8999; www.tourdc.com; tours $12-15

A local travel writer, Mary Kay Ricks, leads a variety of really excellent walking tours around DC neighborhoods, especially around Georgetown and Dupont Circle. Tours focus on such themes as spies and scandal, black heritage, gardens and mansions, and Embassy Row.

TOURMOBILE

☎ 202-554-5100, 888-868-7707; adult/child $18/8; ⓥ 9:30am-4:30pm; Metro: Federal Triangle or Arlington Cemetery

The big boy on the local narrated bus-tour scene, Tourmobile's primary tour runs around the National Mall, Capitol, White House and out to Arlington National Cemetery. You can hop off and reboard for free at any of its 25 stops, which is nice for those who aren't able to walk long distances. Tourmobile also does separate tours of Arlington National Cemetery (adult/child $5.25/2.50), Mount Vernon ($7/3.50) and some black heritage sites ($7/3.50).

WASHINGTON WALKS

☎ 202- 484-1565; http://washingtonwalks.com; adult/child $10/5

Two-hour jaunts include the White House Un-tour (Tuesday to Saturday), plus weekly tours like Haunted Houses and Goodnight Mr Lincoln (great for kids).

NATIONAL MALL

Eating p117; Shopping p174

The National Mall serves as the nation's front yard – where 'We, the People' can enjoy an afternoon picnic, advertise our politics or play a game of pick-up. Here, the US throws its parties, from presidential inaugurations to folk festivals. And here – in the jumble of museums and monuments lining the green – we memorialize our cultural, scientific and political achievements (wars among the latter).

On a day-to-day basis, the Mall hosts sunning tourists, Frisbee-catching dogs, jogging bureaucrats and touting T-shirt salesmen. But this national park is best known for its political gatherings. From suffragettes to victorious soldiers, generations of protesters and celebrants have made the Mall their own. Protesters demonstrated against the Vietnam War during the 1960s; and in 1963, Martin Luther King declared 'I Have a Dream' on the Lincoln Memorial steps. Today gun controllers, 2nd-amendment protectors, pro-lifers, pro-choicers, troop supporters and war protesters are as common as tourists on the Mall.

The national monuments on the Mall are similarly eclectic. When the Vietnam Veterans Memorial opened in 1982, it generated tremendous controversy. But its popularity sparked a monument binge in Washington. Now we have monuments to WWII, the Korean War, women in Vietnam, DC war veterans and more. (An Army canine-corps monument didn't win congressional approval.)

Overkill, critics claim: the excess of monuments detracts from the significance of any one structure. While this criticism is certainly valid, nobody can balk at the big picture.

For all the marble and columns and fountains and lawns, the National Mall is completely breathtaking and totally awe inspiring.

The strange mixture of statuary and buildings offers insight into the ongoing debate over what a national capital – and democracy itself – should be: it's a history lesson in sod and stone.

Transportation

Metro Most sights along the Mall are closest to the Orange Line Smithsonian stop, although if you are headed specifically to the west end, Foggy Bottom-GWU or Farragut West may be closer.

Parking Street parking is not easy but it's not impossible along Constitution and Independence Aves, as well as Jefferson and Madison Drs. Parking becomes legal at 9:30am on weekdays; arrive then or earlier to snag a spot.

Orientation

The National Mall is a 400ft-wide green expanse stretching 3 miles from the Potomac in the west to Capitol Hill in the east. Lined with gravel paths and bordered by tree-shaded avenues (Constitution Ave to the north, Independence Ave to the south), the Mall is fringed by museums and dotted with monuments. The Lincoln Memorial and the Capitol anchor their respective ends of the national park; at the center, the phallic Washington Monument is the axis of the cross formed by these buildings, the White House, and the Thomas Jefferson Memorial. The first half of this section describes the Mall's western extension, officially called West Potomac Park, which incorporates the Reflecting Pool and the many monuments surrounding it, plus the Tidal Basin and its monuments. For our purposes it also includes the Washington Monument. The eastern half of the Mall is the setting for nine of the museums of the Smithsonian Institution, as well as the National Gallery of Art, National Sculpture Garden and United States Botanic Garden. These massive storehouses of culture line the north and south sides of the green. To the south, East Potomac Park extends downward toward the confluence of the Potomac and Anacostia Rivers. East Potomac Park and the Tidal Basin are covered in Southwest DC (p70).

CONSTITUTION GARDENS Map pp246-8

⏱ dawn-dusk; Metro: Smithsonian

Originally planned to be a Rivoli-style amusement park, Constitution Gardens – really just a grove of trees – is a shady place for a stroll. In its midst, a small, kidney-shaped pool is punctuated by a tiny island holding the **Signers' Memorial**, a plaza honoring the Declaration of Independence's signers. At the northeast corner of the gardens, an intriguing, aged stone cottage is a remnant of the days when the Washington City Canal flowed through this area. The 1835 **C&O Canal Gatehouse** was the lockkeepers' house for the lock that transferred boats from the City Canal onto the **C&O Canal** (p74), which begins in Georgetown.

KOREAN WAR VETERANS MEMORIAL

Map pp246-8

☎ 202-426-6841; www.nps.gov/kowa; ⏱ 8am-midnight; Metro: Foggy Bottom-GWU

Dedicated in 1995, this memorial depicts a troop of heavily cloaked soldiers on night patrol in the rice paddies. The life-size statues are shown mid-stride, and realistically exhausted and anxious. Nearby is the small **District of Columbia War Memorial**, commemorating local soldiers killed in WWI. This circular temple, set amid a grove, is a nice place to escape Mall crowds.

LINCOLN MEMORIAL Map pp246-8

☎ 202-426-6841; www.nps.gov/linc; ⏱ 8am-midnight; Metro: Foggy Bottom-GWU

Since its completion in 1922, the memorial to the author of the Emancipation Proclamation has also been a symbol of the Civil Rights movement. Dr Robert Moten, president of historically black Tuskegee Institute, was invited to speak at

---

National Mall Top Five

- **Freer Gallery of Art** (p48) Whistler's Peacock Room.
- **National Air & Space Museum** (p49) Virtual flying, whether in flight simulation or at the IMAX Theatre.
- **National Museum of Natural History** (p50) Examining dinosaur bones up close and personal.
- **National Sculpture Garden** (p50) Surround yourself with surreal sculpture.
- **Vietnam Veterans Memorial** (p47) Shedding a tear and saying a prayer.

---

the memorial's dedication, yet officials sat him in a segregated section of the audience, sparking protests by outraged African Americans.

In 1939, black contralto Marian Anderson, barred from the Daughters of the American Revolution's Constitution Hall, sang from the memorial's steps; the historic 1963 March on Washington reached its zenith here when Martin Luther King Jr delivered his 'I Have a Dream' speech. An engraving of his famed words now marks the spot where MLK stood.

The monument balances the long axis of the Mall, a counterpoint to the Capitol at the eastern end. The 2000ft **Reflecting Pool** stretches in front, its shallow, duck-speckled waters reflecting both the Lincoln and Washington memorials. Designed by Henry Bacon to resemble a Doric temple, the memorial's 36 columns represent the 36 states in Lincoln's union. Within, the seated statue of Lincoln, sculpted by Daniel Chester French, is framed by the carved text of the Gettysburg Address and Lincoln's Second Inaugural.

NATIONAL WORLD WAR II MEMORIAL

Map pp246-8

☎ 800-639-4992; www.wwiimemorial.com; Metro: Smithsonian

On Memorial Day (May 29) 2004, President Bush dedicated a brand-new memorial to honor the 16 million soldiers who served during WWII and the millions of Americans who supported the war effort at home.

The memorial plaza has been constructed around the Rainbow Pool at the eastern end of the Reflecting Pool. It is flanked by two grand arches – the Atlantic and the Pacific – symbolizing victory on two fronts; and 56 granite pillars, one for each state and territory, plus the District of Columbia.

To commemorate the 400,000 Americans who lost their lives, a Freedom Wall sparkles with 4000 sculpted gold stars, the symbol worn by mothers who have lost their sons.

The memorial emphasizes the unprecedented unity of the nation during WWII in hopes of inspiring such nationalism in post-WWII generations.

For Children

DC is filled with fun for kids, including regular exhibits and special events. Here's a list of highlights if you have tots in tow.

Arthur M Sackler Gallery (p47) The Sackler's 'ImaginAsia' is perfect for children aged six to 14.

Arts & Industries Building (p48) The outdoor highlight is the antique carousel; plus the Discovery Theater stages performances and puppet shows that delight kids.

Capital Children's Museum (p68) Inviting hands-on exhibits for kids, including an outdoor sculpture garden and weekends filled with classes and demonstrations.

City Museum of Washington, DC (p52) Features a fun, multimedia show on the city's history.

East Potomac Park (p70) Hain's Point holds a playground and the spooky statue, the *Awakening*, both great for climbing around.

Hirshhorn Museum & Sculpture Garden (p48) 'Young at Art' programs introduce children to artistic study; the regularly scheduled 'Improv Art' classes give kids the chance to make their own artworks.

International Spy Museum (p53) Kids can eavesdrop on bugged conversations and crawl through imitation air ducts.

National Academy of Sciences (p59) Let your kids climb into Einstein's lap and look out at the universe.

National Air & Space Museum (p49) A guaranteed kid favorite – those who dream of being a pilot or an astronaut can test their skills.

National Bureau of Engraving & Printing (p71) Show your kids that money really doesn't grow on trees.

National Geographic Explorers Hall (p77) Interactive exhibits on natural history, dinosaurs, weather, animals and space exploration.

National Museum of American History (p49) Meet Kermit the Frog, see the real ruby slippers and check out any number of special kid features.

National Museum of Natural History (p50) The number one museum for kids, complete with dinosaurs, diamonds and the new Mammal Hall.

National Postal Museum (p65) Send a postcard and learn how it reaches its destination.

National Sculpture Garden & Ice Rink (p50) Kids will delight in the surreal statues and refreshing fountain.

National Zoological Park (p93) An obvious first stop for monkey-lovers and snake-spotters.

Pierce Mill (p94) Kids can watch rangers demonstrate the circa-1820 mill and try it themselves in Rock Creek Park.

Rock Creek Park Nature Center & Planetarium (p94) Hands-on ecological displays, kids' nature hikes and planetarium shows.

Textile Museum (p78) Interactive exhibits that teach all about weaving, dyeing, embroidering as well as patterning fabrics.

Washington Dolls' House & Toy Museum (p95) A marvelous collection of Victorian dollhouses and toys.

Washington National Cathedral (p95) Saturday family programs let kids hear stories and create gargoyles or stained-glass windows to take home.

VIETNAM VETERANS MEMORIAL
Map pp246-8

☎ 202-426-6841; www.nps.gov/vive; ⏰ 8am-midnight; Metro: Foggy Bottom-GWU

Since its dedication in 1982, this somber arrow of black stone has become an American pilgrimage site. A testament to the sacrifice of soldiers during America's least popular war, the memorial was meant to reconcile a divided nation. Designed by a 21-year-old Yale architecture student Maya Lin, its two walls of polished Indian granite meet in a 10ft apex. They are inscribed with the names of the 58,209 soldiers killed in the war, arranged chronologically by date of death. It's an eloquent inversion of the Mall's other monuments: rather than a pale, ornate structure reaching skyward, it's dark, austere and burrows into the earth, symbolizing the war's wound to the national psyche.

Paper indices at both ends help you locate individual names. The most moving remembrances are notes, medals and mementos left by survivors, family and friends; some of these are collected by park rangers and displayed at the National Museum of American History (p49).

In 1984, opponents of Maya Lin's design insisted that a more traditional (and far less interesting) sculpture of soldiers be added nearby. Also nearby is the tree-ringed Women in Vietnam Memorial depicting female soldiers aiding a fallen man.

WASHINGTON MONUMENT Map pp246-8
☎ information 202-426-6841, ☎ reservations 800-967-2283; www.nps.gov/wamo; admission free, reservations $2; ⏰ 9am-5pm, tickets available from 8am; Metro: Smithsonian

This pale obelisk needling the sky near the Mall's west end honors the country's first president and the city's namesake. At 555ft, it's also the tallest structure in DC (by federal law). Inside, an elevator leads to an observation landing with spectacular views. You can descend the 897 steps on foot – the shaft's interior is decorated with inscribed stones.

At the time of research, the monument grounds were closed, and the building was accessible only from 15th St NW. Whether the grounds will reopen or not is the subject of a controversial debate. Same-day tickets for a timed entrance to the monument are available at the ticket kiosk on 15th St and Madison Dr NW. Distribution starts at 8am; arrive early – tickets are limited. Alternatively, you can reserve your tickets for a small fee by calling in advance. Food, drink and large bags are prohibited.

SMITHSONIAN

More than 150 years ol[...] sonian is DC's premier [...] than a complex of mus[...] sonian is also a vast researc[...] institution that cares for a[...] million artworks, scientific [...] facts and other objects – a co[...] that only a tiny percentage of [...] at any time. Its 14 DC muse[...] Smithsonian-run National Zoo[...] together draw millions of visitors[...] and they also offer year-round ca[...] films, lectures, kids' activities a[...] programs, most free.

The **Smithsonian Castle** (Map pp[...] Smithsonian Institution Bldg; ☎ 202[...] 2700; www.smithsonian.org; 1000 Je[...] son Dr SW; ⏰ 9am-4pm Mon-Sat; Me[...] Smithsonian) is the turreted, red-sandsto[...] fairytale building that was designed in 18[...] by James Renwick. The Castle houses the[...] **Smithsonian Visitors Center**. This informative[...] first stop on the Mall is a source for an orientation film, multilingual touch-screen displays and free guides and maps, such as the excellent *Exploring African American Heritage at the Smithsonian* pamphlet.

This section describes the nine Smithsonian museums on the Mall, as well as the non-Smithsonian National Gallery of Art, National Sculpture Garden and United States Botanic Garden. For Smithsonian institutions in other districts see the National Museum of American Art (p55), National Portrait Gallery (p55), Renwick Gallery (p60), National Postal Museum (p65), Anacostia Museum (p66) and National Zoological Park (p93).

ARTHUR M SACKLER GALLERY
Map pp246-8

☎ 202-633-4880; www.asia.si.edu; 1050 Independence Ave SW; admission free; ⏰ 10am-5:30pm, to 8pm Thu Jul & Aug; Metro: Smithsonian

Dedicated to Asian artwork, the Sackler's collection of paintings, sculpture, sacred objects and crafts ranges from the Mediterranean shores to South India to Southeast Asia. Exotic exhibits such as Luxury Arts of the Silk Route Empires explore the cultures of these faraway places. Rotating exhibits focus on contemporary photographic and artistic masterpieces. On the 2nd floor, ImaginAsia is a wonderful interactive exhibit for children aged six to 14. Free lectures, films, gallery talks and tours round out its offerings.

INSTITUTION

...the massive Smith-
...attraction. Far more
...eums, the Smith-
...h and educational
...proximately 140
...ecimens, arti-
...t is on display
...ms and the
...ogical Park
...each year,
...endars of
...d other

246-8;
...357-
...fter-
...ro:

...single mysterious line in the 1826 will of a British chemist who
...ldless, James Smithson wrote, 'I then bequeath the whole of
...ashington, under the name of the Smithsonian Institution,
...mong men.'

...n affair between Elizabeth Macie (a wealthy widow) and the
...self at Oxford, Smithson had an illustrious career as a chemist
...ry that zinc carbonates are minerals rather than zinc oxides. (A zinc
...ndertook more fanciful research as well, on such topics as the chemical
...deal method for making coffee. He had no children, and his nephew died
...American hands.

...ne slammed the British monarchy as a 'contemptible encumbrance' and publicly
...y's ideals – his $508,318 bequest wasn't much of a surprise to anyone but the US
...d this gift horse in the mouth. 'Every whippersnapper vagabond...might think it proper
...ed in the same way,' grumped Senator William Preston, and Senator John C Calhoun argued
...norized to accept the money and that it was 'beneath American dignity to accept presents from
...entiment informed some of this debate: the 1814 British torching of Washington remained fresh in
...nds. Finally, in 1846, Congress deigned to accept the gift and used it to build a museum and research
...d of today's sprawling Smithsonian.

...n is now literally a part of the Smithsonian – his remains lie in a marble bier in the Castle's Crypt Room,
...de the entrance.

ARTS & INDUSTRIES BUILDING
Map pp246-8

☎ 202-357-1500; www.si.edu/ai; 900 Jefferson Dr SW; admission free; ⏱ 10am-5:30pm; Metro: Smithsonian

An exquisite Victorian dream of red brick, multi-colored tiles and fanciful ironwork, the 1881 Arts & Industries Building was the original home of the Smithsonian, back when it was known as the National Museum. Most of its eclectic collection of scientific and industrial artifacts and artworks was later distributed to other Mall museums, but it still hosts excellent, ever-changing exhibits on history, science and society. The **Discovery Theatre** (p156; ☎ 202-357-1500) presents puppet shows, storytelling, music and dance performances for kids.

Outside, kids of all ages will have good, old-fashioned fun on the antique **carousel**. Pick your horse (or lion or tiger) and take her for a spin – literally.

FREER GALLERY OF ART Map pp246-8

☎ 202-633-4880; www.asia.si.edu; 12 St & Jefferson Dr SW; admission free; ⏱ 10am-5:30pm, to 8pm Thu Jul & Aug; Metro: Smithsonian

One of the finest collections of Asian art in the world was donated to the Smithsonian by Charles Lang Freer. This Detroit industrialist and self-taught connoisseur assembled an incredible ensemble of ancient ceramics, screen paintings, sculpture and musical instruments from China, Japan, Southeast Asia and the Near East, which are now on display at the Freer Gallery, built in 1923 to house the collection. He was also a fan of James McNeill Whistler, whose works appear here too. The museum's famed **Peacock Room**, originally designed by Whistler for a London ship owner, features gilded wall murals and an elaborate system of wood shelving that displays prized Chinese porcelains.

HIRSHHORN MUSEUM & SCULPTURE GARDEN Map pp246-8

☎ 202-357-2700; www.hirshhorn.si.edu; 7th St & Independence Ave SW; admission free; ⏱ 10am-5:30pm, to 8pm Thu Jul & Aug; Metro: L'Enfant Plaza

The Smithsonian's cylindrical modern art museum exhibits an impressive array of 19th- and 20th-century sculpture and canvases in chronological fashion, from modernism's early days to the millennium. Highlights include sculpture by Rodin, Brancusi, Calder and Moore, plus canvases by Bacon, Miró, O'Keeffe, Warhol, Stella and Kiefer. Outside and across Jefferson Dr, the sunken Sculpture Garden is a beautifully landscaped setting with a rich collection of works, like Rodin's The Burghers of Calais. The Hirshhorn hosts a wide range of tours, lectures and workshops, including some great events for kids. On Thursday and Saturday, the **Improv Art Room** invites kids to create their own works of art.

NATIONAL AIR & SPACE MUSEUM
Map pp246-8

☎ 202-357-2700; www.nasm.si.edu; 4th St & Independence Ave SW; admission free, IMAX or planetarium adult $7.50, senior & child $6; ☾ 10am-5:30pm, tours 10:15am & 1pm; Metro: L'Enfant Plaza

Every year, eight million people visit the cavernous halls filled with alighted airplanes and soaring spacecraft (including the Wright Brothers' *Flyer*, Charles Lindbergh's *Spirit of St Louis* and the Apollo 11 command module). The 23 galleries of the National Air & Space Museum trace the history of aviation and space exploration through interactive displays and historic artifacts. This place is crazy popular with kids, but adults too will get a kick out of touching the moon rock, walking through the DC-7 cockpit and taking the controls on a flight simulator ride. In 2003, a great new Wright Brothers exhibit opened in honor of the 100th anniversary of their feat.

When You Just Can't Get Enough

As of December 2003, there is even more National Air & Space Museum at the **Steven F Udvar-Hazy Center** (www.nasm.si.edu/museum/udvarhazy) at Washington Dulles International Airport. Visitors can wander across suspended walkways and airborne bridges to get a close-up view of hundreds of fighter planes, space ships and other flying machines suspended from the 10-story ceiling. Of the 200 aircraft and 135 spacecraft, highlights include the *Enola Gay*, SR-71 Blackbird, and space shuttle *Enterprise*. Many engines, rockets, satellites, helicopters and experimental flying machines are on display for the first time. Visitors can also observe ongoing preservation work in the restoration hangar; or hang out in the observation tower and watch the planes take off and land at Dulles airport. A shuttle bus will transport guests from the Air & Space Museum on the Mall to the Dulles airport facility.

The **Lockheed Martin IMAX Theater** features rotating films shown throughout the day. *To Fly*, the grizzled granddaddy of in-your-face IMAX films, still plays here daily, along with newer offerings. Alternative shows at the **Albert Einstein Planetarium** send viewers hurtling through space on tours of the universe. All of these shows sell out (especially the IMAX), so buy your tickets as soon as you arrive at the museum.

NATIONAL GALLERY OF ART
Map pp246-8

☎ 202-737-4215; www.nga.gov; 4th St & Constitution Ave NW; admission free; ☾ 10am-5pm Mon-Sat , 11am-6pm Sun; Metro: Archives-Navy Memorial

Affiliated with but not a part of the Smithsonian, the National Gallery needs two buildings (connected by an underground tunnel) to house its massive collections and the scores of touring exhibitions that go on display here.

The original neoclassical building known as the **West Building** exhibits primarily European works, from the Middle Ages to the early 20th century, including pieces by El Greco, Renoir, Monet and Cézanne. It's the only gallery in America that owns a da Vinci painting *(Ginevra di' Benci)*. Interactive computers in the Micro Gallery allow visitors to design their own tour.

Across 4th St NW, the angular **East Building**, designed by IM Pei, features a Calder mobile as the centerpiece of its four-story atrium. Downstairs, you'll find abstract and modern works. Smaller upstairs galleries hold special exhibits and permanent items like Picasso's *Family of Saltimbanques*. A small Matisse cut-outs gallery on the 3rd floor opens during limited hours.

NATIONAL MUSEUM OF AFRICAN ART
Map pp246-8

☎ 202-357-4600; www.nmafa.si.edu; 950 Independence Ave SW; admission free; ☾ 10am-5:30pm, to 8pm Thu Jul & Aug; Metro: Smithsonian

Enter the museum's ground level pavilion through the Asian moongates and geometric flowerbeds of the beautiful **Enid A Haupt Memorial Garden**. Take note of the African rhythms around you. Then descend into the dim underground exhibit space, connected by tunnel to the Sackler and the Freer. Devoted to ancient and modern sub-Saharan African art, the peaceful galleries display masks, textiles, ceramics, ritual objects and other examples of the visual traditions of a continent of 900 distinct cultures. You can't see it all, but don't miss the eight 'Hot Spots' highlighted at the information desk.

NATIONAL MUSEUM OF AMERICAN HISTORY
Map pp246-8

☎ 202-357-2700; www.americanhistory.si.edu; 14th St & Constitution Ave NW; admission free; ☾ 10am-5:30pm; Metro: Federal Triangle

From venerated historic touchstones like the original American flag to kitschy icons like Dorothy's ruby slippers, the original Kermit the Frog and Fonzie's *(Happy Days)* jacket, the collection of the Museum of American History celebrates

US culture. Among the latest additions is Julia Child's kitchen, transported from Cambridge, Massachusetts and reassembled just as she used it. The museum has come a long way from its beginnings when it was a delightful hodge-podge. Although there is no comprehensive survey from past to present, various exhibits examine the country's history from the perspective of the US presidency, or the development of transportation, or the 240-year 'life' of a New England house. Children will love Hands on Science on the 1st floor, and Hands on History on the 2nd floor (both closed Monday).

NATIONAL MUSEUM OF NATURAL HISTORY Map pp246-8

☎ 202-357-2700; www.mnh.si.edu; 10th St & Constitution Ave NW; admission free, IMAX adult $7.50, senior & child $6; ⏰ 10am-5:30pm, to 7:30pm Jun-Aug, tours 10:30am & 1:30pm; Metro: Federal Triangle
The world's most-visited museum keeps getting better every year. The newest addition is the **Hall of Mammals**, which demonstrates how mammals have evolved by adapting to changing environments. The exhibits are so interactive that visitors actually *feel* the rainstorm on the savannah and *see* what the hunting jaguar is stalking. The old favorites are also still here: the fossilized bones of the gargantuan T-Rex; the glittering 45-carat Hope Diamond; and live tarantula feedings at the insect zoo. The **Discovery Room**, closed for renovation at the time of research, normally contains hands-on science exhibits that enable children to examine – up close and personal – shells, bones, geodes, costumes and more stuff that they are not normally allowed to touch.

The **Johnson IMAX Theater** shows nature extravaganzas like *Bugs! in 3D* daily. Movies sell out so buy tickets as soon as you arrive, or on-line in advance. A fun Friday night adventure – for kids and adults – is to visit the IMAX Jazz Café.

NATIONAL MUSEUM OF THE AMERICAN INDIAN Map pp246-8

☎ 202-287-2020; www.americanindian.si.edu; 4th St & Independence Ave SW; Metro: Smithsonian
The Smithsonian's latest addition is scheduled to open in September 2004 in a sophisticated new building in the southeast corner of the Mall. Its modern shape and rounded lines provide a welcome complement to the National Gallery of Art's East Building directly opposite. The long-awaited institution will be dedicated to the preservation and study of the languages, literature, arts and history of Native Americans.

NATIONAL SCULPTURE GARDEN Map pp246-8

www.nga.gov/feature/sculptgarden/splash.htm; 9th St & Constitution Ave NW; admission free; ⏰ 10am-5pm Mon-Sat, 11am-6pm Sun, to 8pm Fri Jun-Aug; Metro: Archives-Navy Memorial
The National Gallery of Art's delightful 6-acre garden is studded with whimsical sculptures like Roy Lichtenstein's *House*, a giant Claes Oldenburg typewriter eraser and Louise Bourgeois' leggy *Spider*. They are scattered around a fountain – a most welcome place to dip your feet in summer. From November to March the garden's central fountain becomes the quaint **Ice Rink** (adult/child $7/5; ⏰ 10am-10pm). Skate rental is available.

UNITED STATES BOTANIC GARDEN Map pp246-8

☎ 202-225-8333; www.usbg.gov; 100 Maryland Ave SW; admission free; ⏰ 10am-5pm; Metro: Capitol South
Resembling London's Crystal Palace, this iron-and-glass greenhouse provides a beautiful setting for displays of exotic and local plants. It is not technically part of the Smithsonian Institute, but is located at the eastern end of the Mall alongside the Smithsonian museums. Highlights include cycad trees that produce 50lb cones, and the mammoth and smelly Titan Arum. Behind the conservatory, across Independence Ave, is the grand **Bartholdi Fountain**.

Top Five New DC Additions

If this is your first visit to DC in a few years, you may be shocked by the glut of new museums and monuments that are overrunning the nation's capital. Not to mention the renovation and reopening of pre-existing museums, as well as the addition of visitors centers. Where to begin catching up on all that DC has to offer? Here's our guide to the top new sights that everybody's talking about.

- **City Museum of Washington, DC** (p52) The local lowdown on the history of DC. Opened 2003.
- **International Spy Museum** (p53) Interactive exhibits on espionage and intrigue. Opened 2002.
- **National Museum of the American Indian** (p50) Art and history of Native American cultures. Opened 2004.
- **National World War II Memorial** (p46) A tribute to national unity in the Mall. Opened 2004.
- **Steven F Udvar-Hazy Center** (p49) More air and space paraphernalia than you can imagine anywhere but in the air. Opened 2003.

DOWNTOWN

Eating p118; Shopping p175; Sleeping p190

Pennsylvania Ave forms a straight arrow from the US Capitol to the White House: its traffic is inevitably going to or from the legislative or executive headquarters. The Penn Quarter – as this stretch is known – grew up along the way to support and cater to one or both of these institutions. It still reflects such purposefulness: from the grand luxury hotels to the huge federal buildings to the wide avenue itself.

The neighborhood – where life does not revolve around government – is in the streets north of Pennsylvania Ave. That is 'downtown' in its more traditional, non-federal sense, complete with museums, department stores, dance clubs, and loads and loads of restaurants. If DC can claim a theater or art district, they are both here. Indeed, this is the most urban part of DC, perhaps the only place with 'bright lights, big city' in the air.

Also in the air: the aromas of General Tsao and Kung Pao. The streets around 7th and H Sts NW – the colorful Friendship Arch marks the spot – have been the heart of DC's Chinese community since the turn of the century. Chinese restaurants, pharmacies and laundries crowd these streets; spicy smells and Chinese characters add an ethic element to downtown DC.

This lively downtown is a recent development. Like urban areas throughout the country, DC suffered after WWII when residents left the city in droves for the American dream in the suburbs. Despite the federal government's presence just a few blocks away, property values in this area plunged, businesses closed and there was little reason to go downtown.

Improved economic times in the 1990s allowed the DC government to dump serious money into resuscitating the downtown area, and efforts are paying off. The MCI Center – home to DC's professional basketball and hockey teams – opened in the early 1990s, bringing sports fans and concertgoers in droves. Business-types congregate at the vast new convention center north of Mount Vernon Sq. Unfortunately, all this construction has threatened the cohesiveness of Chinatown, but the dwindling community has rallied to preserve its cultural heritage (and this is still the best place to come for Chinese food). As if there is not enough going on, local officials and businesses are dreaming up new ways to lure people downtown outside of working hours: 'art crawl' gallery tours led by local artists; open-air concerts on Pennsylvania Ave; or a hip-hop happening nightclub in the courtyard of a federal building.

Transportation

Metro Every Metro line passes through Downtown, and they all intersect each other around here. McPherson Sq (Blue or Orange Line) is in the neighborhood's northwestern corner, bordering the White House district. Mt Vernon Sq/7th St-Convention Center (Green or Yellow Line) is on the northern border with the Shaw district. On the southern border in the Penn Quarter, Federal Triangle (Orange, Blue) and National Archives-Navy Memorial (Orange, Blue, Yellow, Green) are just north of the National Mall. Metro Center (Red, Orange, Blue) and Chinatown-Gallery Place (Red, Yellow, Green) are in the middle of it all.

Parking Street parking is near impossible around here; use the **PMI parking garage** (727 6th St NW, between F & G Sts; 1325 G St NW).

Orientation

'Downtown' is a portmanteau name loosely applied to the area in the Northwest quadrant that is north of the National Mall and east of the White House (for our purposes, between 1st and 14th Sts NW and Constitution Ave and L St NW).

Immediately north of the Mall, Pennsylvania Ave stretches from the Capitol and heads northwest toward the White House. This stretch is known as the Penn Quarter, and is filled with snazzy restaurants, bureaucratic buildings and tourist spillover from the Mall. As an extreme example of a bureaucratic building, the massive, modern Ronald Reagan Building (the second largest federal building) occupies two entire blocks – from 12th St to 14 St NW – along

Pennsylvania Ave. This southwestern corner of the neighborhood is sometimes called Federal Triangle, after the Metro stop here. Metro Center is a few blocks north.

Downtown's main drag – 7th St NW – runs from the National Archives and Navy Memorial in the south, north to Mount Vernon Sq and beyond to the site of the new City Museum of Washington and the vast new Washington Convention Center complex. Chinatown is at the very center of it all. These days, Chinatown is perhaps more aptly described as MCI-town, as the mammoth sports arena sits in the middle of it; the arena's opening has fueled the revitalization of the area.

East of Chinatown is Judiciary Sq. The square itself is lovely, containing the National Law Enforcement Officers Memorial and fronted by the exquisite National Building Museum. The surrounding streets are overwhelmingly concrete – big boxy buildings crowding the sidewalk and blocking the sun.

ADAS ISRAEL SYNAGOGUE Map pp246-8

☎ 202-789-0900; 701 3rd St NW; admission by donation $3; ⏰ noon-4pm Sun-Thu; Metro: Judiciary Sq, F St exit
Housing the Jewish Historical Society of Greater Washington, this tiny brick 1876 synagogue is DC's oldest. Ring the doorbell and society staff let you into the upstairs sanctuary, which displays its original ark, antique ritual objects and photos of DC's 19th-century Jewish community. The temple once sat at 6th and G Sts NW, but was trucked to its current address in the 1970s.

BEAD MUSEUM Map pp246-8

☎ 202-624-4500; www.beadmuseumdc.org; 400 7th St NW; admission free; ⏰ 11am-4pm Wed-Sat, 1-4pm Sun; Metro: Archives-Navy Memorial
The Bead Society of Greater Washington operates this museum to showcase the aesthetic and symbolic qualities of beads – one of mankind's earliest and most enduring creative expressions. Exhibits are internationally focused and very educational. The society also maintains an impressive library on site.

Downtown Top Five

- **International Spy Museum** (p53) Emulating Bond, James Bond.
- **National Archives** (p54) Revering the documents which keep our nation running.
- **National Building Museum** (p54) Imagining the inaugural balls in the Great Hall.
- **National Museum of Women in the Arts** (p55) The art and the women who made it.
- **Old Post Office Pavilion** (p56) Bird's-eye view of the city.

CHINATOWN Map pp246-8

7th & H Sts NW; Metro: Gallery Pl-Chinatown
The world's largest single-span arch – **Friendship Arch** – was built cooperatively by the Washington city government and its sister city Beijing, and stands as the entrance to and symbol of DC's small Chinatown. Here you will find colorful signs with fancy characters, potent aromas emanating from restaurants, grocery stores, and pharmacies cluttered with exotic-looking fruits and herbs. The Chinese flavor is somewhat diluted with the arrival of the MCI Center and the nearby convention center, but this is still the place to come for dim sum.

CITY MUSEUM OF WASHINGTON, DC

Map pp246-8

☎ 202-785-2068; www.citymuseumdc.org; 800 Mt Vernon Sq; adult $3, senior & student $2, film $6/5, combo$8/6; ⏰ 10am-5pm Tue-Sun, 3rd Thu of month to 9pm; Metro: Mt Vernon Sq/7th St-Convention Center or Gallery Pl-Chinatown
Housed in the historic Carnegie Library at Mount Vernon Sq, this fun, new, interactive museum highlights the local side of DC – the people, events, and communities that shaped the city since its founding. Exhibits explore the growth of specific neighborhoods and ethnic groups, or themes such as cultural identity in sports. An extensive library – which is open to the public – provides access to old photographs, maps and other archives. The DC Historic Preservation Office also operates an archaeology laboratory to work on and display archaeological finds. The film – which is a funny look at the juxtaposition between the federal city and local DC – is a great introduction for kids.

FEDERAL BUREAU OF INVESTIGATION

Map pp246-8

☎ 202-324-3447; www.fbi.gov; 10th St & Pennsylvania Ave NW; ⏰ closed to public; Metro: Archives-Navy Memorial
This massive, neo-brutalist concrete building is officially known as the J Edgar Hoover FBI Building, in honor of the notorious director who led the bureau for 48 years (1924–72)

and transformed the FBI into a huge crime-fighting bureaucracy. These days, the hulking monolith – with security personnel posted on every corner – seems impenetrable; it's hard to believe that hour-long tours were once a highlight of a visit to DC. Unfortunately, the tours have been suspended since 9-11. Check out the virtual tour at www.fbi.gov/aboutus/tour/tour.htm.

City Museum of Washington, DC (p52)

FORD'S THEATRE & PETERSEN HOUSE Map pp246-8

☎ 202-347-4833; www.nps.gov/foth; 511 10th St NW; admission free; ⌚ 9am-5pm (except during rehearsals or matinee performances); Metro: Metro Center

On April 14, 1865, John Wilkes Booth, actor and Confederate sympathizer, assassinated Abraham Lincoln as President and Mrs Lincoln watched *Our American Cousin* in the Presidential Box of Ford's Theatre. The box remains draped with a period flag to this day. The theater is open during the day to wander around on your own or join a tour. Check out the **Lincoln Museum** in the basement, which maps out the assassination's details and displays related artifacts. See also Entertainment (p155).

After being shot, the unconscious president was carried across the street to die at Petersen House, which is also open for walks through; its tiny, unassuming rooms create a moving personal portrait of the president's slow and tragic death. Another assassination-related sight is nearby: Surrat House, now the restaurant **Wok & Roll** (Map pp246-8; 604 H St), is where the Lincoln-assassination conspirators met in 1865. Its owner, Mary Surratt, was eventually hanged at Fort McNair for her part.

INTER-AMERICAN DEVELOPMENT BANK CULTURAL CENTER Map pp246-8

☎ 202-623-3774; www.iadb.org/cultural; 1300 New York Ave NW; admission free; ⌚ 11am-6pm Mon-Fri; Metro: Metro Center

The cultural center was established in 1992 as part of the quincentennial celebration of Columbus' discovery of the Americas. The center showcases outstanding intellectual and artistic contributions from the 46 IADB member countries, with emphasis on Latin America and the Caribbean. The program includes excellent films, art exhibits and public lectures.

INTERNATIONAL SPY MUSEUM

Map pp246-8

☎ 202-393-7798, 866-SPYMUSEUM; www.spymuseum.org; 800 F St NW; adult/senior/child $13/12/10; ⌚ 10am-8pm Apr-Oct, 10am-6pm Nov-Mar; Metro: Gallery Pl-Chinatown

The much-acclaimed museum of espionage opened just in time to fill a void left by the end of FBI tours: spy fans can still get their fill of spy artifacts, anecdotes and interactive displays. All visitors are invited to play the role of a secret agent by adopting a cover at the start of their visit. Throughout the museum, you can try to identify disguises, listen to bugs and spot hidden cameras. Most of the exhibit is historical in nature, focusing on the Cold War in particular (a re-creation of the tunnel under the Berlin Wall is eerie and cool). Gadgets on display are a little out of date to be impressive – we've already seen a lot of this stuff years ago on *Get Smart*.

MARTIN LUTHER KING JR MEMORIAL LIBRARY Map pp246-8

☎ 202-727-1221; www.dclibrary.org/mlk; 901 G St NW; admission free; ⌚ 9:30am-9pm Mon-Thu, 9am-5pm Fri & Sat, 1-5pm Sun; Metro: Metro Center

DC's main library is in Mies van der Rohe's only Washington building, a low, sleek black-glass structure; peek inside to admire the colorful mural portraying the Civil Rights movement. The MLK Library is an important community and cultural center, sponsoring readings, concerts, films and children's activities. You can also access the Internet here.

NATIONAL ACADEMY OF SCIENCE
KECK CENTER Map pp246-8

☎ 202-334-2436; www.nationalacademies.org/nas
/arts.nsf; 500 5th St NW; admission free; ☾ 6-8pm
3rd Thu of month; Metro: Judiciary Sq

In addition to the main building on Constitution Ave, the NAS occupies the less-inspired Keck Center. Its lobby and atrium hold a permanent collection of photography, landscapes and other science-inspired art that is open during the '3rd 3rsday Art Crawl' (p177). Outside, check out Don Merkt's sculpture *Slow Rondo*, which is a nice combination of art and science. Powered by the wind, three concentric circular planes all move independently while sharing the same vertical axis.

NATIONAL ARCHIVES Map pp246-8

☎ 202-510-5400; www.archives.gov; 700 Pennsylvania
Ave NW (enter from Constitution Ave NW); admission
free; ☾ 10am-5:30pm Sep-Mar, 10am-7pm Apr-May,
10am-9pm Jun-Aug; Metro: Archives-Navy Memorial

Inside this grand neoclassical building is a dimly lit rotunda with the three original documents upon which the US government is based: the Declaration of Independence, Constitution and Bill of Rights. Not to mention the 1297 version of the Magna Carta, courtesy of Texas billionaire (and erstwhile presidential candidate) H Ross Perot. Don't expect to linger over the Big Three – guards make you keep moving, but you can study the Magna Carta and other documents at your leisure.

These precious documents are sealed in airtight, helium-filled cases that sink nightly into an underground vault to protect them from attack or theft. After the ongoing renovation at the National Archives, the exhibit will also include 'Public Vaults,' to give visitors the feeling of going inside the stacks at the archives, as well as a theater and gift shop.

The archives themselves preserve reams of essential government documents, from the Louisiana Purchase Treaty to the Emancipation Proclamation. Researchers can access documents from 8:45am to 5pm Monday to Saturday; enter from Pennsylvania Ave.

NATIONAL AQUARIUM Map pp246-8

☎ 202-482-2825; www.nationalaquarium.com; 14th
St & Constitution Ave NW, Dept of Commerce Bldg B-
077 (enter from 14th St) ; adult/senior/child $3.50/3/1;
☾ 9am-5pm; Metro: Federal Triangle

Hidden in the basement of the Department of Commerce Building, this is a poor substitute if you can't make the trek up to the **National Aquarium in Baltimore** (p210). It does have a touch tank, displays on various marine ecosystems (the Chesapeake Bay, marshes) and a few rooms of aquariums. Visit at 2pm, when staff feed piranhas, sharks and 'gators.

NATIONAL BUILDING MUSEUM
Map pp246-8

☎ 202-272-2448; www.nbm.org; Judiciary Sq, 401 F
St NW; admission by donation $5; ☾ 10am-5pm Mon-
Sat, 11am-5pm Sun, tours 12:30pm, family program
2:30pm Sat & Sun; Metro: Judiciary Sq

Devoted to the architectural arts, this underappreciated museum is appropriately housed in an architectural jewel: the 1887 Old Pension Building. Four stories of ornamented balconies flank the dramatic 316ft-wide atrium. The Corinthian columns, which are among the world's largest, rise 75ft high. An inventive system of windows and archways keeps the so-called Great Hall glimmering in natural light. This space has hosted 15 inaugural balls – from Grover Cleveland's in 1885 to George W's in 2001.

The showy space easily overshadows the exhibits, but they're worthwhile nonetheless: 'Washington: City and Symbol' examines the deeper symbolism of DC architecture; 'Tools as Art' features highlights from a fun collection donated by John Hechinger, hardware industry pioneer. Check the website for a schedule of rotating exhibits, concerts and family programs.

Honoring FDR

The beautifully landscaped granite **Franklin Delano Roosevelt Memorial** (p71) on the Tidal Basin is impressive, indeed. But it is a far cry from the wishes of the great president himself. By way of memorial, FDR created the first modern presidential library at his home in Hyde Park, New York. Every president since has followed the tradition, so that libraries are the primary form of presidential commemoration outside the capital. When asked about a more traditional memorial, FDR reportedly responded: 'If any memorial is erected to me, I should like it to consist of a block about the size of this desk and placed in front of the Archives Building. I want it plain, without any ornamentation, with the simple carving *In Memory of*.' This request was honored in 1965, when a small, stone slab was placed at the corner of 9th St and Pennsylvania Ave NW. Though overshadowed by the tribute on the Tidal Basin, the first FDR memorial– the one that remembers FDR the way he wanted – still stands at its designated spot (Map pp246-8).

NATIONAL LAW ENFORCEMENT OFFICERS MEMORIAL Map pp246-8

☎ 202-737-3400; www.nleomf.com; 605 E St NW; admission free; ⏱ memorial 24hr, visitors center 9am-5pm Mon-Fri, 10am-5pm Sat, noon-5pm Sun; Metro: Judiciary Sq

The memorial on Judiciary Sq commemorates the 14,500 US police officers killed on duty since 1794. In the style of the Vietnam Veterans Memorial, names of the dead are carved on two marble walls curving around a plaza; new names are added during a moving candlelight vigil each year in May. Peeking over the walls, bronze lion statues protect their sleeping cubs (presumably as law enforcement officers protect us).

The nearby **visitor center** houses several exhibits about the history of the memorial and the law enforcement officers it honors.

Plans are under way for a National Law Enforcement Museum, which will open across from the memorial in 2008.

NATIONAL MUSEUM OF AMERICAN ART & NATIONAL PORTRAIT GALLERY
Map pp246-8

☎ 202-275-1500; www.americanart.si.edu; 9th & F Sts NW; admission free; Metro: Gallery Pl-Chinatown

These Smithsonian museums are roommates in the 19th-century US Patent Office building, a neoclassical quadrangle that hosted Lincoln's second inaugural ball and a Civil War hospital. Walt Whitman based 'The Wound-Dresser' upon his experiences as a volunteer nurse here. ('The hurt and wounded I pacify with soothing hand/I sit by the restless all the dark night...')

The Portrait Gallery's works include portraits of important Americans and biographical exhibits. The Museum of American Art's holdings include a spirited collection of American folk art.

Note, however, that both museums are closed for renovation until 2006. In the meantime, highlights from the museum are on tour at museums around the country.

NATIONAL MUSEUM OF WOMEN IN THE ARTS Map pp246-8

☎ 202-222-7270; www.nmwa.org; 1250 New York Ave NW; adult $5, senior & student $3, child free; ⏱ 10am-5pm Mon-Sat , noon-5pm Sun; Metro: Metro Center

The only American museum exclusively devoted to women's artwork resides in this magnificent Renaissance Revival mansion. Its collection – 2600 works by almost 700 women

artists from 28 countries – moves from Renaissance artists like Lavinia Fontana to 20th-century works by Kahlo, O'Keeffe and Frankenthaler. The permanent collection is largely paintings, and mostly portraits at that – not as rich a range as one might hope. But special collections are incredibly varied, ranging from Maria Sibylla Merian's natural history engravings to Native American pottery. Rotating exhibits are also extraordinary, gathering works from around the world and introducing them to a wider audience.

National Archives (p54)

NATIONAL PUBLIC RADIO Map pp246-8

☎ 202-513-3232; www.npr.org; 635 Massachusetts Ave NW; admission free; ⏱ tours 11am Thu; Metro: Mt Vernon Sq/7th St-Convention Center

Folks who listen to broadcasters Scott Simon and Bob Edwards every day will enjoy the hourlong tours of NPR headquarters. Visitors see the satellite control center, desks for national, foreign, science and arts news, as well as the studios where shows like 'Morning Edition' and 'All Things Considered' are recorded.

NAVY MEMORIAL & NAVAL HERITAGE CENTER Map pp246-8

☎ 202-737-2300; www.lonesailor.org; 701 Pennsylvania Ave NW, Market Sq; admission free; ⏱ 9:30am-5pm Mon-Sat, film noon; Metro: Archives-Navy Memorial

On Market Sq, the circular plaza is bordered by masts sporting semaphore flags; on its western side, a sculpted seaman – the 'Lone Sailor' – hunches down in his peacoat as a tribute to sea service. The Naval Heritage Center inside displays artifacts and ship models, and has a meditation room and a Navy Memorial Log. At noon daily, its theater screens the gung-ho *At Sea*, which dramatically depicts battle-group maneuvers.

OLD POST OFFICE PAVILION Map pp246-8
☎ 202-606-8691; www.oldpostofficedc.com; 12th St & Pennsylvania Ave NW; admission free; ☺ 9am-7:45pm Mon-Sat, 10am-5:45pm Sun; Metro: Federal Triangle
The landmark 1899 Old Post Office Pavilion – nicknamed 'Old Tooth' for its spiky clock tower – is a downtown success story. Threatened with demolition during much of the 20th century, the Romanesque building was restored in 1978 and became a key attraction. Now its beautiful, bunting-draped, 10-story central atrium holds shops, a large food court, a discount-ticket counter and government agencies. The Park Service operates a glass elevator that takes visitors to the 270ft **observation deck** for a broad view of downtown and a close-up look at the carillon bells. The free tour starts from the northwest corner of the pavilion's ground floor.

RONALD REAGAN BUILDING/ INTERNATIONAL TRADE CENTER
Map pp246-8
☎ 202-328-4748; www.doc.gov; 1300 Pennsylvania Ave NW; Metro: Federal Triangle
This gigantic complex, designed by James Ingo Freed, is mostly office and conference space, but you can visit its downstairs food court and the informative **DC Chamber of Commerce Visitor Information Center** on the ground floor.

Peek into the huge, light-flooded central atrium. Behind it, near Federal Triangle Metro station, is a circular sculpture garden that's a great, quiet place to eat lunch. Every night between April and October, this staid courtyard gets transformed into the happening dance club **Air** (p161).

WHITE HOUSE AREA & FOGGY BOTTOM

Eating p120; Shopping p177; Sleeping p192
The most recognized home in America commands this neighborhood from its roost at 1600 Pennsylvania Ave NW. At first look, the mansion is strikingly accessible – set so close to Pennsylvania that you can almost peek in the windows to see what Dubya or his successor is up to. If you wait around, it seems he might come out the front door to say howdy.

When you step back, however, the majesty of the scene becomes apparent. Forbidding iron gates surround the White House grounds. The Old Executive Office Building and the Treasury Building, on either side of the mansion, are giant-sized and lavishly trimmed. The South Lawn is a wide, green sea separating the president and the people. All around are gargantuan office buildings housing federal agencies and international organizations, stretches of park studded with marble statues, and views of the Capitol or the Washington Monument, or the White House itself. Take it all in: this neighborhood – with its grand architecture and symbolic layout and sweeping views – is befitting the residency of the most powerful leader of the Western world.

Besides the president and his family, not many people live around here. The fancy mansions around Lafayette Sq now house museums, hotels and private clubs, not real people. Thousands of white-collars fill these office buildings each day and keep the US Government ticking. They may hit one of the local pubs for a drink after work, but then they retire to more residential areas like Georgetown or Dupont Circle, or check into a room at a nearby hotel, or hop on the Metro out to the suburbs. These streets are remarkably quiet at night.

By day, however, they bustle with bureaucrats and diplomats, tourists and lobbyists. Helicopters roar above, transporting important people to important places. In-line skaters and street hockey players take advantage of the car-free zone in front of the White House. Lafayette Sq fills up with poster-toting ideologues, chess-playing pensioners and lunch-munching White House staffers (all this goes on and the homeless guy doesn't even wake up).

Orientation

Pennsylvania Ave cuts across Northwest DC on a diagonal from the US Capitol to the White House. These homes of two of the branches of the government balance on either end of the axis, in a visual metaphor of the power balance between the executive and legislative. Pennsylvania Ave continues on its northwestern trajectory into Georgetown, but not without a major detour (where there is no access for cars) around the president's home.

The White House area and Foggy Bottom compile an area that is square (in shape as well as attitude). It is bounded by the blue Potomac River in the west and the green National Mall. These two natural strips of color at the neighborhood's border, however, are a contrast to its interior. Straight streets and grey blocks of office buildings dominate this little piece of the city, lending it a much more urban character than other parts of DC.

The exception is the White House, set back on the lush White House lawns, and flanked by leafy, green Lafayette Sq to the north and the huge Ellipse to the south. Together with the ornate Old Executive Office Building and the colossal Treasury Building, which are on either side of the White House on Pennsylvania Ave, these landmarks comprise the southeast corner of the neighborhood.

For our purposes, the northern boundary of the neighborhood is L St NW, although K St NW – one block south – is a busier, more prominent thoroughfare. K St is punctuated by McPherson Sq at its intersection with 15th St and Vermont Ave NW, and by Farragut Sq at its intersection with 17th St and Connecticut Ave NW.

Further west, the confluence of K St, 23rd St, Pennsylvania Ave and New Hampshire Ave forms Washington Circle. Known as Foggy Bottom, the area's nickname probably derives from the district's original inhabitants (a gasworks, brewery, cement factory and other smoggy industries); modern wits say the name describes the bureaucratic hot air arising from the area's numerous federal agencies.

The campus of George Washington University dominates these blocks south of Washington Circle, but you might not recognize it: the urban campus blends right into the surrounding city with no iron gates or green quad to define it. South of GWU, anchoring the west end of the neighborhood, the Kennedy Center and the Watergate rise over the banks of the Potomac.

Transportation

Metro The Orange and Blue Lines follow I St NW across the top of this neighborhood, stopping at Foggy Bottom-GWU, Farragut West and McPherson Sq. A Red Line stop – Farragut North – is just north of the square at Connecticut Ave and K Sts NW.

Parking There is metered parking on all the major streets in this neighborhood, but it can be difficult to find a spot during the day. Most street parking is legal only after morning rush hour (starting at 9:30am); if you arrive early and find a space remember to feed your meter. Otherwise, there is a parking garage at 1729 G St NW or at 2400 Virginia Ave.

WHITE HOUSE AREA

AMERICAN RED CROSS MUSEUM
Map pp246-8

☎ 202-639-3300; www.redcross.org/museum; 1730 E St NW; admission by donation; ⏰ 8:30am-4pm Mon-Fri, tours 9am Tue & Fri; Metro: Farragut West

Three pillared marble mansions house the national headquarters of the 150-year-old Red Cross. (Check out the colorful Tiffany windows in the main building depicting nurses tending swooning soldiers.)

The museum holds exhibits on disaster relief and the organization's history, including cool old Red Cross posters by Norman Rockwell and NC Wyeth.

A touching new exhibit – opened on the one-year anniversary of 9-11 – demonstrates the ways in which the Red Cross responded to the disaster.

BLAIR & LEE HOUSES Map pp246-8
1653 Pennsylvania Ave NW; ⏰ closed to public; Metro: Farragut West

The 1824 Blair House has been the official presidential guesthouse since 1942, when Eleanor Roosevelt got sick of tripping over dignitaries in her White House. A plaque on the front fence commemorates the bodyguard killed here while protecting President Truman from a 1950 assassination attempt by Puerto Rican pro-independence terrorists.

The neighboring 1858 Lee House was built by the famous general's family. Here scion Robert E Lee declined command of the Union Army when the Civil War erupted.

White House & Foggy Bottom Top Five

- **Corcoran Gallery of Art** (below) Beautiful art classics in a beaux-arts classic.
- **Kennedy Center** (p156) Music, theatre and dance in an elegant setting overlooking the Potomac.
- **National Academy of Sciences** (p59) Sitting on Albert Einstein's lap and looking over his universe.
- **Octagon Museum** (p59) An unusual museum in an unusually shaped house.
- **White House** (p60) Visiting America's most famous address.

CORCORAN GALLERY OF ART
Map pp246-8

☎ 202-639-1700; www.corcoran.org; 500 17th St NW; family/adult/senior/student $8/5/3/1, admission free Mon & 5pm Thu; ☟ 10am-5pm Wed-Mon, to 9pm Thu; Metro: Farragut West vvvvvv

In a beautiful 1897 beaux-arts building overlooking the Ellipse, the Corcoran exhibits American and European masterworks, with an emphasis on 19th- and early-20th century American artists. Special exhibits often focus on particular artists or historical themes, such as Lichtenstein's sculptures and drawings, or the art of the Harlem Renaissance. The Corcoran is particularly known for its surveys of historic and modern photography. The Corcoran also houses the College of Art & Design and mounts intriguing exhibits of its students' work.

Café des Artistes, in the 1st floor atrium, is an elegant restaurant serving light lunch fare. A weekly Sunday gospel brunch features area singers, and jazz musicians play Thursday evenings.

Behind the Corcoran, on E St NW between 18th and 20th Sts NW, pretty **Rawlins Park** is named for US Grant's Secretary of War. With goldfish in its little pond and blooming magnolias in spring and summer, it's among downtown DC's most charming oases.

DAUGHTERS OF THE AMERICAN REVOLUTION Map pp246-8

☎ 202-628-1776; www.dar.org; 1776 D St NW; admission free; ☟ 9:30am-4pm Mon-Fri, 9am-5pm Sat, tours 10am-2:30pm Mon-Fri, 9am-4pm Sat; Metro: Farragut West

The Daughters of the American Revolution is a volunteer women's organization dedicated to promoting patriotism and preserving American history. Its national headquarters (how appropriate that it's at 1776 D St) houses a museum, a library and a concert hall. The DAR museum displays furnishings and decorative arts of pre-industrial America, plus 31 period rooms which showcase American interiors throughout history. The impressive library – a premier center for genealogical research – is worth a peek even if you are not researching family history. Next door, the 3200-seat **Constitution Hall** (☎ 202-628-4780) is a concert/performance venue.

DECATUR HOUSE Map pp246-8

☎ 202-842-0920; www.decaturhouse.org; 748 Jackson Place NW, visitor entrance at 1610 H St NW; admission by donation; ☟ 10am-5pm Tue-Sat, to 8pm Thu, noon-4pm Sun; Metro: Farragut West

At Lafayette Sq's northwest corner, Decatur House was designed in 1818 by Benjamin Latrobe for the naval hero Stephen Decatur (who got himself killed in a duel just a year later). A tour shows you the house's austere architectural charms, and details the lives of not only its famous tenants – including Martin Van Buren and Henry Clay – but also the slaves who waited upon them.

DEPARTMENT OF THE INTERIOR MUSEUM Map pp246-8

☎ 202-208-4743; www.doi.gov/museum /interiormuseum/mission.htm; 1849 C St NW; admission free; ☟ 8:30am-4:30pm Mon-Fri, 1-4pm 3rd Sat of month; Metro: Farragut West

Responsible for managing the US natural resources, the Department of the Interior operates this small but excellent museum to educate the public about its current goals and programs. It includes landscape art, Indian artifacts and historical photos of Indian life, as well as exhibits on wildlife and resource management. Reserve in advance for guided tours of the building itself, which contains 25 tremendous 'New Deal' murals from the 1930s and 1940s. Show a photo ID to enter.

ELLIPSE Map pp246-8
Constitution Ave btwn 15th & 17th Sts NW

The expansive park on the south side of the White House is known as the Ellipse, named for the elliptical road which circles the interior. The park is studded with a random collection of monuments, such as the **Zero Milestone** (the marker for highway distances all across the country) and the **Second Division Memorial**. But the more important function of the Ellipse is to host sporting events, parades and festivals – ranging from the lighting of the national Christmas tree to military drill performances to Lance Armstrong's final ride.

FEDERAL RESERVE Map pp246-8

☎ board 202-452-3149, art 202-452-3778; www.federalreserve.gov; 20th St NW between C St & Constitution Ave; admission free; ⏱ tours by reservation; Metro: Farragut West

'The Fed' conjures up strong images of high-powered businessmen and bureaucrats crafting the economic ebbs and flows of the country. Unfortunately, you won't see too much of that on this tour, which focuses on the architecture of the Eccles Building that houses the Fed. It does feature a film *The Fed Today* and a visit to the Board Room. The tour is recommended for adults only; kids under college age will likely get bored at the Board.

Visitors can also view the Fed's art collection, parts of which are displayed in the atrium of the Eccles Building. The permanent collection is a survey of American art dating from the 1830s to the present. The Board also presents rotating thematic exhibitions of borrowed art on varied themes, such as currency design. A recent exhibit, Complexity, showcased work by artists employing a variety of media to explore complex systems like traffic, the weather and the stock market.

NATIONAL ACADEMY OF SCIENCES
Map pp246-8

☎ 202-334-2436; www.nationalacademies.org/nas /arts.nsf; 2101 Constitution Ave NW; admission free; ⏱ 9am-5pm Mon-Fri; Metro: Foggy Bottom-GWU

The academy advises the government on scientific and technical issues, and also hosts scientific and art exhibitions, concerts and symposia. Recent exhibits have included Under Antarctic Ice, featuring incredible photographs of this harsh but breathtakingly beautiful environment, and An Intimate View of Flowers (self-explanatory). Concerts are often held on Sunday afternoons.

The nicely landscaped grounds along Constitution Ave feature DC's most huggable monument: the **Albert Einstein statue**. The larger-than-life, sandal-shod, chubby bronze reclines on a bench, and little kids crawl all over him. He's elevated on a 'star map' pedestal that depicts the heavens that his theories reshaped for humanity.

OCTAGON MUSEUM Map pp246-8

☎ 202-638 3105; www.theoctagon.org; 1799 New York Ave NW; adult $5, senior & child $3; ⏱ 10am-4pm Tue-Sun; Metro: Farragut West

Designed by William Thornton (the US Capitol's first architect) in 1800, this is a symmetrically winged Federal structure designed to fit an odd triangular lot. Behind it, the American Institute of Architects (AIA) large modern offices wrap around the little house like a protective older brother. Knowledgeable docents show you the Octagon's hidden doorways, twin staircases and period furniture. Upstairs galleries host exhibits on architecture and design; downstairs exhibits explain the careful archaeological work required to restore this and other old houses.

OLD EXECUTIVE OFFICE BUILDING
Map pp246-8

www.whitehouse.gov/history/eeobtour; 17th St NW & Pennsylvania Ave; ⏱ closed to public; Metro: Farragut West

Truman called it 'the greatest monstrosity in America'; Hoover griped that it was an 'architectural orgy.' Yet the ornate Old Executive

---

The Building of Art

In 2001, Frank Gehry – famed architect of the Guggenheim museum in Bilbao, Spain – was commissioned to design a third, sculptural wing on the north side of the existing **Corcoran Gallery of Art** (p58). Three ribbon-like stainless-steel panels will weave around the new entrance on New York Ave. Inside, a soaring, 130ft-high atrium will be connected to exhibition space by suspended walkways. Galleries in the historic beaux-arts building will form a continuum with those in the new wing, doubling the exhibition space at the museum. It will feature new retail space, a library and research center, and state-of-the-art facilities for the College of Art & Design.

A highlight of the new building – besides the dramatic architectural addition – will be the new Children's Center for Art and Technology. The idea is to use new technology and interactive approaches to make art – and learning about art – appealing for kids. Drawing on the college's strong museum education program, the center will stress imagination, creativity and fun, and should be a compulsory stop for future artists.

All of these innovations take time, though. The new wing is expected to open in 2006, and the Corcoran will be closed for some time between now and then. But it will – no doubt – be worth the wait. The Corcoran is already anticipating that the new museum will attract over one million visitors a year.

Office Building (or Eisenhower Executive Office Building, as it is officially known) delights most visitors today. It was designed by Alfred Mullet in the 1870s to house State, War and Navy Department staff. His design was roundly blasted, and poor old Mullet killed himself two years after its completion. Today it houses White House staff. The OEOB is no longer open to the public for tours, but the website's virtual tour offers a glimpse at some of the rooms.

ORGANIZATION OF AMERICAN STATES & ART MUSEUM OF THE AMERICAS Map pp246-8

☎ 202-458-6016; www.oas.org; 201 18th St NW; admission free; ☯ 10am-5pm Tue-Sun; Metro: Farragut West

A sort of forerunner to the UN, the OAS is an international organization founded in 1890 to promote cooperation among North and South American nations. Its main building at 17th St and Constitution Ave is a marble palazzo surrounded by the sculpture-studded **Aztec Gardens**. In the small building behind it, the OAS operates the Art Museum of the Americas, featuring an incredible collection of art that spans the 20th century as well as the Western Hemisphere. Works represent southern interpretations of constructivism and surrealism, as well as more recent pieces of geometric and pop art.

RENWICK GALLERY Map pp246-8

☎ 202-357-2700; www.americanart.si.edu; 17th & Pennsylvania Ave NW; admission free; ☯ 10am-5:30pm; Metro: Farragut West

The Smithsonian's Renwick invites you up the stairs of its regal 1859 mansion and then startles you with wild pieces of artistic whimsy. This is the national crafts museum, displaying woodwork, ceramics, sculpture, metalwork and furniture. But 'crafts' doesn't really describe these pieces – they're wonderfully creative artworks. The many playful pieces make it a wonderful place to introduce kids to art. They especially love Larry Fuentes' *Game Fish*, a sailfish trophy meticulously adorned with beads, buttons, tiles, dominoes, yo-yos etc. Grownups like the Grand Salon and Octagon Room, recently restored in the grand gilded-age styles of the 1870s and 1880s.

ST JOHN'S CHURCH Map pp246-8

☎ 202-347-8766; 1525 H St NW; ☯ 9am-3pm, service 12:10pm, Sun services 8am, 9am & 11am; Metro: McPherson Sq

A small, butter-colored building, St John's isn't DC's most imposing church, but it's among the most charming. St John's is the 'Church of the Presidents' – every president since Madison has attended its services at least once. Designed in 1815 by Capitol architect Benjamin Henry Latrobe, the church reserves a pew (No 54, purchased by Madison) for presidential families. Lyndon Johnson prayed here on the first morning of his presidency, after JFK was killed.

TREASURY BUILDING Map pp246-8

☎ 202-622-2200; www.treasury.gov; 1500 Pennsylvania Ave NW; ☯ closed to public; Metro: McPherson Sq

The 1836 Greek Revival colossus (each of its 30 36ft columns were carved from a single granite block) is decorated as befits a treasury, with golden eagles, ornate balustrades and a two-story Cash Room, constructed with eight types of marble. US currency was printed in the basement from 1863 to 1880. This building no longer prints any money, but it is often confused with the present 'money factory,' the Bureau of Printing & Engraving, south of the Mall. Unfortunately tours of the building have been suspended, but the website offers a virtual tour under 'Education.'

WHITE HOUSE Map pp246-8

☎ 202-456-7041; www.whitehouse.gov; 1600 Pennsylvania Ave NW; ☎ closed to public; Metro: Farragut West

Every US president since John Adams has lived in this 132-room mansion at America's most famous address. Its stature has grown through the years: no longer a mere residence, it's now the central icon of the American presidency.

The Presidential Palace – as it was once known – has changed a great deal over history (and with its changing residents). It was not originally white, for example. After the British burned the building in the War of 1812, it was restored and painted. It was Teddy Roosevelt who later gave official sanction to the executive mansion's popular name.

An overhaul in 1950 gutted almost the entire interior, and Jacqueline Kennedy's extensive redecoration campaign in the 1960s replaced the previous hodgepodge with more tasteful furnishings. Presidents have customized the property over time: Grant put in a personal zoo; FDR added a pool; Truman a balcony; Bush a horseshoe-throwing lane; and Clinton a jogging track. Some residents never leave: it's said that Eleanor Roosevelt and Harry Truman both sighted Lincoln's ghost in Abe's old study.

Back before Herbert Hoover's era, presidents used to open the doors at noon each day to shake visitors' hands. Alas, no longer. Daily tours of the White House have been suspended since 9-11 (although Laura Bush conducts a video tour at the White House Visitor Center). They may commence again in the future. In the meantime, groups of 10 or more may request a tour through their congressperson up to six months in advance. The White House grounds are also occasionally opened for special events, such as **Tee-ball on the South Lawn** and the **Easter Egg Roll**, held every Easter Monday for kids aged three to six.

WHITE HOUSE VISITOR CENTER
Map pp246-8

☎ 202-208-1631; www.nps.gov/whho; 1450 Pennsylvania Ave NW; admission free; 🕙 7:30am-4pm; Metro: McPherson Sq

In lieu of touring the White House itself, visitors can browse exhibits, watch historic reenactments and take a video tour at this center in Malcolm Baldrige Hall of the Department of Commerce building. It's obviously not the same as seeing the real deal first-hand, but it does provide an overview of the building's history, as well as fun anecdotes about the presidential families (and pets!) who have graced its halls. Each month, the visitors center hosts free performances by actors who recreate the lives of presidents and patriots.

FOGGY BOTTOM

KENNEDY CENTER Map pp246-8
John F Kennedy Center for the Performing Arts; ☎ 202-467-4600, 800-444-1324; www.kennedy-center.org; 2700 F St NW; 🕙 10am-midnight, tours 10am-5pm Mon-Fri, 10am-1pm Sat & Sun; Metro: Foggy Bottom-GWU (free shuttle 9:45am-midnight Mon-Sat, noon-8pm Sun)

Overlooking the Potomac, the Kennedy Center was dedicated in 1964 as a 'living memorial' to JFK. The center's theaters, concert hall, opera house and cinema almost single-handedly reversed Washington's former reputation as a cultural desert. (The site had previously housed the Christian Heurich Brewery, makers of Senate-brand beer until 1956.)

Offering lovely river views from the terrace (or from the Roof Terrace Restaurant), the Kennedy Center is a great place to have a drink. Guided tours depart from the gift shop and showcase the main theaters, as well as the impressive Hall of States, which

features the flags of states hung in the order they entered the Union, and Hall of Nations, which features flags of nations recognized by the US. But the best way to see the center is at one of the many festivals, films or concerts held here year-round. The **Millennium Stage** hosts a varied and exciting program of free concerts every day at 6pm. See Entertainment for more information (p156).

ST MARY'S EPISCOPAL CHURCH
Map pp246-8

☎ 202-333-3985; 730 23rd St NW; Metro: Foggy Bottom-GWU

Built in 1887, St Mary's was home to the first black Episcopal congregation in DC. The beautiful red-brick building was designed by James Renwick – designer of the **Smithsonian Castle** (p47) – especially for the congregation.

STATE DEPARTMENT Map pp246-8
US Department of State; ☎ 202-647-3241; www.state.gov; 22nd & C Sts NW; admission free; 🕙 tours by reservation 9:30am, 10:30am & 2:45pm Mon-Fri; Metro: Foggy Bottom-GWU

The State Department is a forbidding, well-guarded edifice, but you can tour its grand Diplomatic Reception Rooms, where Cabinet members and the Secretary of State entertain visiting potentates amid ornate 18th-century American antiques. Call at least a month beforehand to reserve a tour spot, and bring photo ID; no kids under 12 are admitted.

WATERGATE COMPLEX Map pp246-8
☎ 202-965-2300; www.watergatehotel.com; 2650 Virginia Ave NW; Metro: Foggy Bottom-GWU

The riverfront Watergate complex is a posh private community encompassing apartments, designer boutiques and a deluxe hotel. Its curious name derives from a never-realized 1930s' plan to build a ceremonial water gate in the Potomac, a stairway onto which visiting dignitaries could disembark. Now, its name is synonymous with American political scandal: in 1972, a break-in at Democratic National Committee headquarters here was linked to CREEP – the Committee to Re-elect the President – leading to the unprecedented resignation of the sitting president, Richard Nixon. With the Watergate's undulating facade and dragon-tooth balconies, it's among DC's most recognizable landmarks. The upscale restaurant **Jeffrey's at the Watergate** (p122) is a romantic dinner-date destination with a lovely view of the Potomac.

CAPITOL HILL & SOUTHEAST DC

Eating p123; Shopping p178; Sleeping p194

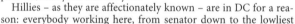

Capitol Hill – synonymous with politics and power and wheeling and dealing – is the geographic center and the political heart of Washington DC. Three years after Jefferson and Hamilton decided upon Washington as the site of the federal city, construction began on the grand Capitol gracing the rise east of the Potomac. Thus was born 'the Hill,' a district of politicos and pundits, lobbyists and lawyers.

Hillies – as they are affectionately known – are in DC for a reason: everybody working here, from senator down to the lowliest staffer, is doing the important work of democracy. They have official-looking identification tags to prove it (if you don't have one, you are obviously a tourist). And they love it.

The Hillies' energy is contagious. Absorb it as you wander these streets, overhearing gossipy staffers exchanging news, and idealistic interns debating views. They are enthusiastic and emotional. Politics excite passion, which is what makes Capitol Hill a uniquely passionate place.

Away from the hallowed halls of the Capitol, the neighborhood's mood mellows; further east it is more laid-back and less politically charged. Many transient Hillies live here, but so do old-timer Washingtonians, low-income minorities and young yuppie families. They might meet for lunch at Jimmy T's and actually *not* discuss the upcoming election. Adding a bohemian element to the otherwise conventional atmosphere, Eastern Market attracts artists, furniture-refinishers and farmers selling their merchandise.

And there are those who are drawn by the neighborhood's brick sidewalks, iron gates and historic architecture: Federal, Greek Revival, Empire-style and Victorian row houses line every street on the Hill. As recently as the 1980s, much of Capitol Hill and Southeast DC was crumbling mansions and crime-ridden streets (visitors still should be careful east of 15th St and south of the Southeast Freeway). Now – in these days of gentrification – stately homes are repaired to their original condition; children and dogs frolic in the parks; and neighbors meet for coffee along 8th St. Revitalized and reenergized, the neighborhood mixes its friendly feel with a sense of historical significance, all in the shadow of the Capitol's dome.

Orientation

The Capitol building presides over its namesake neighborhood from its west end. The building is surrounded by lush green lawns and the obligatory House and Senate office buildings to the north and south. The wide-open plaza north of the Capitol allows an unbroken view of the magnificent beaux-arts Union Station. The Supreme Court, the three Library of Congress buildings and the Folger Shakespeare Library & Theater are immediately east of the Capitol.

From this Hill hub, E Capitol St runs east through the residential neighborhood of Lincoln Park and terminates at the Armory and RFK Stadium. Constitution and Independence Aves do the same to the north and south, respectively. And Pennsylvania Ave juts out to the southeast on a diagonal and heads across the Anacostia River. Outside of the Capitol building itself, most of the neighborhood's activity is clustered up around Union Station and down along Pennsylvania Ave. Eastern Market is on 7th St SE, just south of Independence Ave. Otherwise, the streets are relatively quiet, characterized by architectural gems, parks and glimpses of the Capitol dome. The residential part of Capitol Hill can be tricky to navigate, as different streets in close proximity can have the same letter, depending on whether they are north or south of E Capitol St (ie A St NE is just two blocks north of A St SE). Pay attention to your directionals (NE or SE) to avoid confusion.

Transportation

Metro The Union Station Metro stop is on the Red Line. For destinations on the south side of the Capitol, use Capitol South or Eastern Market, both on the Orange and Blue Lines.

Parking Street parking is possible on the residential streets of Capitol Hill. There is also a parking garage at Union Station, which offers two hours free if you validate your ticket at one of the shops inside.

Southeast is trisected by Pennsylvania Ave and Southeast Freeway both running northwest to southeast across the quadrant. For our purposes, Southeast DC refers to the area south of Pennsylvania Ave and north of the Anacostia River, and bounded by S Capitol St on the west side. The Southeast is an especially disruptive freeway completely severing any continuity between the neighborhoods on either side of the highway. North of the freeway, the 8th St corridor between Pennsylvania Ave and G St SE is bursting with development; just south of G St SE are the tidy Marine Barracks. By contrast, the southern tip of the Southeast quadrant, tucked in between

Capitol Hill & Southeast DC Top Five

- **Capitol** (p63) Seeing Congress at work
- **Eastern Market** (p64) Fresh produce and funky artwork
- **Frederick Douglass National Historic Site** (p66) The life and times of America's greatest abolitionist
- **Library of Congress** (p64) Being awestruck in the Great Hall
- **Supreme Court** (p65) Observing the justices debating and decision-making

the Southeast Freeway and the Anacostia River, is desolate and depressed. The Washington Navy Yard is a well-maintained and heavily guarded oasis in the midst of it.

Anacostia refers to the small piece of Washington DC which is southeast of the Anacostia River. Hwy I-295 – known as the Anacostia Freeway in the south and as Kenilworth Ave further north – cuts across the neighborhood and parallels the river. Anacostia Park occupies much of the riverfront property to the north, while a huge US Naval Station dominates the southern embankment. Southeast of I-295, Anacostia is a confusing mishmash of run-down houses, shops with iron bars on their windows and the odd museum or historic spot. Visitors should not be paranoid, but this isn't a neighborhood for a stroll. You are better off driving or taking public transport to the sites here.

CAPITOL HILL

CAPITOL Map pp250-1
☎ 202-225-6827; www.aoc.gov; admission free;
🕑 9am-4:30pm; Metro: Capitol South

Political center of the US government and geographic center of DC itself, the United States Capitol sits atop a high hill overlooking the National Mall and the wide avenues flaring out to the city beyond. Pierre L'Enfant chose this site for the Capitol in his original city plans of 1791. The Capitol began construction in 1793, as George Washington laid the cornerstone, anointing it with wine and oil in Masonic style.

The story does not continue so smoothly, however. Midway through construction, in 1814 the British marched into DC and burnt the fledgling Capitol to the ground. The dispiriting destruction tempted people to abandon the DC experiment altogether, but the government finally rebuilt it. In 1855 the iron dome (weighing nine-million-pounds) was designed, replacing a smaller one; the House and Senate wings were added in 1857. Everyone breathed a sigh of relief when the final touch, the 19ft Freedom sculpture, was placed atop the dome in 1863.

The House of Representatives meets in the south wing, the Senate in the north wing. When either body is in session, a flag is raised above the appropriate wing. (Appropriately, the House office buildings – Rayburn, Longworth and Cannon – are on Independence Ave south of the Capitol; Senate buildings – Hart, Dirksen and Russell – are on Constitution Ave to the north.)

The east side of the Capitol is undergoing a massive renovation project, which will result in a visitors center, scheduled to open in 2005. In the meantime, the east entrance is closed.

Congress Watching

To watch floor action when Congress is in session is to see history in the making. It's easy to obtain a pass to the galleries. US citizens: call or visit your senator's or representative's office (Capitol switchboard ☎ 202-224-3121). Foreign visitors: request passes from the House or Senate appointment desks on the Capitol's 1st floor.

Committee hearings are often more interesting than open sessions, and some are open to the public. Before your visit, check the *Post*'s 'Today in Congress' listing for details on current hearings and votes, or check www.house.gov and www.senate.gov.

US citizens can also request appointments with their senators and representatives by calling or writing, as early as three months beforehand.

The building is accessible by guided tours, which depart every half-hour. Line up *early* (from 7am in the summer) on 1st St SW, across the street from the United States Botanic Garden. You will receive tickets for a tour at a specific time later in the day. Oversized backpacks and bags are forbidden in the Capitol, as are bottles, cans or any liquids. Tours visit the dramatic Rotunda (with a view of the dome from the inside), Statuary Hall and the old Supreme Court chamber. Docents are knowledgeable. The tour ends downstairs in the Crypt, which has some exhibits on the Capitol's history.

CAPITOL GROUNDS Map pp250-1

The United States Capitol's wide lawns owe their charm to famed landscape architect Frederick Law Olmsted. During the Civil War, Soldiers had camped in Capitol halls and stomped around its lawns. In 1874, spring-cleaning was in order: Olmsted added lush greenery and majestic terraces, creating an elegant landscape indeed. Olmsted's planting schemes gave rise to over 4000 trees from all 50 states and many countries: look for labels on the trunks. Northwest of the Capitol is the charming 1879 **grotto**, a red-brick hexagon with black-iron gates and an interior well.

At the base of Capitol Hill, the **Capitol Reflecting Pool** echoes the larger, rectangular Reflecting Pool at the other end of the Mall. This pool actually caps the I-395 freeway, which dips under the Mall here. The ornate **Ulysses S Grant Monument** dominates its eastern side, showing the general in horseback action.

EASTERN MARKET Map pp250-1

☎ 202-546-2698; www.easternmarket.net; 7th St & North Carolina Ave SE; ⏲ 10am-6pm Tue-Fri, 8am-4pm Sat & Sun; Metro: Eastern Market

Delightful Eastern Market is the heart of the Capitol Hill community. Built in 1873, it is the last of the 19th-century covered markets that once supplied most of DC's food. South Hall has food stands, bakeries, flower stands and delis. North Hall is an arts center where craftspeople sell handmade wares. Weekends are when Eastern Market bursts into full bloom, as craftspeople, food vendors and a flea market spill over the sidewalks outside the market. See also Eating (p124).

FOLGER SHAKESPEARE LIBRARY & THEATRE Map pp250-1

☎ 202-544-4600; www.folger.edu; 201 E Capitol St; admission free; ⏲ 10am-4pm Mon-Sat, tours 11am; Metro: Capitol South

The world's largest collection of the bard's works, including seven First Folios, is housed at the Folger Library: its **Great Hall** exhibits Shakespeare artifacts and other rare Renaissance manuscripts. Most of the rarities are housed in the library's reading rooms, closed to all but scholars, except on Shakespeare's birthday (April 23). But you can take a peek electronically via the multimedia computers in the **Shakespeare Gallery**. The gorgeous **Elizabethan Theatre** replicates a theater of Shakespeare's time. With its wood carvings and sky canopy, the castle is an intimate setting for plays, readings and performances, including the stellar annual PEN/Faulkner readings. East of the building is the **Elizabethan Garden**, full of flowers and herbs that were cultivated during Shakespeare's time. See also p155.

LIBRARY OF CONGRESS Map pp250-1

☎ 202-707-5000; www.loc.gov; Adams Bldg: 2nd St & Independence Ave SE; Jefferson Bldg: 1st & E Capitol Sts SE; Madison Bldg: 1st St SE between Independence Ave & C St SE; admission free; ⏲ 10am-5pm Mon-Sat; Metro: Capitol South

The world's largest library, housed in three different buildings, contains approximately 120 million items, including 22 million books, plus manuscripts, maps, photographs, films and prints. But don't expect to see many books when you visit: most of them are shelved on more than 500 miles of closed library stacks in the three library buildings. Touring the Library of Congress is nonetheless fascinating. In the historic 1897 Jefferson Building, you can wander around the spectacular Great Hall, ornate

Library of Congress (above)

with stained glass and marble, and scope out the three-story Main Reading Room. (Who can get any work done in here?) The visitors center shows a brief film, and there are guided tours. On the 1st floor, 'American Treasures' displays historical documents ranging from Alexander Graham Bell's lab book entry to clips of Groucho Marx on the *Johnny Carson Show*. Both the Jefferson and the Madison Buildings house exhibits, including cool pop-culture in the Bob Hope Gallery of American Entertainment. The reading rooms are open to anyone over 17, but you must first obtain a Reader Identification Card. Take your driver's license or passport to LM-140 in the Madison Building. The Madison Building also hosts concerts and screens classic films in the **Mary Pickford Theater** (p157).

LINCOLN PARK & AROUND Map pp250-1
E Capitol St btwn 11th & 13th Sts SE
Lincoln Park is the lively center of Capitol Hill's east end. Freed black slaves raised the funds to erect the 1876 **Emancipation Memorial**, which portrays the snapping of slavery's chains as Lincoln proffers the Emancipation Proclamation. The **Mary McLeod Bethune Memorial**, DC's first statue of a black woman, honors the educator and founder of the National Council of Negro Women. Near the park, at 14th and E Capitol Sts, the **Car Barn** (now private housing) was DC's 19th-century trolley turnaround. South of here on 11th St SE, an 1860s builder constructed the lovely **Philadelphia Row** (124-54 11th St SE) for his homesick Philly born wife.

NATIONAL POSTAL MUSEUM
Map pp250-1

☎ 202-357-2991; www.postalmuseum.si.edu; **2 Massachusetts Ave NE; admission free;** ⏰ 10am-5:30pm; Metro: Union Station
This place is pretty cool. In the National Capitol Post Office Building, just west of Union Station, the newest Smithsonian museum features kid-friendly exhibits on postal history from the Pony Express to modern times. Also here are antique mail planes, beautiful old stamps, Cliff Clavin's postal carrier uniform (from the television sitcom *Cheers)* and great special exhibits of old letters (from soldiers, pioneers and others).

SEWALL-BELMONT HOUSE Map pp250-1
☎ 202-546-1210; www.sewallbelmont.org; 144 Constitution Ave NE; admission by donation; ⏰ 11am-3pm Tue-Fri , noon-4pm Sat; Metro: Union Station or Capitol South
This historic home is a feminist landmark: it has been the home base of the National Woman's

Supreme Justice
The Supreme Court, the country's highest judicial body, consists of nine justices appointed for life terms. It's referred to by the name of its presiding chief justice (the 'Warren Court,' the 'Rehnquist Court'). The image of stately justices cloaked in black robes is a familiar one, but only recently have the faces of women and African Americans appeared.

The court's high stature began with the appointment of John Marshall as chief justice in 1801. Previously, justices gave separate opinions, but Marshall established the single 'opinion of the court,' which carried much more weight. The Marshall Court issued a number of decisions that upheld Congress' power over the states and affirmed the court's right to declare other governmental branches' actions unconstitutional.

The court's most notorious 19th-century case, in 1857, was Dred Scott v Sandford, a major catalyst to the Civil War. Here the Taney Court ruled that blacks couldn't be US citizens and that Congress couldn't prevent territories in the American West from permitting slavery. In 1896 in Plessy v Ferguson, the court upheld the segregation of the 'white and colored races' under the doctrine of 'separate but equal.' In dissent, Associate Justice John Marshall Harlan wrote that the Constitution recognizes 'no superior, dominant, ruling class of citizens...all citizens are equal before the law.' Not until almost 60 years later did the court say, in Brown v Board of Education of Topeka, that 'separate but equal' was not, in fact, equal.

Perhaps the most controversial 20th-century ruling was the 1973 Roe v Wade decision, which negated state laws denying a woman's right to abortion. The opinions of prospective Supreme Court justices on Roe v Wade are invariably an essential factor in their selection. This case, in addition to many others, draws protesters and advocates alike to the court's marble steps, where they try to sway judicial and public opinion.

Party since 1929, and for 43 years it was the residence of the party's legendary founder, suffragette Alice Paul. Paul spearheaded efforts to gain the vote for women – enshrined in the 19th Amendment – and wrote the Equal Rights Amendment. Docents show you historical exhibits, portraits, sculpture and a library that celebrates feminist heroines.

SUPREME COURT Map pp250-1
☎ 202-479-3030; www.supremecourtus.gov; 1 1st St NE; admission free; ⏰ 9am-4:30pm Mon-Fri; Metro: Capitol South
The Supreme Court of the United States convenes in an imposing 1935 all-marble building designed by Cass Gilbert. The seated figures in front of the building represent the female

Contemplation of Justice and the male Guardian of Law; panels on the 13,000lb bronze front doors depict the history of jurisprudence. The interior grand corridor and 'Great Hall' are no less impressive. Downstairs is an exhibit on the history of the court and a striking statue of John Marshall, fourth Chief Justice.

On days when court's not in session, you can hear lectures about the Supreme Court in the courtroom (and check out its lofty architecture). When court is in session, try to hear an oral argument. Queues form out front starting at 8am: choose the appropriate one depending on whether you wish to sit through the entire argument or observe the court in session for a few minutes. Justices hear arguments at 10am Monday to Wednesday for two weeks every month from October to April. The release of orders and opinions, also open to the public, takes place in May and June. Check the *Post*'s 'Supreme Court Calendar' listing or the Supreme Court website for case details.

UNION STATION Map pp250-1

☎ 202-289-1908; www.unionstationdc.com; 50 Massachusetts Ave NE; ⏱ 10am-9pm Mon-Sat, noon-6pm Sun; Metro: Union Station

The most impressive gateway into Washington, this massive 1908 beaux-arts depot was beautifully restored in 1988 (after years of neglect), and transformed into a contemporary city center and transit hub. Besides Amtrak connections to destinations throughout the East, it has a cinema, food court and 200,000 sq ft of shops.

The huge main hall, the 'Grand Concourse,' is patterned after the Roman Baths of Diocletian (although shields are strategically placed across the waists of the unusually modest legionnaire statues). In the station's east wing is the old Presidential Waiting Room (now B Smith's), where dignitaries and celebrities once alighted when they traveled to DC.

The station's exterior offers vistas of the Capitol and avenues radiating south toward the Mall. Just south along Louisiana Ave NW is **Union Station Plaza**, a grassy park with a large fountain cascade, and the **Taft Memorial Carillon**, whose bells ring every quarter-hour.

SOUTHEAST DC

ANACOSTIA MUSEUM Map pp250-1

☎ 202-287-3306; www.si.edu/anacostia; 1901 Fort Place SE; admission free; ⏱ 10am-5pm; bus W1 or W2 from Anacostia Metro

Originally a neighborhood museum, the Anacostia Museum expanded into a regional heritage

center celebrating black history and culture in DC and the mid-Atlantic states; it is now operated by the Smithsonian Institution and known as the Anacostia Museum & Center for African American History & Culture. Rotating exhibits focus on themes such as the transatlantic slave trade, the earliest free black communities in the New World, and art, photography and sculpture by black artists. The museum usually has full calendars of free concerts, films and workshops during Black History Month (February).

FREDERICK DOUGLASS NATIONAL HISTORIC SITE Map pp250-1

☎ 202-426-5961; www.nps.gov/frdo; 1411 W St SE; admission free; ⏱ 9am-4pm, to 5pm Jun-Aug; bus B2 or B4 from Anacostia Metro

This rather bulky title refers to Cedar Hill, the great abolitionist's Anacostia home, which is maintained by the National Park Service as a museum honoring Frederick Douglass' life and work. Diplomat, author and former slave, Douglass lived here from 1877 until his death in 1895. The house still contains most of his original furnishings, down to his wire-rim eyeglasses on his rolltop desk. Hourly tours are entertaining and informative, touching on Douglass' 5-mile walk to work on Capitol Hill, his authorship of the *Narrative of the Life of Frederick Douglass* and his impressive five-figure salary. The hilltop home has a commanding view of DC. Start at the visitors center embedded in the foot of the hill, where you can see a short biographical film.

MARINE BARRACKS Map pp250-1

☎ 202-433-6060; www.mbw.usmc.mil; 8th & I St SE; ⏱ parade 8:45pm Fri; Metro: Eastern Market

The 'Eighth and Eye Marines' are on largely ceremonial duty at the nation's oldest Marine Corps post. Most famously, this post is home to the Marine Corps Band, once headed by

John Philip Sousa, king of the military march, who was born nearby at 636 G St SE. On Friday evenings in summer, you can watch a two-hour ceremonial drill parade featuring the band, the drum and bugle corps, the silent drill team and the mascot bulldog. Call weeks in advance for reservations or show up for general admission at 8pm.

MARINE CORPS MUSEUM Map pp250-1
☎ 202-433-3840; www.history.usmc.mil; Washington Navy Yard Bldg 58, enter from 11th St SE; admission free; ⏰ 10am-4pm Mon-Fri; Metro: Navy Yard

This small museum within the Navy Yard traces the history of the Marine Corps since its inception in 1775. The exhibit's attempt to personalize the history with profiles of individuals is interesting, but it's not necessarily interactive or eye-catching. A special exhibit honors the 50th anniversary of the Korean War. There are other war artifacts, such as the flag raised by marines over Iwo Jima in WWII.

NAVAL HISTORICAL CENTER Map pp250-1
☎ 202-433-4882; www.history.navy.mil; Washington Navy Yard Bldg 76 (enter from 11th St SE); admission free; ⏰ 9am-4pm Mon-Fri, 9am-5pm Jun-Aug; Metro: Navy Yard

This 600ft-long building – part of the old Gun Factory – produced ordnance and missile components for the navy until 1962. Today, it houses a huge display of artifacts, models and documents, chronicling the navy's history and honoring its heroes. This place is more appealing than the Marine Corps Museum; it includes full-size models of ships and real-to-touch gunmounts and cannons. Outside, tour the decommissioned destroyer USS *Barry*.

BROOKLAND & NORTHEAST DC

Eating p124; Sleeping p196

It was not long ago that most of DC's Upper Northeast district was considered off-limits for casual visitors. Students made a beeline from the Brookland Metro stop back to their dorms on Catholic University or Trinity College campus. Drivers admired the greenery of the National Arboretum from their cars as they drove by on New York Ave, but nobody bothered to stop.

As in many parts of DC, however, times are changing. Brookland is perhaps DC's hottest real estate market, as buyers – driven out of the desirable Northwest quadrant by the now-impossible prices – grab up the large houses with leafy yards. The area around 12th St NE is becoming its own little college town, drawing local residents and students from the nearby campuses. You won't confuse Brookland with Georgetown, by any means. But this is a place in the city where real people can afford to buy homes and hang out at the local pub, all just two Metro stops from Union Station.

The incongruous features of this neighborhood – which are a reminder that Brookland is not Collegetown, USA – are the spectacular National Shrine of Immaculate Conception and the little known Franciscan Monastery. Exquisite landmarks in their own rite, they add a touch of spiritual significance to the neighborhood. Not many college towns attract a steady stream of pilgrims outside of football season!

Orientation

DC's Northeast quadrant is a huge area of mostly peaceful residential streets and green college campuses, but they get rudely interrupted by noisy traffic on unfriendly highways. Bladensburg Rd and Rhode Island Ave (Rte 1), further north, both cut across the quadrant from southeast to northwest, while New York Ave (Rte 50) roars by east to west. For our purposes, the neighborhood includes areas east of N Capitol St and north of L St NE. The neighborhood's eastern boundary is

Transportation

Metro The CUA-Brookland Metro station is two stops past Union Station on the Red Line.

Parking Outside of Brookland, many places are not accessible by public transport, so you may need to drive. Street parking is easy in most parts of the Northeast quadrant (but watch your two-hour limit).

the Anacostia River, and it stretches north to the Maryland line.

Northwest of Rhode Island Ave, the increasingly popular Brookland neighborhood is bursting up around the campuses of Catholic University and Trinity College. There is a little downtown Brookland center along 12th St NE between Monroe and Perry Sts. The shady, green Franciscan Monastery is amid the residential streets a few blocks northeast of here.

Further south, Gallaudet University is squeezed in between New York Ave and Bladensburg Rd. It is flanked on either side by Brentwood Park and Mt Olivet Cemetery, which offer a protective barrier to the roar. And tucked into an unlikely spot in the southeast corner of the quadrant, the pristine US National Arboretum occupies almost all the space between Bladensburg Rd, New York Ave and the Anacostia River.

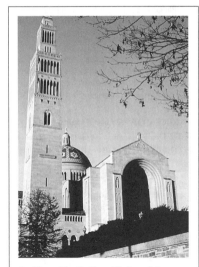

Basilica of the National Shrine of the Immaculate Conception (left)

BASILICA OF THE NATIONAL SHRINE OF THE IMMACULATE CONCEPTION
Map pp252-3

☎ 202-526-8300; www.nationalshrine.com; 400 Michigan Ave NE; ☼ 7am-7pm, Sun Mass 9am, 10:30am, noon, 1:30pm (Spanish), 4:30pm; Metro: Brookland-CU

The largest Catholic church in the Western Hemisphere (and some say the Catholic answer to the Washington National Cathedral), this huge church accommodates 6000 worshipers. In addition to its unearthly size, the Marian shrine sports an eclectic mix of Romanesque and Byzantine motifs, from classical towers to a mosque-like dome, all anchored by a 329ft minaret-shaped campanile. Downstairs, the original, Eastern-style crypt church has low, mosaic-covered vaulted ceilings lit by votives

and chandeliers. Upstairs, the main sanctuary is lined with elaborate saints' chapels, lit by rose windows, and fronted by a dazzling mosaic of a stern Christ. A large gift shop sells religious literature, rosaries and statues.

CAPITAL CHILDREN'S MUSEUM
Map pp252-3

☎ 202-675-4120; www.ccm.org; 800 3rd St NE; adult/senior $7/5; ☼ 10am-5pm daily Jun-Aug, Tue-Sun Sep-May, plus Martin Luther King Day, Presidents' Day, Easter Monday, Columbus Day, Veterans Day & Monday btwn Christmas & Easter; Metro: Union Station

Children can explore a prehistoric cave, make hot cocoa, experience the culture of Mexico, learn why gas is heavier than liquid, star in a cartoon, drive a bus and go to a Japanese school. There is a full calendar of special events and programs for kids.

FRANCISCAN MONASTERY Map pp252-3

☎ 202-526-6800; www.myfranciscan.com; 1400 Quincy St NE; admission by donation; ☼ hourly tours 9am-4pm Mon-Sat, 1-4pm Sun

The Franciscan Monastery is set amid 44 beautifully landscaped acres of gardens that, in spring, explode into a riot of color as tulips, dogwoods, cherry trees and roses bloom. This place isn't just about flowers, however. The Order of St Francis is charged with guardian-

Brookland & Northeast DC Top Five

- Basilica of the National Shrine of the Immaculate Conception (p68) Grandeur and glory to rival Europe's great cathedrals.
- Brookland (p67) Exploring the up-and-coming neighborhood's back streets and byways.
- Franciscan Monastery (p68) The marvels of the Holy Land right in the backyard.
- Kenilworth Aquatic Gardens (p69) Admiring the delicacy of the water lilies.
- National Arboretum (p69) Handsome hollies and magnificent magnolias.

ship of the Holy Land's sacred sites. The monastery has interpreted that task in a unique way, constructing replicas of those sites for the faithful who are unable to visit the Holy Land. Among the glorious blooms are life-size fake-granite reproductions of the Tomb of Mary, the Grotto at Lourdes and other subterranean sacred places. More oddities await inside Mount St Sepulchre itself, including reproductions of the Roman Catacombs under the sanctuary floor. These dark, narrow passages wind past fake tombs and the actual remains of Sts Innocent and Benignus. It's all very creepy and fascinating, like a holy Disneyland.

GALLAUDET UNIVERSITY Map pp252-3
☎ 202-651-5505, TDD 651-5359; www.gallaudet.edu; 800 Florida Ave NE

Established in 1864, Gallaudet University is the world's only accredited liberal-arts school for the hearing-impaired. The college's first hearing-impaired president was appointed after student protests in 1989. Few sports fans know that in 1894, Gallaudet football players invented the American football huddle to prevent their opponents from reading the sign language used to call the plays. Tours of the campus are available by reservation. No Metro station is nearby, so you'll need to drive.

KENILWORTH AQUATIC GARDENS
Map pp252-3
☎ 202-426-6905; www.nps.gov/kepa; 1550 Anacostia Ave NE; admission free; ☺ 8am-4pm; Metro: Deanwood, Douglas St to pedestrian overpass, right on Anacostia Ave; or drive New York Ave (Rte-50) east to Kenilworth Ave south (I-295), right on Douglas St

The only national park devoted to water plants is across the Anacostia River from the National Arboretum, in Anacostia Park. The aquatic gardens were begun as the hobby of a Civil War veteran and operated for 56 years as a commercial water garden, until the federal government purchased them in 1938. Highlights include the lovely water lilies which are the star of an annual festival every July.

POPE JOHN PAUL II CULTURAL CENTER Map pp252-3
☎ 202-635-5400; www.jp2cc.org; 3900 Harwood Rd NE; admission by donation $5 adult, $4 senior & student; ☺ 10am-5pm Tue-Sat, noon-5pm Sun; Metro: CUA-Brookland

This impressive modern building is an unexpected setting for an interactive museum of the Catholic Church. Five galleries explore the history of the church, personal faith, and its relation to science, community and social service. The excellent Gallery of Imagination allows visitors to participate in a carillon-ringing ensemble or to design an electronic stained-glass window.

UNITED STATES NATIONAL ARBORETUM Map pp252-3
☎ 202-245-2726; www.usna.usda.gov; 3501 New York Ave NE; admission free, tram tour adult/student/child $4/3/2; ☺ 8am-5pm, tram tours Sat, Sun & holidays Apr-Oct

Way out in Northeast DC are 446 acres of blooming trees, ornamental plants and lovely verdant meadows. But because it's hard to access the national gardens – they're in a gritty area far from the Metro – they remain among DC's most hidden treasures. Most visitors are locals, not tourists, so it's a really wonderful place to stroll and flower-peep in peace.

Stop at the **Administration Building** near the R St gate for a map and information. Highlights include the **Bonsai & Penjing Museum** (☺ 10am to 3:30pm), east of the Administration Building, and the **Capitol Columns Garden**, south along Ellipse Rd. The latter is studded with Corinthian pillars removed from the US Capitol in the 1950s.

The best times to visit are spring (March to May, when the azaleas bloom) and fall (September to November, for colorful autumn leaves). No direct buses serve the gardens and it's hard to negotiate them on foot, so drive or bike.

SOUTHWEST DC

Eating p125

Historically, Southwest DC is one of the city's most culturally rich neighborhoods, but you would not know it walking around here today. Once out of the touristy area – south of the Mall and around the Tidal Basin – visitors may think they have taken a wrong turn. But there is more to this complex neighborhood than meets the eye; it is worth exploring, whether to take in a sunset from the pleasant waterfront area or to discover the remnants of its varied history.

In response to economic decline in the first half of the century, the city launched in Southwest DC one of its most sweeping urban-renewal clearances. The effort destroyed most of the historic Federal architecture and displaced many of the poor, mostly black residents. The cement office blocks and apartment complexes that went up created the modern – but soulless – residential neighborhood that is here today. IM Pei's **Waterfront Mall** (Map pp254-5), covering the 1100 block of 6th St, is a sleek apartment/commercial complex that epitomizes contemporary Southwest DC.

Still, the area has a few highlights, including the cherry-tree-trimmed Tidal Basin and wide-open East Potomac Park. The stretch along the Mall contains some of DC's most popular attractions, like the National Bureau of Engraving & Printing and the United States Holocaust Memorial Museum. The bustling fish market and peaceful marina are proof that the waterfront area has potential. Whether you dine on crabs while overlooking the Channel, or haggle for your crabs at the colorful market, or even catch them yourself from Hains Point, you can get a taste of it too.

Orientation

Southwest DC – DC's smallest quadrant – is a triangle-shaped area south of Independence Ave (and the National Mall) and west of South Capitol St. The eastern and southern boundaries are the Potomac and Anacostia Rivers respectively.

The 'Federal Rectangle' area just south of the Mall is home to several gigantic federal agencies, such as the US Department of Agriculture, as well as the United States Holocaust Memorial Museum and the National Bureau of Printing & Engraving. The rest of the quadrant is mostly residential, save the riverfront marina area on the Washington Channel and the naval base further south. A finger of land known as East Potomac Park, or Hains Point, stretches south from the Tidal Basin and forms a peninsula between the Washington Channel and the Potomac River.

EAST POTOMAC PARK Map pp254-5
Ohio Dr SW

Local residents flock to this waterside park for biking, running, fishing, golfing and picnicking. Though only a short distance from the National Mall, it is undiscovered by tourists, lending it an unassuming, neighborhood feel. A 5-mile paved trail – great for biking or in-line skating – runs around the park's circumference, paralleling Ohio Dr. The center of the park is the **East Potomac Park Golf Course** (p170). At the park's southern tip, known as Hains Point, an eerie and unexpected sculpture, the **Awakening**, portrays a giant emerging from the earth. Kids love climbing around on this thing, as well as on the nearby playground.

The park sits on a finger of land which extends southward from the Tidal Basin into the Potomac River. On foot, you can access the park

Transportation

Metro To reach the National Bureau of Engraving & Printing, the United States Holocaust Memorial Museum or any of the attractions around the Tidal Basin, the nearest Metro stop is Smithsonian. Use the Waterfront-SEU Metro stop to visit the marina area.

Parking Free parking is available at the north end of East Potomac Park, underneath the bridges. If you wish you go to Hains Point, there is parking further south along Ohio Dr, although it tends to fill up on weekends.

by following trails that lead from the **Thomas Jefferson Memorial** under the bridges. If you drive, you can park on the shoulder of Ohio Dr.

FRANKLIN DELANO ROOSEVELT MEMORIAL Map pp254-5

☎ 202- 426-6841; www.nps.gov/fdrm;
🕒 8am-midnight; Metro: Smithsonian

FDR didn't want a grand memorial. In fact, during his presidency he requested that a slab no larger than his desk be placed outside the National Archives. His wishes were followed; a modest stone still rests there today (p54). Planners later felt the stone wasn't grand enough, however, so this second, 7.5-acre memorial opened in 1997.

On the Tidal Basin's west bank, it is composed of four red-granite 'rooms' that narrate FDR's presidency through statuary and inscriptions, punctuated with cascades and peaceful alcoves. The unique memorial tells the story of the 32nd president, rather than simply displaying a single monumental image.

GEORGE MASON MEMORIAL
Map pp254-5

☎ 202-426-6841; www.nps.gov/gemm;
🕒 8am-midnight; Metro: Smithsonian

This little oasis of flowers and fountains honors the famed statesman and author of the Commonwealth of Virginia Declaration of Rights (a forerunner to the US Bill of Rights). A bronze sculpture of Mason sits in a lovely setting, amid his wise words against slavery and in support for human rights.

NATIONAL BUREAU OF ENGRAVING & PRINTING Map pp254-5

☎ 202-874-3019; www.bep.treas.gov; 14th and C Sts SW; admission free; 🕒 tours 8am-2pm Mon-Fri, plus 3:30-7pm Jun-Aug, visitors center 8:30am-3pm; Metro: Smithsonian

If money does not grow on trees, where does it come from? You can see for yourself at the National Bureau of Engraving & Printing, where all US paper currency is designed, engraved and printed. Forty-minute guided tours demonstrate how $700 million a day is churned out, plus show exhibits on counterfeiting and unusual bills. The sheer thrill of seeing gobs of green makes this a big hit with kids. Line up at the **NBEP ticket kiosk** (Raoul Wallenberg Pl) for tickets; arrive early, as the amount distributed is limited. You can receive up to five tickets for entrance at a designated time on the same day.

Southwest DC Top Five

- **East Potomac Park** (p70) Watching the *Awakening*.
- **Franklin Delano Roosevelt Memorial** (p71) Honoring the memory of the 20th-century's greatest president.
- **National Cherry Blossom Festival** (p72) The Tidal Basin abloom.
- **Seafood Market** (p125) A sensory spectacle of blue crabs and silver fish.
- **United States Holocaust Memorial Museum** (p72) Learning about the horror of the 20th-century's worst tragedy.

THOMAS JEFFERSON MEMORIAL
Map pp254-5

☎ 202-426-6841; www.nps.gov/thje;
🕒 8am-midnight; Metro: Smithsonian

Set on the south bank of the Tidal Basin amid the cherry trees, this memorial honors the third US president, political philosopher, drafter of the Declaration of Independence and founder of the University of Virginia. Designed by John Russell Pope to resemble Jefferson's library at the university, the rounded, domed monument was initially derided by critics as 'the Jefferson Muffin.' Inside is a 19ft bronze likeness, and excerpts from Jefferson's writings are etched into the walls.

TIDAL BASIN Map pp254-5

☎ 202-484-0206; 🕒 8am-dusk; Metro: Smithsonian

Beloved for the magnificent Yoshino cherry trees that ring it, the Tidal Basin attracts joggers, strollers and picnickers to its shady banks. The orchard was a gift from Japan in 1912; since then, every year in late March or early April the banks shimmer with pale pink blossoms.

The enchanting **National Cherry Blossom Festival** (p72) celebrates this event – the first two weeks of April draw 100,000 visitors to DC for the festivities, which culminate in a big parade.

The amoeba-shaped Tidal Basin actually serves a practical purpose as well as being aesthetically pleasing: it flushes the adjacent Washington Channel. At high tide, river waters fill the basin through gates under the Inlet Bridge; at low tide, gates under the Outlet Bridge open and water streams into the channel.

Paddleboats are available for rental on the eastern shore for $7 to $8 per hour.

Neighborhoods – Southwest DC

UNITED STATES HOLOCAUST
MEMORIAL MUSEUM Map pp254-5

☎ 202-488-0400; www.ushmm.org; 100 Raoul Wallenberg Pl SW; admission free; ⏰ 10am-5:30pm, to 7.50pm Tue Apr-Aug; Metro: Smithsonian

The somber, soaring Holocaust Museum is unlike any other DC museum. In remembering the millions murdered by the Nazis, it is brutal, direct and impassioned. Its exhibits leave many visitors in tears and few unmoved. The extraordinary building was designed in 1993 by James Ingo Freed, and its stark facade and steel-and-glass interior echo the death camps themselves.

Apart from the permanent exhibits, the candlelit Hall of Remembrance is a sanctuary for quiet reflection; the Wexner Learning Center offers text archives, photographs, films and oral testimony available on touch-screen computers. If you have young children in tow, avoid the permanent exhibits, which are very graphic; instead, opt for 'Remember the Children,' a gentler kids' installation, on the 1st floor.

Same-day passes (up to four per person) to view the permanentale exhibit are available at the pass desk on the 1st floor. The passes allow entrance at a designated time (arrive early because they do run out). Alternatively, for a surcharge, tickets are available in advance at www.tickets.com or ☎ 800-400-9373.

WATERSIDE PARK & AROUND

Map pp254-5
Metro: Waterfront-SEU

A few historic homes – curiosities in this neighborhood – survived the 1950s urban clearance. The **Law House** (1252 6th St SW) is a Federal-style row house that was built by one of the first DC land speculators in 1796. From the same period, the **Wheat Row houses** (1313-1321 4th St SW, south of N St SW) have human-scale brick facades that add warmth to the neighborhood.

Near the waterfront's south end, Waterside Park contains the **Titanic Memorial** to honor the

National Cherry Blossom Festival

A fluttering gauze scarf of the palest pink encircles the Tidal Basin, at the west end of the National Mall, each spring in late March or early April, as 1300 Japanese cherry trees explode into bloom.

In 1912, the Japanese government presented the forerunners of these trees to President Taft as a goodwill gift. They are mostly of the Yoshino variety, whose blooms are nearly pure white, but a handful of pink-blooming Akebono trees add a shimmer of dawn-like rose to the scene.

Washingtonians immediately adopted the trees as a symbol of their city. When the Tidal Basin was chosen as the site of the Thomas Jefferson Memorial, protesters even chained themselves to trees to prevent their removal. During WWII, the trees were occasionally vandalized, but they thrived anyway. In 1965 the Japanese government provided the US with 3800 more trees, which were planted along the Mall and near the Washington Monument. Later-blooming Kwanzan cherry trees were planted in East Potomac Park.

The city's biggest annual festival, the **National Cherry Blossom Festival** (☎ 202-728-1137; www.nationalcherryblossomfestival.org), is timed to coincide with the trees' blossoming. However, because the blossoming time is somewhat unpredictable, and because Washington's quirky spring weather sometimes pelts the blossoms off the trees with icy rain and wind, the festival doesn't always get its flowers. Nonetheless, the parades, speeches, parties and cultural events draw thousands of tourists and mark the official start of warm weather for Washington.

men who sacrificed their lives to save the women and children aboard the sinking ship. Just south is **Fort Lesley J McNair**, an army post established in 1791 and burned by the British in 1814. The Lincoln-assassination conspirators were hung at McNair in 1865; it now houses the National Defense University and National War College (closed to the public).

GEORGETOWN

Eating p125; Shopping p179; Sleeping p196

Isolated both geographically and historically, Georgetown has long maintained a unique identity in DC. The town of George was a bustling trading port long before the federal city was established; it was annexed by the District of Columbia only in 1871. Even today, just a few avenues traverse the valleys of Rock Creek Park, leaving Georgetown physically cut off from the rest of the city. Frankly, the neighborhood's wealthy

residents like it that way. When DC built the Metro in the 1980s, local residents vetoed a Georgetown stop, condemning future generations of visitors to shuttle buses and the endless pursuit of parking.

Lack of transportation does not keep out the crowds, however. Nor do high rents deter shop owners and restaurateurs, whose trendy ventures are busting out all over this place. Like it or not, Georgetown cannot stop development on and around its cobblestone streets. It is not limited to retail either: older industrial buildings are being converted not only into shopping malls, but also into hotels, office complexes and upscale housing. Considering the under-utilized waterfront area, this development is not likely to stop soon.

Synonymous with Jesuit intellect, blue-blooded gentry and bar-hopping students, Georgetown embraces all of these contrasting features of its old-money, college-town identity. It is home to wealthy bankers and lawyers, as well as poorer students who aspire to be wealthy bankers and lawyers. Its streets contain some of DC's fanciest restaurants and cheapest eats; stately mansions sit alongside dilapidated student row houses; the distinguished university attracts wannabes, both diplomats and basketball players.

Georgetown's bars and boutiques draw swarms of students and suburbanites on weekends. But Georgetown's real treasures are tucked away from the hubbub of Wisconsin Ave and M St NW. Wander the cobblestone streets – lined with flowering arbors and Federal architecture – and soak up a little antebellum charm.

Transportation

Metro The Georgetown community resisted having the Metro in its midst, so the neighborhood is not easily accessible by public transit. The closest stop is Foggy Bottom-GWU, from where a 50c shuttle bus (25c with Metrorail transfer) leaves every 10 minutes during the hours of Metro operation. Route 1 runs down K St NW and up Wisconsin Ave to R St NW before turning around. Route 2 runs all the way down M St NW and crosses the Francis Scott Key Bridge to the Rosslyn Metro station.

Bus Any of the '30' buses (32, 34, 36) travel down Wisconsin Ave from Tenleytown and up M St NW to Washington Circle.

Parking Street parking can be near impossible, especially on weekend evenings. Look for spots on O, P or Q Sts NW between 29th and 31st. The garage beneath Georgetown Park mall is accessible from Wisconsin Ave.

Orientation

Quaint, historic Georgetown is wedged in between Rock Creek Park, Georgetown University and the Potomac River. Only a few streets connect Georgetown to the rest of the city, adding to the neighborhood's unique flavor. Georgetown's commercial heart is the intersection of M St NW and Wisconsin Ave: both streets are walled with ethnic eateries, trendy boutiques, cramped bookstores and happening bars. Further south, the C&O Canal – which used to act as a road – runs east–west between M St and the river.

The walled campus of Georgetown University occupies the southwest corner of the neighborhood, and some of the surrounding streets are populated by university buildings and row houses inhabited by students. But the residential streets also boast some of DC's loveliest homes and gardens.

The grid is at its most effective here: it's impossible to get lost. M through T Sts NW run east–west; and numbered streets from 27th to 37th NW run north–south. Aside from a few small-named streets, the grid is disrupted only by Wisconsin Ave, which cuts across the middle from north to south.

Georgetown Top Five

- **C&O Canal** (p74) Strolling along the towpath or riding in a mule-pulled barge.
- **Dumbarton Oaks** (p74) Gorgeous gardens and a curious collection of art.
- **Georgetown University** (p75) The hallowed halls of the Healy Building.
- **Tudor Place** (p75) Getting a glimpse of Georgetown's bluest blood.
- **Wisconsin & M Sts** Bountiful boutiques, catchy cafés and hip-hop-happening happy hours.

C&O CANAL Map pp256-7

www.nps.gov/choh; between M St & Potomac River; Georgetown shuttle from Foggy Bottom-GWU Metro

From its Georgetown start, the historic Chesapeake & Ohio Canal runs 185 miles upriver to Cumberland, in western Maryland. The towpath alongside, originally for the mules that towed the boats, now accommodates hikers and bikers enjoying the serenity of the canal. It is still a vital transportation link that allows for an easy escape from the city. Rent bicycles and canoes at Fletcher's Boathouse. (See Sports, Health & Fitness, p168 and p170.)

Within Georgetown's central zone, the canal runs parallel to M St a few blocks south. Crisscrossed by walkways and bridges, it is lined on either side with old warehouses and factory buildings that have been renovated into upscale retail and entertainment complexes. Stop by the **C&O Canal Visitors Center** (☎ 202-653-5190; 1057 Thomas Jefferson St; ⏰ 10am-4pm Apr-Oct, weekends only Nov-Mar) to learn about ranger-led walks and canal boat rides (see the boxed text 'Fueled by Mule,' below right).

CONVENT OF THE VISITATION

Map pp256-7

☎ 202-337-3350; www.visi.org; 1524 35th St NW; ⏰ 8am-6pm; Georgetown shuttle from Foggy Bottom-GWU Metro

This beautiful campus – established as a convent in 1799 – is now a girls' prep school. Founders' Hall, at the corner of 35th & P Sts NW, was gutted by a devastating fire in 1993 and totally reconstructed from historic photographs. The oldest building on campus is the 1821 Chapel of the Sacred Heart, south of the entrance on 35th St NW. The convent itself, among the oldest in the country, extends along P St NW.

DUMBARTON HOUSE Map pp256-7

☎ 202-337-2288; www.dumbartonhouse.org; 2715 Q St NW; adult/student $5/free; ⏰ 10am-2pm Tue-Sat, hourly tours 10:15am-1:15pm; Georgetown shuttle from Foggy Bottom-GWU Metro

Often confused with Dumbarton *Oaks*, Dumbarton *House* is a modest Federal historic house, which was constructed by a wealthy family in 1798. It is now run by the Colonial Dames of America. The genteel but gently witty tours focus not only on the house – chockablock with antique china, silver, furnishings, rugs, gowns and books – but also on quaint Federal customs, like passing round the chamber pot after formal dinners so gentlemen could have a group pee.

DUMBARTON OAKS Map pp256-7

☎ 202-339-6401; www.doaks.org; 1703 32nd St NW, enter gardens through R St gate; admission free to collection, gardens adult $5, senior & child $3; ⏰ 2-5pm Tue-Sun; Georgetown shuttle from Foggy Bottom-GWU Metro

This 19th-century mansion houses a fine art museum and research libraries, and is set in 16 acres of terraced gardens. Paths wind down toward Rock Creek amid boxwood and wisteria; 19 pools and fountains add coolness; and banks of cherries, crab apples and forsythias explode with color in spring. Although the gardens are popular, they hold many nooks and corners that let you find your own quiet bower. The museum features renowned Byzantine and pre-Columbian collections. The main house's music room has an intricately painted beamed ceiling and El Greco's *The Visitation*. It was here, in 1944, that the agreement to create the United Nations was forged.

Fueled by Mule

When construction on the C&O (Chesapeake & Ohio) Canal began in 1828, American prosperity depended on its waterways. Thousands of miles of canals provided a means of transportation and trade throughout the growing country. The C&O would join the Chesapeake Bay and the Ohio River, fulfilling a longtime dream to connect the Potomac River basin to the coastal plain. Unfortunately, by the time the project was complete in 1850, the C&O Canal was already obsolete, rendered out of date by the almighty railroad.

Nonetheless, the canal remained in operation for 74 years. Mules trudged along the towpath – originally 12ft wide – pulling boats containing cargo of all types. A series of 74 lift locks raised the boats about 605ft over the course of the 185 miles between Georgetown and Cumberland. The slow boat was not particularly profitable, however, especially as it was vulnerable to weather. After several devastating floods, the canal finally closed in 1924.

Today, bikers and boaters benefit from the canal, now a national park. But you can still experience the canal the old-fashioned way aboard the *Canal Clipper* or the *Georgetown*. Mules pull these barges full of passengers on one-hour journeys along the canal. The historical program includes rangers in period dress and a working lock that raises and lowers the boat 8ft. Barges leave from the visitors center two or three times a day, Wednesday through Sunday from May to October. Fares are adult/senior/child $8/6/5.

GEORGETOWN UNIVERSITY Map pp256-7

☎ 202-687-6538; www.georgetown.edu; 37th & O Sts NW; Georgetown shuttle from Rosslyn Metro

Founded in 1789, America's first Roman Catholic college was originally directed by the country's first black Jesuit, Father Patrick Healy. Today, about 12,000 students pursue degrees here. Notable 'Hoyas' (derived from the Latin *hoya saxa*, 'what rocks') include both Clintons. Georgetown's handsome, shaded campus retains some original 18th-and 19th-century buildings. At the east gate, the imposing, Flemish-style 1879 **Healy Building** is impressive with its tall clock tower. Lovely Dalghren Chapel and its quiet courtyard are hidden behind. Movie buffs might recognize the setting of 1973's shockfest *The Exorcist*: two of little Regan's hapless victims met their fates at the vertiginous **Exorcist Stairs** at 3600 Prospect St NW.

OAK HILL CEMETERY Map pp266-7

☎ 202-337-2835; 30th & R Sts NW; ⏲ 10am-4pm Mon-Fri; Georgetown shuttle from Foggy Bottom-GWU Metro

This 24-acre, obelisk-studded cemetery contains winding walks and 19th-century gravestones set into the hillsides of Rock Creek. The lovely gatehouse and the wee gneiss chapel were designed by James Renwick (both c 1850).

OLD STONE HOUSE Map pp256-7

☎ 202-426-6851; www.nps.gov/rocr/oldstonehouse; 3051 M St; admission free; ⏲ noon-5pm Wed-Sun; Georgetown shuttle from Foggy Bottom-GWU Metro

Sitting incongruously in the midst of the Georgetown shopping drag is DC's oldest surviving building. Built in 1765 as a one-room house, it's since been a boardinghouse, tavern, brothel and shop. It was almost demolished in the 1950s, but a persistent (albeit false) rumor that L'Enfant used it as a workshop while designing DC saved it for posterity. The Park Service now maintains

Georgetown's Black History Sites

Three sites recall the history of Georgetown's 19th-century free black community, who lived in an area known as Herring Hill. Founded in 1816, **Mount Zion United Methodist Church** (Map pp256-7; ☎ 202-234-0148; 1334 29th St NW) is DC's oldest black congregation. Its original site, on 27th St NW, was a stop on the Underground Railroad.

Nearby, at **Mount Zion Cemetery** (Map pp256-7; 2700 Q St NW) and the adjacent **Female Union Band Cemetery** (behind 2515-2531 Q St NW) are the overgrown headstones of many free black residents. The church hid escaping slaves in a vault here. You can reach the cemeteries from Wisconsin Ave by heading east on Q St NW and turning left at the path just before 2531 Q St NW.

it as an example of 18th-century life, exhibiting some of the original architectural features and furniture. The small garden is a peaceful place to recover from too much walking.

TUDOR PLACE Map pp256-7

☎ 202-965-0400; www.tudorplace.org; 1644 31st St NW; house tour adult/senior/student/child $6/5/3/2, self-guided garden tour $2; ⏲ 10am-3pm Tue-Sat, noon-4pm Sun; Georgetown shuttle from Foggy Bottom-GWU Metro

This 1816 neoclassical mansion was owned by Thomas Peter, a landowner and tobacco merchant, and his wife Martha Custis Peter, granddaughter of Martha Washington. The urban estate stayed in the prominent Peter family until opened to the public in 1984, so it preserves pieces of the family's – and the country's – history. Today the mansion functions as a small museum, and features furnishings and artwork from Mount Vernon. Its five acres are beautifully landscaped with gardens, fountains, walkways and orchards.

DUPONT CIRCLE & KALORAMA

Eating p128; Shopping p181; Sleeping p198

World-traveling diplomats and guitar-strumming bohemians, scantily clad gorgeous gays and high-powered pinstripe suits all come together in Dupont Circle, arguably the center of the non-federal universe in DC. The neighborhood is eclectic, ranging from plush ambassadorial estates and refined galleries to gay bars and secondhand bookstores. But it is more than that. Unlike many parts of the city, Dupont Circle bustles around the clock. During the week, workers from the area office buildings descend for a breath of fresh air or a bite to eat; on weekends, shoppers browse

the trendy boutiques and local farmers market; and every night of the week, diners of all dimensions flock to Dupont's lively restaurants and cafés.

A spin around the circle itself displays Dupont's heterogeneous character. At its center, Samuel Francis Dupont, rear admiral of the Union Navy, sits amid sunbathers, chess players, dog walkers and homeless wanderers. At the circle's edge are grand remnants of the days when Dupont was a millionaire's ghetto. The private **Sulgrave Club** (Map pp258-60; 1801 Massachusetts Ave NW) has attracted only the highest society to socialize with each other. The **Washington Club** (Map pp258-60; 15 Dupont Circle), another private club, was once the home of Cissy Patterson, who hosted President and Mrs Coolidge (and, consequently, Charles Lindbergh) while the White House was undergoing renovations in 1927. These turn-of-the-century mansions sit alongside commercial buildings that are home to modern-day millionaires, like the dramatic **Euram Building** (Map pp258-60; 21 Dupont Circle). The **Riggs Bank** (Map pp258-60; 1913 Massachusetts Ave NW) does more retail business in foreign currency exchange than any other bank in the city.

Kalorama adjoins Dupont Circle to the northwest. Greek for 'beautiful view,' it was named for an estate built by Jefferson confidante Joel Barlow that dominated this hilly area in the 19th century. Now Kalorama is a sleepy enclave of embassies and the brick-and-stone mansions and deep gardens of DC's ultrarich. This is the neighborhood of DC's storied 'cave dwellers' (old-money residents). Home to presidents from Wilson to Harding, the area is still thick with powerful politicos and ambassadors.

Orientation

Dupont Circle really is a traffic circle where major thoroughfares Massachusetts Ave and Connecticut Ave intersect with New Hampshire Ave and 19th and P Sts NW. All of these streets are crowded with restaurants and cafés, pubs and clubs. The surrounding number and letter streets (roughly 14th through 22nd Sts NW running north to south, and M through U Sts NW running east to west) are mixed residential and commercial areas, boasting some of DC's loveliest quarters and liveliest corners. Buzzing pockets of activity pop up at the intersection of 18th St and Florida Ave NW, 18th St between P and Q Sts NW, and 22nd and M Sts NW.

Northwest of Dupont Circle, foreign embassies pepper Massachusetts Ave, known here as Embassy Row. Sheridan Circle, at its intersection with 22nd and R Sts NW, is the center of Washington's diplomatic community. Southeast of Dupont Circle, Mass Ave is punctuated by lesser-known traffic circles at 16th and N Sts NW (Scott Circle), and at 14th and M Sts NW (Thomas Circle).

For our purposes, the neighborhood is bounded by Rock Creek Park in the west, Kalorama Rd in the north, 14th St in the east and L St in the south. In the northwest corner (bounded by Massachusetts, Connecticut and Florida Aves, and Rock Creek Park) is the quieter but no less elegant Kalorama. The fashionable West End, full of power-lunch restaurants and luxury hotels, is in the southwest corner between New Hampshire Ave and Rock Creek Park.

Transportation

Metro On the Red Line, the Dupont Circle Metro station is at the center of the action. Farragut North is a few blocks south. If you are headed south of the circle, the Orange Line may be more convenient. Use Foggy Bottom-GWU to reach the West End, and Farragut West or McPherson Sq further east.

Parking There is no reason to drive to this neighborhood. If you must, during the day it is possible to find a meter or to park on residential streets for up to two hours. Street parking becomes much more difficult during evening hours. There are some parking garages (20th St & N St NW).

B'NAI B'RITH KLUTZNICK MUSEUM

Map pp258-60

☎ 202-857-6583; bnaibrith.org; 1640 Rhode Island Ave NW; admission by donation; 🕒 10am-5pm Sun-Fri, to 3:30pm Fri winter; Metro: Dupont Circle

One of the country's largest Judaica collections, covering history and culture from antiquity to present, is on the B'nai B'rith building's ground floor. In its quiet rooms are archaeological artifacts, folk art and beautiful ritual objects, including silver Torah crowns, Kiddush cups, menorahs, Passover platters and rarities like a 1556 Torah scroll. Exhibits address subjects like early Jewish settlement in the US, the Holocaust, and Jews in American history and the arts. The museum's newest exhibit is the National Jewish American Sports Hall of Fame. A tranquil sculpture garden is behind the museum.

CATHEDRAL OF ST MATTHEW THE APOSTLE Map pp258-60

☎ 202-347-3215; www.stmatthewscathedral.org; 1725 Rhode Island Ave NW; ⏰ tours 2:30pm Sun, Mass 5:30pm Sat, 7am, 8:30am, 10am (Latin), 11:30am, 1pm (Spanish) & 5:30pm Sun; Metro: Dupont Circle

The sturdy red-brick exterior doesn't hint at the marvelous mosaics and gilding within this 1889 Catholic cathedral, where JFK's funeral mass was held. Its vast central dome, altars and chapels depict biblical saints and eminent New World personages – from Simón Bolívar to Elizabeth Ann Seton – in stained glass, murals and scintillating Italianate mosaics; almost no surface is left undecorated. Evening's the best time to visit, when flickering candles illuminate the sanctuary, but you can attend Mass on Sunday morning or slip in almost any time to look around.

FONDO DEL SOL VISUAL ARTS CENTER Map pp258-60

☎ 202-483-2777; www.dkmuseums.com/fondo.html; 2112 R St NW; admission by donation; ⏰ 12:30-5:30pm Tue-Sat; Metro: Dupont Circle

This delightful artist-run community museum promotes the Americas' cultural heritage and arts through exhibits of contemporary Latin-American artists' work, pre-Columbian artifacts, *santos* (carved wooden saints) and folk art. In late summer, the Caribbeana Festival features salsa and reggae music.

HEURICH HOUSE Map pp258-60

☎ 202-429-1894; 1307 New Hampshire Ave NW; admission by donation $5; ⏰ tours 12:15pm & 1:15pm Wed; Metro: Dupont Circle

Looking very much like a medieval castle, this 31-room mansion was designed by John Granville Myers for local brewer Christian Heurich. The interior is predominately Renaissance and rococo Revival. A period garden park, a refuge for nearby office workers, offers the perfect spot for contemplation or a quiet lunch break.

ISLAMIC CENTER Map pp258-60

☎ 202-332-8343; 2551 Massachusetts Ave NW; admission free; ⏰ 10am-5pm; Metro: Dupont Circle

The national mosque for American Muslims is a beautiful, though incongruous building in the midst of Embassy Row. Topped with a 160ft minaret, the pale limestone mosque (which faces Mecca) is so delicately inscribed with Koranic verse that it appears to float above Massachusetts Ave. Inside, the mosque glows with bright floral tiling, thick Persian rugs and gilt-trimmed ceilings detailed with more Koranic verse. You can enter to look around; remove your shoes, and women must bring scarves to cover their hair.

NATIONAL GEOGRAPHIC EXPLORERS HALL Map pp258-60

☎ 202-857-7588; www.nationalgeographic.com; 17th and M Sts NW; admission free; ⏰ 9am-5pm Mon-Sat, 10am-5pm Sun; Metro: Farragut North

This natural science museum at National Geographic Society headquarters can't compete with the Smithsonian's more extensive offerings downtown, but it's is worth a stop if you have kids in tow. They'll enjoy its rotating, hands-on exhibits on exploration, adventure and earth sciences. Recent exhibits have included Shackleton's Antarctic-expedition photography and natural history drawings from *National Geographic* magazine's early years.

The society's year-round 'Live...from National Geographic' series at the **Gilbert Grosvenor Auditorium** (☎ 202-857-7700), located in the National Geographic Society Headquarters next to the Explorers Hall, includes films, concerts and lectures by famed researchers and explorers.

PHILLIPS COLLECTION Map pp258-60

☎ 202-387-2151; www.phillipscollection.org; 1600 21st St NW; special exhibits, Artful Evenings & weekends adult $8, student & senior $6, child under 18 free, free to permanent exhibit weekdays; ⏰ 10am-5pm Tue-Sat, noon-7pm Sun, Artful Evenings 5-8:30pm Thu; Metro: Dupont Circle

Founded in 1921, DC's oldest museum of modern art is famed for its extensive collection of Impressionist and Postimpressionist pieces. Monet, Degas, Whistler, van Gogh and Klee are all represented, with Renoir's panoramic *Luncheon of the Boating Party* crowning its holdings. The stately brownstone also draws art lovers for its special exhibits, which in recent years have included Marsden Hartley, Georgia O'Keeffe, Alfred Stieglitz and Pierre Auguste Renoir masterpieces. On Thursdays, the gallery hosts Artful Evenings, featuring live jazz and free appetizers.

Through the end of 2004, many of the European masterpieces are on tour while the gallery undergoes construction of a Center for Studies in Modern Art, a resource and education facility. A series of special exhibits continues to be on display in the Main House.

ST AUGUSTINE CATHOLIC CHURCH
Map pp258-60

☎ 202-265-11470; www.saintaugustine-dc.org; 15th & V Sts NW; ⏱ mass noon Sun; Metro: U Street-Cardozo

Let the spirit move you at DC's oldest and sweetest-sounding black Catholic congregation. St Augustine's gospel choir rocks the house every Sunday at noon. The unrivalled show features the 165-member choir, often clad in Kenti cloth, and talented, spirited soloists singing their hearts out. The Mass is long, but it offers a unique glimpse at the role of religion in contemporary African American society. Plus lively music and a little spiritual nourishment.

Founded in 1858, St Augustine's congregation moved to the Gothic Revival building at 15th and V Sts NW in 1961. It was a bold move, as it also marked a merger with an all-white congregation; the joined churches became known as Sts Paul & Augustine. The name reverted to St Augustine in 1982, but the congregation continues to welcome members of all races and ethnic groups, especially foot-tapping, hand-clapping sopranos and basses who feel the spirit.

SCOTTISH RITE MASONIC TEMPLE
Map pp258-60

☎ 202-232-3579; 1733 16th St NW; admission free; ⏱ 8am-4pm Mon-Fri; Metro: Dupont Circle

The full name of the US Masonic headquarters is 'The Supreme Council of the Inspectors General Knights Commanders of the House of the Temple of...' – well, it goes on like that for a while. Its architectural excesses echo its nomenclature:

patterned in 1911 by John Russell Pope after the Temple of Halicarnassus, it's lofted on a high pedestal of stairs and fronted by lion statues and bronze doors; the interior is frosted with the ersatz Greek and Egyptian arcana beloved by Masons, all rich in numerological meaning.

SOCIETY OF THE CINCINNATI MUSEUM AT ANDERSON HOUSE
Map pp258-60

☎ 202-785-2040; 2118 Massachusetts Ave NW; admission free; ⏱ 1-4pm Tue-Sat; Metro: Dupont Circle

A stately example of Dupont Circle's turn-of-the-century grand manses, this 1902 beaux-arts beauty is now the headquarters of the Society of the Cincinnati. Founded in 1783 by officers who served under Washington in the Continental Army, the society displays European and Asian art and fine furnishings acquired by the Anderson family, plus exhibits on the Revolution. Highlights include Revolutionary musketry and a pretty winter garden.

TEXTILE MUSEUM Map pp258-60

☎ 202-667-0441; www.textilemuseum.org; 2320 S St NW; admission donation $5; ⏱ 10am-5pm Mon-Sat, 1-5pm Sun, tours by reservation 10:15am-3pm Mon-Sat; Metro: Dupont Circle

Near the top of the list for DC's best non-Smithsonian museum, this gem is the country's only textile museum, and is as unappreciated as the art itself. In two historic mansions, its cool, dimly lit galleries hold exquisite fabrics and carpets dating from 3000 BC to the present. Accompanying wall commentary explains how the textiles mirror the social, spiritual, economic and aesthetic values of the societies that made them. Founded in 1925, its collection includes rare kimonos, pre-Columbian weaving, American quilts and Ottoman embroidery. (Find the flaw: Traditional textile artists, from Islamic carpetmakers to Appalachian quilters, weave intentional flaws into their work to avoid mimicking God's perfection.)

Upstairs, the learning center will keep older kids entertained – and learning – for hours. Hands-on (literally!) exhibits demonstrate weaving patterns, dying techniques and more.

WASHINGTON POST Map pp258-60

☎ 202-334-7969; www.washingtonpost.com; 1150 15th St NW; admission free; ⏱ tours by reservation 10am-3pm Mon; Metro: McPherson Sq

Want to see where Woodward and Bernstein toppled a president? Stop by the *Post*'s headquarters. Its free tours don't reveal much of

---

Dupont Circle & Kalorama Top Five

- **Dupont Circle art scene** (p77) From the local artist-run Fondo del Sol to the world-class Phillips Collection.
- **Embassy Row** (p102) The nations of the world come together on one Washington strip.
- **Kramerbooks & Afterwords Café** (p158) Picking up a book or a date at Dupont's trendiest café and bookstore.
- **St Augustine's Catholic Church** (p78) Letting the spirit move you at a gospel service.
- **Textile Museum** (p78) Admiring examples of the world's most practical and universal art forms.

the paper's operations but do show you the busy newsroom and explain how the paper is printed.

WOODROW WILSON HOUSE Map pp258-60
☎ 202-387-4062; www.woodrowwilsonhouse.org; 2340 S St NW; adult/senior $6/4; ⏰ 10am-4pm Tue-Sun; Metro: Dupont Circle
This Georgian Revival mansion offers guided hour-long tours focusing on the 28th president's life and legacy. Genteel elderly docents discuss highlights of Wilson's career (WWI, the League of Nations) and home, which has been restored to the period of his residence (1921–24). The tour features a lovely garden, a stairwell conservatory, European bronzes, 1920s-era china and Mrs Wilson's elegant dresses, all of which offer a glamorous portrait of Roaring '20s DC society.

ADAMS-MORGAN

Eating p132; Shopping p184; Sleeping p202

Funky, ethnic, bohemian Adams-Morgan is a lively mix of cultures and cuisines, scents and sounds, all in a two-block patch of the city. Renamed in 1955 when DC became the first large US city to voluntarily integrate its schools, its moniker comes from two local elementary schools: historically white Adams and black Morgan. Adding to this blend today are immigrants from Latin America, the Caribbean, East Africa and Southeast Asia. All of these groups bring their tingly tastes and sensual sounds to the clubs and restaurants in this global village.

In the early 20th century, Meridian Hill was a very fashionable address. The neighborhood's reigning social queen, Mary Henderson, wife of a Missouri senator, built herself a grand old castle here. (The castle's been demolished, but its crenellated walls still stand on 16th St.) Her favorite architect, George Oakley Totten, built many ornate manses near her castle, such as the 1906 **Pink Palace** (Map p261; 2600 16th St NW), a Venetian-style palazzo.

Since then, the streets around Adams-Morgan have seen their highs and lows, as its population has become more diverse, both ethnically and economically. Today, Adams-Morgan is an edgy 'hood which offers residents a lively, urban atmosphere at (slightly) reduced rents. The surrounding residential streets are home to upper-middle-class folks with an appreciation for the cosmopolitan. The internationals come out to Adams-Morgan by night to get a taste of home or to get their groove on, but most of them retreat before sunrise to their abodes in Arlington or Tacoma or neighboring Mount Pleasant.

By day the place is pretty quiet, although shops selling ethnic ingredients and world music and other imported finery do a brisk business. But nightlife is what's happening here. And nobody can resist the exotic flavors. There is something for everyone: students drinking at **Millie & Al's** (p153), gringos learning a few steps of salsa, gay boys enjoying the famed **Perry's** (p132) drag show, yuppies eating Ethiopian (p133) with their hands...

It's not unusual to see dancin' in the streets around here in September, when DC's largest neighborhood festival takes place. Musicians, vendors, and foodies come out for **Adams Morgan Festival** (p11), a weekend-long street fair.

Orientation

Adams-Morgan is a little international hub on Columbia Rd and 18th St NW, just south of their intersection. The long blocks of 18th St between Florida Ave and Columbia Rd are wallpapered with bars, clubs, new and

Transportation

Metro The nearest Metro stations are Red Line's Woodley Park-Zoo/Adams Morgan or Green Line's U Street-Cardozo. From Woodley Park it's a pleasant 20-minute walk over the Duke Ellington Memorial Bridge to the heart of Adams-Morgan. Alternatively, for 35c (with a rail transfer), you can ride the U Link shuttle, which runs from 6pm Sunday to Friday and from 10am on Saturday until the Metro closes. It travels between the Woodley Park and U Street-Cardozo Metro stops via Calvert, 18th and U Sts NW. The schedule is timed to make the last trains leaving from the Woodley Park Metro.

Parking Sometimes it is possible to find street parking on the other residential streets west of Columbia Rd or east of 18th St NW. Otherwise, use the public lot at 18th & Belmont Sts NW.

Adams-Morgan Top Five

- **18th St** Shopping and bar hopping with an international twist.
- **Habana Village** (p164) Feeling the salsa beat.
- **Meridian Hill Park** (below) Delightful interplay between landscaping and geology.
- **Meskerem** (p132) Eating the Ethiopian way.
- **Perry's drag brunch** (p132) Giving new meaning to 'wearing your Sunday best.'

secondhand bookstores, record stores, retro and nouveau clothing boutiques, sidewalk cafés and rooftop restaurants. The surrounding streets are primarily residential and surprisingly quiet. Be careful walking these streets at night, especially east of 18th St, as crime does spill over from the rougher neighborhoods to the north and east.

East of the hub is Meridian Hill, which marks the geological fall line between the rocky piedmont plateau and the softer coastal plain. Meridian Hill Park, which runs along 16th St NW, marks the eastern boundary of the neighborhood. The western boundary is Rock Creek Park and the zoo. Just north is Mount Pleasant, DC's most Latino neighborhood, where Salvadorean *pupuserías* serve meat-stuffed pastries and Central American groceries line the streets.

MERIDIAN HILL PARK Map p261
Metro: U Street-Cardozo

Unofficially dedicated to Malcolm X, this park scales a hillside from the Shaw neighborhood to Adams-Morgan's upper reaches, and adds much-needed scenery to the area. The park was constructed in the early 20th century, when Meridian Hill was a very fashionable district. Built astraddle the fall line between the piedmont plateau and the Atlantic coastal plain, the park emphasizes its locale with terraced walkways and a waterfall cascade. An eccentric mix of statuary, from Joan of Arc to Dante, enlivens its contoured lawns. It's lovely in springtime, when the dogwoods and azaleas flower, but it isn't safe to visit after dark.

MERIDIAN INTERNATIONAL CENTER
Map p261

☎ 202-667-6800; www.meridian.org; 1630 Crescent Place; admission free; ⏰ 2-5pm Wed-Sun; Metro: U Street-Cardozo

Here in the middle of the city, architect John Russell Pope built this French country chateau, complete with a stately walled entrance, charming cobblestone courtyard and decorated limestone facade. Today, Meridian House – as it is known – is an educational and hospitality center for DC's international community.

The Compliment Man

Ron Miller is a local celebrity in Adams-Morgan, but few people actually know him by name. They know him by his warm smile, his sincere observations and his self-given nickname, the Compliment Man. The moniker is apropos. 'Girl, you look fabulous in that dress,' he might comment, looking you over with approval. Or, 'I love your shoes – they really make that outfit.' If the beneficiary of his comment looks skeptical or confused he explains: 'Don't you know who I am? I'm the Compliment Man.'

And he means it. These are not hoots and hollers tossed out by a leering lout, but thoughtful observations expecting nothing in return. No wonder local residents are always pleased to see the Compliment Man and are usually willing to tip him a buck or two for the positive vibes he emanates.

In recent years, Mr Miller disappeared from the streets of Adams-Morgan, reportedly moving away in search of a job. He has since returned, for better or for worse. Perhaps he discovered that his life calling is right here on 18th St NW, spreading the good word. 'Where do you get your hair cut, girlfriend? It looks great...'

SHAW & THE NEW U DISTRICT

Eating p135; Shopping p185

To walk through Shaw is to walk through the history of black Washington. Starting in the 1890s, Shaw became the political and cultural center of African American DC as black families and opinion makers settled here, driven out of increasingly segregated downtown Washington. Civil rights leaders Archibald and Francis Grimké lived here, as did Calvin Chase, editor of the crusading *Washington Bee*. Black lawyers, doctors and tradesmen

opened offices along U St, which blossomed into a separate downtown for those excluded by racism from DC's other shops.

Civil rights struggles were a constant feature of Shaw life: in the 1950s, Washington's Committee for School Desegregation first met at **John Wesley AME Zion Church** (Map p249; 1615 14th St NW). Their work led to the landmark *Brown v Board of Education*, which mandated school desegregation.

In Shaw's theaters and music halls, a vibrant arts scene sprang up in the 1920s. This 'Black Broadway,' flourished until the 1940s. Duke Ellington grew up on T St; Pearl Bailey waited tables and danced at U St's **Republic Gardens** (p164); Ella Fitzgerald sang at **Bohemian Caverns** (p159), the 11th St jazz club; Louis Armstrong played the Dance Hall at V and 9th Sts; and the **Lincoln Theatre** (p156) and Howard Theatre presented Harlem's and DC's finest to black audiences. Shaw was a high point on the renowned 'chitlin circuit' of black entertainment districts.

By the 1950s, segregation started to ease. Middle-class blacks could live elsewhere, so some moved. Shaw entered a decline that became a tailspin in April 1968, when riots exploded after the murder of Dr Martin Luther King, Jr. Centered on 14th and U Sts, the violence destroyed many black-owned businesses and frightened others away. The neighborhood languished until the late 1980s.

In 1991, the opening of the U Street-Cardozo Metro station started to attract businesses again. The high price of housing in other parts of the city fomented the demand for real estate: young and hip urbanites – especially African Americans – started buying and repairing houses in the surrounding residential streets. Recognizing the historic appeal of the area, bars and clubs opened in the same buildings where the jazz greats used to play.

This renaissance continues today: the New U now houses some of DC's hottest nightspots and trendiest shops, and renovation and construction in the area is nonstop. Nonetheless, this is clearly an area where you should be careful at night – you may feel more comfortable taking a cab home from some of the clubs.

But don't be scared away. Unlike other parts of DC, it is an area of deep roots and reawakening history. Shaw is where black community developed and persevered, and now flourishes in a multicultural setting. And it should come as no surprise that the reawakening has – for accompaniment – the rhythms and melodies of the most vibrant live music scene in DC.

Orientation

Named for Robert Gould Shaw, a Civil War colonel mortally wounded while commanding the famed black 54th Massachusetts Regiment, Shaw is a rectangular block which sits above the downtown district. It stretches from Thomas Circle and Mount Vernon Sq in the south, to Harvard St in the north; and for our purposes, from 14th St NW in the west to N Capitol St in the east. The district

Transportation

Metro The nearest Metro stations are Green Line's U Street-Cardozo and Shaw-Howard U.

Parking There is a paid parking lot near the **9:30 Club** (p158) at 8th & V Sts NW.

is bisected by north–south Georgia Ave, which becomes 7th St south of Florida Ave.

Much of Shaw's northeastern corner is consumed by the Howard University campus and McMillan Park and Reservoir. Funky shops and inexpensive restaurants catering to African American students and scholars are clustered along Georgia Ave and near the Shaw-Howard U Metro station at 7th and S Sts NW. East of here, between 2nd and 7th Sts NW, is LeDroit Park, a small subdivision of Victorian homes from the 1870s. Originally a segregated white enclave, the subdivision later attracted Howard's faculty and other black elite.

Much of Shaw's activity – especially the nightlife – is centered in the 'New U,' along 14th and U Sts NW. Hot clubs and slick boutiques line these streets, illustrating the renaissance taking place in this neighborhood. South of here, at the intersection of Rhode Island and Vermont Aves with 13th and P Sts NW, is Logan Circle, another historic district which is now being rediscovered by yuppies and buppies (Black Urban Professionals).

Shaw & the New U District Top Five

- **9:30 Club** (p158) DC's hottest spot for rock'n'roll.
- **Ben's Chili Bowl** (p135) Chowing down on dogs and chili the old-fashioned way.
- **Duke Ellington's birthplace** (p27) Tracing the footsteps of one of DC's greatest musicians.
- **Howard University** (right) A remarkable center for African American history, culture and learning.
- **New U** (p158) Hearing fresh live music at historic venues.

AFRICAN AMERICAN CIVIL WAR MEMORIAL Map p249

☎ 202-667-2667; www.afroamcivilwar.org; U St & Vermont Ave NW; Metro: U Street-Cardozo

At the center of a granite plaza, the bronze statue of rifle-bearing troops is DC's first major art piece by black sculptor Ed Hamilton. The sculpture is surrounded on three sides by the Wall of Honor, listing the names of 209,145 black troops who fought in the Union Army, as well as the 7000 white soldiers who served alongside them. Use the directory to locate individual names within the regiments.

AFRICAN AMERICAN CIVIL WAR MUSEUM Map p249

☎ 202-667-2667; www.afroamcivilwar.org; 1200 U St NW; admission free; 🕒 10am-5pm Mon-Fri, 10am-2pm Sat; Metro: U Street-Cardozo

In 1862, Abraham Lincoln sanctioned the participation of fully armed, black regiments in the Union army. Thousands of former slaves and free blacks, as well as fleeing slaves, enlisted. This one-room museum highlights the participation of over 200,000 black soldiers who fought for the Union in the Civil War. The permanent exhibit includes photographs and documents, and some audiovisual programs, following African American history from the Civil War through the Civil Rights movement. The Civil War Soldiers and Sailors Project allows visitors to search for ancestors in databases of black troops, regiments and battles. In the near future, the museum is moving to Shaw's historic Masonic Temple, adjacent to the memorial.

BLACK FASHION MUSEUM Map p249

☎ 202-667-0744; bfmdc.tripod.com/about.htm; 2007 Vermont Ave NW; admission by donation; 🕒 by appointment only; Metro: U Street-Cardozo

This eclectic little museum showcases the work of black designers past and present.

Here you can see slaves' dresses, the dress Rosa Parks wore during her historic bus ride, and the handiwork of unsung seamstresses who costumed famous figures from Mary Todd Lincoln to Jackie Kennedy.

HOWARD UNIVERSITY Map p249

☎ 202-806-6100; www.howard.edu; 2400 6th St NW, Welcome Center 1739 7th St NW; Metro: Shaw-Howard U

Anchoring the neighborhood is Howard University, which was founded in 1867. Distinguished alumni include the late Supreme Court Justice Thurgood Marshall (who enrolled after he was turned away from the University of Maryland's then all-white law school), Ralph Bunche, Nobel laureate Toni Morrison and former New York City mayor David Dinkins. Today it has over 12,000 students in 18 schools. There are campus **tours** (☎ 202-806-2900).

Founders' Library, a handsome Georgian building with a gold spire and giant clock, is the campus' architectural centerpiece. It houses the **Moorland-Spingarn Research Center** (☎ 202-806-4237), which boasts the nation's largest collection of African American literature. Also worth visiting is the **Howard University Gallery of Art** (☎ 202-806-7070; Childers Hall), which has an impressive collection of art by African and African American artists, as well as other notable pieces . Both are open 9:30am to 4:30pm Monday to Friday and are free of charge.

Ben's Chili Bowl (p135)

(Continued on page 91)

1 J Paul's (p126) 2 Warren Brown of Cakelove (p13) 3 Eastern Market (p64) 4 Eastern Market (p64)

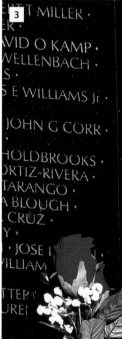

1 Capitol (p63) 2 National Air &
Space Museum (p49) 3 Vietnam
Veterans Memorial (p47)
4 National Museum of Natural
History (p50)

RENCE R SEPULVE
5 · ROBERT S TRUJILLO · ROBER
D · GARY·D FERNANDEZ · PAU
· WOJCIECH WYSOCKI · TIMO
RY · CHARLES L BIFOLCHI · HO
DANIEL R BOWMAN · JAMES L
NE · DENVER D COLBURN Jr · P
EY · HOVEY R·CURRY · LAWRE
ARY P DIETZ · LEONARD E DOR
· ALTON J FENNELL · RICHARD
AN · DANIEL R FULWIDER · ENR
· ROBERT E L HAMILTON · HOW
HREY· DONNEY L JACKSON · B
ES · STEPHEN B KIRSCHNER · R
AMES I MILLER · JONATHAN MIS
LSON · JOHN G NIEDERMEYER
ON · JERRY PATRICK · RONNIE D
· MILLARD E PRICE Jr · GUY J PR
GUEZ · RICHARD A RUMLEY · LC
ON · CHARLES H SMITH · HALL

1 National Museum of Natural History (p50) 2 Washington Monument (p47) 3 Korean War Veterans Memorial (p45)

1 Union Station (p66) *2* Library of Congress (p64) *3* National Gallery of Art (p49) *4* National Gallery of Art (p49)

1 *Smithsonian Castle (p47)*
2 *Washington Dulles International Airport (p222)* 3 *Cox's Row (p104)*
4 *Millennium Stage (p149)*

1 *Georgetown University (p75)*
2 *Mount Zion United Methodist Church (p75)* 3 *Georgetown (p72)*
4 *Arlington National Cemetery (p97)*

1 Adams-Morgan (p79)
2 Musicians, 18th St bar,
Adams-Morgan (p153) 3 Reef
(p153) 4 Islamic Center (p77)

1 *St John's Church (p60)*
2 *Watergate Complex (p61)*
3 *Treasury Building (p60)* 4 *Renwick Gallery (p60)*

(Continued from page 82)

MARY MCLEOD BETHUNE COUNCIL HOUSE Map p249

☎ 202- 673-2402; www.nps.gov/mamc; 1318 Vermont Ave NW; admission by donation; ☺ 10am-4pm Mon-Sat; Metro: McPherson Sq

The Council House, in the Logan Circle Historic District, is the former home of pioneer black educator and activist Mary McLeod Bethune and the first headquarters of the National Council of Negro Women. The Second Empire townhouse, now managed by the National Park Service, is an attractive setting for a collection of Bethune memorabilia and an important archive of black women's historical materials. Rangers lead you on tours here and show you videotapes about Bethune's life. Exhibits, lectures and workshops on black history are held here as well.

UPPER NORTHWEST DC

Eating p133; Shopping p186; Sleeping p202

The winding roads and gentle hills of Upper Northwest DC were once the summer retreats of Washington's political elites, who knew very well – in those days before air-conditioning – that the city was not a pleasant place in the summer. The stucco-covered manor house **Woodley** (Map pp262-3; 3000 Cathedral Ave) was a summer home for Presidents Van Buren, Tyler and Buchanan. In 1881, President Grover Cleveland bought a country house (he hoped anonymously) on Newark St, thus inspiring the naming of the neighborhood Cleveland Park (so much for anonymity).

Despite the respectable residents, it was the trolley cars crossing Rock Creek Park at the turn of the century that brought development to these neighborhoods. Finally, these communities began to attract well-known architects building for lawyers, bureaucrats and journalists who wanted to live here year-round. They had room (and cash) to build large houses with wraparound porches, surrounding them with picket fences and shading them with elms.

The Upper Northwest today is a clear product of this development; in fact, some may wonder how much has changed. Highly educated and well-regarded residents (many of them lawyers, bureaucrats and journalists) reside in the same comfortable homes on these shady streets, enjoying suburban amenities, while the city has grown up around them. Indeed, the suburban amenities are among the attractions that may draw you up here: shopping strips with a selection of stores to rival the suburban mall; classy old-style movie theaters showing artsy and second-run films; miles of rambling, forested parks and paved bike trails; not to mention some of the city's top dining venues.

Orientation

The vast Upper Northwest stretches from W St – just north of Georgetown and Shaw – all the way to the Maryland line, which is marked by the diagonal SW–NE Western Ave. Luscious, green Rock Creek Park runs north–south down the center of the quadrant (although there are few attractions east of the park this far north).

West of the park is mostly affluent residential neighborhoods filled with large homes on quiet, tree-lined streets, with major pockets of development along Connecticut and Wisconsin Aves. Heading up Wisconsin Ave, just north of Georgetown is Glover Archbold Park (named for the park which dominates the neighborhood), a very quaint community of brownstones

Transportation

Metro From Dupont Circle, the Red Line runs through Upper Northwest DC, first following Connecticut Ave through Woodley Park-Zoo/Adams Morgan, Cleveland Park and Van Ness-UDC, then continuing along Wisconsin Ave through Tenleytown-AU and Friendship Heights.

Bus Nos 30, 32, 34 and 36 run up and down Wisconsin Ave between Friendship Heights and Georgetown.

Parking Street parking is not as difficult in this mostly residential neighborhood, but keep in mind that you are still limited to two hours Monday to Saturday.

housing graduate students and young families. Further north is Tenleytown and American University.

Just north of Dupont Circle, Woodley Park and Cleveland Park are upscale communities which occupy the shady streets between Connecticut and Wisconsin Aves. The Washington National Cathedral is tucked in here off Wisconsin Ave. The zoo is nestled in between Connecticut Ave and Rock Creek Park. In DC's far northwestern corner, swanky Friendship Heights borders Chevy Chase, Maryland.

BATTERY KEMBLE PARK & GLOVER ARCHBOLD PARK Map pp262-3
bus D1 from Dupont Circle to Glover Park, D3 or D6 from Dupont Circle to Battery Kemble Park

Glover is a sinuous, winding park, extending from Van Ness St NW in the Tenleytown area down to the western border of Georgetown University. Its 180 tree-covered acres follow the course of little Foundry Branch Creek, along which runs a pretty nature trail. Another good place to access this trail is Reservoir Rd, which crosses the park just north of the university. Further west, skinny Battery Kemble Park, about a mile long but less than a quarter-mile wide, separates the wealthy Foxhall and Palisades neighborhoods of far northwestern DC. Managed by the National Park Service, the park preserves the site of a little two-gun battery that helped defend western DC against Confederate troops during the Civil War.

FORT STEVENS PARK Map pp262-3
www.nps.gov/rocr/ftcircle/stevens.htm; 13th and Quackenbos Sts NW; bus E2, E3 or E4 from Friendship Heights or bus 71 or 72 from Gallery Pl-Chinatown

In a daring raid on July 11, 1864, Confederate General Jubal Early attacked Fort Stevens, the northernmost of the defensive ramparts ringing the city. A small but fierce battle raged until Early's men were forced back across the Potomac. Abraham Lincoln himself was drawn into the shooting: the president, observing the battle from Fort Stevens' parapet, popped his head up so many times that Oliver Wendell Holmes Jr, then a Union captain, yelled: 'Get down, you damn fool, before you get shot!' The fort has been partially restored. Forty-one Union men who died in the Fort Stevens' defense were buried at tiny **Battleground National Cemetery** (6625 Georgia Ave), a half-mile north of the fort. The fort – which was dedicated by Lincoln – has been partially restored. You can

wander around in daylight hours to see the markers and plaques honoring DC's defenders.

HILLWOOD MUSEUM & GARDENS
Map pp262-3

☎ 202-686-8500; www.hillwoodmuseum.org; 4155 Linnean Ave NW; adult/senior/child $12/10/7; ⏱ 9:30am-5pm Tue-Sat, closed Jan; Metro: Van Ness-UDC or Cleveland Park

Housing the biggest collection of Russian imperial art outside Russia itself, Hillwood is the former estate of heiress Marjorie Merriweather Post (of Post cereal fame), who was married to the ambassador to the USSR in the 1930s. By all accounts a formidable woman, Post convinced Stalin and the Soviets to sell her lots of Czarist swag, and her collection includes furniture, paintings, exquisite Fabergé eggs and jewelry. The 25-acre estate features lovely gardens with notable azalea and orchid collections (as well as Post's dog cemetery), a greenhouse and a museum shop. A café serves Russian treats (borscht, blintzes) and afternoon tea. Reservations are required to visit.

KAHLIL GIBRAN MEMORIAL GARDEN
Map pp262-3

3100 Massachusetts Ave NW; Metro: Dupont Circle

In the midst of the wooded ravine known as Normanstone Park, the Kahlil Gibran garden memorializes the arch-deity of soupy spiritual poetry. Its centerpieces are a moody bust of the Lebanese mystic and a star-shaped fountain surrounded by flowers, hedges and limestone benches engraved with various Gibranisms: 'We live only to discover beauty. All else is a form of waiting.' From a trailhead just north of the garden, you can hop onto trails that link to both Rock Creek Park and Glover Archbold Park.

KREEGER MUSEUM Map pp262-3

☎ 202-337-3050; www.kreegermuseum.com; 2401 Foxhall Rd NW; admission by donation adult $8, senior & student $5, no children under 12; ⏰ 1-4pm Sat, tours by reservation 10:30am & 1:30pm Tue-Fri, closed Aug; bus D2 from Dupont Circle to Reservoir & Foxhall Rds NW

In wealthy Foxhall, this exquisite museum is housed in a coolly elegant Philip Johnson-designed building. Among DC's newest and most intimate museums, the Kreeger exhibits 19th- and 20th-century paintings and sculpture collected by David and Carmen Lloyd Kreeger, including works by Miró, Picasso, Monet, Kandinsky and Henry Moore. Seminars, lectures and musical performances round out its offerings.

NATIONAL MUSEUM OF HEALTH & MEDICINE Map pp262-30

☎ 202-782-2200; http://nmhm.washingtondc.museum; 6825 16th St NW, Walter Reed Army Medical Center Bldg 54; admission free; ⏰ 10am-5:30pm; bus 52 from Takoma Metro

Forensics junkies love this 'Library of Congress of the dead,' as described by science writer Gina Kolata, which contains both straightforward scientific exhibits and freakish medical oddities. Visitors can see antique microscopes and surgical instruments, as well as exhibits on renowned scientists and research initiatives. What you come here for, though, is much more thrilling: cannonball-shredded leg bones removed from Civil War soldiers, the bullet that killed Lincoln and fragments of his shattered skull, President Garfield's spinal column, and many other preserved body parts.

NATIONAL ZOOLOGICAL PARK Map pp262-3

☎ 202-673-4800; www.nationalzoo.si.edu; 3001 Connecticut Ave NW; admission free; ⏰ grounds 6am-8pm May-Sep, 6am-6pm Oct-Apr, buildings 10am-6pm May-Sep, 10am-4:30pm Oct-Apr; Metro: Woodley Park-Zoo/Adams Morgan

Founded in 1889 and beautifully planned by Frederick Law Olmsted, designer of New York's Central Park, the zoo's 130 acres follow the natural contours of its woodland-canyon setting. The Smithsonian-operated zoo is intensively involved in worldwide ecological study and species-preservation work, and its exhibits are noted for natural-habitat settings. Tamarins scamper uncaged through the treetops, piranhas hunt in a simulated Amazon and tigers snooze on terraced grass hillsides.

The zoo's higher path, the Olmsted Walk, passes the American prairie exhibit, panda house, elephant/giraffe house, primate and reptile houses. Nearby is **Think Tank**, a wonderful collection of interactive exhibits on animal intelligence and social structure aimed at the six-to-12 set.

Down the trail a bit are open-air lion and tiger enclosures and the dark **Bat Cave**, a perennial kids' favorite. Big cat fans will love the cheetahs' 'What's for Dinner?' display, where overly honest scales inform you who would like to feast on you. ('100lb to 150lb. You're a female warthog. A pack of lions could finish you off in an hour.')

The lower Valley Trail passes the bird house, seal tanks and wetlands displays. In

Panda-monium

DC's most famous celebrities – more popular than any president or politician – are the two giant pandas that have been in residence at the National Zoological Park since 1999. Mei Xiang (meaning 'beautiful fragrance') and Tian Tian ('more and more') are on a 10-year loan from the China Wildlife Conservation Association.

Among the best recognized–but rarest–animals in the world, giant pandas have come to symbolize endangered species and conservation efforts. Only about 1000 giant pandas survive in the mountain forests of central China. They specialize in eating bamboo, so they are suffering from the destruction of the temperate bamboo forest in the mountains of central China. Another 120 are in Chinese breeding facilities and zoos, and about 20 live in zoos outside China.

At the zoo, Mei Xiang and Tian Tian are the focus of an ambitious research, conservation and breeding program designed to preserve this critically endangered species. And, of course, they are monitored closely in the hope that they will produce offspring. It was with great delight that zoo officials reported in April 2003 that the happy couple had mated, albeit for only 15 seconds. Then scientists and panda fans waited with bated breath to see if Mei Xiang was pregnant. It was not so easy to tell. Even if the mating is unsuccessful, the female panda undergoes a pseudopregnancy, in which hormone changes and behavior mimics a true pregnancy. (In fact, Mei Xiang herself did not know if she was with child.) It was only in August that zoo officials announced – much to the great disappointment of panda-fans around the world – that there would be no baby panda this year.

Mei Xiang and Tian Tian are still big hits at the zoo. You can also check them out on panda cam at www.natzoo.si.edu/Animals/GiantPandas.

the tamarins' forest the little primates range free in warm weather. At its eastern end is **Amazonia,** a mini ecosystem complete with aquariums and a conservatory. Piranhas and magnificent fish swim in the water, and the trees are filled with epiphytes, ferns, birds and monkeys.

To beat the zoo crowds, visit early morning on a cloudy, cool, even slightly rainy day. Such weather not only keeps human herds at bay but encourages heat-sensitive or shy animals to venture outside their dens.

US NAVAL OBSERVATORY Map pp262-3
☎ 202-762-1438; www.usno.navy.mil; 3450 Massachusetts Ave NW; admission free; ☾ tours by reservation 8:30pm Mon

Its entrance framed by a pair of stately white ship's anchors, the US Naval Observatory was created in the 1800s 'to determine the positions and motions of celestial objects, provide astronomical data, measure the Earth's rotation, and maintain the Master Clock for the US.' Modern DC's light pollution prevents important observational work these days, but its cesium-beam atomic clock is still the source of all standard time in the US. Tours let you peek through telescopes, yak with astronomers and learn about the Master Clock. They fill up weeks in advance, so reserve early. At other times, the observatory's closed to the public. On observatory grounds above Massachusetts Ave is the official **Vice President's Residence** (Admiral's House), which is closed to the public.

Rock Creek Park

Dropping a slice of wilderness into urban Washington, this national park (Map pp262-3; ☎ 202-282-1063; www.nps.gov/rocr; Metro: Cleveland Park or Woodley Park-Zoo/Adams Morgan) begins at the Potomac's east bank near Georgetown and extends to and beyond the northern city boundaries. Narrow in its southern stretches, where it hews to the winding course of Rock Creek, it broadens into wide, peaceful parklands in Upper Northwest DC. Terrific trails extend along its entire length. Its boundaries enclose Civil War forts and dense forest, recreational facilities and wildflower-strewn fields. Established in 1890, it's one of the country's finest urban parks, and as you walk in its midst you may forget you're in a city altogether.

A great first stop is the **Nature Center & Planetarium** (☎ 202-426-6829; off Military Rd; ☾ 9am-5pm Wed-Sun Sep-May, daily Jun-Aug). Besides informative exhibits on park flora, fauna and history, it has two little nature trails and tons of information on the park, plus maps and field guides to the city. A fun 'touch table' is set up for little kids, and rangers lead kid-oriented nature walks featuring cool activities like poking around in the mud for salamanders.

A bit north of here, on the west side of Beach Dr, is the **Joaquin Miller Cabin**, a little log house that once sheltered the famed nature poet.

Further south, the park's western **Soapstone Valley Park** extension, off Connecticut Ave at Albemarle St NW, preserves quarries where the area's original Algonquin Indian residents dug soapstone for shaping their cookware.

Alongside the creek, the 1820 **Pierce Mill** (☎ 202-426-6908; Tilden St; ☾ 9am-5pm Wed-Sun Sep-May, daily Jun-Aug) is a small, beautiful fieldstone building that was once a water-driven gristmill. Next door, local artists display work in a 19th-century carriage house known as the **Rock Creek Gallery** (☎ 202-244-2482; 2401 Tilden St; ☾ 11am-4:30pm Thu-Sun). The gallery holds poetry readings and art classes, and sells handmade jewelry and crafts.

In summer, pick up an events calendar at the **Carter Barron Amphitheater** (☎ 202-426-6837; www.nps.gov /rocr/cbarron; 16th & Kennedy Sts NW). It's a wonderful 4000-seat outdoor theater where concerts and plays, many of which are free, are held on summer evenings. See also Entertainment (p155).

The remains of Civil War forts are among the park's most fascinating sites. During the war, Washington was, essentially, a massive urban armory and supply house for the Union Army. Its position near the Confederate lines made it vulnerable to attack, so forts were hastily erected on the city's high points. By spring 1865, 68 forts and 93 batteries bristled on hilltops around DC. **Fort DeRussy** is one of the best preserved, with its moat and rammed-earth parapet still apparent. Reach it by following the trail from Military Rd and Oregon Ave NW. The remains of other forts – Battery Kemble near the Potomac, Fort Reno, Fort Stevens and on to Fort Bunker Hill in Northeast DC – are also administered by Rock Creek Park, and some earthworks remain visible. See also **Fort Stevens Park** (p92).

Overlooking Rock Creek in Cleveland Park is the **Klingle Mansion** (☎ 202-282-1063; 3545 Williamsburg Lane; ☾ 7:45am-4:15pm Mon-Fri). Built in 1823 by Joshua Pierce, the 10-room Pennsylvania Dutch fieldstone house is now park headquarters, open for information and permits for special events.

WASHINGTON DOLLS' HOUSE & TOY MUSEUM Map pp262-3

☎ 202-244-0024, 202-363-6400; www.dollshouse museum.com; 5236 44th St NW; adult/senior/child $4/3/2; ☺ 10am-5pm Tue-Sat, noon-5pm Sun; Metro: Friendship Heights

This quirky museum is based on the belief that dolls' houses provide a history of architecture and decorative arts, while antique toys reflect social history. It displays a marvelous collection of antique Victorian dolls' houses and toys: a teeny Capitol; mansions complete with tiny china and linens; and amazingly detailed castles. The museum's miniatures shop sells dolls, accessories and kits so that you can build your own dolls' house.

WASHINGTON NATIONAL CATHEDRAL Map pp262-3

☎ 202-537-6200; www.nationalcathedral.org; Massachusetts & Wisconsin Aves NW; admission by donation, audio tour $5 per person; ☺ 10am-5:30pm Mon-Fri, to 8pm May-Sep, 10am-4:30pm Sat, 8am-6:30pm Sun, tours 10am-3:15pm Mon-Sat, 12:45-2:30pm Sun, main service 11am Sun; Metro Tenleytown or bus 30, 32, 34 or 36

A national cathedral in a country premised upon the separation of church and state is an unusual idea. So, by definition, the National Cathedral, run by the Episcopal diocese but paying tribute to many faiths and peoples, is an unusual place.

The cornerstone of this majestic Gothic cathedral was laid by Teddy Roosevelt in 1908, and construction didn't stop until 1990. Its pale limestone walls, flying buttresses, intricate carving and exquisite stained glass (all intended to

Tea for Tours

Do you take your tea with lemon and sugar, or with a fabulous city view? Two afternoons a week, the National Cathedral's Tour & Tea Program (☎ 202-537-8993; adult/child $22/14; ☺ 1:30pm Tue & Wed) opens up the high West Tower for high tea, following an informative tour of the cathedral and grounds. The tour provides an in-depth look at the cathedral's art, architecture and history. Afterwards, enjoy tea and scones in the beautiful, wood-paneled St Paul Room. Located in the Pilgrim Observation Gallery, it provides magnificent views on a clear day. Reservations are required.

rival Europe's great cathedrals) have won for the cathedral, in many critics' eyes, the title of the country's most beautiful church. Martin Luther King Jr gave his last Sunday sermon here; now it's the standard place for state funerals and other high-profile events.

Take the elevator to the **tower overlook** for expansive city views; posted maps explain what you see. Downstairs in the main sanctuary, chapels honor the Apollo astronauts, MLK, Abe Lincoln, and abstract ideas like peace and justice. The endearing **Children's Chapel** is filled with images of real and imaginary animals. Downstairs in the crypt, famous folks like Helen Keller and Woodrow Wilson are buried. Outside, walk through the charming **Bishop's Garden**, a small English-style garden with winding paths that lend a mood of solitude.

The 11am Sunday service features lovely choral music and a 10-bell peal of the carillon afterwards. Cathedral choristers sing Evensong at 5:30pm Tuesday to Thursday during the school year.

Beasties on the Buttresses: the National Cathedral Gargoyles

Gargoyles serve both a practical function: they're rainwater spouts – their name derives from the French *gargouille*, to gargle. They also serve numerous spiritual functions: they warn churchgoers of hell's terrors, ward off the devil's assaults on the holy and represent pagan deities long ago assimilated by Christian monotheism. They reached their apotheosis on European churches like Notre Dame, but the National Cathedral has raised the gargoyle tradition to comical new heights. On its southern facade perch dogs and cats, boars and donkeys, and beasts wholly imaginary (including a dragon skeleton with a snake lunging from its eye socket). On the western side loom the god Pan, a feasting glutton and a reading elephant. Elsewhere are Darth Vader, a stonemason leering at the Cathedral school girls, a placard-toting hippie, a sobbing tortoise, and caricatures of craftspeople and clergy associated with the cathedral. Like everything else in the National Cathedral, each gargoyle is a handcrafted original, and many were 'donated' by individual supporters of the century-long cathedral-building project. The cathedral hands out three flyers that guide you around its gargoyles and grotesques. Binoculars help. Should you feel the urge to adopt a beast, go to the cathedral's downstairs gift shop for miniature replicas of its critters, plus stuffed gargoyles (for your baby Goth), garden gargoyles (to eat the squirrels), blow-up life-size gargoyles, gargoyle jewelry, gargoyle lollipops ($4) and carve-your-own-gargoyle kits ($23).

ARLINGTON & ALEXANDRIA

Eating p136; Shopping p187; Sleeping p203

During the Civil War, the Potomac waters were a symbolic borderline between North and South: to the north, the capital of the Union; to the south, the Confederate heartland, with General Robert E Lee's mansion commanding the riverside heights. Now, however, Metro links and four bridges almost eliminate the divide between DC and Virginia. In fact, Arlington and Alexandria residents are more apt to identify themselves with DC than with Virginia (*northern* Virginia is not the same as Virginia, they claim).

Arlington absorbs the spillover from the capital: federal agencies that expanded beyond the walls of their downtown buildings; government contractors who aim to be near to their clients (or 'Beltway bandits' as they are known); bureaucrats who work in the city but don't want to live there; even ethnic enclaves that settled in DC, but dispersed as they assimilated. It is the same suburban sprawl that one finds throughout the country, but with a sense of national importance and political awareness that might not exist elsewhere.

Founded in 1699 (predating DC), Alexandria was once a very bustling port city that rivaled New York and Boston; now it plays up its colonial roots for all its worth. The restored Old Town district retains its pre-Revolutionary charm, and many 18th-century houses and colonial sights are open to the public for touring. Old buildings and port warehouses hold upscale restaurants, pubs, shops and hostelries.

Orientation

Arlington's neighborhoods are clustered around Metro stops just across the Potomac River from Northwest DC.

Rosslyn is a bureaucratic, steel and glass district in the north of town, directly across the Francis Scott Key Bridge from Georgetown.

From here, Metro's Orange Line heads west, with stops at Courthouse, Clarendon, Virginia Sq and Ballston: all blossoming neighborhoods with diverse populations and small but lively food and drink scenes.

Metro's Blue Line turns south from Rosslyn and follows the Potomac River.

In addition to Arlington Cemetery and Pentagon, Blue Line stops at Pentagon City and Crystal City: both corporate areas with hotels, high-rises and shopping malls (lots of conveniences but not much character).

Ronald Reagan Washington National Airport is in the southern corner of Arlington on the Potomac River.

Drivers can reach Arlington by crossing the Francis Scott Key Bridge from Georgetown, as well as the Theodore Roosevelt, Arlington Memorial and 14th St (I-395) Bridges further south.

Alexandria is south of Arlington along the Potomac River. The main streets dividing Alexandria are north–south Washington St (George Washington Memorial Parkway) and east–west King St. Addresses are numbered by the 100s (eg Cameron to Queen is the 200 block north).

The historic area, Old Town, is a square bounded by the King St Metro to the west, Slaters Lane to the north, the Potomac River to the east and the Beltway to the south. You will discover that most historic sights lie between Washington St and the river.

Transportation

Metro Arlington is well served by Metro, including Orange Line stops (Rosslyn, Courthouse, Clarendon, Virginia Sq and Ballston) and Blue Line stops (Rosslyn, Arlington Cemetery, Pentagon, Pentagon City, Crystal City and Ronald Reagan Washington National Airport).

Parking Street parking is easier in Arlington than in DC, but still not a given. There is a cheap garage at Pentagon City mall.

ARLINGTON

ARLINGTON HOUSE Map p264

☎ 703-557-0613; www.arlingtoncemetery.net
/arlhouse; admission free; ⓨ 9:30am-4:30pm;
Metro: Arlington Cemetery

Robert E Lee resided in this gracious home set high on the hills overlooking the Potomac River. His home and part of his 1100-acre property were confiscated after he left to command the Confederate Army of Virginia, and Union dead were buried around the house to spite him. After the war, the family sued the federal government for reimbursement: the government paid off the Lees, and Arlington Cemetery was born on their old lands. The historic house has been open since 1817 for public tours, and serves as a tribute to the general who earned the respect of Northerners and Southerners alike.

ARLINGTON NATIONAL CEMETERY

Map p264

☎ 703-607-8052, Tourmobile 888-868-7707; www
.arlingtoncemetery.net; admission free, Tourmobile
adult/child $6/3; ⓨ 8am-5pm Oct-Mar, 8am-7pm
Apr-Oct; Metro: Arlington Cemetery

The 612 acres and 245,000 graves of this national cemetery are a somber counterpoint to the soaring monuments to US history just across the Potomac. It's the burial ground for military personnel and their families, the dead of every war the US has fought since the Revolution, and American leaders, such as JFK, Oliver Wendell Holmes and Medgar Evers.

At the end of Memorial Dr, the first site you'll see is the **Women in Military Service for America Memorial**, honoring women who have served in the armed forces in times of war and peace, from the Revolution onward. The memorial includes an education center and theater.

On the slopes above are the **Kennedy gravesites**. Near the eternal flame that marks the grave of John F Kennedy lie gravestones for Jacqueline Kennedy Onassis and their two children who died in infancy, and Robert Kennedy. The site is one that JFK admired just days before his assassination.

The **Tomb of the Unknowns** holds unidentified bodies from WWI, WWII and the Korean War. Soldiers march before it 24 hours a day, performing an impressive ceremonial changing of the guard every hour (every· half-hour mid-March to September). See the boxed text 'The Known Unknown' (p90). Other memorials include the **Confederate Monument**, the tomb of **Pierre L'Enfant**, the **mast of the battleship USS Maine**,

Arlington & Alexandria Top Five

- **Arlington National Cemetery** (p97) Miles and miles of green rolling hills and white headstones.
- **Gravelly Point** (p98) Ducking as the airplanes roar above.
- **Mount Vernon Trail** (p169) Riding or running along the Potomac and taking in fabulous views of the capital.
- **Old Town Alexandria** (p187) Shopping till you drop in this historic setting.
- **Torpedo Factory Art Center** (p187) Defense conversion at its best.

the **Challenger memorial** and the **Nurses' Memorial**. The **Iwo Jima Memorial**, dedicated to the Marine Corps, is on the cemetery's northern fringes. You can also check out the graves of boxer **Joe Louis**, explorer **Rear-Admiral Richard Byrd Jr** and **President William Taft**. Funerals are held here daily.

FREEDOM PARK Map p264

1101 Wilson Blvd; Metro: Rosslyn

Paying tribute to a free press, Freedom Park features a memorial which honors journalists killed on the job. Icons from political struggles around the world are on display, including chunks of the Berlin Wall. Until recently, the Freedom Forum – a nonpartisan, international foundation dedicated to preserving a free press – operated the state-of-the art **Newseum** (www.newseum.org) here, too. It offered a fascinating, hands-on look at how the news is reported, produced, spun and consumed. In one hall, a block-long screen displayed breaking news; the day's front pages from the world's top newspapers were displayed below it. The interactive newsroom and broadcast studio allowed visitors to create and tape their own broadcasts, and write their own news stories. Thoughtful exhibits examined journalistic ethics, historic events and the journalists who covered them. As of 2006, the Newseum plans to reopen at a prime location at Pennsylvania Ave and 6th St NW in downtown DC.

GEORGE WASHINGTON MEMORIAL PARKWAY Map p264

☎ 703-289-2500; www.nps.gov/gwmp; Metro: Rosslyn

The 25-mile Virginia portion of this highway, honoring the first US president, winds past recreation areas and memorials all the way south to his old estate, Mount Vernon. A national parkland, it's lined with remnants of Washington's life and works, such as his old Patowmack Company canal (in Great Falls National Park) and parks that were once part of his farmlands (Riverside Park, Fort Hunt Park). The road is a pleasant alternative to the traffic-choked highway arteries further away from the river.

The 18½-mile **Mount Vernon Trail** parallels the parkway from Francis Scott Key Bridge to Mount Vernon – it's paved and perfect for biking. Along the way, **Lady Bird Johnson Park** remembers the First Lady who tried to beautify the capital via greenery-planting campaigns and includes a memorial grove dedicated to her husband. Just north of Ronald Reagan Washington National Airport, **Gravelly Point** provides a vantage point for watching the planes take off and land; or check out the natural airborne creatures at the **Roaches Run Waterfowl Sanctuary**.

PENTAGON Map p264
☎ 703-695-1776; www.pentagon.gov; ⏰ closed to public; Metro: Pentagon

The US Department of Defense is housed in what may be the world's biggest office building, built in just 16 months during WWII. About 25,000 people work in this massive polygon, which has more than a dozen miles of corridors and five sides surrounding a 5-acre courtyard. This formidable edifice appears impenetrable, an impression that was proven wrong on September 11, 2001, when American Airlines flight 77 crashed into the side of the building. Between the passengers on the airplane and workers in the building, 184 people were killed in this shocking tragedy. Since 9-11, the Pentagon building is open only for pre-arranged group tours (call several weeks in advance). Virtual tours are on-line at www.defenselink.mil/pubs/pentagon.

PENTAGON MEMORIAL Map p264
☎ 703-695-1776; http://memorial.pentagon.mil; admission free; ⏰ opening fall 2005; Metro: Pentagon

In the fall of 2005 the Pentagon will dedicate a new memorial to the victims of the attack on the Pentagon on September 11, 2001. The poignant memorial plaza will occupy almost two acres on the west side of the Pentagon building, representing each of the 184 victims with a pool of light and an inscription. The memorial design is symbolic down to the details: for example, memorials representing victims who were in the Pentagon will be situated so a visitor sees the engraved name in the same view as the building; memorials to victims who were on flight 77 will face an alternative direction, so the background is only sky. The Age

Wall on the plaza's western edge will grow in proportion to the ages of the victims, who ranged from three to 71.

THEODORE ROOSEVELT ISLAND
Map p264

☎ 703-289-2500; www.nps.gov/this; admission free; ⏰ dawn-dusk; Metro: Rosslyn

This 91-acre wooded island, in the Potomac off Rosslyn, is a wilderness preserve honoring the conservation-minded 26th US president. A large memorial plaza and statue of Teddy dominate the island's center, and trails and boardwalks snake around the shorelines. The island's swampy fringes shelter birds, raccoons and other small animals. A fine place for a hike, it offers great views of the Kennedy Center and Georgetown University across the river. The island is accessible from the Mount Vernon Trail and is a convenient stop on a long bike ride or jog. Note that bikes aren't permitted on the island itself; lock them up in the parking lot.

WASHINGTON & OLD DOMINION TRAIL
W&OD; ☎ 703-729-0596; www.nvrpa.org/wod; admission free; ⏰ dawn-dusk; Metro: East Falls Church

Despite its dense suburbs, northern Virginia is laced with hiking and biking trails. The 45-mile, paved Washington & Old Dominion Trail follows an old railway bed from Shirlington, in southern Arlington, to Purcellville, in Virginia's Allegheny foothills. (For the truly ambitious, it's a short jump from here to the Appalachian Trail and its 2000 miles of trail south

The Known Unknown

For several years after the Vietnam War, the US government had no 'unknown' Vietnam War soldier to inter in Arlington's Tomb of the Unknowns (p97). All recovered remains were identified, albeit slowly, via new forensic techniques. Finally, in 1984, an appropriately anonymous set of remains was located, and Defense Secretary Caspar Weinberger approved their burial in the tomb. The remains joined those of WWI, WWII and Korean War unknowns.

But in 1998, the family of Michael J Blassie, an Air Force lieutenant shot down near An Loc in 1972, discovered via DNA testing that the corpse was that of their lost relative. Blassie was removed in the first-ever Unknowns disinterment and reburied in Missouri. The Vietnam crypt at Arlington, meanwhile, stands permanently empty.

to Georgia and north to Maine.) The scenic, well-maintained trail allows horseback riding between Vienna and Purcellville. Exit right from the East Falls Church Metro station. See also Sports, Health & Fitness (p169).

ALEXANDRIA

ALEXANDRIA ARCHAEOLOGY
MUSEUM Map p265
☎ 703-838-4399; www.alexandriaarchaeology.org; 105 N Union St, Torpedo Factory Art Center No 327; admission free; 🕙 10am-3pm Tue-Fri, 10am-5pm Sat, 1-5pm Sun; Old Town shuttle from King St Metro
Housed in the Torpedo Factory Art Center, this is the laboratory where archaeologists clean up and catalog the artifacts they have unearthed at local digs. First-hand observation of the work, excavation exhibits and hands-on discovery kits allow visitors to witness and participate in the reconstruction of Alexandria's history.

BLACK HISTORY RESOURCE CENTER
Map p265
☎ 703-838-4356; www.alexblackhistory.org; 638 N Alfred St (enter from Wythe St); admission free; 🕙 10am-4pm Tue-Sat, 1-5pm Sun; Metro: Braddock Rd
Paintings, photographs, books and other memorabilia documenting the black experience in Alexandria are on display at this small resource center. Pick up a brochure for self-guided walking tours of important Alexandria black-history sites. In the next-door annex, the **Watson Reading Room** has a wealth of books and documents on African American topics. Operated by the museum, the **African American Heritage Park** (Holland Lane) is worth a stop to see headstones from a 19th-century black cemetery.

CAPTAIN'S ROW & GENTRY ROW
Map p265
The 100 block of Prince St, called Captain's Row, is one of two remaining cobblestone streets in Alexandria. The cobblestones served as the ballast of English ships, and the street was possibly laid by Hessian prisoners of war. It's lined with lovely private homes, many built for sea captains.

Gentry Row, the 200 block of Prince St, is named after the number of imposing private dwellings.

The rosy-colored **Athenaeum** (☎ 703-548-0035; www.alexandria-athenaeum.org; 201 Prince St; 🕙 11am-3pm Wed-Fri, 1-3pm Sat & Sun Mar-Oct) was home to the Bank of the

Old Dominion. Now the Greek Revival building is an art gallery.

CARLYLE HOUSE Map p265
☎ 703-549-2997; www.carlylehouse.org; 121 N Fairfax St; adult/child $4/2; 🕙 10am-4:30pm Tue-Sat, noon-4:30pm Sun, tours Sun every half-hour; Old Town shuttle from King St Metro
It's not hard to believe that merchant John Carlyle's imposing, Georgian-style mansion was the grandest in Alexandria when it was built in 1753. The house's historical significance lies in its use by British General Braddock as headquarters in strategizing the French–Indian War. Guided tours on the half-hour give a peak into 18th-century Alexandria.

CHRIST CHURCH Map p265
☎ 703-549-1450; www.historicchristchurch.org; 118 N Washington St; admission by donation; 🕙 9am-4pm Mon-Sat, 2-4pm Sun; Old Town shuttle from King St Metro
Since 1773, this red-brick Georgian-style church has welcomed worshipers, including George Washington and Robert E Lee. The interesting churchyard cemetery contains the mass grave of Confederate soldiers.

FORT WARD MUSEUM &
HISTORIC SITE
☎ 703-838-4848; www.fortward.org; 4301 W Braddock Rd; admission free; 🕙 9am-dusk, museum 9am-4pm Tue-Sat, noon-5pm Sun; Old Town shuttle from King St Metro
Fort Ward, northwest of Old Town along Braddock Rd, is the best-restored of the 162 Civil War fortifications known as the Defenses of Washington. The Northwest Bastion of the fort has been completely restored, and the remaining earthwork walls give a good sense of the defenses' original appearance. The on-site museum contains interpretive displays and features exhibits on Civil War topics.

Neighborhoods – Arlington & Alexandria

FRIENDSHIP FIREHOUSE MUSEUM

Map p265

☎ 703-838-3891; www.friendshipfirehouse.org; 107 S Alfred St; admission free; 🕑 10am-4pm Fri & Sat, 1-4pm Sun; Old Town shuttle from King St Metro

This 1855 Italianate firehouse displays historic firefighting gear – a great draw for kids. Local legend has it that George Washington helped found this volunteer fire company, served as its captain and even paid for a new fire engine.

GADSBY'S TAVERN MUSEUM Map p265

☎ 703-838-4242; www.gadsbystavern.org; 134 N Royal St; adult/child $4/2; 🕑 10am-5pm Tue-Sat, 1-5pm Sun & Mon Apr-Oct, 11am-4pm Wed-Sat ,1-4pm Sun Nov-Mar; Old Town shuttle from King St Metro

Once a real tavern (operated by John Gadsby from 1796 to 1808), this building now houses a museum demonstrating the prominent role of the tavern in 18th-century Alexandria. As the center of political, business and social life in Alexandria, the tavern was frequented by anybody who was anybody, including George Washington, Thomas Jefferson and the Marquis de Lafayette. The rooms are restored to their 18th-century appearance.

GEORGE WASHINGTON MASONIC NATIONAL MEMORIAL Map p265

☎ 703-683-2007; www.gwmemorial.org; 101 Callahan Dr at King St; admission free; 🕑 9am-5pm, tours on the hour; Metro: King St

Alexandria's most prominent landmark features a fine view from its 333ft tower, where you can see the Capitol, Mount Vernon and the Potomac River. It is modeled after the lighthouse in Alexandria, and honors the first president (who was initiated into the Masons in Fredericksburg in 1752 and later became Worshipful Master of Alexandria Lodge No 22). Artifacts of Washington's life and a striking bronze statue do the job.

LEE-FENDALL HOUSE Map p265

☎ 703-548-1789; www.leefendallhouse.org; 614 Oronoco St; adult/child $4/2; 🕑 10am-4pm Tue-Sat, 1-4pm Sun, tours on the hour; Metro: Braddock Rd

Between 1785 and 1903, generations of the Lee family lived in this house. Guided tours show the house as it probably was in the 1850s and 1860s, showcasing Lee family heirlooms and personal effects. The Georgian-style townhouse across the street (607 Oronoco St; 🕑 closed to public) was Robert E Lee's childhood home from 1810.

LYCEUM Map p265

☎ 703-838-4994; www.alexandriahistory.org; 201 S Washington St; admission free; 🕑 10am-5pm Mon-Sat, 1-5pm Sun; Old Town shuttle from King St Metro

Alexandria's history museum is housed in a Greek Revival building that was restored in the 1970s. The exhibits – which focus on Alexandria since its founding – include prints, photographs, ceramics, silver and Civil War memorabilia.

OLD PRESBYTERIAN MEETING HOUSE Map p265

☎ 703-549-6670; www.opmh.org; 321 S Fairfax St; admission free; 🕑 9am-3pm Mon-Fri; Old Town shuttle from King St Metro

This red-brick building was built in 1775 by a group of Calvinist dissenters. The graveyard holds the **Tomb of the Unknown Soldier of the Revolutionary War**, a little-visited site holding the remains of an unidentified soldier.

STABLER-LEADBEATER APOTHECARY MUSEUM Map p265

☎ 703-836-3713; www.apothecary.org; 105-107 S Fairfax St; adult/child $4/2; 🕑 10am-4pm Mon-Sat, Sun 1-5pm; Old Town shuttle from King St Metro

In 1792, Edward Stabler opened his apothecary – a family business that would operate for 141 years. In 1933, the Depression forced the shop to close; the doors were simply locked, shutting history inside. Over 8000 medical objects and fixtures remained in place. Now the shop is a museum, its shelves lined with 900 beautiful handblown apothecary bottles and strange old items like 'Martha Washington's Scouring Compound.'

TORPEDO FACTORY ART CENTER

Map p265

☎ 703-838-4565; www.torpedofactory.org; 105 N Union St; admission free; 🕑 10am-5pm; Old Town shuttle from King St Metro

Built during WWI to manufacture torpedoes, this complex today manufactures art. At the center of a revamped waterfront with a lively marina, shops and residences, it houses nearly 200 artists and craftspeople who sell their creations directly from their studios.

Walking & Cycling Tours

Walking & Cycling Tours

Washington DC is unusual for its large amounts of green space, its lack of towering buildings, and its miles and miles of off-road walking and biking trails. Its small size and planned layout make it easy to navigate by your own leg power: by foot and by bicycle are the best ways to get around many of the neighborhoods.

This chapter provides some ideal and unusual ways to see Washington DC's most talked-about sites. The White House Walk examines the presidential palace from every angle, but does not skim over the historic homes, pretty parks and notable museums in the area. The Monumental Bike Ride provides a spectacular view of Washington's most famous monuments, plus a few you might have missed if you were in your car.

The other walking tours dive deeper into the neighborhoods that may not be on every visitor's itinerary, but that constitute DC's heart. Strolling along Embassy Row allows an appreciation for the architecture and atmosphere of DC's diplomatic center. The Georgetown Walk-Around explores the storied neighborhood's historical roots, which range from urban black to upper class. The Night Crawl gives visitors a chance to taste the best of DC nightlife, with drinking, dancing and dining venues to suit all tastes. And the Shaw Shuffle dives deep into the heart and soul of DC's African American history.

So lace up your walking shoes and hit the road.

EMBASSY ROW

Neighborhoods p75; Eating p128; Shopping p181; Sleeping p198

Flags of every shape and color fly above the stately mansions along Massachusetts Ave. Embassy Row is an area that is unique in the nation for its combination of distinctive architecture and international flavor. Here tongues of a hundred nations are heard, streets are crowded with sleek sedans sporting embassy plates, and diplomats and dignitaries congregate in hotel bars. The elegant buildings that house the embassies were once mainly private residences dating from the turn of the century – a time when industrialists and financiers were spending their lavish wealth for all to see.

> ### Walk Facts
>
> **Start** Massachusetts Ave and 20th St NW (Metro: Dupont Circle).
> **End** Connecticut Ave and Kalorama Rd NW (Metro: Woodley Park-Zoo/Adams Morgan).
> **Distance** 2.5km.
> **Pit stops** Lebanese Taverna (p134) or Tono Sushi (p135).

Start at the bottom of Embassy Row, where Massachusetts Ave meets Dupont on the circle's west side. The ominous **Blaine Mansion 1** (2000 Massachusetts Ave) was built in 1881 by Republican Party founder 'Slippery Jim' Blaine. It is not actually a diplomatic building, but it ranks as the oldest surviving mansion in the Dupont Circle area.

The Walsh-McLean House (2020 Massachusetts Ave) houses the **Indonesian embassy 2**. The gold-mining magnate Thomas Walsh commissioned this lavish home in 1903, when it was said to be the costliest house in the city (not surprising, considering the gold-flecked marble pillars). To honor his fortune, Walsh embedded in the foundation a gold nugget, which has never been found.

Continue up Massachusetts Ave to the grand **Anderson House 3** (p78; 2118 Massachusetts Ave), which houses the Society of the Cincinnati Museum (p78). Note the military-themed ornamentation above the entrance and the fancy egg-and-dart molding along the roofline. Across the street, a simple **statue of Mahatma Gandhi 4** – a gift from the people of India – sits in front of the Indian embassy.

The rich mansion at 2121 Massachusetts Ave – designed to resemble Petit Trianon at Versailles – has been the headquarters for the **Cosmos Club 5** since 1952. The building is a befitting home for the most prominent social club of DC's intellectual elite: from the rich, wood-paneled library to the sculpted lion overlooking the blooming gardens, it oozes culture and learning.

Back on the south side of Massachusetts Ave, a bronze statue honors **Tomas Masaryk 6**, a leading advocate for Czech independence after WWI and the first president of the new state of Czechoslovakia (1918–35). Nearby is the **Luxembourg embassy 7** (2200 Massachusetts Ave).

Now you are approaching Sheridan Circle, wreathed in lavish embassies and centered on Gutzon Borglum's equestrian statue of Civil War General Philip Sheridan. (Borglum later sculpted Mt Rushmore.) The nearby **plaque 8** remembers the 1976 car-bomb assassination of pro-Allende Chilean exile Orlando Letelier; agents of the Pinochet dictatorship were later connected to the murder.

The **Turkish embassy 9** (1606 23rd St) was commissioned in 1914 by Edward Everett, who made his millions by inventing the grooved bottle cap. Architect George Oakley Totten had just returned from a stint in Turkey, which inspired many of the building's features, such as the 3rd-story balcony. That Mr Everett's widow later sold the property to the Turkish government for its embassy is a happy coincidence.

The **Haitian embassy 10** (2311 Massachusetts Ave) is a little beaux-arts jewel from 1909. Next door, the 1908 Moran House is now the **Pakistani embassy 11** (2315 Massachusetts Ave), another Totten masterpiece.

You are going to turn right on Decatur Pl, but first take a look a little further up Massachusetts Ave. The **Cameroon embassy 12** (2349 Massachusetts Ave) is also the work of Totten. He designed this castle-like mansion for Norwegian diplomat Christian Hauge, who died in a snowshoe accident before its completion. At No 2343, a cross-legged sculpture of St Jerome dreams over his book before the **Croatian embassy 13**.

Now take a detour east on Decatur Pl to 23rd St. The rise up to S St here was deemed too steep for the road, so city planners constructed a delightful pedestrian staircase, which has been dubbed the '**Spanish Steps**' **14** for its resemblance to Rome's Piazza di Spagna. Climb the steps and return to Massachusetts Ave via S St. As you continue north on Massachusetts Ave you will pass the **Zambian embassy 15** at No 2419 and the **Venezuelan embassy 16** at No 2443.

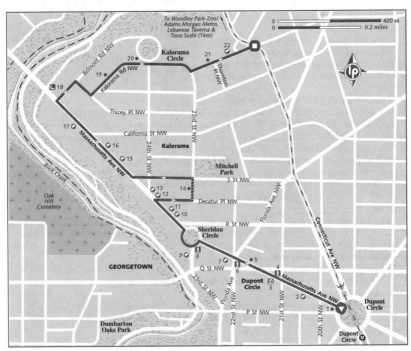

The **Japanese embassy 17** (2516 Massachusetts Ave) cleverly blends Georgian and Asian architectural styles. The beautifully landscaped grounds hold a reconstruction of an antique teahouse, which was brought from Japan in 1960. Its name, Ippakutei, means 'one hundred virtues,' or 'hundredth anniversary,' referring to the US–Japan Treaty of Amity and Friendship that it commemorates.

You will turn right up Belmont Rd, but not before admiring the strikingly ethereal **Islamic Center 18** (p77; 2551 Massachusetts Ave). Now head northwest on Belmont Rd into the interior of Kalorama, where the tree-lined streets and stately homes are among the loveliest in DC.

For this reason – and for its proximity to Embassy Row – many ambassadors' homes are in this neck of the woods. Turn right on Tracey Pl and left on Kalorama Pl to find the **Icelandic ambassador's residence 19** (2443 Kalorama Rd). This half-timbered brick mansion looks built to survive an Arctic winter. DC's oldest extant building is the **Lindens 20** (2401 Kalorama Rd). The Georgian-style mansion was built in Massachusetts in 1754 and shipped to DC in 1934. The magnificent Tudor mansion at 2222 Kalorama Rd is the **French ambassador's residence 21.**

Continue east on Kalorama Rd to Connecticut Ave. Your tour ends here, in front of the **Portuguese embassy 22** (2125 Kalorama Rd). A left on Connecticut will take you across the bridge to the Woodley Park-Zoo/Adams Morgan Metro station. If Embassy Row's international flavor has made you yearn for a further taste of international flavors, check out the restaurants and cafés (p133) clustered around the Metro stop.

GEORGETOWN WALK-AROUND

Neighborhoods p72; Eating p125; Shopping p179; Sleeping p196

The Georgetown Walk-Around starts, quite appropriately, at **Georgetown University 1** (p75), the founding of which, in 1789, capped the good fortune of this already prospering neighborhood.

Enter the campus through the iron gates at 37th and O Sts NW to admire the Gothic spires of the Healy Building and the concrete towers of its modern counterpart, Lauinger Library.

From the gates, walk one block east on O

Walk-Around Facts

Start Georgetown University, 37th and O Sts NW (Georgetown shuttle from Foggy Bottom-GWU or Rosslyn Metro).
End Wisconsin Ave and M St NW (Georgetown shuttle from Foggy Bottom-GWU or Rosslyn Metro).
Distance 4km.
Pit stops Café La Ruche (p126) or **Vietnam Georgetown** (p127).

St and turn right on 36th St. Dating from 1794, **Holy Trinity Church 2** (36th and N Sts NW), was the first Roman Catholic Church in the area. The original church – now housing the convent – is the smaller building at 3525 N St. In the 19th century, this was the only place in Georgetown where black Catholics were welcome to worship; they sat in a designated section of the choir loft, entering through a separate stairway.

Continue south on 36th St to Prospect St. The looooooong flight of stairs leading down to M St is known as the **Exorcist Stairs 3** for its appearance in the horrific film. These stairs continue to torment Georgetown athletes, who often run up them with coaches yelling from below.

Turn left and walk two blocks east on Prospect St. The private **Halcyon House 4** (3400 Prospect St) dates to 1786; in 1900 an eccentric purchased the property and added a ballroom, chapel and theater, plus countless mysterious rooms, doors leading nowhere and stairs ending in solid walls.

Turn left on 34th St and right on N St. On the left, the five Federal houses Nos 3327–39 are known as **Cox's Row 5**, built by the fashionable Georgetown mayor (1823–45) John Cox.

Further down the block, the formal, red-brick **Marbury House 6** (3307 N St) was the home of John and Jacqueline Kennedy before Kennedy became president and they moved into the White House.

Turn left on 33rd St and walk up two blocks to the little house at No 1524. Back in Georgetown's days as a bustling port, this building was known as the **Yellow Tavern 7** (private), a popular stopover for travelers, including Thomas Jefferson.

Take a left at the next corner and walk down Volta Pl to a narrow lane on the left, now known as **Pomander Walk 8**. In the first half of the century, it was a row of tenements called Bell Court, home to domestics, mostly black, who worked in the surrounding mansions. In 1950, the city condemned the buildings and evicted their residents. However unfortunate this history, the row today is a colorful, well-kept corner, representative of the neighborhood's restoration.

Head back east on Volta Pl to Wisconsin Ave. Cross this busy thoroughfare and continue east on Q St to the corner of 31st St. Tucked into five acres of beautifully landscaped grounds, **Tudor Place 9** (p75; 1644 31st St) is the gracious urban estate of the prominent Custis Peter clan (descendents of George Washington). Continue further up 31st St to the intersection with R St. Before you is one of Georgetown's hidden highlights: the eclectic museum and gorgeous gardens of **Dumbarton Oaks 10** (p74).

Turn right and walk east on R St. The intimate and somehow incongruous cobblestone trail on the left was years ago dubbed Lovers' Lane. It leads down into lovely, lush overgrown Dumbarton Oaks Park. Further along R St, tamer Montrose Park hosts the requisite dogs chasing balls and kids on swings. The park's unique feature is the celebrated 'ropewalk,' remaining from the days when this property was used for rope manufacturing. Workers walked up and down the long, straight stretch when fashioning hemp into rope. Adjoining Montrose Park is Oak Hill Cemetery (p75), set on the slopes dropping down to Rock Creek Park.

Continue on R St to its terminus, and turn right to head south on 28th St. Take a quick detour left on Q St to historic **Dumbarton House 11** (p74) at No 2715. Built in 1797, the Federal mansion is one of Georgetown's oldest. Back on 28th St, continue south to P St. The three houses at the corner (2803–11 P St) are protected by **Daw's Fence 12**. Reuben Daw built the storied fence with Mexican War muskets that he found at a pawnshop.

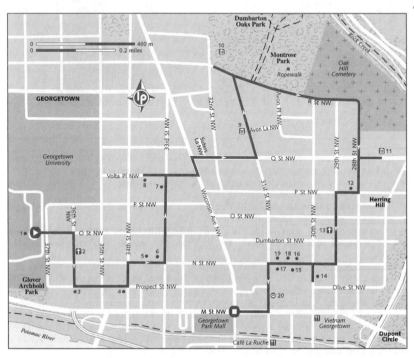

Walk one block west on P St, then turn left to continue heading south on 29th St. This area between 29th St and Rock Creek Park, especially north of P St, is known as Herring Hill. In the early 19th century, it was home to a flourishing free black community. Churches in the area – such as **Mount Zion United Methodist Church 13** (p75; 1334 29th St) – served as stops on the Underground Railroad, defying the neighborhood's reputation as a Confederate bastion during the Civil War.

Continue several more blocks south on 29th St, and turn right on N St to walk west. At 30th St, near the corner on the left-hand side, is a house with a most dubious claim to fame as Georgetown's narrowest house. (It is 11ft wide, in case you are wondering what it takes).

The little row house at 1239 30th St has been dubbed **Spite House 14**, as it was supposedly built to cut off the neighbor's light.

Dumbarton House (p74)

The block of N St between 30th and 31st Sts holds some of Georgetown's most exemplary 18th-century architecture. **Laird-Dunlop House 15**, the red-brick Georgian at No 3014, is now the home of Benjamin Bradlee, the editor who directed the *Washington Post* through the Watergate scandal.

The **Thomas-Beall House 16**, across the street at 3017, has had such prominent residents as the widow Jacqueline Kennedy.

Other architectural gems include: the Federal **Riggs-Riley House 17** at No 3038; the 1780 brick **Beall Mansion 18** at 3033 N St; and the Victorian townhouses of **Wheatley Row 19** (3041 45 N St).

Turn south on 31st St and descend to bustling M St. Don't overlook the elegant facade of the **post office 20** (1215 31st St). When Georgetown was an affluent port, this building served as a lucrative customs house.

The walk-around ends at the intersection of Wisconsin Ave and M St, the heart of Georgetown's commercial activity. We have seen the neighborhood's historical landmarks and architectural masterpieces, but this is the place to experience the buzz of modern Georgetown: shopping, eating and drinking. Pick a spot at a friendly bar or a sidewalk café, and end your walk-around with a sit down.

MONUMENTAL BIKE RIDE

Neighborhoods p61; Eating p120; Shopping p177; Sleeping p192

Washington DC is blessed with fresh air and green space uncharacteristic of an urban setting, as well as hundreds of miles of off-road trails. For the moderately athletic and adventurous, there is no better way to see the city than with two wheels and a pair of pedals. In DC, the Metro makes it easy, allowing bicycles

Bike Ride Facts

Start & End Thompson Boat Center, Rock Creek & Potomac Parkway and I St NW (Metro: Foggy Bottom-GWU).
Distance 10km.
Pit stops Bring a picnic! Otherwise, try **Sequoia** (p127) or **Union Street Public House** (p155).

on the trains except during rush hour and equipping buses with racks to transport bikes.

The bike ride starts at the **Thompson Boat Center 1** (p170), where you can rent a bike if you need to. Exit the boathouse over the small bridge to Rock Creek & Potomac Parkway, and turn right on the parkway trail that runs between the road and the river.

Pedaling along the Potomac, you immediately pass the gargantuan **Watergate Complex 2** (p61) and ride under the overhang of the **Kennedy Center 3** (p61). The trail leads underneath the Theodore Roosevelt Bridge and up a slight incline. Cries of 'Bump, set, spike!' may drift across from the sand **volleyball courts 4**, crowded on weekends with shirtless guys, tanned and buff.

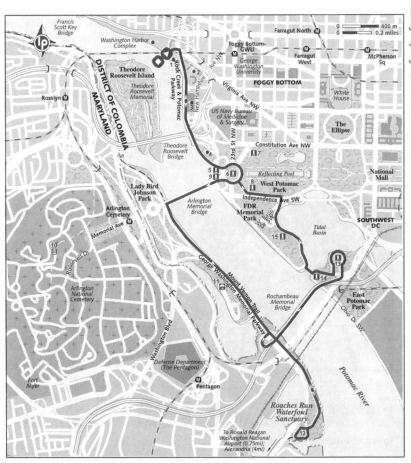

Stop at the top of the hill for a breath and to take in the view (of the environs, not of the guys). The road here is flanked by two bronze statues representing the **Arts of Peace 5**. Aspiration and Literature on the left, Music and Harvest on the right. The wild patch of green across the river is actually Theodore Roosevelt Island (p90) accessible from Arlington. And looming in front of you is the marble-columned **Lincoln Memorial 6** (p45).

Cross the street to your left and follow the pedestrian signs to the front of the memorial. Here it will be difficult to ride with tourists posing for pictures in your path. You can either lock your bike or take it with you as you explore the surrounding memorials on foot. (Either way, be grateful you don't have to find a parking space.) Facing the reflecting pool, the **Vietnam Veterans Memorial 7** (p47) is to your left and the **Korean War Veterans Memorial 8** (p45) is to your right.

After shedding a tear at the granite wall and locating the spot where MLK Jr spoke his famous words, hop back on your bike and ride around to the east side of the Lincoln Memorial. Pick up the path that will take you over Arlington Memorial Bridge on the left side of the road. Before you cross, you will notice the bronze **Arts of War 9**, the counterparts to the Arts of Peace you saw earlier: Valor on the left and Service on the right.

Directly ahead of you, Virginia's rolling hills are covered with the white headstones of Arlington National Cemetery (p97). The mansion on the crest of the hill in the middle of the burial ground is **Arlington House 10** (p97), once owned by Robert E Lee. Once on the Virginia side of the Potomac, turn left to pick up the Mount Vernon Trail (p98) trail heading south. This lovely ride will provide fabulous views of the DC skyline across the river.

The path takes you through Lady Bird Johnson Park (p98), dedicated to the first lady whose efforts beautified many nooks and crannies of the city, including this one. The **LBJ Memorial Grove 11** pays tribute to her husband.

Just before the Rochambeau Memorial Bridge (commonly known as the 14th St Bridge) the bike path forks. Stay left and continue straight under the bridge. Now you are approaching Ronald Reagan Washington National Airport, which will be apparent from the constant roar of airplanes overhead. The park between the bridge and the airport is known as **Gravelly Point 12** (p98) an ideal (if noisy) spot to take a break and pull out your picnic, if you thought to bring one. Flocks of geese and other feathered friends often find their way over from the Roaches Run Waterfowl Sanctuary across the George Washington Memorial Parkway. Even more awesome is watching the iron birds take flight, á la *Bill & Ted's Excellent Adventure*.

If you did not bring a picnic, you might consider continuing south here for a few miles to the heart of Old Town in Alexandria (p99) and a host of lunching options. Otherwise, this is

Korean War Veterans Memorial (p45)

the turn-around point. When your buns are ready, get them back on that bike seat and head from whence you came.

After passing back under the 14th St Bridge, look again for the fork in the path. This time, turn off the path and loop back to the left and over the bridge. Cross the street and pedal around the domed **Thomas Jefferson Memorial 13** (p71) on the banks of the peaceful Tidal Basin. Exiting the memorial, turn right onto Ohio Dr. There is no separate bike path here, so be very careful of cars and pedestrians. Before you cross the small inlet bridge, duck down the path on the left-hand side of the road to discover the hidden **George Mason Memorial 14** (p71).

Cross the inlet bridge and follow the pedestrian signs to the **Franklin Delano Roosevelt Memorial 15** (p71). You must walk your bike through this maze of open-air rooms paying tribute to different eras of the great president's life. Exit the memorial on the northwest side of the Tidal Basin and turn right onto W Basin Dr. The park to your left – FDR Memorial Park – is often the site of polo matches or helicopter landings or other excitement.

Cross busy Independence Ave and go left on the paved walkway along West Potomac Park, back to the Lincoln Memorial. To return to Thompson Boat Center pass between the Lincoln Memorial and the Reflecting Pool to retrace your pedals on the Rock Creek Parkway bike path. After such a ride, you'll need nothing more than to rest your bones and replenish your fluids. Fortunately, the Washington Harbor Complex, just steps from Thompson Boat Center, has a few options to enjoy the breeze off the river and do just that.

NIGHT CRAWL

Neighborhoods p79; Eating p132; Shopping p184; Sleeping p202

So many clubs and pubs, so little time. Here is a sampler plate for night crawlers who are itching to get a taste of all that DC's night-life has to offer. The tour skirts around the edges of up-and-coming Shaw and ever-hip Dupont Circle, before diving into the heart of DC's liveliest nightspot, Adams-Morgan.

Crawl Facts

Start 14th and U Sts NW (Metro: U Street-Cardozo).
End 18th St NW (U Link shuttle to Woodley Park-Zoo/Adams Morgan or U Street-Cardozo Metro).
Distance 2km.

Stops along the way range from swank to dive, from artsy to sporty, from ethnic to American. Keep in mind that this is NOT the city that never sleeps (most of these places close at 2am weekdays, 3am Friday and Saturday). Get an early start to take advantage of happy-hour specials and to take it all in.

Start at the corner of 14th and U Sts NW, two blocks west of the U Street-Cardozo Metro stop. These streets have attracted night crawlers since the 1920s, when music lovers came from all corners of the city to hear the sweet sounds of jazz that emanated from the many nightclubs in the area. One block south of here, the intersection of 14th and T Sts NW was the site of the magical Club Bali, which hosted greats like Louis Armstrong and Sarah Vaughn. Today, the area is enjoying a renaissance as a venue for music, arts and nightlife.

Step into **U-topia 1** (p152; 1418 U St). Part gallery and part bar, it's a place where both artists and musicians have a chance to show off. You can't miss the canvases that decorate the walls; there is also live blues and jazz several nights a week. The action probably won't start until later, though, so have a drink, peruse the paintings and move on.

Walk two blocks west on U St to the intersection of New Hampshire Ave and 16th St NW, a neighborhood – literally and figuratively – on the edge. These northeastern reaches of Dupont Circle sport some of its trendiest spots, like the **Chi-Cha Lounge 2** (p152; 1624 U St). Is it sinking into a plush velvet sofa or smoking a fruity-flavored hookah that makes everybody here so chill? In any case, sit back with a signature *chi-cha* (some South American concoction), pass around the Ecuadorian tapas, and enjoy this eclectic mix of East and West.

When your lungs can't take it any more, continue west on U St to the intersection of 18th St and Florida Ave. The humble little **Staccato 3** (p161; 2006 18th St) provides a friendly introduction to the local music scene. Jazz, folk and rock bands play most nights right in the window, behind the baby grand.

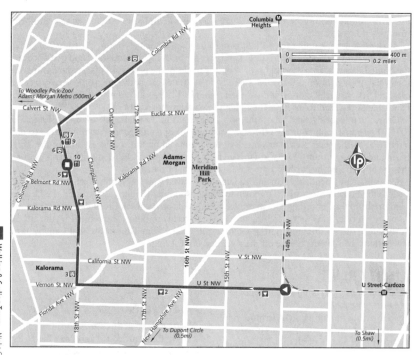

From here, head north on 18th St. The dense strip nestled between Kalorama and Columbia Rds is the epicenter of Adams-Morgan and, arguably, of all nightlife in Washington DC.

Kokopooli 4 (p153) is the Indian character painted on the entrance to 2305 18th St. It is also the name of this sparky sports bar (true, Indian characters don't usually go with sports bars, but we don't want to fence anybody in). Although eight pool tables, festive wall murals and TVs everywhere are good for hours of entertainment, we are not resting here.

Your next stop is 2406 18th St, the **Spy Lounge 5** (p153). Did we warn you to wear your most fashionable duds? Here's where you will need them to get past the crowd-control (and face-patrol) bouncer. Once inside, check out nonstop James Bond on the big screen and enjoy your vodka martini (shaken, not stirred).

Don't get too comfortable, though, as there is a whole world out there. How about a jaunt to Africa? Stroll a few doors down to the **Bukom Café 6** (p160; 2442 18th St), where live juju and other West African beats rock the house.

If world music's not your thing, head across the street to No 2461 for live blues at **Madam's Organ 7** (p160).

When you think you can't take any more fun, hit the streets again. Turn right on Columbia Rd and head up a few blocks to **Chief Ike's Mambo Room 8** (p164; 1725 Columbia Rd). It's three clubs in one, so you're bound to find something you like, be it live bands playing rock or reggae or DJs spinning discs. The catch is that everybody's dancing, so get out there and shake that thang.

By now you must be exhausted and – more urgent – starving. If you need a repose, settle into a comfy booth at the **Diner 9** (p133; 2453 18th St) for a cheesy Western omelet or a juicy burger.

Otherwise walk back to the Metro with a jumbo slice from **Pizza Mart 10** (p133; 2435 18th St NW). It has been argued that this is the best pizza in DC, but nobody has ever eaten it sober, so it's hard to confirm.

SHAW SHUFFLE

Neighborhoods p80; Eating p135;
Shopping p185

Shuffle Facts

Start 12th and U Sts NW (Metro: U Street-Cardozo).
End Vermont Ave NW (Metro: McPherson Sq).
Distance 2.5km.
Pit stops Ben's Chili Bowl (p135) or Café Saint-Ex (p154).

'Before Harlem, there was Shaw,' locals boast about the vibrant African American community that thrived in this part of DC for the first half of the 20th century. Centered around U St NW, the area was home to hundreds of black businesses, churches, schools and civic organizations, not to mention a prominent black university and a magical live music scene.

Start your shuffle through Shaw at the corner of 12th and U Sts NW, just outside the U Street-Cardozo Metro station. Back in its heyday, the True Reformer Building (1200 U St), was the setting for many of the business meetings and social gatherings that kept this community ticking. The grand 1903 Italianate building was designed, built, financed, and ultimately utilized and appreciated by African Americans. Today it houses the **African American Civil War Museum 1** (p82).

Walk south on 12th St past the corner of T St to the **Thurgood Marshall Center 2** (1816 12th St). This community center was built in 1908 to house the nation's first African American YMCA, an institution that nurtured the likes of Langston Hughes, Joe Louis and Georgetown University basketball coach John Thompson.

Head west on T St and stroll past **Duke Ellington's childhood home 3** (1212 T St). The elegant **Whitelaw Hotel 4** (1839 T St) was a luxurious, 1st-class hotel – the first in segregated DC to welcome black travelers.

Now turn right on 13th St and make your way back to U St, the central artery of Shaw. At the corner of 13th and U Sts, Duke Ellington belts out his blue notes from the colorful **mural 5**, painted on the exterior wall of the Metro station by DC artists and students.

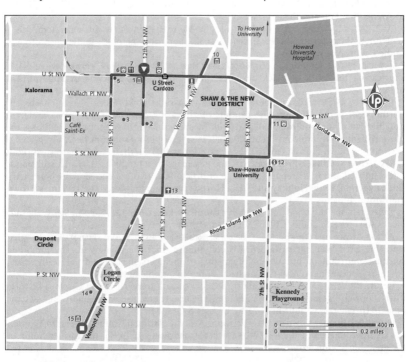

African American Civil War Memorial (p82)

Turn right and head east on U St, passing the historic **Lincoln Theatre 6** (p156; 1215 U St), one of three first-run movie theaters that were clustered here back in its day. Its neighbor, **Ben's Chili Bowl 7** (p135; 1213 U St NW), has been a gathering place for DC's black politicos and community leaders since its opening in 1958.

One block further at the corner of 11th St, the sax-shaped sign and keyboard trim leave no doubt about what goes on inside **Bohemian Caverns 8** (p159). This hip venue for live jazz and soul music is the reincarnation of the fashionable Club Cavern, which occupied the basement here from 1926, and attracted big names from Duke Ellington and Pearl Bailey to Aretha Franklin and the Supremes.

At U St and Vermont Ave, just outside the Metro station's east entrance, is the steel-sculptured **African American Civil War Memorial 9** (p82), honoring the black soldiers who fought in the Union Army.

Turn north to see the eclectic **Black Fashion Museum 10** (p82; 2007 Vermont Ave NW), showcasing the work of black designers past and present. Entry is by appointment only.

Return to U St, walk one block east and turn right down Florida Ave. The blocks northeast of here constitute the campus of Howard University (p82), alma mater of notables like Thurgood Marshall and Toni Morrison. Later in the tour, we will pass the Howard University welcome center, which is several blocks south of here.

Continue down Florida Ave to the intersection with T St, then take a sharp turn right. A key fixture on 'Black Broadway' was the **Howard Theatre 11** (620 T St), which still stands but is unused and in disrepair (although efforts to restore it are occasionally launched). Ella Fitzgerald, Billie Holiday and Lena Horne sang here, followed later by James Brown and Motown bands.

Take a left on 7th St, passing the **Howard University welcome center 12** (1739 7th St). Walk four blocks west on S St and one block south on 11th St.

At the corner of 11th and R Sts, **Lincoln Memorial Church 13** is one of several churches that since the Civil War has sustained this community since the Civil War – by providing spiritual nourishment, but also by organizing its members socially and politically. Black religious institutions were at the forefront of the civil rights movement.

Return to Vermont Ave and walk three blocks south to reach Logan Circle, a historic district of well-preserved Victorian homes. The ornate cream-colored manse at **1 & 2 Logan Circle 14** (private) was built in 1877 by Ulysses S Grant Jr.

One block further down at 1318 Vermont Ave, the National Council of Negro Women has its headquarters at the **Mary McLeod Bethune Council House 15** (p91), the former home of the great black educator.

WHITE HOUSE WALK

Neighborhoods p57; Eating p120; Shopping p177; Sleeping p192

Our stroll through this neighborhood begins where the nightly network news always seems to begin: on the north side of the White House in Lafayette Sq. In the 19th century Lafayette Sq (named for the

Walk Facts

Start Lafayette Sq (Metro: McPherson Sq).
End Aztec Gardens (Metro: Farragut West).
Distance 4km.
Pit stops Café des Artistes (p58) or Teaism (p123).

Marquis de Lafayette, the Revolutionary War hero) was an orchard lined with the mansions of the rich and powerful. The writer Henry Adams, who lived in a mansion on its northern edge, described it thus: 'Lafayette Square was society...Beyond the square, the country began.'

Among the square's remaining Victorian homes is **Decatur House 1** (p58; 748 Jackson Pl). Around the corner at 1 Lafayette Sq, the **Hay-Adams Hotel 2** (p192) is an exclusive, luxurious hostelry that was built on the site of Henry Adams' old mansion.

Across the street, **St John's Church 3** (p60) has a pew permanently reserved for presidential families.

Circle around the square to Pennsylvania Ave NW, which runs between Lafayette Sq and the White House. Until recently, it was a central thoroughfare, but after two threatening incidents in 1994 (a stolen airplane crashed into White House grounds, and a man fired a semiautomatic at the mansion), the portion in front of the White House was closed to car traffic. Now concrete blockades and a heightened security presence add an imposing imperial air to the White House, but they also make the area a more pleasant pedestrian walkway.

Pass in front of the White House, which is almost dwarfed by the wonderfully baroque Old Executive Office Building (p59), where White House staff work. Across the street, the

Walking & Cycling Tours – White House Walk

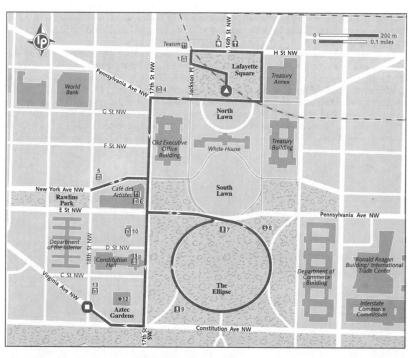

White House protester (p60)

national crafts museum, the **Renwick Gallery 4** (p60), is housed in a historic mansion at the corner of 17th St NW.

Turn left on 17th St and walk three blocks to New York Ave. Walk west on New York Ave to the oddly shaped but appropriately named **Octagon Museum 5** (p59). Across the street, blooming magnolias and gurgling goldfish ponds decorate Rawlins Park – a remarkably peaceful place considering it's named for US Grant's Secretary of War.

Back on 17th St, the beautiful beaux-arts building at No 500 is the **Corcoran Gallery of Art 6** (p58), a magnificent collection of American and European art. If you need a break, the Café des Artistes, on the 1st floor, is a delightful lunch spot.

The Ellipse (p58) is the expansive park across the street. Its northernmost point provides you the classic photo opportunity: the White House facade, in dignified remove across its private South Lawn. Walk around the elliptical road that circles the park.

At the north edge, the **Zero Milestone 7** is the stone marker from which all US highway distances are measured (in case you ever wondered). In December, the National Christmas Tree is illuminated here. Information is available at the **National Park Service Ellipse Visitor Pavilion 8**. Along the southern edge, you cannot miss the **Second Division Memorial 9** with its giant golden hand thrusting forth a flaming sword.

Make your way around the Ellipse and back to 17th St NW. Head south to admire the rest of the monumental buildings along this row: the pillared, marble mansion that serves as the headquarters and museum of the **Red Cross 10** (p57; 1730 E St NW); the stately Memorial Continental Building housing the **Daughters of the American Revolution 11** (p58; 1776 D St); and the **Organization of American States 12** (p60), in the marble palazzo at the corner of Constitution Ave. All have exhibits open to the public, so you can end your tour with a stroll through art galleries and historic rooms. Or kick back in the sculpture-studded Aztec Gardens skirting the OAS.

Eating

Eating

Washington DC is one of the nation's culinary capitals, offering an incredible array of eating options for a city its size. With pleasant weather eight months a year, DC has plenty of opportunities for alfresco dining, including sidewalk cafés (fabulous people-watching) and roof-deck restaurants (fabulous views). Trendy theme restaurants with funky interiors have also become a hot commodity. And DC is undoubtedly the number-one spot in the country for sighting political celebrities out on the town. Between its creative cuisine, delightful decors and powerful patrons, DC dining is bound to stimulate your senses.

Opening Hours

Most restaurants are open for lunch and dinner daily, with some exceptions. Restaurants that depend on weekday business lunch trade (such as in the White House Area) may be open for dinner only on weekends, or not at all. Other restaurants – especially family-owned joints – may close on Sunday or Monday. Unless otherwise noted in this chapter, assume restaurants are open daily 11:30am to 2:30pm for lunch, 5:30pm to 10:30pm for dinner and later (until 11pm or midnight) on Friday and Saturday.

Market stall (p117)

How Much?

Travelers can expect to spend a fair amount of their budgets on eating out. For travelers on a budget, consider the restaurant options listed under Cheap Eats, where you can dine for under $10. Food courts and take-out are also options where large portions are inexpensive. Otherwise, a restaurant dinner with a drink usually starts around $30 and the price goes up as high as you are willing. Lunch runs around $20, although many restaurants offer lunch specials and buffets – a thrifty way to enjoy a nice meal.

Booking Tables

While most restaurants do not require booking a table, it is recommended on weekends, especially at upscale restaurants. Normally, a phone call on the afternoon is sufficient, although some of the hottest, new restaurants require reservations several days or a week in advance.

Tipping

Tipping is an important part of restaurant culture in the US: servers make less than minimum wage and rely on tips to earn their living. Tipping 15% of the total bill is the accepted minimum. If service is good, 20% is a decent average tip, while it is appropriate to tip more if service is exceptional.

Top Five Eat Streets

Excellent eat streets are all over the city, but here's our votes for the best.

- **7th St NW, Downtown** (p118) It's not just for Chinese any more.
- **18th St NW, Adams-Morgan** (p132) Ethnic eateries and good times.
- **M St NW, Georgetown** (p125) Divey to delectable and everything in between.
- **Massachusetts Ave NE, Capitol Hill** (p123) If your senator eats here, why shouldn't you?
- **Pennsylvania Ave NW, Downtown** (p118) Power-dining in the Penn quarter.

Self-catering

Picnicking on the National Mall or on the banks of the Potomac counts among the most pleasant dining experiences in DC. Besides the inspirational setting, DC's **farmers markets** (below) and gourmet stores offer a wonderful selection of fresh produce and exotic eats to pack in your picnic basket.

NATIONAL MALL

Most of the museums offer far overpriced restaurants with mediocre menus; however, there are a few exceptions which we have listed below.

CASCADE CAFÉ Map pp246-8   *Café*
☎ 202-216-2480; East Bldg, National Gallery of Art, 4th St & Constitution Ave NW; lunch from $10; ☒ 10am-3pm Mon-Sat, 11am-4pm Sun; Metro: Archives-Navy Memorial
Your best bet for museum dining on the mall is at one of the National Gallery's lovely cafés. At the Cascade Café in the East Building of the National Gallery, enjoy IM Pei's waterfall while dining. Specialty menus complement current exhibits (eg regional African American dishes in honor of the Art of Romare Beardon).

FULL CIRCLE CAFÉ Map pp246-8   *Café*
☎ 202-633-4674; Hirshhorn Museum, 7th & Independence Ave SW; lunch from $8; ☒ 11am-4:30pm Mon-Fri, to 8pm Thu summer; Metro: Smithsonian
The pleasant Full Circle Café serves soups, salads and sandwiches – plus beer and wine – on a breezy patio.

Farmers Markets

In addition to Eastern Market (the granddaddy of DC open-air markets), numerous local farmers markets offer fresh produce, meats, seafood, flowers, locally made baked goods, jewelry, crafts and even clothing. Try the following:

- **Adams-Morgan Farmers Market** (Map p261; Columbia Rd & 18th St NW, Crestar Bank plaza; ☒ 8am-1pm Sat May-Dec; U Link Shuttle from Woodley Park-Zoo/Adams Morgan or U Street-Cardozo)
- **DC Open-Air Farmers Market** (Map pp250-1; RFK Stadium parking lot, Oklahoma Ave & Benning Rd NE; ☒ 7am-5pm Thu & Sat plus Tue Jun-Sep; Metro: Stadium-Armory)
- **Historic Brookland Farmers Market** (Map pp252-3; 10th & Otis Sts NE; ☒ 4-7pm Tue, 10am-2pm Sun Jun-Oct; Metro: CUA-Brookland)
- **Fresh Farm Market** (Map pp246-8; 8th & E Sts NW, ☒ 3-7pm Thu; Metro: Gallery Pl-Chinatown)
- **Old Town Farmers Market** (Map p265; 301 King St, Old Town, Alexandria; ☒ 9am-2pm Sat; Old Town shuttle from King St Metro)

GARDEN CAFÉ Map pp246-8   *Café*
☎ 202-216-2480; West Bldg, National Gallery of Art, 4th St & Constitution Ave NW; lunch from $10; ◷ 11:30am-3pm Mon-Sat, noon-6:30pm Sun; Metro: Archives-Navy Memorial

The East Building of the National Gallery features the **Cascade Café** (p117) while the West Building has the equally lovely, plant-filled Garden Café. It serves American cuisine and thematic dishes that are related to current exhibitions.

ICE CREAM PARLOR Map pp246-8   *Desserts*
National Museum of American History, 14th St & Constitution Av NW; dessert from $4; ◷ 11am-5pm Mar-Oct; Metro: Smithsonian

No matter where you eat lunch, stop for dessert at this traditional ice-cream parlor. Thick milkshakes, hot-fudge sundaes and the mountainous Star-Spangled Banner Split taste even better in this quaint Victorian-era setting.

PAVILION CAFÉ Map pp246-8   *Café*
☎ 202-289-3660; National Sculpture Garden, 7th St & Constitution Ave NW; lunch from $8; ◷ 11am-3:30pm Mon-Fri, 5-8pm Fri, 11am-4pm Sat, 11am-5:30pm Sun

With a panoramic view of the **National Sculpture Garden** (p50), the Pavilion Café offers specialty pizzas, sandwiches, salads, desserts and assorted beverages, as well as a children's menu. The café also offers a seasonal tapas-style menu on Friday nights in summer, when DC-area jazz musicians put on free concerts.

DOWNTOWN

During the boom years of the 1990s, the neighborhoods north of the Mall transformed themselves. Once this area was a ghost town after dark, but now you can find flourishing restaurant districts in Chinatown, along 7th and 8th Sts NW and close to the White House.

ANDALE Map pp246-8   *Mexican*
☎ 202-783-3133; 401 7th St NW; mains $14-20; ◷ lunch & dinner Mon-Sat; Metro: Archives-Navy Memorial

The executive chef spent the summer in Mexico and was so inspired that she revamped her restaurant – formerly the Mark – into this innovative, contemporary, south-of-the-border gem. Everything here reflects thoughtful effort, from the original artwork and Mexican lanterns adorning the dining room, to the *caldo de mariscos* (spicy seafood stew).

CAFÉ ATLÁNTICO
Map pp246-8   *Pan-Latin*
☎ 202-393-0812; 405 8th St NW; mains $14-20; Metro: Archives-Navy Memorial

Innovative Pan-Latin cooking like chicken polenta canapés and Veracruz-style seafood make this tri-level place one of downtown's most popular. *Caipirinhas* (Brazilian lime drink), *mojitos* (minty, lemon rum drink) and pisco sours wash it all down. On weekends, don't miss the fabulous 'Latin dim sum' brunch.

CAPITAL GRILLE
Map pp246-8   *Steakhouse*
☎ 202-737-6200; 601 Pennsylvania Ave NW; meals from $40; Metro: Archives-Navy Memorial

Is that raw steak you smell, or raw power? Congressional committee heads puff stogies and quaff gin at the bar, cabinet secretaries' limousines purr outside and lobbyists seduce willing prey over buttery beef at the linen-covered tables. If the maitre d' ever deigns to seat you, you can happily tuck into dry-aged 24oz porterhouses, veal chops and other red-blooded fare. It's all extremely delicious, of course, but not half as interesting as the clientele.

DISTRICT CHOPHOUSE & BREWERY
Map pp246-8   *Steakhouse*
☎ 202-347-3434; 509 7th St NW; ◷ 2-11pm Sat & Sun; meals $30; Metro: Archives

More affordable (and some would argue more fun) than most of DC's steakhouses, this lively pub gets points for beef and beer. It's a popular late-night spot, complete with an in-house brewery and cigar humidor, pool tables and Sinatra on the stereo.

JALEO Map pp246-8   *Spanish*
☎ 202-628-7949; 480 7th St NW; tapas $4-8, mains $15; Metro: Archives-Navy Memorial

Although 'Jaleo' can refer to a popular Andalusian dance, in this case the alternative definition is more appropriate: revelry and merrymaking.

Dominated by a large semicircular bar (where you should not pass on a pitcher of sangria), the place is decorated with Andalusian pottery and warm, Mediterranean colors. Dinner can be paella or a few other *platos fuertes* (main dishes), but the star of the menu is the selection of over 40 tapas.

Reservations are highly recommended for dinner.

MARVELOUS MARKET

Map pp246-8   *Self-catering*
☎ 202-628-0824; 730 7th St NW; sandwiches from $6, mains from $8; ⏰ 7am-7pm Mon-Fri, 9am-5pm Sat; Metro: Gallery Pl-Chinatown

This bakery specializes in delicious home-made breads, pastries and cheeses, but also sells sandwiches and dishes to go. Other branches are near the White House (p121) and Dupont Circle (p130)

MATCHBOX Map pp246-8   *Italian*
☎ 202-289-4441; 713 H St NW; meals from $20; ⏰ 11:30am-11pm Mon-Sat; Metro: Gallery Pl-Chinatown

Crispy, thin New York-style pizza – fresh from the brick oven – is drawing DC crowds to this new spot. It's casual and cozy, but in a stylish, contemporary way that attracts hip 20- and 30-somethings, besides families and locals.

POSTE Map pp246-8   *New American*
☎ 202-783-6060; 555 8th St NW; mains $18-24; ⏰ 7am-11pm; Metro: Gallery Pl-Chinatown

This restaurant is named for its previous incarnation as the mail sorting room for the City Post Office. Many of the brasserie's restored architectural features had a practical purpose back in their day – cast-iron ceilings to protect the mail from fire, skylights and a picture window to provide light to sort by, and a portal entry (which now leads to the patio seating) large enough for a horse-drawn carriage. The space is now a fantastic place for a drink (try a 'Skyy Love Letter') or a delightful, French-influenced meal.

RED SAGE Map pp246-8   *Tex-Mex*
☎ 202-638-4444; 605 14th St NW; mains $10-15; ⏰ lunch & dinner Mon-Fri, dinner Sat & Sun; Metro: Metro Center

Georgia O'Keeffe probably inspired these cave-like, rose-stuccoed, subterranean rooms with wood-beam ceilings and fancy ironwork. It's a fine setting to enjoy chef Morou Ouattara's Southwestern-inflected American cuisine (apparently Bill Clinton used to). These are not your typical fajitas and margaritas; chef specialties include red-chile pecan-crusted chicken, grilled diver scallops with saffron, acorn squash risotto, and smoked antelope, bison and ostrich.

TENPENH Map pp246-8   *Asian*
☎ 202-393-4500; 1001 Pennsylvania Ave; mains $15-20; ⏰ lunch & dinner Mon-Fri, dinner Sat; Metro: Federal Triangle

Jewel-toned walls and shimming lights, an abstract painting of an Asian warrior, a 17th-century black Buddha statue: such stylistic touches set the tone for this ultra-hip Asian fusion masterpiece. The food is by no means secondary, however. Jeff Tunks – of DC Coast fame – adds ingredients and spices from China, Thailand and Vietnam to his well-honed traditional techniques, resulting in eclectic but exceptional culinary experiences for his guests.

TONY CHENG'S SEAFOOD RESTAURANT

Map pp246-8   *Chinese & Mongolian*
☎ 202-371-8669; 619 H St NW; dim sum items from $3, lunch from $10, dinner from $25; ⏰ downstairs lunch & dinner, upstairs 11am-3pm lunch & dim sum; Metro: Gallery Pl-Chinatown

This favorite Chinatown eatery is a three in one. Downstairs, Cheng has the first and best build-your-own Mongolian barbecue in town. Upstairs, the Cantonese menu features seafood (which you can see swimming about in tanks), as well as poultry and beef classics. On weekends this place attracts droves of Chinese-Americans for the traditional Hong Kong dim sum.

WOK & ROLL

Map pp246-8   *Chinese & Japanese*
☎ 202-347-4656; 604 H St NW; mains from $8; ⏰ lunch & dinner Mon-Sun, to 3am Fri & Sat; Metro: Gallery Pl-Chinatown

At this inauspicious address, Lincoln's assassins plotted their scheme (and were later hanged for it). These days, much happier plotting takes place here, like deciding whether to order light, fresh sushi or steaming, spicy noodles for lunch. The selection of teas – black and green, hot or cold – is impressive; try one of the delicious and healthy milk teas.

ZAYTINYA Map pp246-8   *Mediterranean*
☎ 202-333-4710; 701 9th St NW; meze $4-8, lunch mains $8-12; dinner mains $15-20; Metro: Gallery Pl-Chinatown

Earth tones, high ceilings and clean lines characterize this elegant bi-level. After stints at Café Atlántico and Jaleo, chef Jose Andres applies his expertise to the fare of Greece, Lebanon and Turkey. The extensive menu of hot and cold mezzes – 'little dishes' – reflect the rich, regional diversity of these cuisines. Reservations recommended for lunch. If you come for dinner, be prepared to wait: reservations are not accepted and this place is all the rage.

Eating – Downtown

ZOLA Map pp246-8 *American*

☎ 202-654-0999; International Spy Museum, 800 F St; lunch from $20, dinner from $35; ☾ lunch & dinner daily, dinner Sat & Sun; Metro: Gallery Pl-Chinatown

A subtle but playful theme of espionage runs through this hip restaurant, named for French author Emile Zola, who championed the case of Alfred Dreyfus when he was falsely accused of being a spy. Located inside the International Spy Museum, it is only appropriate that guests should be able to monitor the kitchen through discreet one-way mirrors in the booths, or slip off to the restroom through a hidden door. Black and white photographs and projections of coded text add further to the mysterious air. In the midst of this secrecy, Zola's cuisine is surprisingly straightforward. Upscale versions of American classics include veal and mushroom meat loaf wrapped in bacon for dinner, or baked ham and smoked gouda grilled sandwich for lunch (not exactly like Mom used to make, but we're not complaining).

Top Five Politico-Spotting Spots

- **Capital Grille** (p118) Could be called the Capitol cafeteria for all its Congressional clients.
- **Jeffrey's at the Watergate** (p122) Rumored to be a favorite of the President and the First Lady (and all those other Texans who moved up here).
- **Monocle** (p124) Sight your senator slinging back a Scotch.
- **Occidental Grill** (p121) 'Where statesmen dine,' per its own motto (and evidenced by the VIP photos covering the walls).
- **Palm** (p130) Do the waiters abuse the VIPs like they will abuse you?

Cheap Eats

The Old Post Office Pavilion's food court is an unbeatable place to get a quick, cheap bite to eat for lunch.

FULL KEE Map pp246-8 *Chinese*

☎ 202-371-2233; 509 H St NW; lunch from $6; ☾ 11-1am Sun-Thu, 11-3am Fri & Sat; Metro: Gallery Pl-Chinatown

At the best dive in Chinatown, fill yourself for next to nothing with a simple noodle dish or gorge on a wondrous stir-fry. Better still, go for one of the rich savory casseroles you won't find at other places, like eggplant and short ribs or pork and bean curd. No alcohol, no credit cards.

TEAISM Map pp246-8 *Teahouse*

☎ 202-638-6010; 400 8th St NW; lunch from $8; ☾ 7am-5pm Mon-Fri; Metro: Archives-Navy Memorial

Simple noodle or bento-box lunches are fresh and delicious, while the teahouse offers a peaceful Zen-like atmosphere to recover from a morning's sight-seeing. There is also a branch near the White House (p123) and one near Dupont Circle.

WHITE HOUSE AREA & FOGGY BOTTOM

Stomping ground of lobbyists and executive-branch power brokers, this area is replete with fancy digs. Needless to say, the restaurants around the White House are among the top spots for spying on politicians while they dine.

White House Area

BOMBAY CLUB Map pp246-8 *Indian*

☎ 202-659-3727; 815 Connecticut Ave NW; mains $14-20; ☾ lunch & dinner Sun-Fri, dinner Sat; Metro: Farragut West

Lauded as DC's best Indian restaurant, this place features cuisine inspired by the subcontinent's diverse cultures. House specialties draw on the best of these, adding the chef's modern touch: spicy seafood curry, succulent chicken tikka masala and hot, hot, hot green chile chicken. The Bombay Club's elegant setting and indulging service allow guests to experience the life of a maharaja, if only for a few hours.

DC COAST Map pp246-8 *Seafood*

☎ 202-216-5988; 1401 K St NW; meals from $40; ☾ lunch & dinner Mon-Fri, dinner Sat; Metro: McPherson Sq

Although the art deco space is rich, the scrumptious seafood is the reason to come to this perennial DC favorite. Who can pass up a 'Tower of Crab' with spicy, citrusy Tabasco butter? It does a serious lawyer-and-lobby lunch trade; the dull roar can be intrusive or exciting depending on your mood.

GEORGIA BROWN'S

Map pp246-8 *Southern*

☎ 202-393-4499; 1 McPherson Sq (15th & K Sts NW); mains $16-24; ☾ 10:30am-2:15pm Mon-Fri, brunch Sun; Metro: McPherson Sq

Sunday brunch at Georgia Brown's has become a veritable DC institution ever since it was rumored to be Bill Clinton's favorite place to get food like down-home. Serious Southern cooking with an emphasis on savory Low Country dishes combines seafood from the Carolina coast with flavors from West Indian plantations. Georgia's is popular with the K St lobbying crowd, with black urban professionals and with anyone else who wants a good plate of grits.

MARVELOUS MARKET

Map pp246-8 *Self-catering*
☎ 202-828-0944; 1800 K St NW; sandwiches from $6, mains from $8; ⏱ 7am-7pm Mon-Fri; Metro: Farragut West
Besides gourmet grocery store items, this chain also carries fresh bread, pastries and sandwiches. There are other branches in downtown (p119) and Dupont Circle (p130).

MAXIM Map pp246-8 *Russian*
☎ 202-962-0280; 1725 F St NW; mains $22-32; Metro: Farragut North
Russian and Georgian specialties, regional wines and vodka, and international panache will take you to the Motherland for dinner. And we're not talking sad-looking Soviet salads here. Thick, rich soups, spicy Georgian treats, like *shashlyk* (shish kebabs) and *khachapuri* (cheesy bread) and – if you can afford it – *bliny* (Russian crepes) with caviar reveal this Old World cuisine as it was meant to be. Euros get their groove on Friday and Saturday nights, making this *the* place to meet Russian-speakers in the DC area.

OCCIDENTAL GRILL

Map pp246-8 *Steakhouse*
☎ 202-783-1475; 1475 Pennsylvania Ave NW; meals from $30; Metro: Metro Center
This DC institution is practically wallpapered with mug shots of congressmen and other political celebs who have dined here throughout the years. Although the Occidental isn't the nerve center it once was, plenty of bigwigs still roll up their pinstripes to dive into hamburgers, chops and steaks.

OLD EBBITT GRILL

.Map pp246-8 *American*
☎ 202-347-4801; 675 15th St NW; meals from $25; Metro: Metro Center
This all-American saloon has been around since 1846, serving local favorites, like Maryland rockfish, crab cakes, steak and burgers.

The brass and wood lends a good ol' boys atmosphere, which is appropriate for the power brokers who show up to dine here. The Sunday brunch menu is a delight.

OLIVES Map pp246-8 *Mediterranean*
☎ 202-452-1866; 1600 K St NW; ⏱ lunch & dinner Mon-Fri, dinner Sat; meals from $40; Metro: Farragut North
Just north of the White House, Boston-based chef Todd English operates this stylish, two-story hotspot. The kitchen-side bar upstairs is a prime seat, especially for solo diners: you can watch the sous-chefs chop and stir, and then order whatever whets your appetite. Handmade pastas are a good bet, if you can resist the aroma of the juicy, wood-grilled steaks and veal.

TABERNA DEL ALABARDERO

Map pp246-8 *Spanish*
☎ 202-429-2200, 1776 I St NW; tapas $5-10, mains $18-24; ⏱ lunch & dinner Mon-Fri, dinner Sat; Metro: Farragut West
Spanish and Basque dishes lure the international-banking and diplomatic sets to this offshoot of a noted Madrid restaurant. The saffron-colored walls and flowery prints provide a sumptuous, old-world setting for a special dinner. Traditional tapas and complimentary wines are the specialty; the attentive waitstaff will help you choose your favorites.

Presidential Nosh

Perhaps it's something about the job, but US presidents seem to have a predilection for odd or even downright unsavory food and drink. Here's a sampler of past White House treats:

Booze Franklin Pierce (who died of cirrhosis).
Hominy grits Ulysses S Grant.
Liver with bacon, kidney stew Theodore Roosevelt.
Anything at all William Taft (who weighed 330lb).
Creamed chipped beef Franklin Roosevelt.
Fresca Lyndon Johnson (who had a tap for it installed in the White House).
Cottage cheese dressed with ketchup Richard Nixon.
Jelly Bellies Ronald Reagan.
XFried pork rinds George Bush père (who ate them as a 'common man' political tactic).

Foggy Bottom

DISH Map pp246-8 *New American*
☎ 202-338-8707; 924 25th St NW, River Inn; mains $12-16; Metro: Foggy Bottom

Casual yet stylish, Dish offers a modern perspective on good old-fashioned American food: start with a bowl of rich tomato soup with goat's cheese croutons; and follow up with Mom's meat loaf with a delectable mushroom sauce, or cheesy, creamy mac and cheese. The decor is light-colored wood and clean lines, with a prominent 8ft photographic diptych of a reclining weimaraner by William Wegman at center stage.

JEFFREY'S AT THE WATERGATE

Map pp246-8 *Tex-Mex*
☎ 202-298-4455; 2650 Virginia Ave, Swissôtel, the Watergate; dinner from $50; Metro: Foggy Bottom

Rumored to be a favorite of President and Mrs Bush, Jeffrey's delivers contemporary Texas cuisine with a spectacular view of the Potomac River. The menu features the culinary specialties of Chef David Garrido: favorites like crispy Texas Gulf Coast oysters, yucca root chips with habanero honey aioli, and Texas beef tenderloin with Roquefort mashed potatoes and caramelized onions. This is a top spot for pre- or post-theater dining.

KAZ SUSHI BISTRO

Map pp246-8 *Japanese*
☎ 202-530-5500; 1915 I St NW; lunch specials $10, meals $16-24; ☺ lunch & dinner Mon-Fri, dinner Sat; Metro: Farragut West

Fusing East and West, chef Kaz Okochi presents his own invention, 'free-style Japanese cuisine.' The sushi on its own is fresh and flavorful and good enough. Many clever combinations, however, add a certain je ne sais quoi to the traditional tastes.

KINKEADS Map pp246-8 *Seafood*
☎ 202-296-7700; 2000 Pennsylvania Ave NW; meals $50; Metro: Foggy Bottom-GWU

The seafood here arrives so fresh you can taste the sea, and it is always artfully combined with inventive spices and sauces. Acclaimed chef Robert Kinkead's imaginative specialties include pepita-crusted salmon, roasted cod with crab imperial, or – as an appetizer – tuna carpaccio. Even if you can't stay for dinner, a half-dozen oysters and a stiff whiskey here are the antidote to your midwinter blues.

LE TARBOUCHE

Map pp246-8 *Mediterranean*
☎ 202-331-5551; 1801 K St NW; meze $5-11, mains $20-30; ☺ lunch & dinner Mon-Fri, dinner Sat; Metro: Farragut West

With its lovely, rich decor of saffron-colored walls accented by ultramarine glassware, Le Tarbouche – meaning 'fez' – serves refined Lebanese-French cuisine with inovative spice and ingredient combinations. Candlelight and lots of nooks and crannies make this a prime spot for romancing. The internationals come out late on Saturday nights to dance to worldbeat Latin and Middle Eastern music.

MARCEL'S Map pp246-8 *French*
☎ 202-296-1166; 2401 Pennsylvania Ave NW; mains $28-40; ☺ dinner; Metro: Foggy Bottom

Located on the edge of Georgetown and the West End, this gem offers French fare with Flemish flair. That translates into fresh fish, farm-raised produce and high-quality ingredients whipped up into dishes like roasted rack of lamb with polenta and goat cheese garlic confit, or pan-seared salmon dusted in coriander and fennel seeds in citrus sauce. One classy touch: Marcel's offers complimentary limousine service to the Kennedy Center and a prix-fixe menu ($48), so this is an ideal spot for pre-theater dining.

TEATRO GOLDONI

Map pp246-8 *Italian*
☎ 202-955-9494; 1909 K St NW; prix-fixe bar lunch $12.50, dinner from $50; ☺ lunch & dinner Mon-Fri, dinner Sat; Metro: Farragut West

A wall decked with harlequin masks and diamond-shaped stained glass creates a festive theatrical decor. Funky lamps, bright blue glassware and tall taste-able centerpieces (elegant vases holding long, slender breadsticks instead of flowers) add to the fun. The cuisine is Venetian: don't pass up the lobster risotto. If you have to wait for a table, check out the incredible vodka selection: 35 at last count, including melon, chocolate and berry flavors.

Cheap Eats

BREADLINE Map pp246-8 *Bakery/Deli*
☎ 202-822-8900; 1751 Pennsylvania Ave NW; sandwiches from $6; ☺ 7am-5pm Mon-Fri; Metro: Farragut West

'Food is ammunition – don't waste it!' commands a WWII-era poster on the wall of this polished bakery and sandwich shop. Chef and local food celebrity Mark Furstenberg uses his ammunition to create fresh and filling sandwiches and to-die-for sweet treats. See the boxed text 'State of the Kitchen' (p14).

TEAISM Map pp120 — Teahouse
☎ 835-2233; 800 Connecticut Ave NW; lunch from $8; ⏰ 7am-5pm Mon-Fri; Metro: Farragut West

This teahouse is unique in the area for its very affordable lunch options – hot noodle dishes and fresh bento-boxes – and its pleasantly relaxing atmosphere. There is also a branch downtown (p120), as well as one located near Dupont Circle.

CAPITOL HILL & SOUTHEAST DC

Capitol Hill offers a mixed bag of dining options: old-boy, cigars-and-gin steakhouses where senators conspire; free-chips-and-cheap-booze eateries where their underpaid staffers drown their sorrows; and the friendliest open-air farmers market in town.

2 QUAIL Map pp250-1 — Continental
☎ 202-543-8030; 320 Massachusetts Ave; meals $40; Metro: Union Station

This place – frilly, romantic and cluttered with chintz and velvet – makes all the romantic-dining shortlists. The food seems to take a back seat to the fancy decor, but nobody is complaining about the fine mains, like roasted duck, seafood pasta or the signature quail.

AMERICA Map pp250-1 — American
☎ 202-682-9555; 50 Massachusetts Ave, Union Station; mains $12-20; Metro: Union Station

Claiming to be DC's 'only 50-star restaurant,' this place takes the theme as far as it goes, with menus shaped like maps and mains from every state in the Union (from New York steak to grilled mahimahi and don't forget Boston cream pie for dessert). The varied menu draws Hill-rats during the week and tourists on weekends.

B SMITH'S Map pp250-1 — Southern
☎ 202-289-6188; 50 Massachusetts Ave, Union Station; mains $16-30; Metro: Union Station

With its spectacular vaulted ceilings, marble floors and Ionic columns, Union Station's former Presidential Waiting Hall is worth a visit for the setting alone. It is a remarkable contrast to the down-home Southern fare that's served here by former model Barbara

Smith (whose unclouded complexion once graced Oil of Olay ads). Which is not to say the food is not delicious: it is. She upgrades Southern classics like fried chicken and blackened shrimp to sophisticated oeuvres (eg jumbo blackened shrimp served over crisp mesclun greens with a tangy soy-lime vinaigrette).

BANANA CAFÉ & PIANO BAR
Map pp250-1 — Caribbean
☎ 202-543-5906; 500 8th St SE; lunch from $10, dinner from $16; Metro: Eastern Market

Amid all the activity on 8th St SE, this funky, colorful cafe mixes it up with traditional Cuban and Puerto Rican dishes and a few Tex-Mex favorites thrown in for good measure. The house specialty 'Cuban' is a Dagwood sandwich with Caribbean flair – juicy roast pork, honey-baked ham and Swiss cheese with all the fixin's. Veggies will love the sweet plaintain timbales stuffed with *picadillo* (pepper and potato hash) and topped with sharp cheddar cheese. On Tuesday to Saturday nights, jazz filters down from the fun piano bar upstairs (p150).

BISTRO BIS Map pp250-1 — French
☎ 202-661-2700; 15 E St NW; mains $20-30; Metro: Union Station

La favorite among DC's beautiful people, this chic bistro inside the **Hotel George** (p195) features nouveau versions of French classics: succulent duck confit with garlic and thyme; seared sea scallops served with roasted eggplant; steak frite with tarragon hollandaise (but with the mandatory *pommes frites*).

IL RADICCHIO & BAROLO
Map pp250-1 — Italian
☎ 202-547-5114, 547-5011; 223 Pennsylvania Ave SE; meals $16 at Il Radicchio, $40 at Barolo; ⏰ lunch & dinner Mon-Sat, dinner Sun; Metro: Eastern Market

Choose your pasta from column A on the menu, choose your sauce from column B, then chow down. It's a simple concept and if you are hungry, you can't go wrong at inexpensive Il Radicchio.

Go upstairs to go upscale at Barolo, where the menu focuses on excellent Piedmontese dishes and Italian wine. This is another place where you are just as likely to spot lobbyists wooing politicians as young Casanovas wooing their dates.

MONOCLE Map pp250-1 *American*
☎ 202-546-4488; 107 D St NE; mains from $20; 🕐 lunch & dinner Mon-Fri; Metro: Union Station
The best place to spot your senator off-duty and glass-in-hand is this good ol' boys' club just behind the Capitol. Besides the clientele, the atmosphere is aided by the dark bar and the walls festooned with politicians' quotes ('If you want a friend in Washington, get a dog'). The food – surf-and-turf American classics like salmon and rib-eye steak – is less interesting than the people-watching.

MONTMARTRE Map pp250-1 *French*
☎ 202-544-1244; 327 7th St SE; meals $40; Metro: Eastern Market
You may mistake Capitol Hill for Paris if you dine on the patio at this charming spot. Apparently the building used to be a post office, but you wouldn't know it now for its pretty dining room and clean-lined bar. Culinary masterpieces include delicious chilled soups in summer, fresh fish seared to perfection and tender, juicy steaks.

TUNNICLIFF'S TAVERN
Map pp250-1 *American*
☎ 202-546-3663; 222 7th St SE; mains $12-20; Metro: Eastern Market
The outdoor patio is often packed with locals enjoying long, drowsy outdoor lunches. Peek inside: it's almost the same, but the happy patrons are seated at the friendly bar. Regulars flock to this neighborhood bar to watch the game and to nosh on upscale pub grub.

WORLD CUISINE CATERING & CAFÉ
Map pp250-1 *American*
☎ 202-546-9433; 523 8th St SE; sandwiches from $6, mains from $9; Metro: Eastern Market
This is the kind of place that stands as proof of a neighborhood's revitalization: $3 coffees; sandwiches with toppings like roasted eggplant and peppers and cilantro pesto; and quiche by the slice. The changing daily menu also includes tried-and-true lunchtime favorites, like chicken salad and ham and cheddar sandwiches.

Cheap Eats
EASTERN MARKET
Map pp250-1 *Self-catering*
www.easternmarket.net; 7th St & North Carolina Ave SE; 🕐 10am-6pm Tue-Fri, 8am-4pm Sat & Sun; Metro: Eastern Market

Fresh meats and cheese, colorful produce and sweet-smelling baked goods fill the cases at Eastern Market. Particularly lively on weekends, it's a treat anytime to buy fresh ingredients straight from their source. See also Neighborhoods (p64).

JIMMY T'S Map pp250-1 *American*
☎ 202-546-3646; 501 E Capitol St; breakfast & lunch from $6; 🕐 7am-3pm Tue-Sun; Metro: Eastern Market
The ultimate in neighborhood joints, this tiny corner diner is jammed on weekends with locals swilling coffee and reading the *Post* at the little counter and in the scuffed-up booths. Breakfast is served all day along with short-order sandwiches and burgers.

MARKET LUNCH
Map pp250-1 *Seafood*
☎ 202-546-2698; 225 7th St SE; lunch $8; 🕐 8am-3pm Tue-Sat, 11am-3pm Sun; Metro: Eastern Market
Inside historic Eastern Market alongside the butchers and bakers and candlestick makers, this unassuming carry-out counter serves some of DC's freshest, tastiest seafood. Crab-cake platters, soft-shell crabs and fried oyster sandwiches don't get much better than this. Saturday and Sunday morning brunch features equally delicious, butter-and-syrup-soaked pancakes (blueberry, buckwheat or bluebucks). Beware: the tough-looking dames behind the counter are reminiscent of *Seinfeld*'s 'Soup Nazi.' Have your orders ready when you reach the front of the line.

BROOKLAND & NORTHEAST DC
The northeast quadrant still does not have too many eating options, but if you are in the neighborhood exploring Catholic University and checking out the Basilica, you will have no trouble sating your appetite at one of these friendly choices.

COLONEL BROOKS' TAVERN & ISLAND JIM'S CRAB SHACK
Map pp252-3 *Southern/Seafood*
☎ 202-529-4002; 901 Monroe St NE; mains $8-12; Metro: Brookland-CU
This friendly bar fills with regulars at lunchtime and happy hour. In the wood-paneled dining room, it serves pub grub and Southern fare. Live jazz bands play in the

evenings. If you are feeling tropical, head to the tiki bar next door. Romp in a palm tree–shaded sandpit or sip umbrella drinks on the outdoor deck. Try the 'Kick Ass Margarita – hot and spicy, cold and icy.' Boogie down to live music on Wednesday evenings. Life is good, mon.

KELLY'S ELLIS ISLAND

Map pp252-3   *American*

☎ 202-832-6117; 3908 12th St NE; sandwiches & salads from $7, mains $12-18; Metro: Brookland-CU

This raucous bar serves up an eclectic array of food in attempt to cater to everybody on Ellis Island: burgers, barbecue, pasta and steaks. This place is a neighborhood favorite for drinking as well as eating.

SOUTHWEST DC

Dining in the Southwest quadrant can be summed up in one word: seafood. Whether seasoned with hot peppers or fruity flavors or nothing at all, it was not too long ago that your dinner was swimming around in the ocean somewhere. This area's lovely views of the Potomac – especially superb at sunset – are a welcome feature of this otherwise drab setting.

CANTINA MARINA

Map pp254-5   *Tex-Mex*

☎ 202-554-8396; 600 Water St SW; meals $20; Metro: Waterfront

This Tex-Mex joint is the exception that proves the seafood rule in Southwest (although you can't go wrong with the BBQ shrimp). Menu highlights are the beef and black bean tostadas and potent margaritas. Outdoor seating in the midst of the marina and live music on weekends makes for an extremely festive atmosphere – the best in the neighborhood.

ZANZIBAR

Map pp254-5   *Afro-Caribbean*

☎ 202-554-9100; 700 Water St SW; mains $16-24; ☽ lunch & dinner Tue-Sun; Metro: Waterfront

Seafood here has a Afro-Caribbean twist: spicy sauces, fruit garnishes and rum drinks characterize the creative menu. The bold, colorful decor complements the African theme. Upstairs there is a large dance floor, often frequented by very elegant-looking African American couples. See Entertainment (p162).

Cheap Eats
FISH WHARF

Map pp254-5   *Seafood*

Waterfront, Washington Channel; meals from $6; ☽ 7:30am-8:30pm Sun-Thu, to 9:30pm Jun-Aug, 7:30am-9pm Fri-Sat, to 10pm Jun-Aug; Metro: L'Enfant Plaza

Just south of the I-395 bridge, barges and stalls sell seafood so fresh that some of it is still moving. Stalls are packed with huge barrels of blue crabs and silver fish. With all the tentacles, smells and flying shells, it's a sensory spectacle even if you're not hungry. The fishmongers will cook for you too: softshell crab sandwiches, oysters on the half-shell and crab cakes are the specialties. Alas, there are no tables, so take your meal south along the channelside walkway where there is bench seating.

GEORGETOWN

Over one hundred eateries line M St and Wisconsin Ave and the surrounding blocks. From fancy French to Viet *pho*, from pub grub to fine wine, Georgetown will feed just about any hungry body.

1789 Map pp256-7   *American*

☎ 202-965-1789; 1226 36th St; mains $19-30; ☽ dinner; Georgetown shuttle from Rosslyn or Foggy Bottom-GWU Metro

Set in a welcoming Federal row house, 1789 is well known to Georgetown students as *the* place to take your visiting parents (or rather, have them take you). Chef Ris Lacoste uses local, seasonal produce and game to create new twists on American classics, such as rabbit and sweetbreads and softshell crabs with corn pudding. You won't pass up dessert if you catch a glimpse of the pastry chefs working in the front window next door. Upstairs you will find the students' favorite drinking spot, **Tombs** (p151).

AU PIED DU COCHON

Map pp256-7   *French*

☎ 202-337-6400; 1335 Wisconsin Ave; mains from $12; ☽ 24hr; Georgetown shuttle from Rosslyn or Foggy Bottom-GWU Metro

Although the food is tasty any time of day, this French bistro is a hotspot for late-night dining, when bar-hoppers form a line to feast on crispy *frites* and eggs Benedict. Thirteen beers are on tap and waitstaff are extremely French.

Top Five Places to See and Be Seen in Georgetown

Ever-trendy Georgetown has long been a favorite place for fashionable internationals, stylish students and other beautiful people to scope each other out. If you want to see who's who, don your shades and check out one of these popular spots.

- **Café Milano** (p126) Prime people-watching with a European flair.
- **Degrees Bar & Lounge** (p151) Industrial renovation at its best: an old incinerator converted into a happening bar.
- **Mie N Yu** (p127) Hotter than the Gobi – and that goes for popularity and patrons.
- **Sequoia** (p127) Fabulous views and a great place to spot the singles.
- **Tombs** (p151) Scope out the Georgetown students scoping each other out.

BISTROT LEPIC   Map pp256-7   *French*
☎ 202-333-0111; 1736 Wisconsin Ave NW; lunch from $20, dinner from $30; ☾ lunch & dinner Tue-Sun; Georgetown shuttle from Foggy Bottom-GWU Metro

Named for the street in Paris where chef/owner Bruno Fortin used to live, this cozy neighborhood bistro is now known throughout the city for its seafood (irresistible sautéed sea scallops) and meats (house specialty braised veal cheeks). The comfortable wine bar upstairs is a recent addition, featuring French wines and 'appeteasers.'

CAFÉ LA RUCHE   Map pp256-7   *French*
☎ 202-965-2684; 1039 31st St; mains from $10, brunch $12; ☾ lunch & dinner, brunch 9am-2:30pm Sat & Sun; Georgetown shuttle from Rosslyn or Foggy Bottom-GWU Metro

Set on a quiet lane away from the crowds and near the canal, La Ruche bills itself as Georgetown's oldest French bistro. This quintessential cafe has a dining room packed with tiled tables and a garden draped in vines. The menu is straightforward, featuring classic items like steamy, spicy, garlic *moules* (mussels) or fresh, tangy salad Niçoise. On weekends, come for brunch and a complimentary mimosa.

CAFÉ MILANO   Map pp256-7   *Italian*
☎ 202-333-6183; 3251 Prospect St; mains $18-24; ☾ 11:30am-midnight Sun-Wed, 11:30am-2am Thu-Sat; Georgetown shuttle from Rosslyn or Foggy Bottom-GWU Metro

Italian food like you find in Italy – not to mention the sidewalk café – draws followers of both mode and mafia. This is a place to see and be seen in Georgetown. Service can be snooty, so if you want a table in the prime seating area, you'd best dress the part.

CITRONELLE   Map pp256-7   *French*
☎ 202-625-2150; 3000 M St NW; dinner from $100; ☾ dinner Sat & Sun; Georgetown shuttle from Rosslyn or Foggy Bottom-GWU Metro

Tucked away inside the **Latham Hotel** (p197), this elegant, bi-level restaurant is among DC's most acclaimed. Chef Michel Richard began his career as a pastry chef, so you can't go wrong with menu items such as shrimp wrapped in filo or, well, dessert. Reserve your table in advance and dress up for the occasion.

DEAN & DELUCA
Map pp256-7   *Café, Self-catering*
☎ 202-342-2500; 3276 M St; lunch $8, coffees $5; Georgetown shuttle from Rosslyn or Foggy Bottom-GWU Metro

The sunny café is enclosed in glass when weather demands it, but otherwise open-air. Sandwiches and snacks are served cafeteria style, but it is fresh and delicious.

The gourmet market is worth a visit just for the pleasure of wandering among the potent cheeses, juicy fruits, fresh-baked breads, smooth mousse spreads and spicy sausages (many of which are available to sample).

J PAUL'S   Map pp256-7   *American*
☎ 202-333-3450; 3218 M Street; mains from $20; ☾ 11:30-2am Mon-Thu, 11:30-3am Fri & Sat, 10:30-2am Sun; Georgetown shuttle from Rosslyn or Foggy Bottom-GWU Metro

Most people come to J Paul's for the aphrodisiac raw bar or for the affable beer bar: happy hour is definitely happy at this modern-day saloon. It's worth coming for dinner, though, especially if you order a house favorite like jumbo lump crab cakes.

MENDOCINO GRILLE & WINE BAR
Map pp256-7   *American*
☎ 202-333-2912; 2917 M St; lunch $20, dinner $35; ☾ lunch & dinner Mon-Sat, dinner Sun; Georgetown shuttle from Rosslyn or Foggy Bottom-GWU Metro

California meets Georgetown. From its extensive selection of West Coast wines to its use of organic ingredients and free-range birds, Mendocino is a happy answer to the demand for nouveau cuisine. With a welcoming window overlooking M Street and decor suggesting a West Coast winery, the popular restaurant also succeeds in capturing the laid-back California spirit. Reservations recommended.

MIE N YU

Map pp256-7 *Fusion*
☎ 202-333-6122; 3125 M St; mains from $25;
🕑 lunch & dinner Mon-Fri, dinner Sat & Sun; Georgetown shuttle from Rosslyn or Foggy Bottom-GWU Metro

The eclectic menu and exotic decor in this hot, new bar and restaurant evoke the Silk Road. Depending where you are seated, you might dine in a Bedouin camp or in the sultan's harem, but rest assured you will be surrounded by colorful pillows and waited on hand and foot. Don't leave without checking out the fancy, unisex toilet in the basement. Reservations recommended.

NEYLA Map pp256-7 *Mediterranean*
☎ 202-333-6353; 3206 N St; meze from $5, mains from $20; 🕑 dinner; Georgetown shuttle from Rosslyn or Foggy Bottom-GWU Metro

Meet Neyla, the Mediterranean spirit of prosperity, abundance and success. She has already blessed diners at this sleek but pricey Mediterranean grill. The menu reflects all the cultures of the Phoenician coast, from traditional Lebanese mezes to French-inspired grilled meats to Turkish coffees and pastries. Reservations recommended on weekends.

PAOLO'S Map pp256-7 *Italian*
☎ 202-333-7353; 1303 Wisconsin Ave; mains from $12; Georgetown shuttle from Rosslyn or Foggy Bottom-GWU Metro

This upscale Italian bistro is famous for its wine collection, but its pizzas, grilled meats and pastas offer excellent fare to complement it. Brick-oven baking, an outdoor patio and big street-side windows draw in both Georgetown residents and the international set.

PEACOCK CAFÉ

Map pp256-7 *Mediterranean*
☎ 202-625-2740; 3203 Prospect St NW; sandwiches, salads from $6, mains from $12; 🕑 9am-2pm Sat & Sun; Georgetown shuttle from Rosslyn or Foggy Bottom-GWU Metro

The Peacock was born 12 years ago as a tiny juice and sandwich bar. Since then chef Maziar Farivar has expanded his menu to include delectable soups, salads, pastas and meat

dishes. Preparation techniques are simple, but the ingredients are fresh and the results rewarding. Regulars return for the outdoor seating and the friendly staff who encourage guests to linger.

Mie N Yu (left)

SEQUOIA Map pp256-7 *American*
☎ 202-944-4200; Georgetown Harbor, 3000 K St; mains $18-24; 🕑 11:30-midnight Mon-Thu, 11:30-1am Fri & Sat, 10:30-midnight Sun; Georgetown shuttle from Foggy Bottom-GWU

The reasons to come to Sequoia extend beyond the decent but not particularly inspired menu. In a prime location on Georgetown Harbor, the highlight of this steak and seafood joint is really great views, of sunsets over the Potomac River and of singles on the DC scene.

VIETNAM GEORGETOWN

Map pp256-7 *Vietnamese*
☎ 202-337-5588; 2928 M St NW; lunch buffet $6.45, dinner mains from $12; Georgetown shuttle from Rosslyn or Foggy Bottom-GWU Metro

Come here for steaming bowls of noodles and deep-fried crispy rolls: spicy and satisfying. The lunch buffet is particularly good value. The staff and setting are charming, if somewhat frazzled. The garden out back is decked with colorful lights and is especially attractive on a summer evening. (Minus the garden, this place is nearly interchangeable with its next-door neighbor, the Saigon Inn.)

Cheap Eats

You'll find the cheapest options at the Georgetown Park food court, on the lower level of the mall at M St and Wisconsin Ave.

BOOEYMONGER

Map pp256-7   *Sandwiches*
☎ 202-333-4810; 3265 Prospect St NW; sandwiches from $4; ⏰ 8am-10pm; Georgetown shuttle from Rosslyn or Foggy Bottom-GWU Metro
Create your own sandwich or choose one from the big board. Ingredients are fresh and service is quick, which explains why this local institution is often packed at lunchtime.

MOBY DICK HOUSE OF KABOB

Map pp256-7   *Middle Eastern*
☎ 202-333-4400; 1070 31st St; sandwiches from $4, platters from $6; ⏰ 11am-10pm Sun-Thu, 11am-4am Fri & Sat; Georgetown shuttle from Rosslyn or Foggy Bottom-GWU Metro
Why it's called Moby Dick is a mystery, but this is another hole-in-the wall joint serving tasty Persian food into the wee hours. The highlight is the pita bread, fresh and warm from the clay oven. Daily lunch specials are $6.25.

DUPONT CIRCLE & KALORAMA

Dupont Circle demonstrates the best of DC's dining scene. Classy nouveau cuisine and upscale ethnic eateries cater to the flocks of diplomats and businesspeople, and casual cafés cater to the more bohemian.

ADDIS ABABA Map pp258-60 *Ethiopian*
☎ 202-232-6092; 2106 18th St NW; meals from $12; Metro: Woodley Park-Zoo/Adams Morgan
Come to this nondescript-looking restaurant for the real-deal Ethiopian eats, not for any exotic decor. Ambience is provided by the East African expats watching news from home and chowing down on *injera* (pancake-like bread) and *wat* (a mélange of simmered vegetables or meat in sauce) and with much more style than most of us can manage while eating with our hands.

AFTERWORDS CAFÉ & KRAMERBOOKS Map pp258-60 *American*
☎ 202-387-1462; 1517 Connecticut Ave; mains from $12; ⏰ 8:30am-1:30am Sun-Thu, 24hr Fri & Sat; Metro: Dupont Circle
Some locals would claim this independent bookstore with café attached is the center of the DC universe. The café changes its moods throughout the day: in the morning, people schmooze over lazy cups of coffee and muffins; in the afternoon and early evening, readers dally over newspapers and new-bought novels; at night, it's a bar scene with live music. The food is good, if slightly overpriced. But the real treat here is to see and be seen.

Top Five Late-Night Dining Spots

It's not New York, but DC is good for late-night dining if you know where to go.
- **Afterwords Café** (p128) Coffee, books and café fare all night long (how very Dupont).
- **Annie's Paramount Steakhouse** (p128) One of DC's hottest gay spots after 3am.
- **Au Pied du Cochon** (p125) Late-night like they do it in Paris.
- **Diner** (p133) Classic post-clubbing cuisine at any hour.
- **Pizza Mart** (p133) Grab a jumbo slice to go.

ANNIE'S PARAMOUNT STEAKHOUSE
Map pp258-60   *Steakhouse*
☎ 202-32-0395; 1609 17th St NW; meals $16-30; ⏰ 11:30am-11:30pm Mon-Thu, 24hr Fri-Sun; Metro: Dupont Circle
This neighborhood steakhouse attracts a predominately gay clientele, which says more about its location than anything else. After hours on weekends the place is at its best, hopping with clubbers grabbing a burger or breakfast on their way home. Waitstaff are friendly making this one of the best places to meet and greet the gay community.

ASIA NORA Map pp258-60 *Asian*
☎ 202-797-4860; 2213 M St NW; mains from $24; ⏰ dinner Mon-Sat; Metro: Foggy Bottom-GWU
At this younger sister of Nora, organic, seasonal seafood is given an Asian twist. The setting is beautiful, with dark-green walls and handmade furnishings. Critics complain that portions are small for the price. But what this place lacks in value, it makes up for in taste and style.

BISTROT DU COIN

Map pp258-60   *French*

☎ 202-234-6969; 1738 Connecticut Ave; meals from $15; Metro: Dupont Circle

Ou est Phillipe? At this happening bistro, no doubt. This raucous room looks like the real thing, the waiters gargle their Rs and the food on the plate smells and tastes just as it should. The dishes are heavy on rich sauces, with perfect *frites* and greens on the side.

CITY LIGHTS OF CHINA

Map pp258-60   *Chinese*

☎ 202-265-6688; 1731 Connecticut Ave; meals from $15; Metro: Dupont Circle

It's not much to look at, but City Lights is consistently named among the top Chinese restaurants in DC. The house specialty is Peking duck, but all the old favorites are here. For the more health conscious, the menu now offers some of the old favorites, like General Tsao's chicken, with sautéed white meat instead of deep-fried batter and served with steamed broccoli and brown rice.

COPPI'S PIZZA Map pp258-60   *Italian*

☎ 202-319-7773; 1414 U St NW; meals $20-24; ⏰ dinner; Metro: U Street-Cardozo

One of the pioneers in the rebirth of U St, this bicycle-themed pizza parlor serves wood-fired pizzas and calzones made with a range of top-quality ingredients, some traditional and some less so. Brace yourself for the noise and the wait if it's crowded.

DUPONT GRILLE

Map pp258-60   *New American*

☎ 202-939-9596; Jury's Hotel Dupont, 1500 New Hampshire Ave NW; meals from $30; Metro: Dupont Circle

The glassed-in dining room and sidewalk seating are perfect places to sit and observe Dupont's bustle, sampling chef Cornell Coulon's innovative dishes, prepared with hints of New Orleans, Italy and Asia. Seasonal produce, fresh meats and seafood, and complementing wines make for a delectable dining experience.

FIREFLY Map pp258-60   *New American*

☎ 202-861-1310; 1310 New Hampshire Ave NW; dinner $50; ⏰ 8am-10pm; Metro: Dupont Circle

This happening bistro boasts that it is 'lighting up the neighborhood,' and it does draw consistent crowds. They are coming to taste the creations of chef John Wabeck, who's known from his days at Nora for his use of fresh, sea-

sonal ingredients. Low lights and earth tones lend an intimate atmosphere indoors, while the sunny terrace is also pleasant.

GALILEO Map pp258-60   *Italian*

☎ 202-293-7191; 1110 21st St NW; meals $50; ⏰ lunch & dinner Mon-Fri, dinner Sat & Sun; Metro: Foggy Bottom-GWU

Owned by DC's Italian-cuisine wonder kid, Roberto Donna, Galileo tops many DC foodie lists for its wonderful pastas, risottos and grilled meats. For extra special occasions, book the Laboratorio, where 10 to 12 guests dine in a private space and observe the preparation of their custom meal.

GRILLFISH Map pp258-60   *Seafood*

☎ 202-331-7310; 1200 New Hampshire Ave NW; meals $30; Metro: Farragut North

The fresh fish straight from the grill is simple but divine. The funky decor – featuring a huge, colorful mural behind the bar – is not so straightforward, but fun nonetheless. It draws a boisterous, young crowd most nights a week.

JOHNNY'S HALF SHELL

Map pp258-60   *Seafood*

☎ 296-2021; 2002 P St NW; mains $12-20; Metro: Dupont Circle

Johnny's is the place to come for local specialties: Maryland crab cakes; fried oyster po'boys; and sautéed soft-shell crabs. The barbecued shrimp with *asiago* cheese grits are 'better than my mother's,' according to one Southern patron. The friendly bar also boasts strong drinks, but don't come here without sampling the seafood.

LAURIOL PLAZA Map pp258-60   *Tex-Mex*

☎ 202-387-0035; 1835 18th St NW; lunch specials $7, dinner from $10; Metro: Dupont Circle

This lively spot is popular for its pitchers of margaritas, its huge rooftop terrace and its gentrified Tex-Mex dishes. Grilled marinated quail and pork roasted in Seville's bitter oranges are among the fancier items on the menu. But never fear, there are enchiladas and fajitas here too.

LOCAL 16 Map pp258-60   *New American*

☎ 202-265-2828; 1602 U St NW; dinner from $30; ⏰ dinner daily, to 2am Fri & Sat; Metro: U Street-Cardozo or Dupont Circle

Ruby-colored walls, clean lines and jazz music strike the mood at this trendy restaurant-lounge.

Mains such as balsamic filet mignon and pan-seared salmon fulfill mouthwatering expectations. The lounge upstairs and the roof deck further up promise to be the hottest spots on the block for a drink.

MARVELOUS MARKET

Map pp258-60   *Self-catering*
☎ 202-332-3690; 1511 Connecticut Ave; ⏰ 8am-9pm; bus D2 from Dupont Circle

Besides fresh produce and grocery-store items, this chain also carries sandwiches, pizzas and coffees. There are branches near the White House (p121) and downtown (p119).

MIMI'S

Map pp258-60   *American & Middle Eastern*
☎ 202-464-6464; 2120 P St NW; lunch $20, dinner $30; Metro: Dupont Circle

It calls itself an 'American bistro' but the menu and decor argue otherwise: walls are elegantly draped with Persian rugs; an appetizer for sharing, called the 'Peace Meal,' features hummus and *baba ganouj* (eggplant dip); and the last Sunday of the month Mimi's hosts an Arab–Jewish dialogue for anyone that wishes to participate. The novelty at Mimi's, however, is the waitstaff, who are all starving musicians. They occasionally break from waiting tables to sing opera or play jazz piano.

NORA

Map pp258-60   *New American*
☎ 202-462-5143; 2132 Florida Ave; mains from $25, tasting menu $64; ⏰ dinner; Metro: Dupont Circle

Nora is the queen of the Washington food scene. She has made her reputation serving food from local farmers and ranchers, usually organic and always fresh, and combining ingredients in innovative ways. All this happens in a quaint carriage house on one of Dupont's loveliest corners.

OBELISK & PIZZA PARADISO

Map pp258-60   *Italian*
☎ 202-223-1245; 2029 P St NW; mains from $12 at Pizza Paradiso, prix-fixe $50 at Obelisk; Metro: Dupont Circle

You can spend a boatload for an amazing prix-fixe Italian meal from Peter Pastan at Obelisk, or you go next door and spend a whole lot less for one of his deceptively simple pizzas or perfect panini. Crispy, thin-crust pizzas are cooked in a wood-burning stove and topped with your choice of the freshest toppings.   ·

PALM

Map pp258-60   *American*
☎ 202-293-9091; 1225 19th St NW; mains from $20, steaks from $30; ⏰ lunch & dinner Mon-Fri, dinner Sat & Sun; Metro: Dupont Circle

Fun for people-watching as well as meat-eating, this classic American steakhouse is a media and political celebrity magnet (Larry King likes to hang out here). Everyone's lunch seems to consist of sirloin, straight-gin martinis and cigar smoke. Its waitstaff are renowned for giving their customers a hard time.

PESCE

Map pp258-60   *Seafood*
☎ 202-466-3474; 2016 P St NW; dinner $40; Metro: Dupont Circle

The colorful fish decor gives away the menu, which features all things with fins – bluefish, salmon, grouper – all perfectly fresh and simply prepared. The dishes at this crowded café have a Mediterranean twist: seafood pastas, Provençal fish soup, grilled sardines and scallop ceviche are among the specialties.

RAKU

Map pp258-60   *Asian*
☎ 202-265-7258; 1900 Q St; tapas from $4, mains from $9; ⏰ lunch & dinner Tue-Sun; Metro: Dupont Circle

If you are wondering what tapas are doing on an Asian menu, look again. These 'Pan-Asian tapas' are treats like mussels sautéed in a ginger-black bean sauce, or shrimp and crab dumplings in a Thai chile sauce. The menu also offers a selection of sushi, salads, noodles and other mains. The Asian fusion concept extends to the drinks, too. How about a green tea martini?

SESTO SENSO

Map pp258-60   *Italian*
☎ 202-785-9525; 1214 18th St NW; meals from $20; ⏰ lunch & dinner, plus 11pm-2am Fri & Sat dancing; Metro: Dupont Circle

Early in the evening, this restaurant is ideal for a business lunch or a romantic dinner. The Northern Italian menu is authentic and affordable, featuring delicious, lightly fried calamari, fresh vegetarian pastas and thin, crispy pizzas. After hours, the Euros show up in all their finery to dance the night away.

TABARD INN

Map pp258-60   *New American*
☎ 202-331-8528; 1739 N St NW; mains around $20; Metro: Dupont Circle

This delightful oasis consists of a warm, dark bar inside or a sun-dappled, walled garden outside. Eclectic mains include fish stew, pastas and chops for dinner, which you might enjoy on a rainy night next to the roaring fire in the lounge. Or come for beignets with vanilla whipped cream or chocolate-almond pancakes for brunch in the garden. Life is sweet.

THAIPHOON Map pp258-60 *Thai*
☎ 202-667-3505; 2011 S St NW; lunch mains from $6, dinner from $10; Metro: Dupont Circle

The quality of the food does not always match the sleek decor, which features a wall of windows, a colorful interior and a funky bar. But Thaiphoon's seafood and veggie dishes are good enough to draw crowds, giving the place a buzz to match the tingle of Thai spices.

UNI Map pp258-60 *Sushi*
☎ 202-833-8038; 2122 P St NW; meals $20; ✿ lunch & dinner Mon-Sat, dinner Sun; Metro: Dupont Circle

This modern sushi bar – decorated in subdued green hues and trimmed in metal and wood – looks down on P St from its 2nd-floor perch. Jazz plays from the speakers and diners feast on sushi and innovative 'small dishes.' Monday through Friday, enjoy Sake-tini happy hour, featuring $1 sushi and $3.50 sake martinis.

WAZURI Map pp258-60 *Afro-Caribbean*
☎ 202-797-4930; 1836 18th St NW; meals $30; ✿ lunch & dinner Tue-Sun; Metro: Dupont Circle

Unlike its Ethiopian counterparts, this bi-level restaurant features West African cuisine, with hints of the Caribbean and of Brazil. The art-decked walls and welcoming staff make for an inviting atmosphere. If the weather is fine, don't miss the opportunity to dine on the roofdeck.

Cheap Eats

CAKELOVE Map pp258-60 *Desserts*
☎ 202-588-7100; 1506 U St NW; desserts $2-10; ✿ 8am-8pm Mon-Fri, 10am-6pm Sat, 11am-5pm Sun; Metro: U Street-Cardozo

Warren Brown loved making cakes so much he left his job as an attorney and opened this shop, and DC loves him for it. Come for cake, love or any number of delectable desserts. A new café across the street has seating and sandwiches. See 'For the Love of Cakes' (p13).

JAVA HOUSE Map pp258-60 *Café*
☎ 202-387-6622; 1645 Q St NW; coffee & drinks from $3; ✿ 7am-11pm Sun-Thu, 7am-midnight Fri & Sat; Metro: Dupont Circle

Delicious coffees, all-day breakfast and sidewalk seating draw the local boys to this otherwise nondescript spot. One coffee lets you sit all day...so bring a book, sip your cappuccino and watch the world go by.

LUNA CAFÉ & SKE[...]
Map pp258-60
☎ 202-387-4005; 1633 P [...] 11pm Mon-Thu, 8am-1am [...] 11pm Sun; Metro: Dupont [...]

You can't beat this [...] fast any time of day, [...] Wednesday and Sun [...] same owners, differ[...] Eastern fare, like meat kabobs and falafels, are fresh and tasty.

WELL DRESSED BURRITO
Map pp258-60 *Tex-Mex*
☎ 202-293-0515; 1220 19th St NW (enter through the alley); lunch $8; ✿ 11:45am-2:15pm; Metro: Dupont Circle

Brought to you by CF Folks, across the street, this hidden gem is arguably the best Tex-Mex in the neighborhood. The gigantic 16oz El Gordo burrito – stuffed with marinated beef, chicken or vegetables, plus beans and cheese – receives rave reviews.

ZORBA'S CAFÉ Map pp258-60 *Greek*
☎ 202-387-8555; 1612 20th St NW; sandwiches from $5, mains from $8, pizza from $10; Metro: Dupont Circle

Generous portions of moussaka and souvlaki, as well as pitchers of Rolling Rock, make this Greek diner a popular spot. Contrary to the menu's promise, you will probably not confuse yourself for being in the Greek Isles (despite the bouzouki music). But the fresh food and quick service make this family-run place a good option.

Top Five Roof Decks in Dupont Circle & Adams-Morgan

You'll be on top of the world when you stop for a drink or a bite at one of the many rooftop venues in Adams-Morgan and Dupont Circle. Here's our pick for the top of the top spots.

- **Lauriol Plaza** (p129) Tangy margaritas and sweet sangria, al fresco.
- **Local 16** (p129) Beautiful views and beautiful people.
- **Perry's** (p132) Possibly the longest-running hot spot in Adams-Morgan, because views like this never go out of style.
- **Reef** (p153) Belgian beers and organic eats under the stars.
- **Wazuri** (p131) When it's as hot as Africa, why not add some red pepper and a juju beat?

ORGAN

...rgan is Washington's interna-
...norgasbord. Here you can dine
e *goreng* (Indian noodle dish), shish
...bs, *yebeg alicha* (Ethiopian lamb stew),
...alzones, jerk chicken, ceviche, *pupusas*
(Salvadoran meat-stuffed pastry) and, of
course, Happy Meals.

ANZU Map p261 *Mediterranean*
☎ 202-462-8844; 2436 18th St NW; pizzas from $8,
tapas from $5; 🕐 dinner daily, brunch Sat & Sun;
Metro: Woodley Park-Zoo/Adams Morgan

This sophisticated new wine bar features
modern European fare: thin-crust pizzas,
homemade raviolis, seared seafood and seasonal veggie tapas. Order several items and
pass them around the table.

CASHION'S EAT PLACE
Map p261 *New American*
☎ 202-797-1819; 1819 Columbia Rd NW; mains $18-
24; 🕐 dinner Tue-Sun, brunch Sun; Metro: Woodley
Park-Zoo/Adams Morgan

Restaurateur and chef Ann Cashion is somewhat of a local celebrity for the original menu
and inviting decor she has invented at this
little bistro. Cashion's serves food that can be
light and rich at the same time (or just rich
and rich, as in duck breast served with foie
gras). The mismatched furniture and flower
boxes create an unpretentious setting to
enjoy her work.

FELIX Map p261 *New American*
☎ 202-483-3549; 2406 18th St NW; mains $18-24;
Metro: Woodley Park-Zoo/Adams Morgan

Urban but elegant, this steel-and-glass restaurant has a varied, eclectic menu. You might
feast on duck confit, while your companion
dines on brisket and matzoh-ball soup. Next
door, the mysteriously swanky Spy Lounge is
one of the hippest places to sip a martini and
wait for your table.

MANTIS Map p261 *Asian*
☎ 202-667-2400; 1847 Columbia Rd NW; tapas $5-8;
🕐 5:30pm-2am; Metro: Woodley Park-Zoo/Adams
Morgan

Chic Mantis offers a new take on Pan-Asian:
tapas ranging from classic beef satay to nouveau crab-stuffed wontons with chile dipping
sauce. Servings are small so you can sample a
bunch of them. Sit at the bar or lounge on the
cool, low couches.

MESKEREM Map p261 *Ethiopian*
☎ 202-462-4100; 2434 18th St NW; meals from $16;
🕐 noon-midnight Sun-Fri, noon-1am Sat; Metro:
Woodley Park-Zoo/Adams Morgan

To many folks, Adams-Morgan means just one
thing: Ethiopian food. You can eat it at several
restaurants, but the leading place is Meskerem,
named for the first month of the Ethiopian
calendar. This place goes for an exotic atmosphere, with traditional woven straw-basket
tables and camel-leather hassocks. Use your
hands to sample beef, poultry, lamb, seafood
and vegetarian dishes, which are served on
whole-wheat *injera*.

Felix (left)

PASTA MIA Map p261 *Italian*
☎ 202-328-9114; 1790 Columbia Rd NW; meals $20;
🕐 dinner Mon-Sat; Metro: Woodley Park-Zoo/Adams
Morgan

People line up on the sidewalk for generous
servings of 20-some kinds of pasta made the
way your mother does (if she is an Italian gour-
mand). The heaps of delicious pasta are worth
the long waits and brusque treatment, which
are all part of the experience.

PERRY'S Map p261 *Asian*
☎ 202-234-6218; 1811 Columbia Rd NW; meals $30;
Metro: Woodley Park-Zoo/Adams Morgan

You can do sushi at Perry's, but the creative fusion fare really deserves your tongue's attention.

The only problem is deciding whether to dine in the funky lounge or under the stars. For the very adventurous, the Sunday drag-queen brunch is a hoot. This place can be hard to spot because there's no real sign – the doorway canopy uses rebus symbols (like a pear) to spell out the name.

Cheap Eats

DINER Map p261   *American*
☎ 202-232-8800; 2453 18th St NW; breakfast from $5, sandwiches from $6; ⏰ 24hr; Metro: Woodley Park-Zoo/Adams Morgan

Late-night breakfast and satisfying comfort food hit the spot around the clock. Crowds of bar-hoppers agree, as they flock to this retro diner for refueling. Cartoons on the big screen are a nice touch.

MAMA AYESHA'S

Map p261   *Middle Eastern*
☎ 202-232-5431; 1967 Calvert St NW; meals $10; Metro: Woodley Park-Zoo/Adams Morgan

This neighborhood institution has changed little since it opened 50 years ago, neither prices nor decor. Mama's specializes in Syrian takes on hummus, kebabs and other Levantine classics.

PIZZA MART Map p261   *Italian*
☎ 202-234-9700; 2435 18th St; pizza from $4; ⏰ 11-3am Sun-Thu, 11-4am Fri & Sat; Metro: Woodley Park-Zoo/Adams Morgan

Any place that sells 'jumbo' slices (and we mean jumbo) until the wee hours in the middle of bar-hopping central is bound to be a hit; believe it or not, this pizza is actually pretty good, at least after enough beers.

UPPER NORTHWEST DC

Despite its distance from the city center, Upper Northwest DC has its fair share of excellent eateries. Most are clustered around the Metro stops in Cleveland Park, Tenleytown and Woodley Park, although several are in Glover Park, just north of Georgetown.

ARDEO'S Map pp262-3   *New American*
☎ 202-244-6750; 3311 Connecticut Ave NW; meals from $30; Metro: Cleveland Park

Prices at this slick joint are quite reasonable, considering the posh decor and the sophisticated menu. The latter features a few rich pastas, lots of fresh fish and juicy meat selections, plus a few salads and sandwiches.

Try a local specialty like succulent, pan-roasted rockfish, served with a ragout of prosciutto, sweet corn and plantains.

CACTUS CANTINA

Map pp262-3   *Tex-Mex*
☎ 202-686-7222; 3300 Wisconsin Ave; mains from $12; bus 30, 32, 34, 36 from Tenleytown-AU or Foggy Bottom-GWU Metro

This Mexican cantina is a perennial favorite, especially with kids, for its festive atmosphere, complete with Christmas lights and palm trees. Adults like it, too, for such top-notch treats as mesquite-grilled quail, juicy tamales and potent pitchers of margaritas.

Dinner on a Pancake

DC is among the world's best places – outside East Africa – to sample Ethiopian and Eritrean cuisine. Beginning in the early 1980s, East African immigrants began opening DC restaurants that showcased their spicy, inexpensive, fun-to-eat cuisine and they won an instant place in the hearts of hungry Washingtonians.

An Ethiopian meal consists of *injera* (spongy, pancake-like bread rounds made with *tef*, or buckwheat flour) and *wat* (a mélange of simmered vegetables or meat in sauce). *Wat* has two varieties: red, fiery *kay wat* and milder, yellowish *alicha wat*. It can include meat, like savory *doro wat* (chicken stew, often with a hard-boiled egg sitting in its center) and *sega wat* (lamb stew). Ethiopian cuisine is also beloved by vegetarians, who dig into vegetable *alicha wat*, *yemiser wat* (spicy lentil stew) and *fitfit* (tomato-and-chile salad).

A traditional meal is served to diners seated on low divans or hassocks. A cloth-covered wicker table *(mesab)* is placed among them. On top of the table is a large platter blanketed by a single round of *injera*; upon the *injera* are scoops of *wat*. To the side rests a platter heaped with folded *injera*. Diners take up an *injera*, tear off a piece with their fingers and use it to fold a bit of *wat* into their mouths. (Waitstaff sometimes proffer a copper basin in which to wash your hands before the meal, plus baby wipes to wipe down afterward.) Once the *wat* is gone, the bottom *injera* itself is eaten – there's something very satisfying about eating your 'tablecloth'! It all goes down well with *tej* (gentle, honey-sweetened white wine) or lager.

Which DC restaurant offers the best East African cuisine? That's a matter of rollicking debate. On 18th St NW are two perennial favorites: **Meskerem** (p132), which is wall-to-wall with diners most nights and offers traditional mesabs upstairs and **Addis Ababa** (p128), a plainly decorated joint drawing more East African customers.

FACCIA LUNA TRATTORIA

Map pp262-3   *Italian*

☎ 202-337-3132; 2400 Wisconsin Ave; meals $20-25; bus 30, 32, 34, 36 from Tenleytown-AU or Foggy Bottom-GWU Metro

Delicious wood-fired pizzas and cheap Chianti make this a favorite standby for a night out, even with the kids in tow. Pizzas can come *margherita* or *blanco* (with tomato sauce or not) and both choices are delicious. Inside, booths are roomy, and the pleasant outdoor seating is not right on the sidewalk, allowing for fresh air without the traffic

INDIQUE Map pp262-3   *Indian*

☎ 202-244-6600; 3512-14 Connecticut Ave NW; mains $9-16; Metro: Cleveland Park

The cool, white decor is highlighted by rich Indian tapestries, frescoes and furniture at this upscale bistro and wine bar. Specializing in 'unique Indian flavors,' the menu features creations like *biriyani*, a flavorful long-grained basmati cooked with herbs and spices and lamb, chicken, shrimp or veggie.

LEBANESE TAVERNA

Map pp262-3   *Middle Eastern*

☎ 202-265-8681; 2641 Connecticut Ave; meze from $5, mains from $10; Metro: Woodley Park-Zoo/Adams Morgan

This family-run Middle Eastern joint ranks among our favorite DC restaurants. Make a whole meal out of meze, like creamy *lebneh* cheese, tangy grape leaves, *kibbeh* (beef-stuffed pasta) and garlicky *foole m'damas* (fava-bean dip), which please both vegetarians and meat eaters. An outdoor patio makes this a fine summertime choice.

NEW HEIGHTS Map pp262-3   *New American*

☎ 202-234-4110; 2317 Calvert St NW; mains $22-32; ⏱ dinner daily, brunch Sun; Metro: Woodley Park-Zoo/Adams Morgan

This airy 2nd-floor restaurant, winner of the American Institute of Architects (AIA) design award, has a prime perch overlooking Rock Creek Park. Here, acclaimed chef Arthur Rivaldo serves up delicious new American dishes with Asian and Mediterranean influences and complementary wines. Specialties range from the well known – local jumbo lump crab cakes (and they do mean jumbo) – to the exotic Opaka-Paka – Hawaiian red snapper grilled with black trumpets and grapefruit. The signature appetizer, black-bean and goat cheese pâté, is a rich, creamy delicacy.

PETITS PLAT Map pp262-3   *French*

☎ 202-518-0018; 2653 Connecticut Ave; dinner $40, 3-course early-bird special $23; ⏱ dinner; Metro: Woodley Park-Zoo/Adams Morgan

This petite French bistro fits a warm, welcoming atmosphere into its little rooms. The traditional French menu gets high marks for delicious appetizers, salads and desserts. But this place is so charming you might not care what you eat, so long as the waiter continues to pour your wine.

SUSHI-KO Map pp262-3   *Sushi*

☎ 202-333-4187; 2309 Wisconsin Ave; dinner $30; ⏱ lunch & dinner Tue-Fri, dinner Sat-Mon; bus 30, 32, 34, 36 from Tenleytown-AU or Foggy Bottom-GWU Metro

DC's first sushi bar, this stripped-down, modern place is still beloved for impeccably fresh fish. The kitchen serves the basics (tuna belly, California roll) and the exotic (raw-trout napoleons).

YANŸU Map pp262-3   *Pan-Asian*

☎ 202-686-6968; 3435 Connecticut Ave; mains from $20, tasting menu $40-75; Metro: Cleveland Park

Chef Jessie Yan fuses Asian flavors from China, Malaysia, Vietnam and Thailand with seasonal ingredients to create works of art on the plate. Signature dishes include juicy Peking duck, or 'Big Duck' as she calls it, and 'Dancing Crab,' crispy soft-shell crab seasoned perfectly with peppers and scallions. Decorated with beautiful murals and Japanese fabrics, the setting is delightful. If you have the time and money, try one of the tasting menus.

Cheap Eats
BRICKS TAVERN

Map pp262-3   *Italian*

☎ 202-362-8440; 3421 Connecticut Ave; sandwiches, pizza from $8; Metro: Cleveland Park

'Bricks' means the ovens in which the gourmet pizzas are baked and topped with the freshest of toppings: grilled chicken with sun-dried tomato and lemon-dressed arugula; roasted eggplant with sweet peppers and goat cheese; and classics like tomato, basil and fresh mozzarella. Salads, sandwiches and pastas round out the menu beautifully. You can enjoy your meal at the long, friendly bar or alternatively upstairs on the rooftop.

ROCKLANDS BARBECUE

Map pp262-3   *Southern*

☎ 202-333-2558; 2418 Wisconsin Ave; meals from $8; bus 30, 32, 34, 36 from Tenleytown-AU or Foggy Bottom-GWU Metro

Order up some spicy ribs and choose your favorite side dish from Southern classics like potato salad or collard greens. While you wait for your order, check out the huge selection of hot sauces ('From the Depths of Hell'). Then take a seat at the wooden counter in the window and watch the passers-by drool.

TONO SUSHI Map pp262-3   *Asian*

☎ 202-332-7300; 2605 Connecticut Ave; sushi from $2, lunch from $7, dinner from $10; Metro: Woodley Park-Zoo/Adams Morgan

This place is pretty nondescript to look at, but the menu is a feast for the eyes (and palate). It offers great bargain lunch specials, as well as reasonably priced sushi and noodles throughout the day and evening. Besides, who needs a fancy decor if you sit outside and enjoy the sidewalk scene.

ZOO BAR Map pp262-3   *American*

☎ 202-232-4225; 3000 Connecticut Ave; kids' menu $3.50, sandwiches from $6; Metro: Woodley Park-Zoo/Adams Morgan

This neighborhood pub is really more of a drinking establishment, but the zoo theme and value-minded menu make it an ideal lunch spot on your way out of the zoo. This place welcomes kids, which is apparent by the animals on the walls, the patient waitstaff and the unprecedented cheap kids' menu. See Entertainment (p153).

SHAW & THE NEW U DISTRICT

Not exactly a culinary center, Shaw nonetheless has a few gems, including two of DC's longest-running restaurants. Come here for spicy Jamaican or down-home soul food.

FLORIDA AVENUE GRILL

Map p249   *Southern*

☎ 202-265-1586; 1100 Florida Ave NW; mains from $8; ⏰ lunch & dinner Tue-Sat; Metro: U Street-Cardozo

A Washington institution that has been around for almost 60 years, this place has a loyal clientele from around the city who swear by its down-home grits, meatloaf and barbecued ribs. It's a greasy spoon in the truest sense and that's part of the charm. Its walls are lined with signed photos of singers, actors and politicos who have enjoyed its soul food, as well as Southern memorabilia and kitsch.

HAMBURGER MARY'S

Map p249   *American*

☎ 202-32-7010; 1337 14th St NW; burgers $8; Metro: U Street-Cardozo

Colorful Christmas lights, 1950s pin-ups and counter seating give Mary's a retro feel – an inviting place for a burger and a beer. This place attracts a lot of gay regulars, partly for the bar Titan's upstairs.

ISLANDER CARIBBEAN

Map p249   *Caribbean*

☎ 202-234-4971; 1201 U St NW; meals from $20; Metro: U Street-Cardozo

Spicy cuisine and tropical drinks will whisk you to the islands – a perfect spot to be on a humid, DC August evening. Service is decidedly laid-back, but it's worth the wait for grilled fish, fried plaintains and rum smoothies, all set to a Caribbean beat.

KAFFA HOUSE

Map p249   *Caribbean*

☎ 202-462-1212; 1212 U St NW; meals $10-20; ⏰ 4-11pm; Metro: U Street-Cardozo

Marley lives on at this collective, strangely named for a coffee-bean region of Ethiopia. Spicy Jamaican cuisine, fruity drink specials and reggae music attracts a politically aware young crowd.

Cheap Eats
BEN'S CHILI BOWL

Map p249   *American*

☎ 202-667-0909; www.benschilibowl.com; 1213 U St; dogs from $4; ⏰ lunch & dinner daily, to 4am Fri & Sat; Metro: U Street-Cardozo

Newlyweds Ben and Virginia Ali launched this neighborhood institution in 1958. It became a lunch staple for all the locals, including the stars who were playing at the neighborhood clubs. Everyone from Redd Foxx to Duke Ellington to Bill Cosby has eaten at Ben's. Despite radical changes in the neighborhood, Ben's Formica counters and bright booths still look pretty much the same. And the spicy dogs ('Our chili will make a hot dog bark!') are always drawing crowds at lunchtime.

ARLINGTON & ALEXANDRIA

Both Arlington and Alexandria have respectable (and growing) culinary scenes that will sate your hunger if you happen to be on this side of the Potomac. Arlington's restaurants are clustered around the Metro stops, especially Clarendon, Courthouse and Crystal City.

Arlington

HARRY'S TAP ROOM
Map p264 *New American*
☎ 703-778-7788; 2800 Clarendon Blvd; meals $30; Metro: Clarendon

Set on two levels, this swanky new brasserie features steaks, salads and sandwiches, all with a delicious, modern interpretation. The very classy decor – polished wood furniture, sun-catching windows, mosaic-tile bar and fireplace – is remarkable for casual Clarendon.

IL RADICCHIO
Map p264 *Italian*
☎ 703-276-2627; 1801 Clarendon Blvd; meals from $16; Metro: Clarendon

This spaghetteria is Arlington's counterpart to the Capitol Hill favorite (p123).

KABOB BAZAAR
Map p264 *Middle Eastern*
☎ 703-522-8999; 3133 Wilson Blvd; mains from $6; Metro: Clarendon

That this place is often crowded with swarthy men and Middle Eastern families is proof that the spicy meat skewers and fresh veggie salads are top-notch. Cool green walls and faux marble columns add to the exotic atmosphere, not to mention the open kitchen, which allows guests to catch a glimpse – and a whiff – of the juicy meats roasting over the flame.

LEBANESE VILLAGE
Map p264 *Middle Eastern*
☎ 703-271-9194; 549 S 23rd St; mains from $10; Metro: Crystal City

This family-run Middle Eastern joint represents the best of Crystal City's restaurant row: friendly service and top-notch food at prices that are bargains by DC standards. Charcoal-grilled kabobs and rotisserie-roasted shawarma are highlights of the menu; or one could easily fill up on classic meze, like *baba ganouj*, hummus and *fattoush* (salad).

QUEEN BEE
Map p264 *Vietnamese*
☎ 703-527-3444; 3181 Wilson Blvd; mains from $8; Metro: Clarendon

The name does not lie – Queen Bee is indeed the best of the little Vietnamese places around. By way of warning, you don't come here for atmosphere (the red and pink is actually a step up from its previous decor). But the food consistently rates among DC's Asian favorites, especially the crispy spring rolls.

RED HOT & BLUE
Map p264 *American*
☎ 703-276-7427; 1600 Wilson Blvd; sandwiches from $6, ½-slab ribs $12; Metro: Rosslyn

The logo featuring pigs in sunglasses jamming on guitars says it all: Memphis-style barbecue. The traditional spicy dry ribs are undeniably the best, but you can also get them smothered in sauce. In any case, they are smoked over hickory wood for hours and hours, and served with beans, coleslaw or other classic Southern side dishes.

RUTH'S CHRIS STEAK HOUSE
Map p264 *Steakhouse*
☎ 703-979-7275; 2231 Crystal Dve, Crystal Park Bldg No 3; mains $16-30; ☺ lunch & dinner Mon-Fri, dinner Sat & Sun; Metro: Crystal City

The 11th-floor perch gives this branch of the national chain a unique attribute: fabulous views of the DC skyline, from the Capitol dome to the marble monuments. Whether you prefer juicy prime rib or thick filet mignon, you can expect it tender, tasty and perfectly cooked. Put on your fancy clothes and treat yourself.

STARS & STRIPES
Map p264 *American*
☎ 703-979-1872; 567 S 23rd St; mains $12-16; Metro: Crystal City

If your touring of the National Mall and Arlington Cemetery have inspired your patriotism, you may want to dine at this all-American eatery. Red and blue track lighting and an enormous American flag set the mood for classic American cooking – burgers, steaks and hearty sandwiches. This place is an anomaly in the midst of Crystal City's mostly ethnic restaurant row.

Alexandria

219
Map p265 *Creole*
☎ 703-549-1141; 219 King St; mains $18-25; Old Town shuttle from King St Metro

If you are longing for the Big Easy, 219 King St might be your best chance to get a dose:

feast on succulent oysters on the half-shell or spicy barbecue shrimp in one of Old Town's most romantic settings; or descend to the **Basin Street Lounge** (p159) to hear live jazz and blues.

CHART HOUSE

Map p265   *Seafood*

☎ 703-684-5080; 1 Cameron St; lunch mains $15-20, dinner mains $20-30; Old Town shuttle from King St Metro

While feasting on seafood, why not feast your eyes on lovely views of the lazy Potomac? You'll pay for them here, but the fresh seafood and waterfront setting are worth the price. A daily changing selection of fresh fish can be prepared to your liking. The menu also features some innovations, like crunchy, macadamia-crusted mahimahi, served with a sweet, warm peanut sauce. Prime rib and steaks are also available for landlubbers, but vegetarians will be at a loss.

ELYSIUM DINING ROOM

Map p265   *New American*

☎ 703-838-8000; 116 S Alfred St, Morrison House; meals $55; Old Town shuttle from King St Metro

Inside the posh hotel **Morrison House** (p204), the highlight of the Elysium is its one-of-a-kind Chef of Your Own experience. Chef Ulrich visits with each Elysium guest before preparing a custom-made meal, designed to fulfill each guest's desires. Suggested wines complement his creations. It's quite a dining adventure.

FISH MARKET

Map p265   *Seafood*

☎ 703-836-5676; 105 King St; lunch from $12, dinner from $16; Old Town shuttle from King St Metro

The sign on the window advertises: 'We serve shrimps, crabs, tall people and nice people too!' With its seafood menu and balconies overlooking King St, the Fish Market harkens to New Orleans. This is the place to come in Old Town for crab cakes or fried oysters. There is also live entertainment featured in the evening.

GADSBY'S TAVERN RESTAURANT

Map p265   *American*

☎ 703-548-1288; 138 N Royal St; dinner from $30; Old Town shuttle from King St Metro

Set in the building of an 18th-century tavern, Gadsby's is named for the Englishman who

actually operated the tavern from 1796 to 1808 (it was then the center of Alexandria's social life). This place tries hard to emulate an 18th-century hostelry. The overall effect is rather kitsch, but it's all good, clean and historical fun. Besides, who isn't curious to try 'George Washington's Favorite,' duck stuffed with tart fruit and topped with sweet Madeira gravy?

GENEROUS GEORGE'S POSITIVE PIZZA & PASTA PLACE

Map p265   *Italian*

☎ 703-370-4303; 3006 Duke St; pizzas from $12; Metro: King St

This is positively the very best place in the DC area for kids, Generous George will fill them up with his big, crispy-crusted pies. If you can't decide between pizza and pasta, never fear; oddly enough, pasta is also served on pizza crust. It's crowded, chaotic and a little crazy. You will find it about 5km west of Old Town Alexandria.

KING STREET BLUES

Map p265   *Southern*

☎ 703-836-8800; 112 N Saint Asaph St; early bird special $7, mains from $10; Old Town shuttle from King St

This is a crazy Southern 'roadhouse' diner which serves really good baked meat loaf,' country fried steak, Southern fried catfish and other diner favorites. It is strewn with colorful papier-maché figures which float across its three levels. Shiny chrome furniture and multicolored tablecloths lend it an attractive retro air. Live blues is played on Thursday night.

MAJESTIC CAFÉ

Map p265   *New American*

☎ 703-837-9117; 911 King St; dinner from $30; Old Town Shuttle from King St Metro

It's hard to say what's more appealing, the Majestic's modernized diner setting, or its mouthwatering but modern diner menu.

The art-deco cafe has already been recognized by the American Institute of Architects (AIA) for the extremely slick renovation of its historic building. But the menu is no afterthought: it changes regularly, depending on what is fresh and seasonal, but it is always perfectly divine.

Sautéed softshell crabs are a perennial favorite, as are the desserts.

Cheap Eats

HARD TIMES CAFÉ Map p265 *American*

☎ 703-528-2233; 3028 Wilson Blvd, Arlington; chile from $5, kids' menu $3; Metro: Clarendon

This menu features four distinct chiles: traditional Texas; hot and sweet Cincinnati (traditionally served over spaghetti); hearty vegetarian; and the house original Terlingua Red, a tribute to the ghost town that hosted the first chile cook-off. Experimental types may want to try chile on a dog, in a tortilla, or even over a bowl of Frito's, known as 1940s Frito Pie. Monday to Friday happy hours feature half-price draughts.

PIP CAFÉ Map p265 *Café*

☎ 703-519-8886; 106 S Union St, Alexandria; sandwiches, salads from $6, coffees from $3; ☯ 10:30am-8pm Mon-Thu, 10:30am-9:30pm Fri & Sat, 11am-6pm Sun; Old Town shuttle from King St

Nothing goes with a good book like a piping hot coffee; and if you need a snack while you're perusing the pages you can get that here, too. Located upstairs in **Olsson's** (p187) bookstore, this little café ('Proof In the Pudding,' in case you are wondering what PIP means) serves fancy coffees and fruity smoothies, crispy, thin pizzas and gourmet sandwiches.

1 Busker, Eastern Market (p64)
2 Tryst (p153) 3 Georgetown (p72)
4 Tomb of the Unknowns,
Arlington National Cemetery (p97)

1 *Mie N Yu (p127)* 2 *Performing waitstaff, Mimi's (p130)* 3 *Meskerem (p132)* 4 *Cakelove (p131)*

COCO-PINA
$1.50

SUNRISE
$1.50

1

2

4

1 *Friendship Arch, Chinatown (p52)* 2 *Happy hour, Adams-Morgan (p150)* 3 *Dean & Deluca (p126)* 4 *Old Post Office Pavilion (p56)*

3

1 Busker, National Museum of American History (p49) 2 Kennedy Center (p156) 3 Bohemian Caverns (p159) 4 Lincoln Theatre (p156)

1 *United States National Arboretum (p69)* **2** *Lafayette Sq (p56)* **3** *C&O Canal Towpath (p168)* **4** *Jogger, Rock Creek Park (p94)*

1 Climber, Carderock Recreation Area, C&O Canal Towpath (p171) 2 Blader, Capitol (p63) 3 Jogger, Lincoln Memorial (p45) 4 Cyclist, Rock Creek Park (p168)

1 Secondhand bookstore near
Eastern Market (p178) **2** Zenith
Gallery (p177) **3** Eastern Market
(p178) **4** Beadazzled (p181)

1 Inner Harbor, Baltimore (p209)
2 Chesapeake Bay (p212) 3 Mount
Vernon (p207) 4 Oriole Park,
Baltimore (p209)

Entertainment

Entertainment

Although DC is known for politics not culture, all those bureaucrats and diplomats know how to have some fun, too. In fact, theater and music in the nation's capital are thriving. Although the cultural element is not as daring as its New York or San Francisco counterparts, DC offers plenty of nightlife options, from the Kennedy Center to the Capitol Steps and from Euro clubs to bluesy pubs.

The drinking age in DC – as in the rest of the US – is 21. Many clubs and bars don't let anyone under that age through the door. Some 'over-18' clubs let you enter to dance or see shows, but don't give you the hand-stamp that lets you buy alcohol. Bring a photo ID to prove your age: a driver's license is the usual kind.

The best place to find out what's happening is the free weekly *Washington City Paper* (issued Thursday) or the monthly *On Tap*. Both are available in heaps at the entrances of stores and clubs. A more mainstream resource is the 'Weekend' section of the Friday *Washington Post*. The free *Washington Blade*, available at stores and clubs, gives the scoop on gay and lesbian happenings.

Union Station (p66)

Tickets

Most venues sell discounted tickets on the nnnday of the performance, either for standing room or obstructed view spots. Call the box office for details. Discounted tickets are also available at **Ticketplace** (Map pp246-8; ☎ 202-842-5387; www.cultural-alliance.org/tickets; 1100 Pennsylvania Ave NW, Old Post Office Pavilion; ☺ 11am-6pm Tue-Sat; Metro: Federal Triangle), which sells day-of-performance tickets to citywide concerts and shows for half-price plus 10%. Available tickets are listed on a board hanging in the office. **Ticketmaster** (Map pp246-8; ☎ 202-432-7328; www.ticketmaster.com; 2000 Pennsylvania Ave NW, Tower Records; ☺ 9am-midnight Mon-Sat, 10am-10pm Sun; Metro: Foggy Bottom-GWU) has information on, and sells full-price tickets to, citywide events.

DRINKING

Considering the city's small size, the number of bars and pubs in DC is staggering; and they may leave you staggering, too.

DOWNTOWN

701 Map pp246-8

☎ 202-393-0701; 701 Pennsylvania Ave NW; ⏰ 11:30am-3pm Mon-Fri, 5:30-10:30pm Mon-Thu, 5:30-11:30pm Fri & Sat, 5-9:30pm Sun; Metro: Archives-Navy Memorial

Two large round bars, cushy chairs and modern art set the mood at this Penn Quarter sophisticate. Mo's Bar offers specialty martinis, while the Caviar Lounge features domestic and Russian roe, chilled champagnes and DC's best selection of vodka.

BUTLERS CIGAR BAR Map pp246-8

☎ 202-637-4735; 1000 H St NW, Grand Hyatt; ⏰ 5pm-2am Mon-Sat; Metro: Metro Center

Comfy couches, large-screen TVs showing jazz concerts and 1920s-era artwork lend an air of nostalgia to this swanky lounge. Drink specialties include designer martinis served in individual shakers and the house microbrew, Butlers Private Reserve. Monday to Friday happy hour (5pm to 7pm) attracts a sophisticated crowd.

ESPN ZONE Map pp246-8

☎ 202-783-3776; 555 12th St NW; ⏰ 11:30am-midnight Sun-Thu, 11:30am-1am Fri & Sat; Metro: Metro Center

This three-floor, 200-TV emporium features the Sports Grill, a massive screening room with speakers in its chairs and a 16ft TV that looks like a war-room missile monitor. Next door, the Sports Arena is packed with video games, air hockey and other table games. This is a happening place to watch a game (any game), but it's often crowded with tourists.

FADÓ IRISH PUB & RESTAURANT

Map pp246-8

☎ 202-789-0066; 808 7th St NW; ⏰ 11:30-2:30am; Metro: Gallery Pl-Chinatown

This place sticks out in Chinatown like James Joyce in Shanghai. Somehow the Chinese restaurants are not so conducive to drinking, so Fadó packs in the thirsty, especially after games at the nearby MCI Center. Every room in this Disney-esque pub is decked out in its own unique Celtic style – country library, medieval castle etc.

GREEN LANTERN & TOOL SHED

Map pp246-8

☎ 202-347-4533; 1335 Green Court NW; ⏰ 9pm-2am Wed-Thu, 9pm-3am Fri & Sat, 6pm-2am Sun; Metro: McPherson Sq

The gay Green Lantern is downstairs, with leather-lovers' Tool Shed on the 2nd floor. This bi-level place attracts a slightly older crowd. Shirtless men get free beer on Thursday night.

WHITE HOUSE AREA & FOGGY BOTTOM

BOTTOM LINE Map pp246-8

☎ 202-298-8488; 1716 I St NW; ⏰ 11:30-1:30am Mon-Thu, 11:30-2:30am Fri & Sat; Metro: Farragut West

This long, dark and friendly basement bar draws prosperous patrons for lunchtime and happy hour. It's more grown-up than most pubs in the area and many folk appear to be conducting business-related tête-à-têtes.

FROGGY BOTTOM PUB Map pp246-8

☎ 202-338-3000; 2141 Pennsylvania Ave NW; ⏰ 11:30-1:30am Mon-Thu, 11:30-2:30am Fri & Sat; Metro: Foggy Bottom-GWU

This popular GWU hang-out attracts students with their grub-and-pub specials, like Saturday's $10 all-you-can-eat-&-drink. Happy-hour specials run 5pm to midnight.

Top Five Free Entertainment Options

In DC, it's easy to entertain yourself for next-to-nothing (or for nothing, for that matter). All-free-all-the-time **Smithsonian** (☎ 202-357-2020) sponsors evening lectures, films, concerts and other performances that are often free. In summer, the city becomes one giant outdoor venue for free concerts and fun. Here are five options for culture vultures with empty pockets.

- **Carter Barron Amphitheater** (p155) Shakespeare in the Park or music after dark.
- **Mary Pickford Theater** (p157) Historical and artsy films, Tuesday, Thursday and Friday at 7pm.
- **Millennium Stage** (p156) Live jazz, blues, folk, world-beat or classical music at the Kennedy Center – every night at 6pm.
- **Monday Night at the National** (p155) Mini-productions of music and drama every Monday at 6pm and 7:30pm.
- **Pavilion Café** (p118) Jazz wafting from the woolly mammoth or surrounding the sculptures on Friday evening.

MACKEY'S PUBLIC HOUSE Map pp246-8
☎ 202-331-7667; 1823 L St NW; ⏰ 11:30-2am Mon-Fri, noon-2am Sat; Metro: Farragut North

The fireplace and easy chairs recall an Irish country pub – one where the whole town puts on suits and comes to drink every afternoon around 5pm. Mackey's is welcoming and comfortable, especially when the bartenders are drawing you pints of Guinness, Harp and Caffrey.

CAPITOL HILL & SOUTHEAST DC

BANANA CAFÉ & PIANO BAR
Map pp250-1
☎ 202-543-5906; 500 8th St SE; ⏰ 11:30am-2:30pm & 5-10:30pm Mon-Thu, 11:30am-2:30pm & 5-11:30pm Fri, 5-11:30pm Sat, 11am-3pm & 5-10:30pm Sun; Metro: Eastern Market

Nestled above its namesake restaurant (p123), enter through the side door on E St and you will find this warmly lit gathering spot has a Caribbean flavor, drawing an older gay and straight mix for its nightly offerings of live jazz. Lounge in an oversize wicker chair, sip a martini beneath the palm fronds and take in the show.

CAPITOL LOUNGE Map pp250-1
☎ 202-547-2098; 229-31 Pennsylvania Ave SE; ⏰ 11-2am Sun-Thu, 11-3am Fri & Sat; Metro: Eastern Market

Cigars and martinis make the Capitol Lounge

more upscale than the other pubs in the neighborhood, but not too upscale to host 10c wing night (Tuesday) or to pack in the suits after work. Pool tables, sports on TV and familiar faces draw the Hillies in droves. One recent visit turned up drunken Library of Congress staffers engaged in a most fierce pool tourney – good to see that librarians get loose, too.

HAWK & DOVE Map pp250-1
☎ 202-543-3300; 329 Pennsylvania Ave SE; ⏰ 11-12:30am Mon-Thu, 11-2:30am Fri, 4pm-3am Sat; Metro: Eastern Market

Reputed to be a Republican hang-out, the Hawk & Dove has been a Capitol Hill institution since the 1960s. It's not really a partisan place, though. Everybody eventually finds their way here, including congressional staffers and even some of the younger representatives of all parties. Friday nights are particularly lively: pick up a date or just a game of pool and enjoy the happy-hour specials.

KELLY'S IRISH TIMES Map pp250-1
☎ 202-543-5433; 14 F St NW; ⏰ 11-1:30am Sun-Thu, 11-2:30am Fri & Sat; Metro: Union Station

Kelly's implores: 'Give me your tired, your hungry, your befuddled masses.' And the masses respond. Fans of the on-tap Guinness and Wednesday to Saturday live music tend to be younger than the patrons next door at the Dubliner – students and staffers and other suds-drinkers.

LOUNGE 201 Map pp250-1
☎ 202-544-5201; 201 Massachusetts Ave NE; ⏰ 6pm-2am Tue-Sat; Metro: Union Station

Decidedly retro decor and brightly colored martinis go hand-in-hand at this swanky, new cocktail lounge. The menu claims that 'To drink is human, to lounge is divine' and you will certainly believe it after spending an evening here sipping martinis and munching on gourmet finger food.

POLITIKI Map pp250-1
☎ 202-546-1001; 319 Pennsylvania Ave SE; ⏰ 4pm-1:30am Mon-Thu, 4pm-2am Fri & Sat; Metro: Eastern Market

Mixing politics with Southeast Asia sounds dangerous, but this place pulls it off nicely. The bar provides tiki torches, pool tables and a jukebox; and the politics are provided – of course – by the Hilly clientele. Daily happy-hour specials and a fiercely competitive trivia night challenge are the highlights.

RED RIVER GRILL Map pp250-1

☎ 202-546-7200; 201 Massachusetts Ave NE; 11:30-2am Sun-Thu, 11:30-3am Fri & Sat; Metro: Union Station

This smoky Tex-Mex joint packs in young Hill rats and even younger students, most in high mating mode. The drinks are dirt cheap, the decor divey, and the food greasy and good.

REMINGTON'S Map pp250-1 🕺

☎ 202-543-3113; 639 Pennsylvania Ave SE; 4pm-2am Mon-Thu, 4pm-3am Fri, 8pm-3am Sat, 5pm-2am Sun (also 1hr before kick-off on Redskins game days); Metro: Eastern Market

Conveniently located next to Red River Western Wear, this Texas type draws DC's country & western aficionados for tall drinks and two-stepping. Boots and bolo ties blend with T-shirts and jeans at this mostly male watering hole, decked out with the requisite antlers and wagon wheels. Grab your partner and hit the dance floor, or shoot a round of pool or pinball in the upstairs video bar.

GEORGETOWN

CLYDE'S Map pp256-7

☎ 202-333-9180; 3236 M St NW; 11:30am-midnight Mon-Thu, 11:30-1am Fri, 10-1am Sat, 9am-midnight Sun; Georgetown shuttle from Foggy Bottom-GWU

A true Georgetown warhorse, Clyde's has been around for almost 40 years. Back in the day, it used to cater mainly to Georgetown students, but Clyde's has gone upscale in recent years; now yuppies are more likely than students to drink in this classy saloon. The Railroad Bar, salvaged from a Baltimore station and tucked into the back of the bar, is the best spot in the house. The food is not your typical pub fare (eg ginger-steamed rockfish with soba noodles, apricots and veggies), although it serves burgers and sandwiches, too.

DEGREES BAR & LOUNGE Map pp256-7

☎ 202-912-4100; 3100 South St NW, Ritz-Carlton Hotel; 2:30pm-12:30am; Georgetown shuttle from Foggy Bottom-GWU

In the lobby of the new Ritz-Carlton (p198), this trendy place captures the history of the incinerator with exposed brick walls and black slate floors. The lounge is all the rage among the businesspeople that work in the area and come here to sip the signature fiery red martini.

GARRETT'S Map pp256-7

☎ 202-333-8282; 3003 M St NW; 11:30-1:30am Mon-Thu, noon-2:30am Fri & Sat, noon-1:30am Sun; Georgetown shuttle from Foggy Bottom-GWU

This English-style pub has a teeny bar downstairs, a roomier 2nd floor and an outdoor patio. Its bar is copper-topped, its floors wooden and its mood welcoming. One of the most popular drinking spots for Georgetown students, it's also not a bad place to grab some cheap pub grub.

MR SMITH'S Map pp256-7

☎ 202-333-3104; 3104 M St NW; 11-2am; Georgetown shuttle from Foggy Bottom-GWU

Dark and welcoming, Mr Smith's is really an old-timers' bar, although daily specials like half-price burgers and all-you-can-eat fish and chips draw students too. The crowded, friendly front bar (you'll rub bodies with at least two strangers while drinking) hides a more spacious rear seating area with a fireplace and open patio.

TOMBS Map pp256-7

☎ 202-337-6668; 1226 36th St; 11:30-2am Mon-Thu, 11:30-3am Fri, 11-3am Sat, 9:30-2am Sun; Metro: Georgetown shuttle from Rosslyn or Foggy Bottom-GWU

Downstairs from 1789 (p125), the Tombs is Georgetown students' favorite drinking spot: it's close enough to be a regular stop for Hoyas on their way home from the library. In fact, the profs like to come here too, knowing they're bound to get some free drinks from pet students. Crew memorabilia hangs on the wall, pitchers flow freely and students scope each other out.

DUPONT CIRCLE & KALORAMA

BIG HUNT Map pp258-60

☎ 202-785-2333; 1345 Connecticut Ave NW; 4pm-2am Mon-Thu, 4pm-3am Fri, 5pm-3am Sat, 5pm-2am Sun; Metro: Dupont Circle

Yes, that name gets played for all the puns it's worth: the bar advertises itself as the 'happy hunting ground for humans in pursuit of a mate, food and drink.' But it's not really all that cruisey. Most patrons focus on the 27 on-tap beers and bar-eats deals, amid cheesy Hemingway decor: animal-print upholstery, mosquito nets. Coin-operated pool tables are on the 2nd floor.

BRICKSKELLER INN Map pp258-60
☎ 202-293-1885; 1523 22nd St NW; ⏰ 11:30-2am Mon-Thu, 11:30-3am Fri, 6pm-3am Sat, 6pm-2am Sun; Metro: Dupont Circle

This underground beer paradise has 900 varieties, listed on a menu heavy enough to cause trouble after the fifth pint or so. Shandies, stouts, darks, lights, lagers and creams – it claims the world's largest selection. Its subterranean red-brick warren is usually choked with college-age folks arrayed around big circular tables. Most bottles cost around $4, but true exotics can cost up to $15. It also offers accommodations (p201).

BUFFALO BILLIARDS Map pp258-60
☎ 202-331-7665; 1330 19th St; ⏰ 4pm-2am Mon-Thu, 4pm-3am Fri, 1pm-3am Sat, 1pm-1am Sun; Metro: Dupont Circle

Thirty pool and snooker tables pull college kids and yuppies into this bright, below-street-level cave. Tables are kind of costly – about $12 for two people playing for an hour. There is usually a wait for a table – pull up a loungey chair and play Score Four while you are waiting.

CHI-CHA LOUNGE Map pp258-60
☎ 202-234-8400; 1624 U St NW; ⏰ 5:30pm-2am Sun-Thu, 5:30pm-3am Fri & Sat; Metro: U Street-Cardozo

On first thought, Arabic *arguilehs* (hookahs) and Andean food don't seem a felicitous combination, but Chi-Cha makes it work. Curl into velvet settees, nibble Ecuadorian tapas and order a pipeful of Bahrainian fruit-and-honey-cured tobacco. Ah, East and West do combine beautifully. Hookahs are available weekdays only.

COMMON SHARE Map pp258-60
☎ 202-588-7180; 2003 18th St NW; ⏰ 5:30pm-2am Sun-Thu, 5:30pm-3am Fri & Sat; Metro: Woodley Park-Zoo/Adams Morgan

This is DC's cheapest bar that doesn't involve brown paper bags, a place that commendably considers the buzz a basic human right. It sells every beer (even nice ones like Guinness) and mixed drinks for just $2 to $3. Beaten-up curbside freebies furnish the place, but at these prices, who's complaining?

FOX & HOUNDS Map pp258-60
☎ 202-232-6307; 1533 17th St NW; ⏰ 11-2am Sun-Thu, 11-3am Fri, 10-3am Sat; Metro: Dupont Circle

The huge patio is the main draw at this casual, divey bar, especially for scoping the boys on 17th St on summer eves. Beer is the usual choice of potable, but something called 'Winston Whirlie's World-Famous Whimwham' is poured too.

JR'S Map pp258-60
☎ 202-328-0090; 1519 17th St NW; ⏰ 2pm-2am Mon-Thu, 2pm-3am Fri, noon-3am Sat, noon-2am Sun; Metro: Dupont Circle

At JR's weekday happy hour you might think you've stepped into a living Banana Republic ad: chinos and button-downs are de rigueur at this popular gay hang-out frequented by the 20- and 30-something, work-hard and play-hard set. Some DC residents claim that the crowd at JR's epitomizes the conservative nature of the capital's gay scene; but even if you love to hate it, as many do, JR's is the happy-hour spot in town and is packed more often than not.

SIGN OF THE WHALE Map pp258-60
☎ 202-785-1110; 1825 M St; ⏰ 11:30-1am; Metro: Dupont Circle

This cozy, Brit-style pub has a giant fireplace, high beamed ceilings and a long wooden bar, with boars' heads overlooking the scene. It's popular for happy-hour specials and a weekend brunch that features unlimited mimosas for $9 or a Bloody Mary bar for $10.

STETSON'S FAMOUS BAR & RESTAURANT Map pp258-60
☎ 202-667-6295; 1610 U St NW; ⏰ 5pm-1am; Metro: U Street-Cardozo

'Famous' might be a bit of a stretch, but Stetson's can lay claim to fame as *the* neighborhood bar in the U St area. It is basic – the ratty pool table and the jukebox are the primary amenities – and comfortable, with good and tasty burgers and cheap happy-hour specials.

U-TOPIA Map pp258-60
☎ 202-483-7669; 1418 U St NW; ⏰ 11-2am Mon-Thu, 11-3am Fri, 5pm-3am Sat, 11am-11:30pm Sun; Metro: U Street-Cardozo

This narrow bar – which began its life as a gallery – is a very relaxed place which attracts an eclectic crowd of bar-crawling youngsters, gay couples and older urban homesteaders. On display is the work of local painters, and these are usually for sale. Its eclectic menu leans toward Cajun (gumbo, jambalaya), and there is live blues or jazz on Thursday and Sunday.

ADAMS-MORGAN

KOKOPOOLI'S Map p261
☎ 202-234-2306; 2305 18th St NW; pool $10 per hr; ⏰ 11-2am Mon-Thu, 11-3am Fri, 2pm-3am Sat, 2pm-2am Sun; Metro: Woodley Park-Zoo/Adams Morgan

A popular pool joint with eight tables and colorful murals, Kokopooli's is the best place to shoot pool in Adams-Morgan, especially if you come during happy hour (3pm to 7pm) when it's half-price. Sports on TV and bar games should keep you entertained if the tables are full.

MILLIE & AL'S Map p261
☎ 202-387-8131; 2440 18th St NW; ⏰ 4pm-2am Mon-Thu, 4pm-3am Fri & Sat; Metro: Woodley Park-Zoo/Adams Morgan

This comfortably worn dive is an Adams-Morgan institution, famous for its $2 drafts, Jell-O shots and hit-the-spot pizza (best consumed in that order). Two TVs show a constant stream of sports.

PHARMACY BAR Map p261
☎ 202-483-1200; 2337 18th St NW; ⏰ 5pm-1:30am Mon-Thu, 5pm-2:30am Fri & Sat; Metro: Woodley Park-Zoo/Adams Morgan

As tribute to this building's previous incarnation as a drugstore, this cool bar is decorated with old medicine jars on the walls and pills embedded in the tabletops. A quiet contrast to the wild Adams-Morgan scene, it's an ideal spot for a late-night snack or a nightcap.

REEF Map p261
☎ 202-518-3800; 2446 18th St NW; ⏰ 4pm-2am Sun-Thu, 4pm-3am Fri & Sat; Metro: Woodley Park-Zoo/Adams Morgan

A new edition to Adams-Morgan, the Reef has out-the-door lines waiting to climb up to its huge roofdeck upstairs and to meditate on the gigantic, colorful fish tanks downstairs. Owner Brian Harrison is somewhat of a beer connoisseur and it shows in his all-draft beer selection: a few standards are supplemented by Belgian-style specialty beers and organic ales.

SPY LOUNGE Map p261
☎ 202-483-3549; 2406 18th St NW; ⏰ 5:30pm-2am; Metro: Woodley Park-Zoo/Adams Morgan

The Spy Lounge is one of the hottest spots in Adams-Morgan and it very cleverly plays on everyone's secret desire to be suave, sneaky and – well – more like James Bond. Espionage is in; conveniently, so are martinis: both are on tap at this swanky lounge, next door to funky Felix.

TRYST Map p261
☎ 202-232-5500; 2459 18th St NW; ⏰ 6:30-2am Mon-Thu, 6:30-3am Fri & Sat, 8-12:30am Sun; Metro: Woodley Park-Zoo/Adams Morgan

This Greenwich Village–style place is probably the best coffeehouse in DC. The couches, armchairs and bookshelves scattered about and the light flooding through streetside windows lure patrons so faithful they probably should pay rent. Sweet alcoholic concoctions flow along with caffeine (sometimes in the same glass), nice complements to the menu of waffles, muffins and cake. It's a great place to meet up with old friends or make new friends.

UPPER NORTHWEST DC

AROMA COMPANY Map pp262-3
☎ 202-244-7995; 3417 Connecticut Ave NW; ⏰ 5:30pm-1am; Metro: Cleveland Park

There's a pronounced fascination with the 1950s at this sleek retro club: it's filled with those kidney-shaped coffee tables and old sofas; the tiled bar serves up the Scotch and ciggies. Live jazz plays here on Friday nights.

IRELAND'S FOUR PROVINCES
Map pp262-3
☎ 202-244-0860; 3412 Connecticut Ave NW; ⏰ 5pm-1am Sun-Thu, 4pm-2am Fri, 5pm-2am Sat; Metro: Cleveland Park

This landmark Irish bar offers live Celtic and folk music, 21 beers on tap, relentless emerald-shamrock decor and a friendly scene of late-20s neighborhood professionals cruising and schmoozing. Come on a hot summer night to sit on the streetside patio, or during weekday happy hour for a $4 20oz Guinness.

ZOO BAR Map pp262-3
☎ 202-232-4225; 3000 Connecticut Ave NW; ⏰ 11:30-2:30am; Woodley Park-Zoo/Adams Morgan

When you just can't take any more cuddly animals, ditch the zoo and head across the street to the Zoo Bar, a friendly neighborhood beer-drinkin' dive with live music Friday and Saturday, and happy hour 3pm to 7pm. See Eating (p135).

SHAW & THE NEW U DISTRICT

CAFÉ SAINT-EX Map p249

☎ 202-265-7839; 1847 14th St NW; ✆ 5:30pm-1am Sun-Wed, 5:30pm-2am Thu-Sat; Metro: U Street-Cardozo
Reminiscent of the Parisian Latin Quarter, Saint-Ex attracts a mix of ages, ethnicities and orientations. Different DJs spin tunes every night and there is no cover charge. A bar salvaged from a 1930s Philadelphia pub, seats from an old movie theater and classic movies running on the TVs all lend a nostalgic air. The downstairs lounge, Gate 54, plays up the aeronautic theme with a wooden propeller from the owner's grandfather's WWI fighter plane (author Antoine de Saint-Exupery was also a pilot).

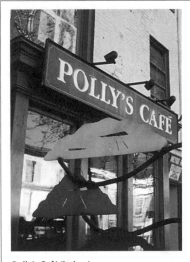

Polly's Café (below)

KING PIN Map p249

☎ 202-588-5880; 917 U St NW; ✆ 8pm-2am; Metro: U Street-Cardozo
This late-night bar doesn't really get going till after midnight, when patrons from the **Velvet Lounge** (p161) and the **9:30 Club** (p158) stop for drinks while their eardrums recover from the show. But there is a deal if you come early: a domestic beer and a shot go for $5, Monday to Friday 8pm to 10pm.

POLLY'S CAFÉ Map p249

☎ 202-265-8385; 1342 U St NW; ✆ 6pm-2am Mon-Thu, 6pm-3am Fri, 10am-3am Sat, 10-1am Sun; Metro: U Street-Cardozo

This friendly, no-attitude, basement-level bar was a New U pioneer: it's been around for more than a decade. Exposed brick walls and fireplace coziness make it a fine place to rendezvous before or after a night of music. Polly serves reasonably priced pints and a menu of basic eats like salads and burgers.

TITAN Map p249

☎ 202-232-7010; 1337 14th St NW; ✆ 5pm-2am; Metro: U Street-Cardozo
Upstairs from Hamburger Mary's, this crazy place hosts gay Family Feud, which is wildly popular among the Dupont set. State Department and World Bank types – officially Gays & Lesbians in Foreign Affairs – meet here for happy hour every month (third Thursday).

ARLINGTON & ALEXANDRIA

BILBO BAGGINS Map p265

☎ 703-683-0300; 208 Queen St, Alexandria; ✆ 11:30am-10:30pm Mon-Sat, 11am-9:30pm Sun; Old Town shuttle from King St Metro
Half-bar and half-restaurant, this Old Town neighborhood café gets high marks for eating or drinking. The light-filled, wood-paneled room makes for a wonderful, romantic setting to enjoy global cuisine and an extensive wine list.

FOUNDERS' BREWING CO Map p265

☎ 703-684-5397; 607 King St, Alexandria; ✆ 11am-midnight Mon-Thu, 11-1am Fri & Sat, 10am-8pm Sun; Old Town shuttle from King St Metro
Founders' four brews (and counting) play off themes of local Alexandria history (such as Smoot's Stout, named for a 19th-century mayor). The beers are smooth and refreshing, a nice complement to the all-American menu.

GUA RAPO Map p264

☎ 703-528-6500; 2039 Wilson Blvd, Arlington; ✆ 5-10:30pm Mon-Thu, 5-11:30pm Fri & Sat, lounge 9pm-1:30am Thu-Sat; Metro: Courthouse
Rich gem tones and plush couches lend an air of luxury to this laid-back restaurant and lounge, brought to you by the folks responsible for **Chi-Cha** (p152). This place is more upscale with tapas and hookah pipes, and live music in the upstairs lounge Thursday to Saturday.

IRELAND'S FOUR COURTS Map p264

☎ 703-525-3600; 2051 Wilson Blvd, Arlington; ✆ 11-2am Mon-Sat, 10-2am Sun; Metro: Courthouse
Buckets of Guinness lubricate the O'Connors and McDonoughs at Arlington's favorite Irish

pub. The sidewalk seating draws a lunchtime crowd for shepherd's pie and fish-and-chips, while the green green interior attracts an evening crowd for cold drafts and live tunes.

UNION STREET PUBLIC HOUSE

Map p265
☎ 703-548-1785; 121 S Union St, Alexandria; ⌚ 11:30-1am Mon-Sat, 11-1am Sun; Old Town shuttle from King St Metro

Gas lamps out front welcome tourists and locals into this spacious taproom for frosty brews, raw-bar delights and nightly dinner specials. Inside, the atmosphere is equally inviting: a wide bar, heavy wooden furniture and exposed brick hark back to Alexandria's days as a bustling colonial port.

WHITLOW'S ON WILSON Map p264

☎ 703-276-9693; 2854 Wilson Blvd, Arlington; ⌚ 11:30-2am Mon-Fri, 9-2am Sat & Sun; Metro: Clarendon

Occupying almost an entire block just east of Clarendon Metro, Whitlow's has something for everyone: burgers, brunch and comfort food on the menu; happening happy hours and positive pick-up potential; plus 12 brews on tap, a pool table, jukebox, live music and an easy-going atmosphere.

THEATER

DC theater divides into three camps: the renowned Kennedy Center, presenting world-famed companies and productions; a second string of well-established theaters, which often host Broadway national runs; and a third group of adventurous small stages, presenting cutting-edge works whose quality ranges from totally fabulous to sophomoric.

ARENA STAGE Map pp254-5

☎ 202-488-3300; www.arenastage.org; 1101 6th St SW; tickets from $35; Metro: Waterfront

The three theaters at Arena State (including a theater-in-the-round) are top venues for traditional and experimental works, especially American classics, premieres of new plays and contemporary stories. It was DC's first racially integrated theater and it has continued its progressive tradition through performances addressing African American history.

CARTER BARRON AMPHITHEATER

Map pp262-3
☎ 202-426-0486; www.nps.gov/rocr/cbarron; 16th & Colorado Ave NW, Rock Creek Park; tickets free or $18; ⌚ box office show days noon-9pm; bus S2 or S4 from McPherson Sq

The outdoor amphitheater in Rock Creek Park is the venue for Shakespeare Free for All, a free series staged by the Shakespeare Theatre, as well as music festivals and concerts throughout the summer. For free shows, tickets are distributed from 4pm on the day of the show. For more information about Rock Creek Park see Neighborhoods (p94).

FOLGER SHAKESPEARE LIBRARY & THEATRE Map pp250-1

☎ 202-544-7077; www.folger.edu; 210 E Capitol St SE; tickets from $30; Metro: Capitol South

The magnificent Globe-style theater attached to the Folger Shakespeare Library stages classic and modern interpretations of the Bard's plays. Exhibitions, poetry readings and great programs for kids are all part of the repertoire, in addition to world-class Shakespearean theater. For more information see Neighborhoods (p64).

FORD'S THEATRE Map pp246-8

☎ 202-218-6500, 800-955-5566; www.fordstheatre.org; 511 10th St NW; tickets $25-40; ⌚ box office 10am-6pm Mon-Fri; Metro: Gallery Pl-Chinatown

The historical theater – where John Wilkes Booth killed Abraham Lincoln – has staged world premier musicals, mostly about Lincoln's life and times. The theater also hosts a series on 'American Originals': influential individuals who have played significant cultural roles. For more information see Neighborhoods (p53).

NATIONAL THEATRE Map pp246-8

☎ 202-628-6161, 800-447-7400; www.nationaltheatre.org; 1321 Pennsylvania Ave NW; ⌚ box office 10am-9pm Mon-Sat, noon-8pm Sun; Metro: Federal Triangle

Established in 1835 and renovated in 1984, the National is Washington's oldest continually operating theater. This is where you would catch Les Misérables and Rent. Half-price tickets are available for students and seniors. Monday nights at the National are good value as they feature free performances at 6pm and 7:30pm.

SHAKESPEARE THEATRE Map pp246-8

☎ 202-547-1122; www.shakespearetheatre.org; 450 7th St NW; tickets $16-60; ☯ box office 10am-6pm Mon-Sat, noon-6pm Sun; Metro: Archives-Navy Memorial

Under artistic director Michael Kahn, this little theater on Gallery Row has been called 'one of the world's three great Shakespearean theaters' by the *Economist*. Its home company stages a half-dozen works annually, plus a free summer Shakespeare series in Rock Creek Park (see **Carter Barron Amphitheater**, p155).

WARNER THEATRE Map pp246-8

☎ 202-783-4000; www.warnertheatre.org; 1299 Pennsylvania Ave NW; tickets $25-55; ☯ box office 10am-4pm Mon-Fri, noon-3pm Sat; Metro: Federal Triangle

The beautifully restored 1924 art-deco theater was originally built for vaudeville and silent films, but it now stages headliner concerts, comedians and national runs of Broadway musicals.

Smaller venues and troupes include:

Asian Stories in America (☎ 703-979-0875; www.asianstoriesinamerica.com) Performing primarily at venues in Arlington, highlights the work of playwrights from Asia and the Pacific Rim.

Catalyst Theater (Map pp250-1; ☎ 202-547-6839; 545 7th St SE; Metro: Eastern Market) Part of the Capitol Hill Arts Workshop, which stages theater, cinema and musical events.

DCAC (Map pp261; ☎ 202-462-7833; www.dcartscenter.org; 2438 18th St NW; Metro: Woodley Park-Zoo/Adams Morgan) A 50-seat black box theater hosting the improvisational interactive Playback.

Discovery Theatre (Map pp246-8; ☎ 202-357-1500; www.discoverytheatre.si.edu; Smithsonian Arts & Industries Bldg; Metro: Smithsonian) Stages delightful productions for kids, such as puppet shows.

Gala Hispanic Theatre (Map p261; ☎ 202-234-7174; www.galatheatre.org; 1625 Park Rd NW; Metro: Columbia Heights) Maintains a 25-year tradition of four annual Spanish-language productions.

Lincoln Theatre (Map p249; ☎ 202-328-9177, 328-6000; 1215 U St NW; Metro: U Street-Cardozo) Historic cinema recently renovated to host music and theater.

Source Theatre Company (Map pp258-60; ☎ 202-462-1073; www.sourcetheatre.com; 1835 14th St NW; Metro: U Street-Cardozo) In the heart of the new U district, hosts the Annual Washington Theatre Festival.

Stanislavsky Theatre (Map pp258-60; ☎ 800-494-8497; www.sts-online.org; 1742 Church St NW; Metro: Dupont

Circle) The best of world theater, especially Russian, with a twist.

Studio Theatre (Map pp258-60; ☎ 202-332-3300; www.studiotheatre.org; 1333 P St NW; G2 bus from Dupont Circle) Twenty-five years of producing Pulitzer Prize-winning and premiere plays.

Theater J (Map pp258-60; ☎ 202-777-3229; www.dcjcc.org/theaterj.htm; 1529 16th St NW; Metro: Dupont Circle) Addresses urban American Jewish experience.

West End Dinner Theatre (☎ 703-370-2500; www.wedt.com; 4615 Duke St, Alexandria; tickets $30-35; ☯ dinner 6pm Tue-Sun, show 8pm) The area's largest dinner-theater stage, featuring Broadway musicals and comedies. The theater is on Duke St west of Old Town Alexandria.

Woolly Mammoth Theatre Co (Map pp258-60; ☎ 202-393-3939; www.woollymammoth.net; 917 M St NW; G2 bus from Dupont Circle) The edgiest of the experimental group.

Kennedy Center

DC's main cultural jewel, the **Kennedy Center** (Map pp246-8; ☎ 202-467-4600, 800-444-1324; www.kennedy-center.org; 2700 F St NW; Metro: Foggy Bottom-GWU), is given credit for transforming DC from a cultural backwater to an artistic contender in the late 20th century. The stately white-marble building overlooking the Potomac holds two big theaters, a theater lab (where new or experimental theater is staged), cinema, opera house and concert hall (and the fine Roof Terrace Restaurant to boot). It's home to the National Symphony Orchestra, the Washington Chamber Symphony (both directed by Leonard Slatkin), the Washington Opera directed by Placido Domingo and the Washington Ballet; film festivals and cultural events are frequent highlights. About 3000 performances are held here annually.

Orchestra seats cost about $40 for concerts, $60 for theater, $140 for opera. On the day of the performance, reduced-rate tickets are sometimes available for students and for obstructed-view seats. Order tickets by phone or purchase them at the box office.

The Kennedy Center also hosts the **Millennium Stage**, a series of daily free music and dance. First-rate performances take place every day at 6pm in the Grand Foyer and cost absolutely nothing. Pick up a schedule at the Kennedy Center, or check the website.

A free shuttle bus runs between Foggy Bottom-GWU Metro station and the Kennedy Center every 15 minutes from 9:45am to midnight Monday to Saturday, noon to 8pm Sunday. There's also paid parking underneath the Kennedy Center. See also Neighborhoods (p61).

DANCE

Performance dance in Washington DC is surprisingly limited. The premier dance venue is the Kennedy Center, home of the Washington Ballet, but the lesser-known, and oddly located, Dance Place experiments with some more quite daring choreography.

DANCE PLACE Map pp252-3

☎ 202-269-1600; www.danceplace.org; 3225 8th St NE; tickets $18; Metro: Brookland

The only truly cutting-edge dance space in the capital is quite hidden in a rather obscure neighborhood in Northeast DC. Run by five resident modern-dance companies offering a year-round calendar of new work, which includes festivals featuring African dance, tap dancing and other genres. It also hosts the work of top-notch national companies, such as the Joe Goode Performance Group.

WASHINGTON BALLET Map pp246-8

☎ 202-467-4600, 800-444-1324; www.kennedy-center.org; 2700 F St NW; Metro: Foggy Bottom

Housed at the Kennedy Center, the Washington Ballet hasn't been known for any groundbreaking productions, although its reputation is beginning to change as it explores the work of younger choreographers. The center also hosts fine visiting groups like Merce Cunningham and Alvin Ailey. See the boxed text 'Kennedy Center' (p156) for details on tickets.

FILM

Washington offers a few excellent opportunities for film buffs to see some unusual work. Unfortunately the American Film Institute has relocated from the political capital to the movie capital, Hollywood, but DC still plays host to some top-notch festivals. The Smithsonian, the Library of Congress and other museums round out the programming by offering a great variety of international, historical and educational films. Of course, Hollywood's finest are on view here, too.

AMC 9 THEATRES Map pp250-1

☎ 202-703-998-4AMC; www.amctheatres.com; 50 Massachusetts Ave; child/senior/adult matinee $5.50/6.50/6.50, evening $5.50/6.50/8.50; Metro: Union Station

This giant theatre shows the latest and greatest from Hollywood from romantic comedy to action-adventure.

CINEPLEX ODEON

☎ 333-FILM; www.cineplex.com; matinee $5.25, adult $5, child & senior $5

This chain operates several cinemas that show a mixture of popular and art-house movies. Branches include: **Uptown** (Map pp262-3; 3426 Connecticut Ave NW; Metro: Cleveland Park); **Janus** (Map pp258-60; 1660 Connecticut Ave NW; Metro: Dupont Circle); and **Outer Circle** (Map pp262-3; 4849 Wisconsin Ave NW; Metro: Tenleytown-AU).

DC Film Festivals

FilmFest DC (☎ 202-628-3456; www.filmfestdc .org; late Apr) International film festival with themes such as Politics in Film.

Reel Affirmations (☎ 202-986-1119; www .reelaffirmations.org; Oct) The best of new gay, lesbian, bisexual and transgender films from around the world, plus late-night camp films, lively parties and a women's filmmaker brunch.

Washington Jewish Film Festival (☎ 202-777-3248; www.wjff.org; late Nov/early Dec) Films about contemporary Jewish-American themes.

LOEWS CINEPLEX Map pp256-7

☎ 202-342-6441; www.enjoytheshow.com; Wisconsin Ave & K St NW; matinee $6.50, evening adult $9, child & senior $6.50; Georgetown shuttle from Foggy Bottom-GWU

Housed in a refurbished old industrial building on the waterfront, this modern, comfortable cinema has 10 theaters offering Hollywood's finest.

MARY PICKFORD THEATER

Map pp250-1

☎ 202-707-5677; www.loc.gov/rr/mopic/pickford; 101 Independence Ave SE, 3rd Floor, Madison Bldg; admission free; ⚏ shows 7pm Tue, Thu & Fri; Metro: Capitol South

The Mary Pickford Theater at the Library of Congress screens films on historical or cultural themes, relevant to current events. Seating is limited to only 64 people, but reservations can be made by telephone up to one week in advance.

CLASSICAL MUSIC & OPERA

The Kennedy Center is the premier venue for classical music and opera, but performances also take place at venues around town, including the National Gallery of Art, National Building Museum, Corcoran Gallery and Library of Congress, as well as at local universities and churches.

NATIONAL SYMPHONY ORCHESTRA & WASHINGTON CHAMBER SYMPHONY Map pp246-8

☎ 202-467-4600, 800-444-1324; www.kennedy-center.org; 2700 F St NW; Metro: Foggy Bottom

Both directed by Leonard Slatkin, these classic instrumental ensembles perform at the **Kennedy Center** (p156) and at **Wolf Trap Filene Center** (right) in summer.

WASHINGTON OPERA

☎ 202-295-2400, 800-876-7372; www.dc-opera.org

Normally housed at the **Kennedy Center** (p156), the Washington Opera took residence at **Daughters of the American Revolution Constitution Hall** (p58) while the Opera House was closed for renovation. But the company returns home in March 2004 in time for *La Traviata* and *A Streetcar Named Desire*.

COMEDY

Washington DC is not exactly Comedy Central, but the follies of the federal government provide fodder for some fun.

CAPITOL STEPS POLITICAL SATIRE

Map pp246-8

☎ 202-312-1427; www.capsteps.com; Ronald Reagan Bldg & International Trade Center Amphitheater; tickets $31.50; ☺ shows 7:30pm Fri & Sat; Metro: Federal Triangle

This troupe claims to be the only group in America that tries to be funnier than Congress. It's actually comprised of current and former Congressional staffers, so they know their stuff. The best of political comedy, this DC tradition pokes satiric bipartisan fun at both sides of the spectrum (as evidenced by former Speaker of the House Newt Gingrich's observation 'I think I like it better when you make fun of Clinton').

IMPROV Map pp258-60

☎ 202-296-7008; www.dcimprov.com; 1140 Connecticut Ave; Sun-Thu $15, Fri & Sat $17; ☺ shows 8:30pm Tue-Thu, 8pm & 10:30pm Fri & Sat, 8pm Sun; Metro: Farragut North

This is comedy in the more traditional sense, featuring stand-up by comics from Comedy Central, Mad TV and HBO, among others. The Improv also offers workshops for those of us who think we're pretty funny. Six two-hour weekly sessions are $180.

LIVE MUSIC

Washingtonians have long had a love affair with jazz and blues, but in this most international of American cities, you'll also find abundant places to groove to reggae, salsa, African beats and world-music fusion.

Mega Venues

Many of metro DC's larger concert venues are outside the city in the suburbs of Maryland and Virginia.

MCI Center (Map pp246-8; ☎ 202-628-3200; www.mcicenter.com; 601 F St NW; Metro: Gallery Pl-Chinatown) The giant 20,000-seat sports and concert venue in downtown DC.

Merriweather Post Pavilion (☎ 301-596-0660; www.mppconcerts.com; 10475 Little Patuxent Pkwy, Columbia, Maryland) An outdoor venue in suburban Maryland with pavilion and lawn seating.

Nissan Pavilion (☎ 703-754-6400; www.nissanpavilion.com; 7800 Cellar Door Dr, Bristow, Virginia) A huge outdoor venue with lawn and pavilion seating.

Wolf Trap Filene Center (☎ 703-255-1860; www.wolf-trap.org; 1645 Trap Rd, Vienna, Virginia) A beautifully landscaped 4000-seat outdoor venue.

9:30 CLUB Map p249

☎ 202-3-930-930; www.930.com; 815 V St NW; admission $10-35; ☺ 7:30pm Sun-Thu, act 1 8:30pm, act 2 9:15pm, headline 10-10:30pm, 9pm Fri & Sat, act 1 9:45pm, act 2 10:15pm, headline 11:30pm; Metro: U Street-Cardozo

In 1996, DC's premier live rock venue moved from its small downtown digs to this spanking new warehouse, which holds 1200 patrons and has two levels and four bars. (If you've been in DC awhile, you'll recognize the basement bar, salvaged from 9:30's old home.) The calendar is packed with big names – and a wide variety, too, like Joan Armatrading, Blur, Dwight Yoakam, the Samples, Steel Pulse and Third Eye Blind. Shows are standing-room-only on the main floor, but you can sit upstairs in the balcony.

BASIN STREET LOUNGE Map p265
☎ 703-549-1141; 219 King St, Alexandria; admission Fri & Sat $5; ⏰ shows 8pm Tue-Thu, 9pm Fri & Sat; Old Town shuttle from King St Metro

Wire-rimmed glasses and black turtlenecks may be the uniform at this sophisticated jazz venue. Downstairs from the Creole restaurant **219** (p136), the lounge maintains the same French Quarter Victorian decor, which is appropriate for the swinging piano, saxophone and bluesy jazz performances.

BIRCHMERE
☎ 703-549-7500; www.birchmere.com; 3701 Mt Vernon Ave (off Glebe Rd), Alexandria, Virginia; admission $15-35; ⏰ box office 5-9pm, shows 7:30pm; bus 10A from Pentagon City

Known as 'America's Legendary Music Hall,' this is the DC area's premier venue for folk, country, Celtic and bluegrass music. Mary Chapin Carpenter, Lyle Lovett, Shawn Colvin and kd lang are some of the musicians who have performed here. It is located north of Old Town Alexandria off Glebe Rd. Unlike other venues, there is no standing room or dancing; seating is general admission.

BLACK CAT Map p249
☎ 202-667-7960; www.blackcatdc.com; 1811 14th St NW; admission $5-12; ⏰ box office 8pm-midnight; Metro: U Street-Cardozo

Co-owned by Foo Fighter Dave Grohl, the Black Cat is head kitty of DC's indie-rock clubs. Set in a beat-up old warehouse, it draws fans of grunge and industrial rock – most of whom are aged under 30 – to listen to the likes of Garbage, Girls Against Boys, Radiohead, the Squirrel Nut Zippers and Superchunk. The cover charge varies with the band, but there's no cover in the Red Room bar, where there's a good selection of Belgian beer, pool tables and a jukebox.

BLUES ALLEY Map pp256-7
☎ 202-337-4141; www.bluesalley.com; 1073 Rear Wisconsin Ave; admission $13-40; ⏰ shows 8pm & 10pm; Georgetown shuttle from Foggy Bottom-GWU

The city's preeminent jazz and blues club is tucked into a dark alley off Wisconsin Ave in the heart of Georgetown. Inside, this elegant, candlelit supper club has attracted such artists as Ahmad Jamal and the late Dizzy Gillespie. Current performers include Nancy Wilson, Danilo Pérez and various Marsalises. The cover charge is steep, as are the drinks and Creole specialties. The crowd is largely professional.

BOHEMIAN CAVERNS Map p249
☎ 202-299-0801; www.bohemiancaverns.com; 2001 11th St NW; admission $15 ⏰ 6pm-2am Wed-Sat; Metro: U Street-Cardozo

This legendary jazz club – where Miles Davis, John Coltrane, Ella Fitzgerald and Duke Ellington once played – reopened in 2000, after 32 years of decline and decay since the 1968 riots. The new club maintains the mysterious cave-like decor in the basement lounge and features weekly open-mic nights, poetry readings, and live jazz and blues Wednesday to Saturday.

Bohemian Caverns (above)

BOSSA Map p261
☎ 202-667-0088; 2463 18th St NW; admission free-$10; ⏰ 6pm-1am Sun-Thu, 6pm-2am Fri-Sat; Metro: Woodley Park-Zoo/Adams Morgan

Latin jazz, flamenco and bossa nova are on the music menu at this new addition to Adams-Morgan. The music is upstairs in the dark, candle-lit lounge, but the 1st-floor dining room – with high ceilings and art-canvassed walls – is also worth a visit. Come drink mojitos and martinis, and taste the delectable tapas during happy hour.

Going to a Go-Go

Go-go is a unique brand of percussion-driven dance music with both its funky boots planted squarely in DC's black neighborhoods. The go-go scene hit its peak in the mid-'80s and never gained a national following, but fame and recorded tracks aren't really the point with go-go, whose essence is the live jam and the dance party.

African-derived rhythms, loud brass and bass drums and audience call-and-response ('Are you ready to go? Hell, no!') keep the floor moving at go-go shows. The musicians trace their influences back to the pre-1970s de facto segregation of DC. White clubs wouldn't admit black patrons, so they flocked to neighborhood dance halls and black-run venues like the Howard Theatre and Northeast Gardens, which gave rise to a vibrant new soul music played by bands such as the Young Senators and Black Heat. Go-go's daddies, Chuck Brown and the Soul Searchers, emerged from this club culture. In the mid-'70s, Brown mixed disco's nonstop format with funk, syncopated African and Latin rhythms and call-and-response, and the infectiously danceable result spawned other great go-go bands, such as Rare Essence, Trouble Funk and Experience Unlimited.

Shootings at a few shows in the late '80s gave the whole scene a bad (and rather unfair) rep for violence, as did the 1985 film *Good to Go*, which used a go-go soundtrack for its story of rape and murder. The rise of hip-hop soon overshadowed go-go. But the music plays on. Some of the scene has migrated into the suburbs, especially Maryland's Prince Georges County, but you can still hear go to a go-go at DC clubs like **2:K:9** (p164). Check out current music in *City Paper*'s Go-Go section in the CityList. Look for shows by Rare Essence, DJ Kool, the Backyard Band and Northeast Groovers.

BUKOM CAFÉ Map p261
☎ 202-265-4600; 2442 18th St NW; admission free; ⏰ shows 9pm Mon-Thu, 10pm Fri & Sat; Metro: Woodley Park-Zoo/Adams Morgan

Adams-Morgan is known for East African establishments, but Bukom taps the other side of the continent. It draws a stylishly dressed crowd of West Africans and African Americans to share its excellent cuisine and sexy late-night club scene, where bands play African

and Caribbean music: reggae, highlife, funky jazz. There's hardly any room to dance, so everyone kind of stands in place, bounces to the music and rubs against their neighbors.

ELLINGTON'S ON 8TH Map pp250-1
☎ 202-546-8308; 424 8th St SE; admission free; ⏰ 5-10pm Wed, 5-11pm Thu, 5pm-midnight Fri, 11am-midnight Sat, 3-9pm Sun; Metro: Eastern Market

Suffering from a split personality, Ellington's is a pleasant garden café and champagne lounge that attracts a mixed though mostly female clientele. The café has a small menu featuring Southern and Caribbean fare; the loungey side serves smoothies and frappés and fancy desserts to accompany a schedule of poetry readings, and jazz and world-music performances.

IOTA Map p264
☎ 703-522-8340; www.iotaclubandcafe.com; 2832 Wilson Blvd, Arlington; tickets $8-15; ⏰ 11am-2am; Metro: Clarendon

With shows almost every night of the week, Iota is the best spot for live music in Clarendon's music strip. Tickets are available at the door only (no advance sales) and this place packs 'em in. Iota also hosts poetry readings every second Sunday and open-mic night every Wednesday.

LIVE ON PENN Map pp246-8
www.liveonpenn.com; Pennsylvania Ave btwn 3rd & 6th Sts NW; admission $3; ⏰ 4-10pm Jul-Sep; Metro: Archives-Navy Memorial

Every Friday in summer, Pennsylvania Ave turns into a giant outdoor stage that hosts big names (Better than Ezra, Blues Traveler, Everclear and They Might Be Giants all played here in 2003) for practically nothing. Considering the great tunes and incredible price, this has quickly become one of DC's favorite summertime venues.

MADAM'S ORGAN Map p261
☎ 202-667-5370; www.madamsorgan.com; 2461 18th St NW; admission $1-10; ⏰ shows 9:30pm Mon-Thu, 10pm Fri & Sat; Metro: Woodley Park-Zoo/Adams Morgan

It's easy to find this anagrammatic blues and jazz club – look for the wall mural of the bodacious red-haired mama with the club's name painted across her overflowing décolletage. Inside there is more funky decor, with stuffed animals, bizarre paintings and, upstairs, Daddy's Love Lounge & Pickup Joint (actually dedicated to pool-playing) and a deck. Redheaded women – natural or dyed – get half-price Rolling Rocks. Wednesday there's a fine bluegrass jam with much whoopin' and stompin'. Who says DC's got no soul?

RAGTIME Map p264
☎ 703-243-4003; www.ragtimerestaurant.com; 1345 North Courthouse Rd, Arlington; admission free; ⏰ 11am-1am; Metro: Courthouse

Fun happy hours (4pm to 8pm) and diverse live music acts bring out the Arlington music lovers. This place is a bit classier, and likewise the crowd is older and more professional, than at the venues around Clarendon. Acts feature a wide range of blues, jazz and acoustic music. Sunday at 9pm is a popular open-mic night.

SALOUN Map pp256-7
☎ 202-965-4900; 3239 M St NW; admission $3-5; ⏰ 5:30-2am Sun-Thu, 5:30pm-3am Fri & Sat; Georgetown shuttle from Foggy Bottom-GWU

More casual and cheaper than the better-known Georgetown venue Blues Alley, the Saloun attracts patrons who are younger, less polished, but more fun. The mostly local acts play jazz during the week and blues and Motown on weekends. Eighteen beers on tap and Cajun food round out the joint.

STACCATO Map pp258-9
☎ 202-232-2228; www.staccatodc.com; 2006 18th St NW; admission free-$8; ⏰ 7pm-1am; Metro: Woodley Park-Zoo/Adams Morgan

The stage is right in the window, alongside the beautiful baby grand. Acts are mostly acoustic, though they range from rock to jazz to classical. The place gets packed, but the balcony affords a good, comfortable view. Tuesday is open-mic night from 8pm to 1am and Sunday has relaxing, live jazz starting at 9pm.

VELVET LOUNGE Map p249
☎ 202-462-3213; www.velvetloungedc.com; 915 U St NW; admission $5; ⏰ 8pm-2am; Metro: U Street-Cardozo

DC bands on their way up play at this tiny club with a big dedication to local talent. Emerging grungey acts play to alt-rock fans in the Velvet's upstairs hall; downstairs is a dark little pit of a bar.

CLUBBING

Clubbing in DC can be a wide-ranging experience – from the beautiful people who don their fanciest duds to go Downtown, to the exuberant jeans-clad kids running around Georgetown, to the chicly dressed Euros dancing in Dupont. Rest assured, the music is pumping and the crowd is jumping all around the city.

Top Five Clubs

There's no shortage of clubbing options in DC, but here's your best bet for getting down.

- **18th Street Lounge** (p163) Where the beautiful people go to dance and lounge around.
- **Air** (p161) Who can resist dancing in the moonlight?
- **Habana Village** (p164) Once you feel the salsa beat you won't sit down.
- **Nation** (p162) The biggest dance floor in the Nation – um, the city.
- **Polly Esther's** (p162) Were the '70s really so much fun?

DOWNTOWN

AIR Map pp246-8
www.airclubdc.com; 1300 Pennsylvania Ave NW, Ronald Reagan Bldg & International Trade Center; admission $10; ⏰ 9pm-2am Fri & Sat; Metro: Federal Triangle

On weekend nights from June to October, this sober courtyard turns into a high-speed, high-class open-air dance club. The attempt to lure people Downtown after hours is brilliant; city dwellers and suburbanites flock to this space, which pumps with sounds of R&B, house, hip-hop and disco. Comfy lounge chairs – plastic in case of rain – are scattered around the courtyard. Colored lights decorate the marble facade of the Ronald Reagan Building, and tunes blend with the sound of the breeze in the trees. Get on the guest list by signing up on the website in advance.

PLATINUM Map pp246-8
☎ 202-393-3555; www.platinumclubdc.com; 915 F St NW; admission $10; ⏰ 10pm-3am Thu-Sun; Metro: Metro Center

One of the moment's hottest clubs is a three-floor operation housed in a grand former bank, where beautiful people all dressed up dance to the usual mélange of world and electronic music. Theme nights include College night and Latin night, but check the website in advance as the schedule changes. Sign up in advance to get on the guest list, in which case there is no cover charge before 11pm.

POLLY ESTHER'S Map pp246-8
☎ 202-737-1970; www.hustlepass.com; 605 12th St NW; admission Fri $8, Sat $10; ☾ 5pm-2am Thu, to 3am Fri & Sat; Metro: Metro Center
Are you dying to hear Donna Summer or craving Culture Club? Whether you bust out the bellbottoms or just love legwarmers, you'll find a home at this dance club that has a special dance floor for each decade. The crowd is generally mixed, but young – these kids can't possibly remember the underlying romantic tension between the Professor and MaryAnn. But they sure like to boogie down. Sign up online so you don't have to wait at the door.

VIP CLUB Map pp246-8
☎ 202-347-7200; www.vipclubdc.com; 932 F St NW; admission $10-15; ☾ 9pm-3am Fri-Sun; Metro: Gallery Pl-Chinatown
An old department store has been cleverly converted into four wide-open floors rocking to the beats of reggae, hip-hop, Latin and house music. The distinction between VIP Fridays, Plush Saturdays and Glamour Sundays is not really clear, but rest assured, you'd best wear something tight and don't forget your dancing shoes any night of the week.

Friday is ladies' night – open bar 9pm to 11pm and free admission if you arrive before midnight.

WHITE HOUSE & FOGGY BOTTOM

BRAVO BRAVO Map pp246-8
☎ 202-223-5330; 1001 Connecticut Ave NW; admission $5; 10pm-4am Wed-Sat; Metro: Farragut North
The mood is flirty, the dancers are polished, and both men and women wear their best clothes to this salsa and Latin-dance club for the under-30 set. Set in an enormous basement club, the place gets going after midnight. Thursday night features live go-go music.

CAPITOL HILL & SOUTHEAST DC

NATION & VELVET NATION Map pp250-1
☎ 202-554-1500; www.nationdc.com; 1015 Half St SE; price varies with show Sun-Fri, $8-15 Sat; ☾ 8pm-2am Sun-Thu, 10pm-5am Fri & Sat; Metro: Navy Yard
DC's largest dance and live music club has six bars scattered over several levels and a monster outdoor deck with unparalleled views of the Capitol. Live music happens on weekdays, dance parties on weekends. The music is all over the map – house, funk, electronica – with a gargantuan techno party on Friday.

On Saturday, the late-night gay dance party known as 'Velvet Nation' now ranks as one of the hottest gay venues in town. On the immense dance floor, the pumped-up and shirtless pulse in unison to the sounds of hard house, hi-energy and trance under a suspended disco ball the size of a small planet. This swanky affair attracts everyone from circuit boys and drag queens to hip dykes, club kids and cruisers. Velvet Nation doesn't really start kicking till around 12:30 am on Saturday and dancing goes on till 5am.

BROOKLAND & NORTHEAST DC

DREAM Map pp252-3
☎ 202-636-9030; www.masouda.com; 1350 Okie St NE; admission $10-15; ☾ 9pm-4am Thu, 6pm-4am Fri, 9pm-4am Sat; bus D3 or D4 from Union Station
This huge new venue has four floors, each with its own dance floor and style of music: R&B and hip-hop on the 1st floor, Latin on the 2nd; and international or Arabic dance music on the 3rd. The result is a pretty good mix of people, all dressed up and getting down. Weekly events include Friday night singles' parties and Saturday international night. Check out the website in advance to get on the list.

SOUTHWEST DC

ZANZIBAR Map pp254-5
☎ 202-554-9100; 700 Water St SW; admission $10; ☾ 5pm-1am Wed-Thu, 5pm-4am Fri, 9pm-4am Sat, 6pm-1am Sun; Metro: Waterfront
This elegant waterfront dance club draws a well-dressed, primarily black clientele. Dance the night away to live bands or DJ spins, depending on the night. Wednesday is among

the most popular Latin nights in the city; other nights feature techno, zouk, Caribbean and world-beat. See also the Eating chapter (p125).

GEORGETOWN

RHINO BAR & PUMP HOUSE
Map pp256-7
☎ 202-333-3150; 3295 M St NW; admission free; ⏱ 4pm-2am; Georgetown shuttle from Foggy Bottom-GWU Metro

The previous bar on this site, Winston's, was legendary for its dance-and-grope scene. The Rhino Bar has sanitized the premises a bit, but the college-age crowd still checks its inhibitions at the door. DJs play dance music Thursday to Saturday. There are great happy-hour specials – if you can call 9pm to midnight happy hour – include 10c wings on Monday, and half-price burgers and beers on Friday.

THIRD EDITION Map pp256-7
☎ 202-333-3700; 1218 Wisconsin Ave NW; admission $5; ⏱ 5pm-1am Mon-Thu, 5pm-2am Fri, 11:30-2am Sat & Sun; Georgetown shuttle from Foggy Bottom-GWU Metro

For a cinematic college-bar experience, visit this place, which was featured in the 1985 film St Elmo's Fire. This is a pretty serious singles' scene: people are listening closer to pick-up lines than to the music. When you get tired of the crowded dance floor, relax out on the back patio at the tiki bar. Nearly everyone who graduates from Georgetown has some comedic or tragic story about this place.

DUPONT CIRCLE & KALORAMA

18TH STREET LOUNGE Map pp258-60
☎ 202-466-3922; 1212 18th St NW; admission free-$20; ⏱ 9:30pm-2am Tue-Wed, 5:30pm-2am Thu, 5:30pm-3am Fri, 9:30pm-3am Sat; Metro: Dupont Circle

The lack of a sign on the door proclaims the exclusivity of this swanky yet cozy club. In a beautiful mansion that once housed Teddy Roosevelt, its sleek dance floors are ruled by hip-hop and dub. The club is famed for bouncers leaving lesser patrons waiting in the cold; wear your teeniest skirt to avoid any problems.

APE Map pp258-60
☎ 202-296-0505; 1415 22nd St NW; admission $5 before 10pm, $10 after 10pm; ⏱ 9pm-2am Tue, Thu-Sun; Metro: Dupont Circle

Crown jewel of the gay, P-St dance club scene, Ape brings out the college kids and buff boys in droves, especially on Friday. Don't come here to cruise, though; everybody is far too busy getting his groove on to be bothered. This is a popular spot for after-hours dancing on Friday and Saturday.

CLUB CHAOS Map pp258-60
☎ 202-232-4141; www.chaosdc.com; 1603 17th St NW; admission free; ⏱ 5pm-2am Mon-Fri, 5pm-3am Sat & Sun; Metro: Dupont Circle

Thursday's Latin night packs the gay boys and draws a fair number of women into this steamy basement for dancing to salsa and merengue. Saturday night is also popular. Early evenings midweek, live comedy and drag shows attract a more mature crowd.

COBALT & 30 DEGREES Map pp258-60
☎ 202-462-6569; www.foodbardc.com; 1639 R St NW; admission free Sun-Thu, $5 Fri & Sat; ⏱ 5pm-2am; Metro: Dupont Circle

The latest, greatest addition to the 17th-St gay scene is a reincarnation of a club that burned down in 1998. Reopened and renovated, the ground floor now has Food Bar, which gets mixed reviews for its menu. The 1st-floor lounge 30 Degrees has been dubbed the

'Pottery Barn' for its oh-so-tasteful decor. Cobalt is the disco ballroom where pretty boys get down and let loose.

MCC III Map pp258-60

☎ 202-822-1800; 1223 Connecticut Ave NW; admission $5-22; 🕑 4pm-2am Tue-Thu, 4pm-3am Fri, 6pm-3am Sat; Metro: Farragut North

This is the place in DC where you're most likely to see an Icelandic beauty tangoing with a suave Pakistani subconsul. DC's internationalistas, many of them Embassy Row residents, congregate in this beautifully designed club (the name is the street address in Roman numerals). Patrons sip martinis while waiting for DJs to start at 11pm to play world-beat and techno so they can shimmy onto the dance floor. Sunday night is a popular gay night.

ADAMS-MORGAN

BLUE ROOM Map p261

☎ 202-332-0800; 2321 18th St NW; admission $5 after 10pm Fri & Sat; 🕑 9:30pm-2am Wed-Thu, 9:30pm-3am Fri & Sat, 9:30pm-2am Sun; Metro: Woodley Park-Zoo/Adams Morgan

This place is characterized by its cool blue artwork adorning the walls and its cool clientele decorating the three floors of the club (restaurant, dance floor and lounge). The small 3rd-floor bar is open weekends only, but it's an intimate spot to share a drink. The techno dance floor attracts a sleek, upscale clientele.

CHIEF IKE'S MAMBO ROOM Map p261

☎ 202-332-2211; 1725 Columbia Rd NW; admission downstairs/upstairs $4/8; 🕑 9pm-2am; Metro: Woodley Park-Zoo/Adams Morgan

Despite the mixed crowd of young students and older professionals, ain't nobody getting dressed up here. The decor here is *Day of the Dead* meets *Night of the Living Dead*: blinking lights, monster comics laminated onto the tables and voodoo critters on the walls. Dance on weekends and drink all week. Two additional clubs are upstairs: punk Chaos and hip-hop Cosmo Lounge.

HABANA VILLAGE Map p261

☎ 202-462-6310; 1834 Columbia Rd NW; admission $5 Fri & Sat men only, lesson $10; 🕑 7pm-1am Wed-Thu, 7pm-2am Fri & Sat, lesson 7-9pm Wed; Metro: Woodley Park-Zoo/Adams Morgan

DC's best Latin club is in an old townhouse with a cosmopolitan bar and romantic back room where you can sip a mojito and nibble tapas in front of the fireplace. After 10:30pm the scene on the upstairs dance floor explodes, as DJs spin salsa, merengue, mambo, tango and bossa nova to a mixed Latin and white crowd.

HEAVEN & HELL Map p261

☎ 202-667-4355; 2327 18th St NW; Heaven/Hell $5/free; 🕑 Hell: 7:30pm-2am Sun-Thu, 7:30pm-3am Fri & Sat, Heaven: 7:30pm-2am Tue-Thu, 7:30pm-3am Fri & Sat; Metro: Woodley Park-Zoo/Adams Morgan

Heaven (appropriately, upstairs) has three bars and painted cherubs on its walls. Its big draw is Thursday 1980s night (when girls who can tease their hair to make it as big as possible), but it has techno and house DJs most nights. Dress up to get past the gatekeeper (St Peter?). Hell is the darker downstairs pub, where wee devils poke pitchforks at you from the walls. Here you can play pool and dress however you want.

SHAW & THE NEW U DISTRICT

2:K:9 Map p249

☎ 202-667-7750; 2009 8th St NW; admission $12; 🕑 5pm-2am Thu, 5pm-3am Fri, 5pm-4am Sat; Metro: Shaw-Howard University,

Techno and hip-hop rule in a sleekly converted warehouse near the Howard campus. The club promotes itself as multicultural and the under-30 crowd indeed seems equally drawn from white and black neighborhoods. Go-go dancers gyrate in cages elevated above the downstairs dance floor, which has a superloud sound system.

REPUBLIC GARDENS Map p249

☎ 202-232-2710; www.republicgardens.com; 1355 U St NW; 🕑 5:30-11:30pm Tue, 5:30pm-2am Wed-Thu, 5:30pm-2:30am Fri, 6:30pm-2:30am Sat; Metro: U Street-Cardozo

This historic club (where Pearl Bailey waited tables in the 1940s) has recently reopened after a renovation and it looks fabulous. Exposed brick walls, shiny wood floors and modern leather furniture give this place a look of slick sophistication. The program was still being developed at the time of research, so keep your eye on the website.

Sports, Health & Fitness

Sports, Health & Fitness

Considering DC's young population and expansive parkland, it comes as no surprise to see urban outdoorsmen and women running up the Capitol steps, biking around the Jefferson Memorial and skating in front of the White House.

Fierce rugby matches on the Ellipse, studly two-on-two volleyball near the Lincoln Memorial and league softball on the Mall: all take place on any given sunny weekend in DC. Where else in the world can you pant and sweat and groan in the shadow of such majesty?

If you are more of an outdoor-type person and you don't find the plethora of monuments and marble inspirational, Rock Creek Park, the Potomac River and the C&O Canal Towpath are some really fantastic venues for hiking, biking and kayaking – unique ways to escape the city, right in the city.

Carderock Recreation Area, C&O Canal Towpath (p74)

All this goes on, while the keenest of sports fans are planted in front of their TVs. Watching the Redskins. When it comes to spectator sports, DC exposes its Southern roots: this is football country.

Other sports have their fans, to be sure (especially during a strong season). The Wizards' and the Hoyas' most loyal fans are urban kids who – when they're not watching hoops – are playing hoops. The Caps are kept alive by northern transplants (of which there are more than a few).

Hometown baseball, too, is a real fantasy of those who remember it from somewhere else, or from the distant days of the Senators. But the Redskins reign supreme among Washington teams.

'Sports' means different things to different people and DC is no exception. The happy result is that every sportsperson – from in-line skater to face-painter – will find something to cheer about in the nation's capital.

WATCHING SPORT

Offensive maneuvering, defensive strategizing and stiff competition: politics and sports have a lot in common. Watching sport in Washington DC may be second to following politics, but it is still a popular pastime. Professional football, basketball, hockey and soccer teams, as well as competitive college basketball, keep DC sports fans busy year-round.

FOOTBALL

The Washington Redskins are a populist religion in DC, no matter whether they're winning or losing. 'Skins games empty the city, drawing streams of people into sports bars and living rooms to cheer the punting and the grunting.

The Redskins play September through January at **FedEx Field** (☎ 301-276-6050; www.redskins.com; 1600 Raljon Rd, Landover, Maryland; tickets $50-85), but rare is the opportunity to actually see them play here.

There is a miles-long waiting list to buy season tickets, so there are never tickets left for individual games. The only exception is when tickets are returned to the box office by the opposing team, which you can find out by calling the stadium two or three days before the game. If you have your heart set on seeing the 'Skins in person, many online ticket agents will be pleased to sell you tickets with a hefty markup.

www.dreamtix.com; ☎ 703-931-0916

www.thefootballticket.com

www.ticketmonster.org; ☎ 301-669-9659, 800-637-3719

www.tickets-redskins.com; ☎ 301 953-1163, 800-528-4257

If you do manage to secure tickets. you can drive to FedEx Field by taking the Central Ave exit from I-495, or take the $5 shuttle from the Landover or Addison Rd Metro station. Otherwise, enjoy the game from a bar stool at **ESPN Zone** (p149) or **Stetson's** (p152), which are bound to be equally spirited.

BASKETBALL

All of DC's basketball teams – including the National Basketball Association (NBA) Washington Wizards, the women's team (WNBA) Washington Mystics and the Georgetown University Hoyas – play at the **MCI Center** (Map pp246-8; ☎ 202-628-3200; www.mcicenter.com; 601 F St NW; ✆ box office 10am-5:30pm Mon-Sat; Metro: Gallery Pl-Chinatown).

The Washington Wizards play November through April. Tickets are as cheap as $10 for the nosebleed section; $50 for decent seats in the upper concourse; $80 to $90 for the club concourse; and up and up.

The women's team – the Washington Mystics – plays May through September and ticket prices are cheaper ($8 to $50). The Georgetown Hoyas are part of the National College Athletic Association (NCAA), which plays during the same season as the NBA, ending with the NCAA tournament in March.

Tickets to regular season games are $5 to $35, but they can be hard to come by for the games against the Hoya's toughest rivals like Syracuse and Boston College. Tickets for all teams are available at the MCI Center box office, or through **Ticketmaster** (☎ 432-SEAT; www.ticketmaster.com), for which you will have to pay a service charge.

Also in the NCAA, the University of Maryland Terrapins has a pretty fierce basketball team. Season-ticket holders buy up all the seats at the sleek, new **Comcast Center** (Map p244-5; ☎ 410-314-7070; Paint Branch Dr, College Park, Maryland). If students do not pick up their entire allotment, single-game tickets may go on sale about two weeks before the game. But it's recommended that you call the ticket office to find out.

BASEBALL

Short of a miraculous acquisition of the Montreal Expos (p15), DC baseball fans must trek up to Baltimore to cheer on the Orioles at **Oriole Park Camden Yards** (☎ 410-685-9800, 888-848-BIRD; www.theorioles.com; 333 W Camden St, Baltimore; ✆ box office 10am-5pm Mon-Sat, noon-5pm Sun).

During the regular season (April to September), tickets are readily available at the box office or through **Ticketmaster** (☎ 432-SEAT; www.ticketmaster.com) for a service charge. If you don't have a car, you can get to Camden Yards by MARC or Amtrak trains from Union Station, or take a $9 bus ride from the Greenbelt Metro station.

HOCKEY

DC's National Hockey League team, the Washington Capitols, take to the ice at the **MCI Center** (Map pp246-8; ☎ 202-628-3200; www.mcicenter.com; 601 F St NW; ☺ box office 10am-5:30pm Mon-Sat; Metro: Gallery Pl-Chinatown). From October to May, tickets are $25/40/55 and up for the upper-upper/upper/club concourse. Again, they are available from the box office or through **Ticketmaster** (☎ 432-SEAT; www.ticketmaster.com) for a service charge.

SOCCER

Three-time National Major League soccer champions DC United play April through October at **RFK Stadium** (Map pp250-1; ☎ 703-478-6600; East Capitol St; Metro: Stadium-Armory). Tickets are $16 to $36, but the only way to get them is by purchasing a season-long package (with tickets to six or nine games) or by paying the service charge and going through **Ticketmaster** (☎ 432-SEAT; www.ticketmaster.com).

The women's team, Washington Freedom, was led by Mia Hamm for three seasons until the Women's United Soccer Association was disbanded in 2003.

OUTDOOR ACTIVITIES

Washington DC has an ideal climate for outdoor activities. The city's geography, centered around the Potomac River and covered with parks and green space, allows plenty of opportunities to take advantage of the mild temperatures. Whether it's hiking, biking, running, sunning, canoeing, kayaking, horse riding or rock climbing, you'll find a place to do it in DC.

CYCLING

Acres of parkland along the Potomac and around the National Mall and a relatively flat landscape make for great bike touring around DC. The kicker is the miles and miles of off-road bike trails, many of which were converted as part of Rails to Trails. Now that Metro allows bicycles on trains and buses, there is almost no place in DC that you can't reach by bike.

In **Rock Creek Park** (p94), Beach Drive, between Military and Broad Branch Rds, closes to traffic on weekends. South of

Broad Branch, a paved trail parallels the parkway past the zoo and all the way to the Potomac. The trail is narrow in spots and gets crowded on weekends, but it's an easy way to traverse the city by bike. Access the trail at 27th and P Sts NW, or at Connecticut Ave and Calvert St NW.

C&O Canal Towpath (below)

From Georgetown, take the 10-mile **Capital Crescent Trail** (Map pp256-7; www.cctrail.org) along the Potomac and into downtown Bethesda, Maryland. This paved trail – a recent addition to DC's Rails to Trails – is among the best maintained in the city. It has some beautiful lookouts over the river, and winds through woodsy areas and upscale neighborhoods. The southern trailhead is at the east end of K St (called Water St here) under the Francis Scott Key Bridge. From downtown Bethesda, the trail continues for another 2 miles to northern Rock Creek Park, but it is not paved. For maps, call the **Coalition for the Capital Crescent Trail** (☎ 202-234-4874).

The **C&O Canal Towpath** (p74) starts in Georgetown and stretches 184 miles northwest to Cumberland, Maryland. This wide dusty path parallels the Capital Crescent Trail for a few miles. The latter turns west, while the towpath continues 14 miles north to **Great Falls** (p217) and beyond. Note that the towpath is not paved, so wider tires are a boon.

Ohio Dr starts at the Tidal Basin and circumnavigates the peninsula that contains **East Potomac Park** (p70). A wide, paved sidewalk runs parallel for bikers who are not comfortable sharing the road with cars. The five-mile loop runs along the Washington Channel on one side and the Potomac River on the other.

Across the Potomac, the **Mount Vernon Trail** (Map p264) is a beautiful paved riverside path that's a favorite among local bikers. From the Francis Scott Key Bridge, it follows the river south past Roosevelt Island, Arlington Cemetery and National Airport, through Old Town Alexandria, all the way to Mount Vernon (18 miles). The course is mostly flat, except the long climb up the hill to George Washington's house at the end. The scenery is spectacular – DC skylines and all – and the historical element is certainly unique. Old Town Alexandria provides a much-appreciated opportunity to take a break for a drink or a snack.

Also in Virginia, the **Washington & Old Dominion Trail** (W&OD; Map pp244-5; www .wodfriends.org) starts in southern Arlington and follows the old railway bed through historic Leesburg and on to Purcellville, in the Allegheny foothills. Its 45 miles are paved and spacious, winding their way through the Virginia suburbs. The easiest place to pick up the trail is outside the East Falls Church Metro station: exit right and turn right again onto Tuckahoe St, then follow the signs. Vienna and Leesburg are pleasant places to stop along the way.

If you prefer to ride, the **Custis Trail** (Map pp256-7) connects the W&OD to the Mount Vernon Trail or to Washington DC via the Francis Scott Key Bridge.

The **Monumental Bike Ride** (p107) is the best way for cyclers to take in Washington's memorial sights.

If you would like a guide, **Bike the Sites** (Map pp246-8; ☎ 842-BIKE; www.bike thesites.com; 1100 Pennsylvania Ave, Old Post Office Pavilion; adult/child $40/30; ☯ tours 9am & 1pm; Metro: Federal Triangle) offers professionally guided tours of the National Mall, plus off-Mall specialty tours. The price includes bike and equipment. For more information, pick up *Short Bike Rides In & Around Washington, DC*, by Michael Leccese, or *ADC's Washington Area Bike Map*.

The **Washington Area Bicyclists' Association** (WABA; ☎ 202-628-22500; www.waba.org)

has information on bike-advocacy, bike maps and group rides.

On the last Friday of every month, WABA organizes a Solidarity Ride to promote cycling in Washington, DC. Bikers meet in Dupont Circle at 6pm and leave promptly at 6:15pm on a pre-determined, 5- to 10-mile route.

For a list of bike-rental outlets see the Directory (p222).

Top Five Nonpolitical Races

- **Cherry Blossom 10-Miler** (p10) Race around the Tidal Basin when the blossoms are in bloom.
- **Drag Race** (p11) DC's fastest and prettiest, racing through Dupont in high heels.
- **Marine Corps Marathon** (p11) Twenty-six tough miles from the Monument of Iwo Jima around DC and back again.
- **Rolling Thunder** (p10) Thousands of Vietnam Vets descend on the Mall on motorcycles.
- **Seagull Century** (p215) Cycle a century – not 100 years but 100 miles – along the Eastern Shore.

HIKING & RUNNING

Besides the trails mentioned under Cycling (opposite), many miles of unpaved trails provide walkers and runners a softer terrain and uninterrupted time on their feet. **Rock Creek Park** (p94) has 15 miles of unpaved trails. On the west side of Rock Creek, the 4.5-mile green-blazed **Western Ridge Trail** winds through the forest; pick it up at Beach Dr near the intersection with Porter St NW (Metro: Cleveland Park). On the east side, the 5.5-mile blue-blazed **Valley Creek Trail** runs closer to the creek; pick it up at Park Rd near the **tennis courts** (Metro: Cleveland Park). The trails are lightly trafficked and clearly blazed. Maps are available at the **Nature Center** (☎ 202-426-6829). There is also a 1.5-mile exercise trail behind the **Omni Shoreham Hotel** (2500 Calvert St NW; Metro: Woodley Park-Zoo/Adams Morgan), with 18 exercise station stops.

Extensive trail networks connect Rock Creek Park to the other northwestern DC parks – Normanstone, Montrose, Dumbarton Oaks, Whitehaven, Glover Archbold and Battery Kemble – so you can take a terrific cross-city parkland ramble. A good map, *Trails in the Rock Creek Park Area*, is published by the Potomac Appalachian Trail Club.

Other good books include *Hikes in the Washington Region*, also by the Potomac Appalachian Trail Club, and the *Washington, DC Running Guide*, by Don Carter. For organized road races, check out www.runwashington.com or www.dcfront runners.org.

IN-LINE SKATING

The 1995 closure of Pennsylvania Ave to car traffic opened an unprecedented opportunity: a huge stretch of flat, smooth pavement – a parking lot without the cars – right in front of DC's most prime of prime real estate. It did not take long for in-line skaters to discover this outdoor roller rink.

Nowadays, Pennsylvania Ave is a meeting place for bladers of all types. The **Washington Area Roadskaters** (www.skatedc.org) is a loose organization of avid skaters that leads group skates, ranging from the beginners' monument loop to an advanced night skate. Their goal is to promote safe skating, but they also have a great time skating and socializing together, often finishing up the skating outings with beers at the **Froggy Bottom Pub** (p149). They meet in front of the White House on Wednesday and Friday at 7pm and Sunday at 11am from April to October. The White House also hosts informal roller hockey pick-up games, often on Thursday evening and also on weekends.

In-line skates are available for rental from the **Ski Center** (Map pp262-3; ☎ 202-966-4474; www.skicenter.com; 4300 Fordham Rd NW; per day $15; Metro: Tenleytown-AU) and the **Ski Chalet of Arlington** (☎ 703-521-1700; www.skichalet.com; 2704 Columbia Pike; per hr/day $5/15; 16 bus from Pentagon Metro), southwest of Arlington Cemetery.

KAYAKING & CANOEING

Kayaks and canoes can cruise on the waters of both the Potomac River and the C&O Canal. The canal is ideal for canoeing between Georgetown and Violettes Lock (Mile 22); canoeists must portage around each lock. The Potomac is for the more adventurous, but it is a great vantage point from which to admire the city skyline. North of Georgetown, white-water areas can be dangerous, especially between Great Falls and Chain Bridge.

ATLANTIC KAYAK Map pp254-5
☎ 703-479-0707; www.atlantickayak.com; 600 Water St, Gangplank Marina; 2hr tour $32; ⏰ 10am-8:30pm; Metro: Waterfront

Atlantic Kayak offers beginners' kayaking classes, as well as tours of the Washington Channel, Anacostia River and Potomac River. Romantic moonlight tours are offered every month. Atlantic's main facility is in **Alexandria, Virginia** (Map p265; ☎ 703-838-9072, 800-297-0066; 1201 N Royal St, Alexandria).

FLETCHER'S BOATHOUSE Map pp244-5
☎ 202-244-0461; www.fletchersboathouse.com; 4940 Canal Rd NW; canoe per hr/day $11/21; ⏰ 9am-7:30pm Mar-Nov; bus D5 from Foggy Bottom-GWU Metro.

This boathouse is a few miles upriver from Georgetown (accessible by bike from the C&O Canal Towpath or by car from Canal Rd). Canoes, rowboats and bicycles are available.

POTOMAC PADDLESPORTS
☎ 301-831-8270, 877-529-2542; www.potomacpaddlesports.com; Potomac, Maryland

Whitewater and sea-kayaking lessons are the focus of Potomac Paddlesports. It also leads flat-water trips for beginners, like a fall foliage tour, a moonlight tour of the Potomac and nature-lovers' tours through a wildlife refuge ($98 each).

THOMPSON BOAT CENTER Map pp256-7
☎ 202-333-9543; 2900 Virginia Ave NW; watercraft per hr $8-13, day $22-30; ⏰ 6am-6pm; Metro: Foggy Bottom-GWU

Just across the street from the Kennedy Center, Thompson Boat Center rents canoes and kayaks, and offers rowing classes. This is also a convenient place to rent bicycles (p223).

GOLF

DC's three public golf courses are all fine places to enjoy a spring afternoon in the city.

EAST POTOMAC PARK Map pp254-5
☎ 202-554-7660; Ohio Dr SW; 18 holes weekday/ weekend $20/25, 9 holes $12/16; ⏰ dawn-dusk; Metro: Smithsonian

This busy place is a bit scrubby, but where else can you golf in sight of the Jefferson Memorial and the Washington Monument, with big ol' jet airliners flying low overhead? The downside is it can be loud (thanks to aircraft) and windy. There are three courses: the par-72 18-hole

Blue; nine-hole White; and 12-hole Red, which is in the best condition.

LANGSTON Map pp252-3
☎ 202-397-8638; 26th St NE & Benning Rd NE; 18 holes weekday/weekend $15/19; ✆ dawn-dusk; bus X1, X2 or X3 from Union Station

Considered by many to be DC's best public course, Langston opened in 1939 as a course for African American golfers and is still predominately played by black golfers. Fairways are flat, with lots of trees on the back nine.

ROCK CREEK PARK Map pp262-3
☎ 202-882-7332; 1600 Rittenhouse St NW; 18 holes weekday/weekend $16.50/22, 9 holes $11/14; ✆ 6am-9pm Apr-Oct, 7am-5:30pm Nov-Mar; bus S1, S2, S4

This 18-hole course does not get great reviews for the upkeep of its tee boxes or fairways. But this 'citadel of working person's golf' offers convenience and value. Low hills and narrow fairways offer a bit of a challenge, but there are no water hazards.

HORSE RIDING
For the horse rider, 13 miles of wide dirt trails crisscross the northern part of Rock Creek Park, with a large **Equitation Field** (Map pp262-3) nearby. The **Rock Creek Horse Center** (Map pp262-3; ☎ 202-362-0117; 5100 Glover Rd NW; per hr $25; ✆ 3pm Tue-Thu, noon, 1:30 & 3pm Sat & Sun) offers guided trail rides, lessons and pony rides for kids. Reservations are required.

ROCK CLIMBING
In DC, rock climbers head for **Rock Creek Park** (p94). The boulder area underneath the bridge at Massachusetts Ave and Whitehaven Rd is 20ft high and 50ft wide, large enough for four defined routes and the potential for more. Other climbing spots are at Carderock Recreation Area on the **C&O Canal Towpath** (p74) and **Great Falls** (p217). Indoor climbing walls are at the **National Capital YMCA** (p171) and **Results the Gym** (p172).

TENNIS
The city maintains over 50 free public courts, including Montrose Park at 31st and R Sts NW and Rock Creek Park at 24th and N Sts NW. Call the **DC Dept of Parks and Recreation** (☎ 202-698-2250; http://dpr.dc.gov).

ROCK CREEK PARK Map pp262-3
☎ 202-722-5949; 16th & Kennedy Sts NW; courts per hr from $4; ✆ 7am-11pm; bus S1, S2 or S4

Both hard- and soft-surface courts (25 in total) are open to the public, but they must be reserved from April to October. For more about the park, see Neighborhoods (p94).

HEALTH & FITNESS
When in DC, there is no need to forego your regular routine of running or reflexology. The city has plenty of fitness centers and health spas to meet the work-out and chill-out needs of any visitor.

SWIMMING POOLS
When air-conditioning isn't enough, get relief from the summer heat at one of these facilities.

Capitol East Natatorium (Map pp250-1; ☎ 202-724-4495; 635 N Carolina Ave SE; adult/child $7/4; ✆ 6:30am-9pm Mon-Fri, 10am-5pm Sat & Sun; Metro: Eastern Market) Indoor 25m facility.

Francis Pool (Map pp258-60; ☎ 202-727-3285; 2500 N St NW; adult/child $7/4; ✆ 1-8pm Mon & Wed-Fri, noon-6pm Sat & Sun; Metro: Dupont Circle) Outdoor pool open June to August.

Georgetown Pool (Map pp256-7; ☎ 202-282-2366; 3400 Volta Pl; adult/child $7/4; ✆ 1-8pm Tue-Fri, noon-6pm Sat & Sun; Georgetown shuttle from Foggy Bottom-GWU Metro) Outdoor pool open June to August and crowded with kids.

GYMS & FITNESS CENTERS
In the dead of winter or the dripping, humid heat of summer, DC gyms are packed with type-As. The good news is that you can join them. DC has enough visitors and transient residents that most gyms allow for short-term (as short as one-day) memberships.

Fitness First (Map pp246-8; ☎ 202-659-1900; www.fitnessfirstclubs.com; 1075 19th St NW; day/month pass $10/75; ✆ 5am-11pm Mon-Thu, 5am-10pm Fri, 8am-8pm Sat & Sun; Metro: Farragut North) All the weight machines and cardiovascular equipment you could hope for, plus free weights; kickboxing, aerobics, spinning, Pilates and yoga classes; sauna and steam room.

National Capital YMCA (Map pp258-60; ☎ 202-862-9622; www.nationalcapitalymca.org; 1711 Rhode Island Ave; day pass/steam room $15/20; ✆ 5:30am-10:30pm Mon-Fri, 8am-6:30pm Sat, 9am-5:30pm Sun; Metro: Farragut North)

Seven floors of fitness and fun, including squash courts, basketball courts, indoor track, rock-climbing wall, free weights, cardio machines and classes.

Results the Gym: Capitol Hill (Map pp250-1; ☎ 202-234-5678; www.resultsthegym.com; 315 G St SE; day pass $18; 🕒 5am-11pm Mon-Fri, 8am-9pm Sat & Sun; Metro: Capitol South) Light-filled cardio room; rotating climbing wall; specialty classes for abdominals as well as varying levels of yoga, and urban funk.

Results the Gym: Dupont Circle (Map pp258-60; ☎ 202-518-0001; 1612 U St NW; Metro: U Street-Cardozo)

Spiral Flight (Map pp256-7; ☎ 202-965-1645; www .spiralflightyoga.com; 1726 Wisconsin Ave NW; 60/90 min $16/18; 🕒 classes vary seasonally; Georgetown shuttle from Foggy Bottom-GWU Metro) Center for yoga and tai chi, in art-gallery setting.

YWCA (Map pp246-8; ☎ 202-626-0710; www.ywcanca .org; 624 9th St NW; day pass $12; 🕒 6:30am-9pm Mon-Fri, 8:30am-4:30pm Sat, 10am-4:30pm Sun; Metro: Gallery Pl-Chinatown) Free weights, machines and a 25m lap pool; women and men welcome.

MASSAGE & DAY SPAS

Every now and then, everyone needs to indulge. Hair gets frizzy, feet get sore, minds grow weary and nothing but a little pricey self-indulgence can fix matters. Here's a list of good day spas where you can spoil yourself:

Andre Chreky Salon (Map pp246-8; ☎ 202-293-9393; 1604 K St NW; Metro: McPherson Sq) A sleek business-district spa fixing up skin, hair and nails. It has a coffee bar to keep you awake while you're fussed over.

Aveda Georgetown (Map pp256-7; ☎ 202-965-1325; 1325 Wisconsin Ave NW; Georgetown shuttle from Foggy Bottom-GWU Metro) Does nice herbal things to skin, body and hair.

EFX/Blue Mercury (Map pp256-7; ☎ 202-965-1300; 3059 M St NW; Georgetown shuttle from Rosslyn or Foggy Bottom-GWU Metro) A small Georgetown spa drawing a hip young clientele. It has facials, massages, friendly, low-key staff and better-than-average piped-in music.

Four Seasons Fitness Club/Spa (Map pp256-7; ☎ 202-944-2022; 2800 Pennsylvania Ave NW; Georgetown shuttle from Foggy Bottom-GWU Metro) Part of the luxurious Four Seasons Hotel. You can't use the gym itself unless you stay overnight, but exercise classes and spa treatments are available to nonguests.

Jolie (☎ 301-986-9293; 7200 Wisconsin Ave NW, Bethesda; Metro: Bethesda) One of the area's better-known spas. It's pretty affordable, despite its expensively frilly decor, and offers all the services: massage, vitamin facial wraps and pedicures. It's close to Bethesda Metro.

Tara Salon (Map pp256-7; ☎ 202-333-8099; 2715 M St NW; Metro: Foggy Bottom-GWU) Offers all sorts of skin and hair stuff, from basic leg waxes to massage and electrolysis.

Shopping

Shopping

When it comes to shopping, the nation's capital is a souvenir-lovers paradise. From rubber Nixon masks to stars-and-stripes underpants, Washington shops sell the ultimate in kitsch and memorabilia. And there are the classic souvenirs, too: stuffed pandas from the National Zoological Park, shredded money from the Bureau of Printing & Engraving, balsa-wood airplanes from the National Air & Space Museum.

Less giddy shoppers will appreciate the plethora of museum stores. They offer books, jewelry, crafts, art and souvenirs from across the US. Imported goods, such as textiles and art, are available at museum stores and import shops throughout the city.

World-music buffs and multilinguists will find music, literature and newspapers from the four corners of the planet.

Secondhand shops, clothing boutiques, bookstores and art galleries will keep a shopper busy for hours in Georgetown or Dupont Circle.

Opening Hours

Generally, stores are open 10am to 7pm weekdays and Saturday; noon to 5pm Sunday, although some shops close on Sunday. Smaller shops may close at 5pm every day, or stay open until 7pm one night a week, eg Thursday. Museum shops are open according to museum hours.

Consumer Taxes

Sales tax is 5.75% in DC, 4.5% in Virginia and 5% in Maryland.

NATIONAL MALL

ARTHUR M SACKLER GALLERY

Map pp246-8   *Museum Shop*

☎ 202-633-4800; www.asia.si.edu; 1050 Independence Ave SW; ☺ 10am-5:30pm, to 8pm Thu Jul & Aug; Metro: Smithsonian

The Arthur M Sackler Gallery shop features Asian art posters and limited edition prints, jewelry and crafts from around the world, and lots of books and educational materials.

FREER GALLERY OF ART

Map pp246-8   *Museum Shop*

☎ 202-633-4800; www.asia.si.edu; 1050 Independence Ave SW; ☺ 10am-5:30pm, to 8pm Thu Jul & Aug; Metro: Smithsonian

As well as prints, posters, jewelry and crafts, world music enthusiasts will find an extensive selection of traditional and contemporary music from Asian countries. Fun kits for kids teach them about brush painting, origami and haiku.

HIRSHHORN MUSEUM

Map pp246-8   *Museum Shop*

☎ 202-357-2700; 7th St & Independence Ave SW; ☺ 10am-5:30pm; Metro: Smithsonian

The Hirshhorn has a small but excellent store for books on modern art. Exhibition catalogs make great souvenirs and are terrific to share with others.

NATIONAL AIR & SPACE MUSEUM

Map pp246-8   *Museum Shop*

☎ 202-357-2700; 6th St & Independence Ave SW; ☺ 10am-5:30pm; Metro: Smithsonian

This gift shop is more like a gift mall: it's a three-floor emporium offering books, toys, posters, model aircraft and such iconic DC souvenirs as freeze-dried Astronaut Ice Cream (tasting like cotton candy squished by a steamroller). It has an incomparable selection of books on all aspects of aviation – it would be hard to find such a collection in any other US bookstore. All kinds of kites roost here, too, from classic diamond shapes to neon butterflies.

NATIONAL GALLERY OF ART

Map pp246-8   *Museum Shop*

☎ 202-737-4215; www.nga.gov; 4th St & Constitution Ave NW; ☺ 10am-5pm Mon-Sat, 11am-6pm Sun; Metro: Archives-Navy Memorial

If you're in the market for art reproductions of any kind, browse the elongated shops lining

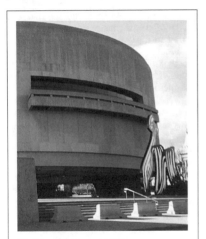
Hirshhorn Museum (p174)

the underground corridors linking the East and West Buildings. The collection here is quite extensive, with framed and unframed reproductions of the museum's best-known works, greeting cards, jewelry and loads of books. A good children's section has crafty kits to encourage your kid's creative tendencies.

NATIONAL MUSEUM OF AFRICAN ART
Map pp246-8   *Museum Shop*
☎ 202-357-2700; 950 Independence Ave SW;
🕐 10am-5:30pm; Metro: Smithsonian
This museum shop carries an incredible selection of African Art, including textiles, baskets, musical instruments and dolls.

NATIONAL MUSEUM OF AMERICAN HISTORY Map pp246-8   *Museum Shop*
☎ 202-357-2700; 14th St & Constitution Ave NW;
🕐 10am-5:30pm; Metro: Smithsonian
In the spirit of consumerist America, the American History offers four (and counting) venues for your wallet to 'celebrate' American history. The main museum shop has reproductions of old war posters and newspapers with newsworthy headlines from the 20th century. There is an excellent selection of crafts, including Navajo pottery and Inuit statues. Other stores in the museum focus specifically on presidents, music and – in keeping with the museum's latest exhibit – transportation. The museum also has the Smithsonian's largest collection of books and videos on all aspects of American culture and history.

NATIONAL MUSEUM OF NATURAL HISTORY Map pp246-8   *Museum Shop*
☎ 202-357-2700; 10th St & Constitution Ave NW;
🕐 10am-5:30pm; Metro: Smithsonian
This museum is another gift emporium with four different specialty shops, including the main store on the ground floor. The Tricera Shop is totally devoted to dinosaur merchandise (now that's specialized). The glittering Gem Store – outside the Geology Hall – has a huge selection of fine and costume jewelry, including beautiful amber samples which are millions of years old. The newest Mammals Museum Store, designed to represent four continents (Asia, Australia, North & South America), carries toys, crafts, posters and books focusing on mammals and evolution.

DOWNTOWN

APARTMENT ZERO Map pp246-8   *Housewares*
☎ 202-628-4067; 406 7th St NW; 🕐 11am-7pm Wed-Sat, noon-5pm Sun; Metro: Archives-Navy Memorial
Selling clean-lined furniture – think George Jetson meets Danish Modern – this little design shop prides itself on functionality (many items are modular or foldable).

BEAD MUSEUM
Map pp246-8   *Jewelry & Accessories*
☎ 202-624-4500; www.beadmuseumdc.org; 400 7th St NW; 🕐 11am-4pm Wed-Sat, 1-4pm Sun; Metro: Archives-Navy Memorial
The shop reflects the museum's educational mission by offering one-of-a-kind contemporary

Top Five Shopping Strips

These top shopping locales are good for souvenirs, galleries, bookstores and specialty shops. Serious consumers, however, should head to the suburban malls where you will find huge selections of clothing, electronics, books and furniture stores (see the boxed text 'Shoppin' in the Suburbs: Local Malls', p188).

- **7th St NW, Downtown** Department stores like Hechts and H&M (coming soon), plus an up-and-coming art district.
- **Connecticut Ave & Around, Dupont Circle** DC's best collection of art galleries and import shops.
- **M St NW, Georgetown** Art galleries, boutiques and bookstores galore.
- **National Mall** Souvenirs, souvenirs, souvenirs.
- **Union Station** Hundreds of stores selling Americana-themed souvenirs and gifts (and regular stuff you might need too).

Top Five Kitschy Souvenirs

- **Arlington National Cemetery Gift Shop** (p97) Commemorative JFK-gazing-into-the-distance photographs.
- **Best of DC Shop, Union Station** (p179) White House snowstorm globes.
- **International Spy Museum** (p176) Rear-view sunglasses.
- **NRA Firearms Museum Gift Shop** (11250 Waples Mill Rd, Fairfax, Virginia) National Rifle Association terrycloth baby bibs.
- **Vendor carts** (17th St NW, near the White House) 'I'm with Bubba' Bill Clinton T-shirt.

and ethnic beaded jewelry, books, posters and videos that relate to the exhibits.

CELADON Map pp246-8 *Beauty Products*
202-347-3333; 1180 F St NW; 9am-7pm Mon-Fri, 8am-4pm Sat; Metro: Metro Center
This rather luxurious spa also carries a very impressive array of beauty products by such upscale designers as Peter Thomas Roth and Jack Black.

CITY MUSEUM OF WASHINGTON
Map pp246-8 *Books*
202-785-2068; 800 Mt Vernon Sq; 10am-5pm Tue-Sun, to 9pm 3rd Thu of month; Metro: Mt Vernon Sq-Convention Center or Gallery Pl-Chinatown
The museum's unique bookstore has an extensive selection of books on all aspects of DC history, including specific neighborhoods, ethnic groups and historical periods.

HECHT'S Map pp246-8 *Department Store*
202-628-6661; 1201 G St NW; 10am-8pm; Metro: Metro Center
This is the mid-Atlantic region's version of Macy's: a big department store selling a full range of mid-priced clothing, cosmetics, shoes and housewares.

INTERNATIONAL SPY MUSEUM
Map pp246-8 *Museum Shop*
202-393-7798, 866-SPYMUSEUM; 800 F St NW; 10am-8pm Apr-Oct, 10am-6pm Nov-Mar; Metro: Gallery Pl-Chinatown
Let's face it – everyone needs a pair of reverse-mirrored sunglasses once in a while, whether you are being followed or you just want to check out the hottie behind you in the elevator. Now you know where to get

them, and piles of other nifty spy gadgets. The store claims that such paraphernalia is 'bound to make your life, well, more cool,' and who can argue with that? Other Bond-gear that might come in handy includes concealed video and listening devices, disguise kits, microcameras and recorder pens.

NATIONAL BUILDING MUSEUM
Map pp246-8 *Museum Shop*
202-272-2448; www.nbm.org; 401 F St NW; 10am-5pm Mon-Sat, 11am-5pm Sun; Metro: Judiciary Sq
This museum shop is an amateur architect's dream, with small furniture pieces, rich coffee-table books, paper models of famed buildings, and a collection of books on American and international architecture.

NATIONAL MUSEUM OF WOMEN IN THE ARTS Map pp246-8 *Museum Shop*
202-222-7270; www.nmwa.org; 1250 New York Ave NW; 10am-5pm Mon-Sat, noon-5pm Sun; Metro: Metro Center
This unique institution dedicated to women artists has an equally unique shop. A small room left of the museum entrance, it holds books, prints, posters, jewelry and handicrafts – all made by women.

NATIONAL PLACE Map pp246-8 *Mall*
202-662-1250; 14th & F Sts; 10am-7pm Mon-Sat, noon-5pm Sun; Metro: Metro Center
This little mall has a handful of boutiques and a decent food court. It's not worth a special trip, but it is useful to fulfill some basic needs (eg birthday card, watch band, button-down shirt) if you happen to be in the neighborhood.

NUMARK GALLERY Map pp246-8 *Art*
202-628-3810; 625 E St NW; 11am-6pm Tue-Sat; Metro: Judiciary Sq
In its flashy new street-level space, Numark is one of several galleries in this downtown art district, showcasing mainly local artists' work.

OLD POST OFFICE PAVILION
Map pp246-8 *Mall*
202-289-4224; 12th St & Pennsylvania Ave NW; 9am-7:45pm Mon-Sat, 10am-5:45pm Sun; Metro: Federal Triangle
It's not exactly a shopping center, but it does have a tourist-crowded food court, as well as souvenir shops, newsstands and stores. It's worth a visit just for a look around the gorgeous central atrium. For more details see p56.

Shopping – Downtown

TOUCHSTONE GALLERY Map pp246-8   *Art*
☎ 202-347-2787; www.touchstonegallery.com; 406 7th St NW; ⓒ 11am-5pm Wed-Fri, noon-5pm Sat & Sun; Metro: Archives-Navy Memorial
One location encompasses several galleries, including the spacious, artist-owned Touchstone Gallery, which exhibits the work of its 35 to 40 members. Exhibits are contemporary and varied.

VEGA Map pp246-8   *Housewares*
☎ 202-589-0140; 819 7th St NW; ⓒ 11am-6pm Mon-Sat, noon-5pm Sun; Metro: Gallery Pl-Chinatown
Decorate your pad with furniture and light fixtures from this slick interior design gallery.

ZENITH GALLERY Map pp246-8   *Art*
☎ 202-783-0050; www.zenithgallery.com; 419 7th St NW; ⓒ 11am-4pm Mon, 11am-6pm Tue-Fri, noon-7pm Sat, noon-5pm Sun; Metro: Archives-Navy Memorial
Margery Eleme Goldberg's gallery has been an anchor of the DC art scene for several decades, showcasing new and established artists from both local and national (and some international) artists. She hosts exhibits of interesting paintings and sculpture, as well as three-dimensional mixed media works – unusual tapestries, fine crafts and furniture, and wearable art.

3rd 3rsday Art Crawl

On the third Thursday of each month, at 6pm to 8pm, local artists lead free tours of the downtown galleries and art businesses (www.culturaldc.org /3rdthursday.html). The tours often feature special exhibits, poetry readings and lectures by the artists about their work – an incredible opportunity to get a first-hand insider's view of the downtown art scene. Tours begin at **Goethe-Institut Inter Nationes** (Map pp246-8; 814 7th St NW). The crawl route is subject to change, but it usually goes like this:

- **Vega** (p177) 819 7th St NW
- **Starbucks PoetryFest** 800 7th St NW
- **National Academy of Sciences** (p59) 500 5th St NW
- **Numark Gallery** (p176) 625 E St NW
- **HNTB Companies** 421 7th St NW
- **Zenith Gallery** (p177) 419 7th St NW
- **Apartment Zero** (p175) 406 7th St NW
- **Artists' Museum** 406 7th St NW
- **Touchstone Gallery** (p177) 406 7th St NW

After the tour, stop by **Andale** (p118) or the **District Chophouse & Brewery** (p118) to socialize with the artists and take advantage of 3rd 3rsday happy-hour specials from 8pm to 10pm.

WHITE HOUSE AREA & FOGGY BOTTOM

ABC MAP & TRAVEL CENTER
Map pp246-8   *Maps*
☎ 202-628-2608; 1636 I St NW; ⓒ 9am-6:30pm Mon-Thu, 9am-5:30pm Fri, 9am-5pm Sat; Metro: Farragut West
This wee downtown storefront is packed with everything from DC activity guides to bus-route maps to huge foldout sheet maps of the district.

CHAPTERS Map pp246-8   *Books*
☎ 202-347-5495; 1512 K St NW; ⓒ 10am-6:30pm Mon-Fri, 11am-5pm Sat; Metro: McPherson Sq
The best bookstore in this area is dedicated almost exclusively to literary fiction; it has one of the liveliest reading calendars in town and an active book club that meets monthly. Blocks from the White House, it is a favorite of white-collars, as well as tourists.

INDIAN CRAFT SHOP Map pp246-8   *Art*
☎ 202-208-4056; 1849 C St NW, No 1023 Dept of Interior; ⓒ 8:30am-4:30pm Mon-Fri; Metro: Farragut West
This crowded one-room shop sells gorgeous but costly basketry, weavings and jewelry made by Native Americans. Show picture ID to enter the building.

RENWICK GALLERY
Map pp246-8   *Museum Shop*
☎ 202-357-2700; 17th St & Pennsylvania Ave NW; ⓒ 10am-5:30pm; Metro: Farragut West
In one of DC's best museum shops, handmade textiles and hand-dyed silks are available, as is glasswork, woodwork and unique jewelry, much of it quite affordable (a pair of hand-blown ruby-glass earrings costs $12). Its excellent choice of books includes how-to manuals on jewelry- and fabric-making, ceramics, glass-blowing and cabinetry, many appropriate for kids. In this store you can learn as well as buy; it feels like an organic extension of the crafts museum upstairs.

RITZ CAMERA Map pp246-8   *Cameras*
☎ 202-861-7710; 1750 L St NW; ⓒ 8am-6:30 pm; Metro: Farragut North
This shop is well stocked with cameras, photography gear and photogs who can repair yours if need be.

SECURITY INTELLIGENCE TECHNOLOGIES

Map pp246-8   *Espionage Essentials*

☎ 202-887-1717; 1001 Connecticut Ave NW, No 530; 🕘 9am-6pm Mon-Fri by appointment; Metro: Farragut North

Wannabe G-men won't find a better place to pick up surveillance and countersurveillance gear. Some patrons seem to be here for a laugh, but others are very serious indeed. Check out the Predator VI night-vision goggles, Air Tasers, line-bug detection devices – everything your paranoid little heart desires.

WHITE HOUSE HISTORICAL ASSOCIATION GIFT SHOP

Map pp246-8   *Souvenirs*

☎ 202-737-8292; 740 Jackson Pl NW, Lafayette Sq; 🕘 9am-4pm Mon-Fri; Metro: Farragut West

Peruse a wide selection of books, videos, gifts, posters, Christmas ornaments, jewelry, postcards and educational materials, all on the theme of the big house across the square. This is the place to buy your dad a White House necktie. There is a similarly stocked store in the White House Visitors Center.

WORLD BANK INFOSHOP

Map pp246-8   *Books*

☎ 202-458-5454; www.worldbank.org/infoshop; 1818 H St NW, No J1-060; 🕘 9am-5pm Mon-Fri; Metro: Farragut West

The controversial multilateral lender runs the excellent World Bank InfoShop, which sells a vast collection of books and documents on all aspects of development and economics.

CAPITOL HILL & SOUTHEAST DC

ANACOSTIA MUSEUM

Map pp250-1   *Museum Shop*

☎ 202-287-3306; www.si.edu/anacostia; 1901 Fort Pl SE; 🕘 10am-5pm; bus W1 or W2 from Anacostia Metro

This small shop has a thoughtful collection of African and African American toys, books and crafts.

BACKSTAGE Map pp250-1   *Fancy Dress*

☎ 202-544-5744; 545 8th St SE; 🕘 11am-7pm Mon-Sat; Metro: Eastern Market

This costume and theatrical store caters to both the drag crowd and government types in search of fancy dress for parties. It rents outfits, and you can buy funky face paints, wigs and masks.

EASTERN MARKET

Map pp250-1   *Food & Beverages, Art, Antiques*

☎ 202-546-2698; www.easternmarket.net; 225 7th St SE; 🕘 10am-6pm Tue-Fri, 8am-4pm Sat & Sun; Metro: Eastern Market

Eastern Market's **South Hall** is the closest DC gets to foodie heaven: in its friendly confines are a bakery, dairy, fish counter, poultry counter, butcher, produce vendors and flower stands. Put together a real Southern feast here – the Southern Maryland Seafood Company serves up the blue crabs and shrimp; over at Union Meat Company are fresh chitterlings, pigs' trotters and all kinds of sausage and steak. To get it all blessed, stop by Calomiris, the Greek produce stand, which sells Orthodox icons among its cucumbers and oranges.

Next door, **Market 5 Gallery** is a space used by local artists to exhibit visual and performing arts. On weekends, both the artists and the farmers markets spill out onto the sidewalks. Besides fresh produce, you can pick up hand-made scarves, prints, smelly soaps and candles, colorful pottery, painted ceramics and unusual jewelry. Across the street at the weekend **flea market**, vendors hawk cool refinished (or not) furniture

GOVERNMENT PRINTING OFFICE & BOOKSTORE Map pp250-1   *Books*

☎ 202-512-0132; 710 N Capitol St; 🕘 8am-4pm Mon-Fri; Metro: Union Station

Perhaps you needed to pick up a title published by the US government. (You never know...there are 15,000 of them.) Here, you can peruse blockbusters like *Selling to the Military* and *Nest Boxes for Wood Ducks* (among many others).

NATIONAL POSTAL MUSEUM

Map pp250-1   *Museum Shop*

☎ 202-357-2991; www.postalmuseum.si.edu; 2 Massachusetts Ave NE; 🕘 10am-5:30pm; Metro: Union Station

Perhaps it goes without saying, but philatelists should head to the National Postal Museum shop for current US stamps and poster-size blow-ups of unique historical stamps.

TROVER SHOP Map pp250-1   *Books*

☎ 202-547-2665; 221 Pennsylvania Ave SE; 🕘 7am-8pm Mon-Fri, 7am-7pm Sat, 7am-3pm Sun; Metro: Eastern Market

This two-level goldmine is a DC institution for books, cards and gifts. It also has a wide selection of books-on-tape, which are rentable. Unsurprisingly, its section on politics is primo.

UNION STATION Map pp250-1 *Mall*

☎ 202- 289-1908; www.unionstationdc.com; 50 Massachusetts Ave NE; ⏱ 10am-9pm Mon-Sat; noon-6pm Sun; Metro: Union Station

Not only an architectural landmark and a train depot, Union Station is also a good-sized mall, complete with multiscreen cinema, food court, restaurants and hundreds of shops. Stores include your standard mall chains, but there is also a great selection of boutiques that sell toys, jewelry and DC souvenirs. Highlights include the National Zoo Store, Appalachian Spring for arts and crafts, Discovery Store, the Great Train Store (selling train memorabilia and toys) and the Best of DC souvenir shop. Two-hour validated parking is available for shoppers. See also Neighborhoods (p66).

GEORGETOWN

APPALACHIAN SPRING Map pp256-7 *Art*

☎ 202-337-5780; 1415 Wisconsin Ave NW; ⏱ 10am-8pm Mon-Fri, 10am-6pm Sat, noon-6pm Sun; Georgetown shuttle from Rosslyn Metro

Touting their motto 'celebrating American craft,' this local chain features fine handmade pottery, woodcarvings, quilts and jewelry.

BALDAQUIN Map pp256-7 *Bed, Bath & Table*

☎ 202-625-1600; 1413 Wisconsin Ave NW; ⏱ 10am-6pm Tue-Fri, 10am-5pm Sat; Georgetown shuttle from Rosslyn Metro

Finely woven tablecloths, fluffy terrycloth bathrobes and fine duvets are on display at this classy shop.

BETTER BOTANICALS

Map pp256-7 *Ayurvedic Goods*

☎ 888-224-3727; 3066 M St NW; ⏱ 9am-6pm Mon-Fri; Georgetown shuttle from Foggy Bottom-GWU Metro

Feeling stressed by your travels? This unique shop prepares custom-made Ayurvedic herbal products (oils, soaps, shampoos, scents); its service and knowledge has been recommended by readers. The stuff isn't cheap ($15 for 8oz of lotion), but staff are dedicated and give you helpful tips.

BEYOND COMICS

Map pp256-7 *Books & Toys*

☎ 202-333-8651; 1419 Wisconsin Ave NW; ⏱ 11am-8pm Mon & Tue, 11am-9pm Wed-Fri, 10am-9pm Sat, 11am-6pm Sun; Georgetown shuttle from Rosslyn

This small shop is crowded with new and used comics, plus trading cards, figurines and quite hooligan-looking teens.

BIG WHEEL BIKES

Map pp256-7 *Bikes*

☎ 202-337-0254; 1034 33rd St NW; ⏱ 11am-7pm Tue-Fri, 10am-6pm Sat & Sun Mar-Nov, 11am-7pm Fri, 10am-6pm Sat & Sun Dec-Feb; Georgetown shuttle from Foggy Bottom-GWU Metro

Among the biggest and best bike stores in the city, Big Wheel has a huge selection of bikes and biking accessories. It also does tune-ups and repairs, and is accessible to the Mount Vernon, Rock Creek Park and Capitol Crescent Trails. For a list of bike-rental outlets see p222.

Big Wheel Bikes (above)

COMMANDER SALAMANDER

Map pp256-7 *Funky Clothing & Accessories*
☎ 202-337-2265; 1420 Wisconsin Ave NW; 10am-9pm Mon-Thu, 10am-10pm Fri & Sat, 11am-7pm Sun; Georgetown shuttle from Rosslyn

This Georgetown institution has been a friend to street punks and wannabes for decades. Back when Friday night in Georgetown meant seeing *The Rocky Horror Picture Show* at the Key Theatre, this was the place everyone showed off for black lipstick and handcuffs. It now sells funky makeup, all colors of hair dye, Goth-wear, and baggy clothes from such brands as Moschino and Hook-Ups.

COWBOY WESTERN WEAR

Map pp256-7 *Western Wear*
☎ 202-298-8299; 3147 Dumbarton Ave NW; 10am-7pm Mon-Sat, noon-5pm Sun; Georgetown shuttle from Foggy Bottom-GWU Metro

This little Western shop will guarantee you are dressed to the nines for that night out two-steppin'. Even if you don't know how to 'swing your partner,' it has a great selection of boots and other Western wear.

Clothing Sizes

Measurements approximate only, try before you buy.

Women's Clothing

Aust/UK	8	10	12	14	16	18
Europe	36	38	40	42	44	46
Japan	5	7	9	11	13	15
USA	6	8	10	12	14	16

Women's Shoes

Aust/USA	5	6	7	8	9	10
Europe	35	36	37	38	39	40
France only	35	36	38	39	40	42
Japan	22	23	24	25	26	27
UK	3½	4½	5½	6½	7½	8½

Men's Clothing

Aust	92	96	100	104	108	112
Europe	46	48	50	52	54	56
Japan	S		M	M		L
UK/USA	35	36	37	38	39	40

Men's Shirts (Collar Sizes)

Aust/Japan	38	39	40	41	42	43
Europe	38	39	40	41	42	43
UK/USA	15	15½	16	16½	17	17½

Men's Shoes

Aust/UK	7	8	9	10	11	12
Europe	41	42	43	44½	46	47
Japan	26	27	27½	28	29	30
USA	7½	8½	9½	10½	11½	12½

CREIGHTON-DAVIS GALLERY

Map pp256-7 *Art*
☎ 202-333-3050; 3222 M St NW, Georgetown Park; 10am-9pm Mon-Sat, noon-6pm Sun; Georgetown shuttle from Foggy Bottom-GWU Metro

Georgetown's largest gallery, the Creighton-Davis acts as a sort of catchall for 20th-century works of art, from Picasso to Hockney.

DEAN & DELUCA Map pp256-7 *Gourmet Food*
☎ 202-342-2500; 3276 M St NW; 10am-8pm Sun-Thu, 10am-9pm Fri & Sat; Georgetown shuttle from Foggy Bottom-GWU Metro

The New York gourmet chain has an overwhelming and mouthwatering selection of produce, meat and baked goods in this revamped, brick warehouse (all costly; this is a place for Black Angus beef and caviar). Outside is a lovely canopied dining area for noshing on its ready-made sandwiches and pastries.

DEJA BLUE Map pp256-7 *Jeans*
☎ 202-337-7100; 3005 M St NW; 10am-7pm Mon-Sat, noon-5pm Sun; Georgetown shuttle from Foggy Bottom-GWU Metro

Looking for vintage jeans? This place has stacks of 'em, plus salespeople who can take one glance at you and throw you several pair that fit like they were tailored for your booty alone. They usually run between $30 and $40, but they're worth it.

GEORGETOWN PARK Map pp256-7 *Mall*
☎ 202-298-5577; Wisconsin Ave & M St NW; 9am-9pm Mon-Sat, noon-6pm Sun; Georgetown shuttle from Foggy Bottom-GWU Metro

This elegantly designed upscale mall is on the north bank of the C&O Canal. It has a nice downstairs food court (with splashing fountains) and more than 100 shops, including FAO Schwarz, J Crew and Victoria's Secret. Here, too, is 250-year-old Caswell-Massey, an apothecary that once sold soaps and toiletries to George Washington.

HATS IN THE BELFRY Map pp256-7 *Millinery*
☎ 202-342-2006; 1250 Wisconsin Ave NW; 10am-9pm Mon-Thu, 10am-midnight Fri & Sat, 10am-8pm Sun; Georgetown shuttle from Foggy Bottom-GWU Metro

From fashionable (but affordable) bonnets to costume caps, this shop has been topping off Georgetown's heads for years. The place has lots of mirrors and you are welcome to try on the goods.

INGA'S ONCE IS NOT ENOUGH

Map pp256-7   *Used Clothing & Accessories*

☎ 202-337-3072; 4830 MacArthur Blvd NW;
🕐 10am-5pm Mon-Sat; bus D5 from Foggy Bottom-GWU Metro

This fine consignment shop has many items, mostly for women, coming in from residents of its chichi upper northwest neighborhood. Inga herself, who is a fashion consultant for the local Fox channel, takes her customers firmly in hand, showing them what they really want to buy in her very crowded shop, which is thick with designer labels (from Armani to Prada). It's easiest to drive here.

PARISH GALLERY

Map pp256-7   *Art*

☎ 202-944-2310; 1054 31st St NW; 🕐 noon-6pm Tue-Sat; Georgetown shuttle from Foggy Bottom-GWU Metro

This is among conservative Georgetown's more contemporary galleries, featuring the work of African Americans and other minority artists. Many locals artists are represented.

SECONDHAND ROSE

Map pp256-7   *Quality Used Clothing*

☎ 202-337-3378; 1516 Wisconsin Ave NW;
🕐 11:30am-6pm Mon-Sat; Georgetown shuttle from Foggy Bottom-GWU Metro

Somewhat pricey for a secondhand shop, Rose offers consignment women's clothing that's no more than two years old. This isn't a place for bargain-hunters – no $10 dresses here – but this Georgetown store has a fast turnover and all items are in good condition.

SEPHORA Map pp256-7   *Perfumery*

☎ 202-338-5644; 3065 M St NW; 🕐 10am-9pm Mon-Sat, noon-6pm Sun; Georgetown shuttle from Foggy Bottom-GWU Metro

This two-floor cosmetics-and-scents shop is a lot of fun: upstairs are huge racks of pencils, liners and powders in all colors of the rainbow, and downstairs the walls are lined with nearly every perfume imaginable.

SUGAR

Map pp256-7   *Women's Apparel*

☎ 202-333-5331; 1633 Wisconsin Ave NW; 🕐 10am-7pm Mon-Sat, noon-5pm Sun; Georgetown shuttle from Rosslyn

This fresh women's boutique is modern without being too trendy, a great place to check out clothing by smaller-name designers.

VILLAGE ART & CRAFT

Map pp256-7   *Imported Goods*

☎ 202-333-1968; 1353 Wisconsin Ave NW; 🕐 10am-8pm; Georgetown shuttle from Foggy Bottom-GWU Metro

This tiny shop is so packed with jewelry, rugs and textiles that you can hardly move around it. But if you can navigate the piles of rugs and tables covered with knickknacks, you will find pashmina shawls and other clothes, finely woven kilims, and cool stuff imported from Morocco, India and Turkey.

DUPONT CIRCLE & KALORAMA

BEADAZZLED Map pp258-60   *Jewelry*

☎ 202-265-2323; 🕐 10am-8pm Mon-Sat, 11am-6pm Sun; 1507 Connecticut Ave NW; Metro: Dupont Circle

Crafty types and jewelry lovers should not miss this specialty shop, which carries all things small and stringable. The selection from around the world ranges from 5¢ clay doohickeys to expensive pearls. Helpful staff will tell you how to put them together, and classes are offered on weekends.

BEST CELLARS Map pp258-60   *Wine*

☎ 202-387-3146; 1643 Connecticut Ave NW;
🕐 10am-9pm Mon-Thu, 10am-10pm Fri & Sat; Metro: Dupont Circle

For a libation to complete your gourmet feast, go to this elegantly designed vintner's shop. Arranged by taste categories (sweet, fruity, bold) rather than by type, it is helpful for vino novices, particularly since lots of bottles are under $15. The shelves display fun little wine facts, too, like a Renaissance pope's desire to have his corpse washed in Orvieto.

CANDEY HARDWARE

Map pp258-60   *Hardware*

☎ 202-659-5650; 1210 18th St NW; 🕐 8:30am-6:30pm Mon-Fri; Metro: Dupont Circle

This family-owned hardware shop – around since 1891 – is like something out of small-town USA. It survives in transient DC by offering friendly service and everything the locals need around their homes.

CASA PEÑA Map pp258-60   *Latin Treats*

☎ 202-462-2222; 1636 17th St NW; 🕐 8am-11pm; Metro: Dupont Circle

This Latin specialty food store will carry anything you need to whip up a Mexican feast: chiles, South American spices and five different brands of *yerba maté* (tealike beverage).

CHOCOLATE MOOSE

Map pp258-60 *Cards & Gifts*

☎ 202-463-0992; 1800 M St NW; ⏱ 10am-6pm Mon-Sat; Metro: Dupont Circle

Funny cards and kitsch gifts – from rubber chickens to inflatable dolls – are the specialty of this novelty shop.

DESIGNER ART & CRAFT USA, INC.

Map pp258-60 *Imported Goods*

☎ 202-462-5489; 1709 Connecticut Ave NW; ⏱ 10am-10pm; Metro: Dupont Circle

Why 'USA' is included in the name of this shop is not clear, as it carries clothing, textiles and jewelry from everywhere else. The selection of pashmina shawls and woven kilims is huge.

GINZA Map pp258-60 *Japanese Housewares*

☎ 202-331-7991; 1721 Connecticut Ave NW; ⏱ 11am-7pm Mon-Sat, noon-6pm Sun; Metro: Dupont Circle

Japan is the theme here. There is a nice selection of beautiful (looking and sounding) indoor fountains, scented candles and other interesting elements of Asian decor.

GUITAR SHOP

Map pp258-60 *Musical Instruments*

☎ 202-331-7333; 1216 Connecticut Ave NW; ⏱ noon-7pm Mon-Fri, 11am-6pm Sat; Metro: Dupont Circle

Although it's the size of a phone booth, this is DC's most impressive instrument retailer and repairer. Around since 1922, this store

Kramerbooks (right)

has serviced Springsteen and Dylan. The dedicated staff help musicians – be they novice or star – to find what they really need. And you will need help, as the incredibly dense collection ranges from top-of-the-line Martins to off-brand cheapies.

HIMALAYAN HOUSE

Map pp258-60 *Imported Goods*

☎ 202-223-3366; www.himalayanhouse.com; ⏱ 9am-9pm Mon-Sat, noon-8pm Sun; 1319 Connecticut Ave NW; Metro: Dupont Circle

This place oozes positive karma, probably because the handicrafts, jewelry and clothing all come straight from Nepal and Tibet. The Tibetan ritual crafts are fun to investigate even if you are not buying.

KRAMERBOOKS Map pp258-60 *Books*

☎ 202-387-1400; 1517 Connecticut Ave NW; ⏱ 8:30am-1:30am Sun-Thu, 24hr Fri & Sat; Metro: Dupont Circle

With the Afterwords café and bar behind the shop, this round-the-clock bookstore is as much a spot for schmoozing as for shopping. You can listen to live bands, drink a pint, check email for free on its public terminal, nosh and flirt with comely strangers (the store is a fabled pick-up spot for straights and gays). This flagship independent – which leapt into First Amendment history when it firmly refused to release Lewinsky's book-buying list to Starr's snoops – features fine current literature, travel and politics sections.

LAMBDA RISING Map pp258-60 *Gay Bookstore*

☎ 202-462-6969; 1625 Connecticut Ave NW; ⏱ 10am-10pm Sun-Thu, 10am-midnight Fri & Sat; Metro: Dupont Circle

This landmark in gay and lesbian DC sells CDs and videos, as well as books. The flyers and free giveaways near its door are a good way to learn about happenings in gay DC.

LAMMAS Map pp258-60 *Women's Bookstore*

☎ 202-775-8218; 1607 17th St NW; ⏱ 10am-6pm Mon-Sat; Metro: Dupont Circle

This women's bookstore offers a good stock of lesbian, feminist and spiritual titles.

LYNELLE BOUTIQUE

Map pp258-60 *Clothing & Accessories*

☎ 202-223-4222; 1800 M St NW; ⏱ 10am-6pm Mon-Fri, 11am-4pm Sat; Metro: Dupont Circle

This boutique complements its fun fashions

with a little bubbly at its weekly Champagne and Shopping Thursday.

MEEPS FASHIONETTE

Map pp258-60 *Vintage Clothier*
☎ 202-265-6546; 1520 U St NW; ⏰ 4-7pm Tue-Thu, noon-8pm Fri, 1-6pm Sun; Metro: U Street-Cardozo

This vintage clothier appeals to both boy and girl denizens of the New U club district with its 1950s and '60s swinger-style clothes: puffy skirts for dancing, suede-lapelled blazers, and such accessories as funky hats and beaded purses. Items are moderately priced (dresses around $30) and in decent shape.

MELODY RECORD SHOP

Map pp258-60 *Records & CDs*
☎ 202-232-4002; 1623 Connecticut Ave NW; ⏰ 10am-10pm Mon-Thu, 10am-11pm Fri & Sat, noon-10pm Sun; Metro: Dupont Circle

Serving Dupont Circle its daily CD and vinyl requirements for nearly 30 years, the deceptively small storefront hides a very wide range of discs.

MOTO PHOTO

Map pp258-60 *Photo Processing*
☎ 202-797-9035; 1601 Connecticut Ave NW; ⏰ 8am-9pm Mon-Fri, 9am-8pm Sat, 11am-6pm Sun; Metro: Dupont Circle

This national chain offers very reliable, high-quality one-hour photo processing. This is one of many city locations.

NEWSROOM & INTERNATIONAL LANGUAGE CENTER

Map pp258-60 *Periodicals & More*
☎ 202-332-1489, 332-2894; 1803 Connecticut Ave NW; ⏰ 7am-9pm; Metro: Dupont Circle

The Newsroom offers thousands of magazines and newspapers from all over the world. Upstairs at the International Language Center you will find dictionaries, audio and video programs, and other resources in over 200 languages, which might help you to read the periodicals downstairs!

OLSSON'S BOOKS & RECORDS

Map pp258-60 *Books & Music*
☎ 202-785-1133; 1307 19th St NW; ⏰ 10am-10pm Mon-Wed, 10am-10:30pm Thu-Sat, noon-8pm Sun; Metro: Dupont Circle

This is a local chain which offers both books and music. Its indie mood is sparked by the book-obsessed staff who are full of great recommendations and opinions.

PHILLIPS COLLECTION

Map pp258-60 *Museum Shop*
☎ 202-387-2151; 1600 21st St NW; ⏰ 10am-5pm Tue-Sat, noon-7pm Sun; Metro: Dupont Circle

The museum shop has a good collection of posters, pop and scholarly art books, and knickknacks imprinted with famous paintings, such as umbrellas sporting Renoir's *Luncheon of the Boating Party* and Monet water-lily mugs.

PROPER TOPPER

Map pp258-60 *Millinery*
☎ 202-842-3055; 1350 Connecticut Ave NW; ⏰ 9am-9pm Mon-Fri, 10am-7pm Sat, noon-6pm Sun; Metro: Dupont Circle

This great shop sells tops to both men and women. Fedoras, floppy-brimmed picture hats, berets – if it sits on your head, they're gonna have it.

SECOND STORY

Map pp258-60 *Used Books & Music*
☎ 202-659-8884; 2000 P St NW; ⏰ 10am-10pm; Metro: Dupont Circle

Up to its eyeballs in dusty used tomes, this is a Dupont Circle fixture that also offers used LPs and CDs, and a small stock of Asian antiques. It's a good place to stop on your way to the local cafés, and an impromptu pick-up scene flourishes among its shelves. It's such a beloved DC institution that Defense Secretary William Cohen wrote a cheesy poem in its honor ('Hieroglyphics heaped/in deep layers of ink...').

SECONDI

Map pp258-60 *Secondhand Clothing*
☎ 202-667-1122; 1702 Connecticut Ave NW; ⏰ 11am-6pm Mon-Tue, 11am-7pm Wed-Fri, 11am-6pm Sat, 1-5pm Sun; Metro: Dupont Circle

This classy secondhand shop markets high-end used clothing for men and women, including formal wear. A $200 Vera Wang on the rack here probably cost its Kalorama-matron first owner a few thousand.

TABLETOP

Map pp258-60 *Home Furnishings*
☎ 202-387-7117; 1608 20th St NW; ⏰ noon-8pm Mon-Sat, Sun noon-6pm; Metro: Dupont Circle

This funky, modern design shop carries 'functional objects for all surfaces.' In some cases, the functionality element is debatable, but it does not detract from its style.

ADAMS-MORGAN

ALL ABOUT JANE
Map p261   *Women's Clothing*
☎ 202-797-9710; 2438 18th St NW; ⏰ noon-9pm
Mon-Sat, noon-7pm Sun; Metro: Woodley Park-Zoo/
Adams Morgan

For chic fashion, this popular women's boutique is a great stop. Prices are reasonable and designs are truly unique – something that's hard to come by these days.

BAZAAR ATLAS
Map p261   *Imported Goods*
☎ 202-332 4911; 2405 18th St NW; ⏰ noon-8pm;
Metro: Woodley Park-Zoo/Adams Morgan

This little shop really does resemble a bazaar when you step inside: the floors and the walls are covered with African art, Moroccan ceramics, Indian furniture, and tables displaying beads and jewelry.

BETTY Map p261   *Women's Clothing*
☎ 202-234-2389; 2439 18th St NW; ⏰ Mon, Wed &
Thu noon-8pm, noon-9pm Fri & Sat, noon-6pm Sun;
Metro: Woodley Park-Zoo/Adams Morgan

This little boutique sells stylish women's clothing, much of it by local designers. The pieces are sexy, elegant and reasonably priced.

BRASS KNOB Map p261   *Hardware*
☎ 202-332-3370; 2311 18th St NW; ⏰ 10:30-6pm
Mon-Sat, noon-5pm Sun; Metro: Woodley Park-Zoo/
Adams Morgan

This unique two-floor hardware shop sells 'rescues' from old buildings: fixtures, lamps, tiles, stained glass, mantelpieces, keyplates, mirrors. This place is a fantasy-land for anybody renovating (or just living in) an old house. Staff can help you find whatever you need.

DC CD Map p261   *Music*
☎ 202-588-1810; 2343 18th St NW; ⏰ 10am-midnight; Metro: Woodley Park-Zoo/Adams Morgan

This is Adams-Morgan's best music shop. It's unique in that it showcases Washington talent. It has new and used CDs, plus stacks of vinyl, and you can listen to anything before buying it.

FLEET FEET Map p261   *Sports Footwear*
☎ 202-387-3888; 1841 Columbia Rd NW; ⏰ 10am-
8pm Mon-Fri, 10am-7pm Sat, noon-4pm Sun;
Metro: Woodley Park-Zoo/Adams Morgan

Shoes for every sporting activity are on sale

Shake Your Booty (p185)

here; staff provide lots of personal service to match customers' feet with their activity of choice.

IDLE TIME BOOKS
Map p261   *Used Books*
☎ 202-232-4774; 2467 18th St NW; ⏰ 10am-10pm;
Metro: Woodley Park-Zoo/Adams Morgan

Three creaky wood floors are stuffed with used literature and nonfiction, including the best secondhand political and history collection in the city. Its sci-fi, sports and humor sections are top-notch, and there's a good newsstand in its front window. A sweet-tempered old cat patrols its upper floors.

KOBOS Map p261   *African Clothier*
☎ 202-332-9580; 2444 18th St NW; ⏰ 11am-8pm
Mon-Sat; Metro: Woodley Park-Zoo/Adams Morgan

Not your average clothing shop, Kobos is an African clothier. The Afro boutique carries a good selection of kente cloth, as well as cool tapestries and African music.

LOGAN'S ANTIQUES
Map p261   *Antiques*
☎ 202-483-2428; 3118 Mount Pleasant St NW;
⏰ 10am-6:30pm Tue-Sat; Metro: Columbia Heights

North of Adams-Morgan in Mount Pleasant, this crowded antique/junk shop is stuffed to its rafters with old housewares and furniture.

Some of it is beat, but you might also discover a gem: while away a rainy afternoon picking through the place.

MISS PIXIE'S FURNISHINGS & WHATNOT

Map p261   *Antiques*

☎ 202-232-8171; 1810 Adams Mill Rd NW; ⏰ noon-9pm Thu, noon-7pm Fri-Sun; Metro: Woodley Park-Zoo/Adams Morgan

This whimsical little joint purveys old housewares, furniture and doodads, all cheap and presided over by Miss Pixie herself.

OYA MINI BAZAAR

Map p261   *Imported Goods & Souvenirs*

☎ 202-667-9853; 2420 18th St NW; ⏰ noon-11pm; Metro: Woodley Park-Zoo/Adams Morgan

Another day in Adams-Morgan, another bazaar. This one also has decidedly domestic goods like Washington DC T-shirts.

SHAKE YOUR BOOTY

Map p261   *Women's Shoes*

☎ 202-518-8205; 2324 18th St NW; ⏰ noon-8pm Mon-Fri, noon-9pm Sat, noon-6pm Sun; Metro: Woodley Park-Zoo/Adams Morgan

'Booty' here means boots...and pumps and sandals and any other accessories you might need to hit the town (and then shake your other booty). The footwear here is trendy and fun, but it's only for women.

SKYNEAR & CO

Map p261   *Home Furnishings*

☎ 202-797-7160; 1800 Wyoming Ave NW; ⏰ 11am-7pm Mon-Sat, noon-6pm Sun; Metro: Woodley Park-Zoo/Adams Morgan

Explore four (count 'em four!) levels of rooms crowded with 'stressed' armoires, funky sofas and kitschy coffee tables. The stuff is really unique and prices are reasonable.

YAWA BOOKS & GIFTS

Map p261   *African American Books*

☎ 202-483-6805; 2206 18th St NW; ⏰ 11am-7pm Mon-Fri, 11am-9pm Sat; Metro: Woodley Park-Zoo/Adams Morgan

The focus here is on the books – lots of 'em – addressing African American political, social and cultural issues. Sports, spirituality, sex...absolutely nothing is overlooked. There is also a good selection of fiction by African American writers.

SHAW & THE NEW U DISTRICT

GO MAMA GO! Map p249   *Art*

☎ 202-299-0850; www.gomamago.com; 1809 14th St NW; ⏰ noon-7pm Mon, 11am-7pm Tue-Sat, noon-5pm Sun; Metro: U Street-Cardozo

These 'moms with an attitude' offer pottery and art handcrafted by Asian and African artisans. The unique dinnerware is green, blue, cobalt: clear, strong colors with very simple shapes.

HOME RULE Map p249   *Housewares*

☎ 202-797-5544; 1807 14th St NW; ⏰ 11am-7pm Mon-Sat, noon-5pm Sun; Metro: U Street-Cardozo

Tired of Pottery Barn homogeneity around your house? Check out Home Rule's amusingly original stock: frog-shaped toothbrush holders with sucker feet for sticking on the wall, brightly colored martini glasses, animal-shaped salt-and-pepper sets, and rugs and linens, too. The mosaic decorating the front counter symbolizes the U St district's revitalization – it's made up of smashed glass from the 1968 riots.

MAD T MUSICBOX Map p249   *Music*

☎ 202-328-1456; 2009 14th St NW; ⏰ 10am-8pm Mon-Sat, noon-5pm Sun; Metro: U Street-Cardozo

This record shop has a great selection of rock, hip-hop and techno-flavored music. It's popular among DC's DJs, so it must be good.

PULP Map p249   *Gifts*

☎ 202-462-PULP; 1803 14th St NW; ⏰ 11am-7pm Mon-Sat, noon-5pm Sun; Metro: U Street-Cardozo

This quirky, kitschy gift shop has all kinds of things you were not looking for – funky frames, funny cards, silly toys, smelly candles and retro art. It's a good place to come looking for a gift (as long as you don't know what you are looking for).

SHOP POP Map p249   *Clothing & Accessories*

☎ 202-332-3312; 1803 14th St NW; ⏰ 11am-7pm Mon-Sat, noon-6pm Sun; Metro: U Street-Cardozo

This brand-new boutique for women and men features designers like Ben Sherman and Tipton Charles.

UP AGAINST THE WALL

Map p249   *Hip-Hop Clothing*

☎ 202-234-4153; 2301 Georgia Ave; ⏰ 10am-9pm Mon-Thu, 10am-10pm Fri & Sat, noon-6pm Sun; Metro: Shaw-Howard U

The music-blaring boutique is one of DC's top funky fashion spots for the hip-hop set.

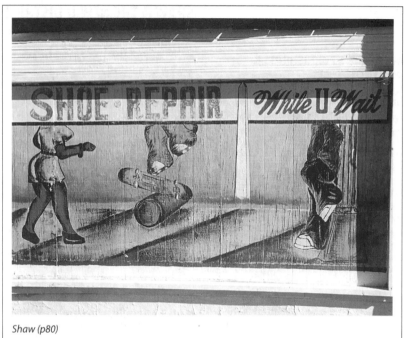
Shaw (p80)

VASTU Map p249   *Housewares*
☎ 202-234-8344; 1829 14th St NW; ⏱ 11am-7pm
Tue-Sat, noon-5pm Sun; Metro: U Street-Cardozo
This upscale furniture design store and art
gallery looks slightly out of place on rough-
and-tumble 14th St, but it's a sign of what's to
come in this neighborhood. The sleek, modern
furniture is not cheap, but it looks great in revitalized old buildings.

Get the Poop

The zoo's animals collectively produce hundreds of
pounds of manure every day. Most is trucked off to
the dump, but some is made into DC's most unusual
souvenir: ZooDoo fertilizer. Composted animal dung
(only from plant-eating beasties) is mixed with wood
chips, straw and leaves, and sold in buckets decorated
with little drawings of animal butts. Buy ZooDoo at
any zoo information booth, or order it from **Friends
of the National Zoological Park** (☎ 673-4989); a
1lb bucket costs about $5. The zoo uses ZooDoo on
its own beautiful grounds, so you can see how well
it works – and you'll probably be the only person on
your block with genuine zebra poop in your zinnias.

UPPER NORTHWEST DC
KRÖN CHOCOLATIER
Map pp262-3   *Edible Treats*
☎ 202-966-4946; Mazza Gallerie, 5300 Wisconsin Ave
NW; ⏱ 10am-9pm Mon-Fri, 11am-7pm Sun; Metro:
Friendship Heights
This shop is known for hand-dipped truffles
and amusing novelties, like edible chocolate
baskets, and milk-chocolate telephones and
cars.

NATIONAL ZOOLOGICAL PARK
Map pp262-3   *Museum Shop*
☎ 202-673-4800; 3001 Connecticut Ave NW;
⏱ 10am-6pm May-Sep, 10am-4:30pm Oct-Apr;
Metro: Woodley Park-Zoo/Adams Morgan
The zoo has several shops on its grounds that
sell toys and products featuring all manner of
charismatic megafauna: ostriches, seals, tigers,
wolves, elephants and the inevitable pandas.
(Bring home a plastic hyena for less-beloved
relatives.) It also has the Zoo Bookstore, in the
Education Building on the Connecticut Ave
NW side, which has a pretty good natural history and field-guide section.

POLITICS & PROSE BOOKSTORE

Map pp262-3   *Books*

☎ 202-364-1919; 5015 Connecticut Ave NW; ⏰ 9am-10pm Mon-Thu, 9am-11pm Fri & Sat, 10am-8pm Sun; bus L1 or L2

Way up in Northwest DC is a key literary nexus and coffeehouse. This active independent has a really excellent selection of literary fiction and nonfiction – it's fiercely supportive of local authors – plus dedicated staff, high-profile readings and 15 active book clubs.

RODMAN'S

Map pp262-3   *Low-Priced Exotic Condiments*

☎ 202-363-3466; 5100 Wisconsin Ave NW; ⏰ 9am-10pm Mon-Sat, 10am-7pm Sun; Metro: Friendship Heights

One of DC's odder food shops, this little place sells Thai spices, Indian pickles, pastas, chocolates, pâtés and other foodstuffs in a discount-dimestore atmosphere: with its crowded, dusty aisles, it feels like the junkshop of gourmet markets.

SULLIVAN'S TOY STORE Map pp262-3 *Toys*

☎ 202-362-1343; 3412 Wisconsin Ave NW; ⏰ 10am-6pm Mon, Tue & Sat, 10am-6pm Wed-Fri, noon-5pm Sun; bus Nos 30, 32, 34, 36

This independent toy store specializes in European and educational toys that are a nice antidote to the video-games fare of many children's toy stores.

TRAVEL BOOKS & LANGUAGE CENTER

Map pp262-3   *Travel Books*

☎ 202-237-1322; 4437 Wisconsin Ave NW; ⏰ 10am-6pm Mon-Sat; Metro: Tenleytown-AU

This specialty bookstore carries a gargantuan selection of guidebooks, maps and foreign-language publications.

VACE ITALIAN Map pp262-3 *Food & Beverages*

☎ 202-363-1999; 3315 Connecticut Ave NW; ⏰ 9am-9pm Mon-Fri, 9am-8pm Sat, 10am-5pm Sun; Metro: Cleveland Park

This neighborhood favorite deli offers fresh pastas, cheeses, gnocchi and Italian sweets.

WAKE UP LITTLE SUZIE Map pp262-3 *Gifts*

☎ 202-244-0700; 3409 Connecticut Ave NW; ⏰ 11am-7pm Mon-Fri, 11am-6pm Sat, noon-5pm Sun; Metro: Cleveland Park

This funny and original gift shop sells stuff like neon clocks, bright chunky metal-and-ceramic

---

Money Can Buy You Music

The musically inclined may want to check out the **House of Musical Traditions** (☎ 301-270-9090, 800-540-9090; www.hmtrad.com; 7040 Carroll Ave, Takoma Park, Maryland; ⏰ 11am-7pm Tue-Sat, 11am-5pm Sun & Mon; Metro: Takoma Park), which carries an impressive array of acoustic instruments from around the world, including harps, concertinas, drums, dulcimers and flutes – and a lot of other instruments that you have never heard of. Inquire about Friday evening jam sessions and other concerts.

---

jewelry, polka-dotted pottery, cards and T-shirts. If you have a need for an *Invasion of the Monster Women* lunch box or boxing-rabbi windup doll, Suzie's your woman.

ALEXANDRIA
OLSSON'S BOOKS & RECORDS

Map p265   *Books & Music*

☎ 703-684-0077; 106 S Union St; ⏰ 10am-10pm Mon-Thu, 10am-11pm Fri & Sat, 11am-8pm Sun; Old Town shuttle from King St Metro

DC's best local chain of bookstores has an outlet in the heart of Old Town. Besides a great bookstore and a smaller selection of music, the **PIP Café** (p138) is upstairs.

TEN THOUSAND VILLAGES

Map p265   *Imported Goods*

☎ 703-684-1435; 824 King St; ⏰ 10am-7pm Mon-Wed, 10am-9pm Thu-Sat, noon-6pm Sun; Old Town shuttle from King St Metro

A unique nonprofit store, Ten Thousand Villages imports handicrafts from a developing country for a fair price, so you won't find any incredible bargains here. On the other hand, the craftsmanship on furniture, pottery and textiles is of a high quality, and you can rest easy knowing your purchase helps to pay for food, education, health care or housing for somebody who needs it.

TORPEDO FACTORY ART CENTER

Map p265   *Gallery Shop*

☎ 703-838-4565; www.torpedofactory.org; 105 N Union St; ⏰ 10am-5pm; Old Town shuttle from King St Metro

Built during WWI to manufacture torpedoes, this complex today manufactures art. At the center of a revamped waterfront with a

Shoppin' in the Suburbs: Local Malls

Several big malls on DC's outskirts draw shoppers in search of chain stores and bargains. All of this fits within the famous, or infamous, Capital Beltway (I-495), the sometimes high-speed, sometimes traffic-clogged highway that rings the city.

Mazza Gallerie (Map pp262-3; ☎ 202-966-6114; ☺ 10am-8pm Mon-Fri, 10am-7pm Sat, noon-5pm Sun; 5300 Wisconsin Ave NW; Metro: Friendship Heights), on the Red Line at the Maryland border at Bethesda, is upscale. Anchored by Neiman-Marcus and patronized by matrons in search of the perfect cocktail dress, the mall has a variety of costly boutiques focusing on women's fashion and jewelry, plus a Williams-Sonoma. Downstairs is a seven-screen movie theater, but there's no food court. There's a Hecht's department store just across Western Ave from the mall.

Pentagon City (Map pp244-5; ☎ 703-415-2400; 1100 S Hayes St, Arlington; ☺ 10am-10pm Mon-Sat, 10am-8pm Sun; Metro: Pentagon City) houses 160 shops, including Macy's, Nordstrom, Gap, a cinema and a food court. It's not distinguished by anything, but this was where Monica Lewinsky got busted by Ken Starr's troopers back in '98.

Potomac Mills (☎ 703-490-5948; Woodbridge, Virginia; ☺ 10am-9:30pm Mon-Sat, 11am-7pm Sun), a fire-breathing monster of mid-Atlantic outlet malls, is just a half-hour drive south of DC. It features about 250 discount shops: Ikea, Saks, Marshall's and Spiegel, among others. This place now draws more tourists and tour buses (about 24 million per year) than Williamsburg or Virginia's other historic sites, which might say something about Americans' priorities. Take Exit 158-B off I-95.

Tysons Corner (☎ 703-893-9400; 1961 Chain Bridge Rd, McLean; ☺ 10am-9:30pm Mon-Thu, 10am-10pm Fri & Sat, 10am-8pm Sun), further north in Virginia and just west of the Beltway, is a gigantic shopping complex that has, over the years, metastasized into its own strange, sidewalk-less suburban Edge City. With about 250 stores, there are few human needs Tysons can't fill: it has over 20 restaurants, big department stores from Bloomie's to Nordstrom, and smaller shops from Abercrombie & Fitch to Georgetown Tobacco. The adjacent, swanker complex has Louis Vuitton, Gucci, Fendi, Chanel and Hermés. You'll need to drive here.

marina, shops, parks, walkways, residences, offices and restaurants, it houses nearly 200 artists and craftspeople who sell their creations directly from their studios.

VIRGINIA SHOP Map p265 *Souvenirs*
☎ 703-836-3160; 104 S Union St; ☺ 10am-8pm Mon-Thu, 10am-9pm Fri & Sat, 11am-6pm Sun; Old Town shuttle from King St Metro

You might get all of your gifts out the way in one stop, if you care to give Virginia peanuts, wines and other food items. Books and souvenirs representing the Commonwealth are also for sale.

WHY NOT? Map p265 *Toys*
☎ 703-548-4420; 200 King St; ☺ 10am-5:30pm Mon-Sat, noon-5pm Sun; Old Town shuttle from King St Metro

Kids and parents alike will have a field day in this little shop, crowded with children's books, toys and cute clothing.

Sleeping

Sleeping

Tourism is Washington's bread and butter, so the city offers the complete range of accommodations, from dormitory-hostels to five-star historic hotels.

Most DC hotels, particularly upscale chains, have no set rates. Instead, rates vary week to week and even day to day, depending on season and availability. Hotel rates are generally lower on weekends (Friday and Saturday) than on weekdays. Rates often vary seasonally as well, with peak seasons being late March through mid-July and September through October. Discounts are often available for seniors, children, government employees and just about anybody if business is slow, so don't be shy about asking.

Unless otherwise noted, prices cited in this chapter are average high-season charges for a standard room, DC room tax (14.5%) not included. Accommodations listed under 'Cheap Sleeps' run $85 or less for a double room.

Keep in mind that calling the hotel is rarely the best way to find the cheapest rate. When quoting prices, hotels will often offer their rack rate, which is a base rate with no discount or special criteria applied. No smart traveler should ever pay rack rates, however. Better rates are undoubtedly available via booking services (p225), hotel websites, and bidding and discount websites (p191).

> ## Rental & Roommate Services
>
> If you're in DC for a while and need a roof over your head, your first option is, of course, the *Post* or *City Paper* classifieds, but you also might try these services:
>
> **Roommates Preferred** (Map pp262-3; ☎ 202-965-4004; Suite 136, 3000 Connecticut Ave NW; Metro: Woodley Park-Zoo/Adams Morgan)
>
> **Spectrum Apartment Search** (☎ 800-480-3733; www.apartmentsearch.com; 7629 Old Georgetown Rd, Bethesda, Maryland; Metro: Bethesda); **Alexandria, Virginia** (291 S Van Dorn St; Metro: Van Dorn St)

DOWNTOWN

With the construction of the Convention Center, Downtown has become hotel central for business travelers. The obvious result is that accommodations are expensive in this area, although there is certainly no shortage of options.

HAMILTON CROWNE PLAZA
Map pp246-8   *Business*

☎ 202-682-0111; www.crowneplaza.com; 1001 14th St NW; weekend/weekday from $99/199; Metro: McPherson Sq

This newly restored 1920s building looks lovely and the rooms inside are nothing to scoff at. They woo guests with 'seven-layer beds,' soft duvets and fluffy feather comforters. Marble baths and royal blue bathrobes add to the luxury. For practical matters, the rooms have high-speed Internet access and CD players. The 24-hour fitness center also has a sauna. Off its lobby, the new restaurant/bar 14K serves contemporary Italian fare and has a pretty patio overlooking Franklin Sq.

HENLEY PARK HOTEL
Map pp246-8   *Boutique*

☎ 202-638-5200; 800-222-8474; www.henleypark.com; 926 Massachusetts Ave; rack rates s/d $195/215, specials from $109; Metro: Mt Vernon Sq/7th St-Convention Center

A beautiful Tudor building with gargoyles and stained glass makes a fine setting for this historic hotel. The rooms – decked in flowery prints and brass furniture – are as elegant as the edifice. They are all up-to-date, featuring dataports and dual-phone lines, coffeemakers and minibars.

HOTEL HARRINGTON Map pp246-8   *Family*

☎ 202-628-8140, 800-424-8532; www.hotel-harrington.com; 436 11th St NW; s/d with bathroom from $89/99, f $89; Metro: Federal Triangle

As one of the most affordable options near the Mall, this hotel is popular among school groups, families and international guests. And why not? All rooms have cable TV; there are several restaurants and laundry facilities on site. The place is not particularly attractive, but it is serviceable and friendly, and good value for the budget-minded.

HOTEL MONACO
Map pp246-8   *Boutique*

☎ 877-202-5411; www.monaco-dc.com; 700 F St NW; r around $199; Metro: Gallery Pl-Chinatown

The Kimpton Group's Hotel Monaco artfully combines modern and historic in the grand Corinthian-columned, all-marble 1839 Tariff Building. Bold, colorful artwork and modern furniture blend masterfully in the wood-paneled lobby; funky prints and jewel tones add new life to the arched ceilings and wood molding in the guestrooms. Each room is equipped with a cordless speakerphone, high-speed Internet access, Italian coffee, luxurious bathrobes and, in case you need company, a resident goldfish. (The hotel is otherwise pet-friendly, by the way, stocking dog-walking maps and offering room service for pets.) The on-site restaurant **Poste** (p119) is one of DC's hottest.

MORRISON-CLARK INN
Map pp246-8   *Boutique*

☎ 202-898-1200, 800-332-7898; www.morrisonclark .com; 1015 L St NW; r incl breakfast $99-199; Metro: Mt Vernon Sq/7th St-Convention Center

Conjuring the spirit of the South, this inn is listed in the National Register of Historic Places and often shows up on lists of DC's best hotels. Combining two 1864 Victorian residences, the boutique hotel has 54 rooms and suites furnished with fine antiques, lace, chintz, marble fireplaces, polished wood floors and all modern conveniences. Outside are two shady verandas; inside, the Morrison-Clark Restaurant serves highly praised Southern cuisine.

Cheap Sleeps
HOSTELLING INTERNATIONAL–WASHINGTON DC
Map pp246-8   *Hostel*

☎ 202-737-2333, 800-909-4776; www.hiwashingtondc .org; 1009 11th St NW; dm incl breakfast members/ nonmembers from $29/32, Internet special $23; Metro: Metro Center

Well organized and centrally located, this HI-AYH hostel has 250 beds (linens provided) in various-sized rooms. Although this neighborhood is not as exciting as, say, Adams-Morgan, it is closer to the action during the day and is convenient to many transportation options. Well-kept facilities include modern bathrooms and kitchen, dining and lounge rooms with a big-screen TV, coin laundry, storage lockers and free Internet access. A programming office organizes often free and always unique outings: night tours of the monuments, political

Room Service in the 21st Century

In recent years, the Internet has revolutionized many aspects of travel, not the least of which is finding and booking hotel rooms. Savvy surfers now visit bid-for-booking sites and discount hotel sites before they travel, guaranteeing a significantly reduced hotel room rate. These sites can be used for hotels all over the country – if not the world – so anybody who is online has access to hotels' cheapest rates. Here are the best sites and how they work.

www.biddingfortravel.com The goal of this website is to promote informed bidding when using the services of www.priceline.com (below). Visitors are invited to post their successful bidding history on specific hotels so that others learn the lowest acceptable prices. The site is monitored by an administrator, who answers questions and gives advice to subscribers who want to bid.

www.hoteldiscounts.com Enter your destination and dates and the website will provide information and prices for hotels with rooms available. You can book through the website at the discounted rate offered.

www.hotels.com This website uses the same system as www.hoteldiscounts.com and seems to come up with the same results.

www.hotwire.com Choose your dates and your preferred neighborhood (up to four) and www.hotwire.com will provide a general location, list of amenities, price and star-rating for several options. You learn the hotel name and exact location only after you buy your reservation.

www.priceline.com Choose your desired neighborhood, desired star-rating and desired price; enter dates and credit card info. If www.priceline.com finds something that meets your criteria, your reservation is automatically booked and you learn the hotel specifics afterwards. There's nothing to stop you from starting very low and gradually increasing your bid so you get the best price possible. Use this site in conjunction with www.biddingfortravel.com for a great hotel deal.

panel discussions, concerts at the Kennedy Center and the like. The on-site travel office is also helpful and convenient. Reservations highly recommended March to October.

SWISS INN Map pp246-8   *Family*

☎ 202-371-1816, 800-955-7947; www.theswissinn.com; 1204 Massachusetts Avenue NW; r $69-99 Mar-Oct, $55-79 off-peak; Metro: Metro Center

This restored brownstone houses a delightful family-run, budget inn. The rooms, which can sleep one to four people, all have a kitchenette, TV, telephone and private bath. They are nothing fancy, but they are all crispy clean, with sparkling tiles, and new carpeting and windows. This place – which is one of DC's friendliest – draws lots of internationals and travelers. Pets and kids are welcome.

WHITE HOUSE AREA & FOGGY BOTTOM

Foggy Bottom and the White House area do not have much 'neighborhood' feeling, but they do have lovely, luxurious, often historic hotels (charging luxurious rates). They usually cater to visiting dignitaries and high-profile politicians, so if you can afford to stay here you will be among good company.

White House Area

HAY-ADAMS HOTEL Map pp246-8   *Business*

☎ 202-638-6600, 800-853-6807; www.hayadams.com; 1 Lafayette Sq; rack rates from $525; Metro: McPherson Sq

This landmark hotel, where 'nothing is over-looked but the White House,' was named for two mansions that once stood on the site (owned by Secretary of State John Hay and historian Henry Adams). In their day, they hosted the political and intellectual elite at Washington's leading salons. Today, it has 145 subtly luxurious rooms, a palazzo-style lobby and a tasteful soupçon of Washington scandal: back in the 1980s, this hotel was a site where Oliver North wooed contributors to his illegal contra funding scheme.

HOTEL SOFITEL LAFAYETTE SQUARE

Map pp246-8   *Business*

☎ 202-730-8800, 800-763-4835; www.sofitel.com; 806 15th St NW; r from $119; Metro: McPherson Sq

This historic building, erected in 1880, contains 220 modern rooms with plush down comforters and practical perks like high-speed Internet access. One child stays free with parents and so do pets! Downstairs are a refined French restaurant and a spiffy fitness center.

ST REGIS WASHINGTON

Map pp246-8   *Business*

☎ 202-638-2626, 800-562-5661; www.luxurycollection.com; 923 16th St NW; weekend/weekday from $285/370; Metro: McPherson Sq

With crystal chandeliers hanging from the coffered ceilings to the Oriental rugs on the parquet floor, the lobby of the St Regis reflects the grandeur of a Renaissance palace. Its 200 rooms and suites have every provision, from dataports to marble baths, and there's a butler on each floor. Room No 1012 is infamous as the place where Monica Lewinsky spilled details of her shenanigans with President Clinton to Ken Starr's investigators.

Foggy Bottom

GEORGE WASHINGTON UNIVERSITY INN Map pp246-8   *Family*

☎ 202-337-6620, 800-426-4455; www.gwuinn.com; 824 New Hampshire Ave NW; weekend/weekday from $199/259, discounts from $99; Metro: Foggy Bottom-GWU

Set on a quiet tree-lined street, this boutique hotel has guest rooms and suites featuring colonial-style furniture and two-line phones with dataports. While some suites have full kitchens, all rooms include refrigerators, microwaves and coffeemakers. The GW Inn is only a block away from the Foggy Bottom Metro stop, but its immediate vicinity is residential and academic, offering a pleasant retreat from the city.

HOTEL LOMBARDY Map pp246-8 *Business*
☎ 202-828-2600, 800-424-5486; www.hotellombardy; 2019 I St NW; summer weekend/weekday from $99/119, peak $139/179; Metro: Foggy Bottom-GWU

Done up in funky Venetian decor (shuttered doors, warm gold walls), and beloved by World Bank and State Department types, this European boutique hotel has a multilingual staff and an international mood – you hear French and Spanish as often as English in its halls. Many of the 125 rooms have original artwork, Chinese and European antiques, as well as kitchens and dining areas. On-site are the well-reviewed Café Lombardy and the decadent Venetian Room Lounge (with a fireplace, tasseled hassocks and velvet banquettes).

HOTEL WASHINGTON
Map pp246-8 *Independent*
☎ 202-638-5900, 800-424-9540; www.hotelwashington .com; 15th & Pennsylvania Ave; s/d from $195/215; Metro: McPherson Sq

DC's oldest continuously operating hotel has sat just around the corner from the White House since about 1918, and retains the elegance and refinement with which it was built. Newly restored rooms are adorned with marble baths, mahogany furniture, and historic print fabrics and wallpaper (the latter lending a distinctly old-fashioned feel). This hotel is most famous for its fabulous view from the rooftop Sky Terrace Lounge.

LINCOLN SUITES DOWNTOWN
Map pp246-8 *Suites*
☎ 202-223-4320, 800-424-2970; www.lincolnhotels .com; 1823 L St NW; r weekend incl breakfast $99-199; Metro: Farragut North

This centrally located hotel's newly renovated entrance and lobby are bold and modern, but its 95 suites are more traditionally decorated. Still, its spacious studio suites are a good bet for families who will appreciate the fully stocked kitchenettes, space for kids to play and complimentary snacks. Room rates include a pass to a nearby gym.

MELROSE HOTEL Map pp246-8 *Business*
☎ 202-955-6400, 800-MELROSE; www.melrosehotel.com; 2430 Pennsylvania Ave NW; weekend/weekday $159/189; Metro: Foggy Bottom-GWU

A few blocks from the Metro, steps from Rock Creek Park and just over the bridge from Georgetown, this luxury hotel sits on one of Pennsylvania's nicest stretches. The revamped 14-storey building has 400 fancy rooms with original artwork, terry bathrobes, dataports and wireless access. Off the elegant lobby is a bar – the warm, wood-paneled Library – and restaurant, as well as a fine fitness center.

Hay-Adams Hotel (p192)

ONE WASHINGTON CIRCLE

Map pp246-8   *Suites*

☎ 202-872-1680, 800-424-9671; www.onewashingto
ncirclehotel.com; 1 Washington Circle; weekend/
weekday $139/239; Metro: Foggy Bottom-GWU

At its eponymous address, this sleek, modern all-suite hotel has always attracted high-profile guests; for example, Nixon maintained offices here after the Watergate scandal totaled his presidency. Some of the features of these suites (besides the expected kitchen) are entertainment centers, with CD player and Nintendo, and walk-out balconies with views of Washington Circle. Facilities like the sophisticated Circle Bistro and the outdoor pool are also welcome.

RIVER INN Map pp246-8   *Boutique*

☎ 202-337-7600, 800-424-2741; www.theriverinn.com;
924 25th St NW; off-peak/peak rates from $105/130;
Metro: Foggy Bottom-GWU

On a quiet residential street (despite the name, it's not on the river) a block from the Kennedy Center, this generic-looking brick facility has 126 stylish suites inside. They all have sleek-lined, modern furniture, black-and-white photographs, entertainment centers with Nintendo and video/CD libraries, workstations with dataports, and full kitchens with marble floors. The new American restaurant DISH is already popular for the theater crowd. Fitness center, laundry and parking are available.

SWISSÔTEL WATERGATE

Map pp246-8   *Business*

☎ 202-965-2300; www.watergatehotel.com; 2650
Virginia Ave NW; weekend from $169; Metro: Foggy
Bottom-GWU

Here you can lodge in the company of political scandal. (Nixon's operatives tried to bug Democratic National Committee headquarters here back in 1972; its famed residents have included Bob Dole and Monica Lewinsky.) The hotel is luxurious but, apart from its notoriety, unremarkable. Bonuses include a gym with a spectacular indoor swimming pool, great Potomac views and a fine location just downriver from Georgetown. A whole self-enclosed village of swank – couture shops, the restaurant **Jeffrey's at the Watergate** (p122) – is here, too.

WILLARD INTER-CONTINENTAL
HOTEL Map pp246-8   *Business*

☎ 202-628-9100; www.washington.intercontinental
.com; 1401 Pennsylvania Ave NW; r from $259, specials
from $209; Metro: Federal Triangle

Here, in DC's most history-laden hotel: MLK wrote his 'I Have a Dream' speech; the term 'lobbyist' was coined (by President Grant to describe political wranglers trolling the lobby); and Lincoln, Coolidge and Harding all stayed. Nathaniel Hawthorne observed that it could 'much more justly [be] called the center of Washington...than either the Capitol, the White House, or the State Department.'

Today the very luxuriously restored 1904 beaux-arts hotel – the third to be built on this site – is still favored by power brokers, and its chandelier-hung hallways are still thick with lobbyists and corporate aristocrats buffing their loafers on the dense carpets. It offers a gym, business center, concierge, airline and car-rental desks, upscale shops, the Willard Room restaurant and the marvelous Round Robin Bar, which claims to be the birthplace of the mint julep.

Cheap Sleeps

ALLEN LEE HOTEL Map pp246-8   *Family*

☎ 202-331-1224; www.allenleehotel.com; 2224 F St
NW; s/d $45/58, with bathroom $62/74; Metro: Foggy
Bottom-GWU

If your expectations are modest, this plain, institutional-looking lodging is a great deal. Staff are friendly, and rooms are clean and have phones, TVs and rather worn furnishings. Guests are young and international – it's a nice place to meet students and travelers.

CAPITOL HILL
& SOUTHEAST DC

Capitol Hill can be divided into two accommodations areas. The northwest side of the Capitol, bordering Downtown, is an area of upscale hotels – most of them large chains with hundreds of rooms. These hotels are catering mainly to lawyers and lobbyists who have business at the Capitol. By contrast, Capitol Hill itself (east of the Capitol building) is a residential area with many gorgeous Victorian mansions that house B&Bs.

BULL MOOSE BED & BREAKFAST

Map pp250-1   *B&B*

☎ 202-547-1050, 800-261-2768; www.bullmoose-b-and
-b.com; 101 5th St NE; s with/without bathroom from
$129/89, d $20 extra, ste from $169, weekly from $350,
incl breakfast; Metro: Eastern Market

Named after the nickname for the Progressive Party founded by Teddy Roosevelt in 1912, this turreted red-brick 1892 Victorian has a lovely interior with 10 redecorated guest rooms that echo Teddy's times. Common areas include nice kitchen facilities and a parlor with an exquisite 100-year-old oak mantelpiece. Proprietors Jim Pastore and JoAnn McInnis – like the neighborhood – are very friendly.

CAPITOL HILL SUITES HOTEL

Map pp250-1 *Suites*
☎ 202-543-6000; www.capitolhillsuites.com; 200 C St SE; ste incl breakfast from $109; Metro: Capitol South
This 152-room, all-suite property is ideally located in the heart of Hill legislative action (it's the only hotel that is actually *on* the Hill). It's heavily favored by congressional interns, and even a few congressmen and senators rent suites. And no wonder, the place is good value, especially since weekly and monthly rates are available. Rooms are newly renovated and quite chic. All have a kitchen or kitchenette; laundry facilities are on-site. Rates include passes to a nearby gym.

DOOLITTLE GUEST HOUSE

Map pp250-1 *B&B*
☎ 202-546-6622; www.doolittlehouse.com; 506 E Capitol St; r incl breakfast $110-175; Metro: Eastern Market
This exquisite 1860s Romanesque row house has three antique-furnished rooms, all with private baths and one with a fireplace. An onsite library has a fax and computer. Scrumptious breakfasts feature organic products from a local farmers' market and homemade goodies.

HOTEL GEORGE Map pp250-1 *Independent*
☎ 202-347-4200; www.hotelgeorge.com; 15 E St NW; weekend/weekday from $139/199; Metro: Union Station
George was really the first DC hotel to take the term 'boutique' to a daring, ultra-modern new level. The stylish interior features clean lines, chrome and glass furniture, and modern art. The 139 rooms have all the niceties, including high-speed Internet access, cotton duvets, leather chairs, marble baths and terry bathrobes. The 24-hour gym has men's and women's steam rooms. Off the lobby is the stylish French **Bistro Bis** (p123).

MAISON ORLEANS Map pp250-1 *B&B*
☎ 202-544-3694; maisonorln@aol.com; 414 5th St SE; r incl breakfast $95-135; Metro: Eastern Market
In a Federal-front row house built in 1902, this little B&B has architecture and decor that echo New Orleans' French Quarter, where owner Bill Rouchell grew up. Its three rooms (plus a studio apartment) are furnished with family heirlooms, giving the feel of your grandmother's house. The highlight of this place is the private patio, overflowing with gurgling fountains, fish ponds and colorful blooms.

PHOENIX PARK HOTEL

Map pp250-1 *Business*
☎ 202-638-6900, 800-824-5419; www.phoenixpark hotel.com; 520 N Capitol St; weekend/weekday from $119/209; Metro: Union Station
If you are not a fan of the American corporate hotel, check out this 'Center of Irish Hospitality' upstairs from the Dubliner pub. Although it's set in the midst of hotel row, it is homier than the other behemoth options on the block. It has also been home away from home for visiting Irish politicians like Gerry Adams. The hotel's 150 rooms feature period furnishings, Irish linens, cable TV and computer hookups. Other facilities include a small business center, a gym and laundry. Kids under 16 stay free.

SIMPKINS HOSTEL Map pp250-1 *Hostel*
☎ 202-387-1328; 2411 Benning Rd NE; dm $10; bus X1, X2 or X3 from Union Station (use H St exit)
'Georgetown East' – as it was labeled – is a bit of a stretch to describe this edgy community on the far northeastern edge of Capitol Hill. But it does have easy access to nice river stretches along the Anacostia River, and a few fun pubs and clubs. And if revitalization goes as planned, this whole stretch of waterfront property and the commercial district along H St NE will be a nucleus of development activity in the coming years. In the meantime, Simpkins' new hostel offers an ultra-inexpensive place to stay. Rooms are comfortable, with more privacy than your standard hostel (two-bed rooms). Facilities like laundry and high-speed Internet access are on-site.

THOMPSON-MARKWARD HALL

Map pp250-1 *Long-term*
☎ 546-3255; www.ywch.org; 235 2nd St NE; r $700 per month; Metro: Union Station
Young women visiting the city on long stays might consider this communal option, which is open to women 18 to 34 who are working or studying in Washington. (In summertime, 90% of its guests are Hill interns.) The minimum stay is two weeks; rates include two meals a day plus Sunday brunch. That's good value,

considering the average price of a sublet apartment in Washington, so reserve at least two to three months in advance. All rooms are small, furnished singles with phones, computer hookups and shared bath. The mood is like that of an upscale dorm, with a spacious courtyard, sundeck, pretty dining room and sitting areas. Coin laundry is available.

Drawbacks: you can't drink, smoke or bring male guests above lobby level. (Thompson-Markward's second name is 'The Young Woman's Christian Home,' but apart from these rules, you'd never know it.) If you start missing the Y-chromosome set, the Capitol Hill bar scene is just a couple of blocks away.

BROOKLAND & NORTHEAST DC

Northeast DC is pretty far off the beaten track, which is to say that it feels like a quiet town in middle America, not like a neighborhood of the nation's capital. But the advantages of staying out here are noteworthy: besides the obvious (cheap, cheap, cheap), Northeast also has a friendly local feel that does not exist in many parts of DC. Furthermore, these places are just a few Metro stops past Union Station, a quick easy commute to the center of it all.

Cheap Sleeps

INDIA HOUSE TOO   Hostel
☎ 202-291-1195; www.dchostel.com; 300 Carroll St; dm/d $18/40; Metro: Takoma

Laid-back and super-friendly, this hostel is in the bohemian, politically leftish neighborhood of Takoma Park, in far northeast DC. Set in a century-old Victorian, the hostel is frequented by crowds of backpackers from all over the world. The backyard barbie and hammock inspire frequent impromptu parties. Nine dorm rooms have four or six bunks and shared baths. Facilities include lockers, laundry, an old-fashioned kitchen, a lounge with TV and a computer with high-speed Internet access, all overseen by the affable Brit Angus Chapman and his partners. Don't be frightened off by the hostel's distance from downtown: India House is across the street from the Metro, which gets you to Capitol Hill in about 15 minutes. Besides, Takoma has its own strip of antique shops and vegetarian restaurants to explore.

MCMILLAN HOUSE Map pp252-3   B&B
☎ 202-636-9399; www.mcmillanhouse.net; 1201 Perry St NE; r without bathroom incl breakfast $64; Metro: Brookland-CUA

Set in a stately colonial in up-and-coming Brookland, this friendly B&B has three rooms with shared baths. Host Albert Ceccone speaks English, Spanish and Italian, and goes to great lengths to ensure his guests' comfort.

SOUTHWEST DC

It may not be DC's most exciting neighborhood, but staying in Southwest has its advantages. Although isolated by highways and riverways, it is remarkably close to the National Mall and the Tidal Basin, which makes for easy access to the major sights. The livelier nightlife is across town, but the waterfront area does boast a few restaurants, the Arena Stage, the colorful seafood market and a pleasant waterfront park.

CHANNEL INN Map pp254-5   Family
☎ 800-368-5668; www.channelinn.com; 650 Water St SW; weekend/weekday from $105/150; Metro: Waterfront

Overlooking the Washington Channel, this modern hotel features many rooms with balconies facing the water, offering fabulous sunset views. It also has a restaurant and swimming pool. Close at hand are lively marinas, tour-boat operators and giant seafood restaurants drawing tour-bus crowds.

LOEWS L'ENFANT PLAZA
Map pp254-5   Business/Family
☎ 202-484-1000; www.loewshotels.com; 480 L'Enfant Plaza SW; weekend/weekday from $129/199; Metro: L'Enfant Plaza

A big convention and business-traveler hotel sits atop the L'Enfant Plaza Metro station, two blocks south of the Mall. It is primarily an office building, so it bustles during the day, but empties out at night. It has a gym, year-round pool, business center and a few restaurants. Pet and child care are arranged via outside agencies, making this a friendly place for both.

GEORGETOWN

Georgetown is one of DC's loveliest neighborhoods and its accommodations options match its character: elegant and expensive. Keep in mind that staying in Georgetown is not convenient to visiting other parts of the city, as the Metro is not close.

Georgetown (p72)

FOUR SEASONS HOTEL

Map pp256-7   *Business*

☎ 202-342-0444; www.fourseasons.com; 2800 Pennsylvania Ave NW; rack rates from $350; Georgetown shuttle from Foggy Bottom-GWU Metro

Topping most 'best hotels in Washington' lists, the ultra-luxurious Four Seasons Hotel is perched atop Rock Creek Park's south end. This five-star property looks boxy and plain on the outside (it has none of the architectural charms of, say, the Willard). But inside, the 260 spacious rooms and suites are strewn with antiques; a full-service gym and day spa tones and pampers the guests; and the staff are extraordinarily attentive. Kids' activities and babysitting are provided.

GEORGETOWN INN Map pp256-7   *Family*

☎ 202-333-8900, 800-424-2979; www.georgetowninn .com; 1310 Wisconsin Ave NW; d $175-255; Georgetown shuttle from Rosslyn Metro

The blue-blooded Georgetown Inn is a gorgeous property favored by Georgetown University alumni and parents on college weekends. The inn spreads 95 rooms through a collection of restored 18th-century townhouses and its stately decor (four-poster beds, furniture with feet on it) is matched by stately service.

GEORGETOWN SUITES

Map pp256-7   *Suites*

☎ 202-298-7800; www.georgetownsuites.com; 1111 30th St NW; ste from $175; Georgetown shuttle from Foggy Bottom-GWU Metro

Although rather soulless, this is a convenient choice for families or longer-term visitors, who will appreciate a private kitchen and studio, and one- and two-bedroom suites. The pleasant location on the C&O canal is also convenient to M St and the Foggy Bottom Metro.

HOTEL MONTICELLO

Map pp256-7   *Boutique*

☎ 202-337-0900, 800-388-2410; www.monticellohotel .com; 1075 Thomas Jefferson St NW; s/d $209/219, specials $129/139; Georgetown shuttle from Foggy Bottom-GWU Metro

An attractive boutique hotel popular among European visitors, Hotel Monticello is just off M St near the C&O Canal. Each of its stylish 47 suites has a fully equipped kitchen, brass-and-crystal chandeliers, colonial-reproduction furniture and tasteful flower arrangements. A continental breakfast is included in the price of the room, as is parking (a real find in Georgetown).

LATHAM HOTEL Map pp256-7   *Boutique*

☎ 202-726-5000; www.thelatham.com; 3000 M St NW; r from $150; Georgetown shuttle Foggy Bottom-GWU Metro

In the midst of the M St scene is the red-brick Latham Hotel, a charming boutique hotel with 142 rooms, including two-storey 'carriage house' suites. The hotel boasts a pleasant rooftop sundeck and pool, as well as one of DC's finest restaurants, **Citronelle** (p126)

RITZ-CARLTON GEORGETOWN

Map pp256-7 *Business*

☎ 202-835-0500; www.ritzcarlton.com; 3100 South St NW; r incl breakfast from $325; Georgetown shuttle from Foggy Bottom-GWU Metro

Georgetown's newest hotel is discreetly tucked into the revitalized waterfront of the harbor. Its slick design incorporates the surrounding industrial buildings, including a towering incinerator smokestack and several historic houses: the result is a modern, luxurious but understated setting. Rooms feature feather duvets, goose-down pillows and oversized marble baths; many also offer fabulous views of the Potomac. The hotel bar, Degrees, crawls with white-collars from area offices during happy hour.

DUPONT CIRCLE & KALORAMA

Convenient transportation, lively night-life and endless options make Dupont Circle the ideal destination for sleeping in DC. Shops, restaurants, museums and galleries are all at the doorstep of most hotels and B&Bs in this vicinity. The Metro, too, is easily accessible, as there are several stations in the neighborhood. Kalorama is not quite as convenient to Metro, as it lies in the northern part of the neighborhood and further from the Dupont Circle Metro.

Dupont Circle

CARLYLE SUITES Map pp258-60 *Suites*

☎ 202-234-3200, 800-944-5377; fax 387-0085; 1731 New Hampshire Ave NW; r from $129; Metro: Dupont Circle

The art-deco decor lends a retro air to this all-suite hotel, but its facilities are modern. All 170 suites have full kitchens, TVs, phones and brightly colored furnishings. Laundry and health club facilities are on the premises. This is a great place for families: kids under 18 stay free.

DUPONT AT THE CIRCLE

Map pp258-60 *B&B*

☎ 202-332-5251, 888-412-0100; www.dupontatthecircle.com; 1604 19th St NW; r $140-180, ste $225, incl breakfast; Metro: Dupont Circle

This upscale inn is housed in a stately brick Victorian row house, one block north of the circle. Its seven fully equipped guest rooms and suite are furnished with tasteful antiques; all have private baths with clawfoot tubs or Jacuzzis. Breakfasts are modest affairs: muffins, granola, fruit.

EMBASSY INN Map pp258-60 *Family*

☎ 202-234-7800, 800-423-9111; www.windsorembassyinns.com; 1627 16th St NW; r from $79 off-peak, s/d $99/119 peak; Metro: Dupont Circle

This 38-room boutique hotel, a couple of blocks east of Dupont Circle, has the feel of a small, European hotel. The furniture is mostly tasteful reproductions, but the mosaic at the entrance and the marble stairway are originals from 1910. Rooms are pleasantly furnished, and have cable TV, phones and private baths. Continental breakfast and an evening sherry are included in the rates.

FAIRMONT WASHINGTON DC

Map pp258-60 *Business*

☎ 202-429-2400; www.fairmont.com; 2401 M St NW; weekend/weekday rack rates $259/309; Metro: Foggy Bottom-GWU

This luxurious option in the West End has 415 spacious rooms and an atrium lobby overlooking a flowery courtyard. The full health club features a lap pool and ball courts. Every room has three phones and a fridge in addition to the usual comforts.

HILTON WASHINGTON EMBASSY ROW Map pp258-60 *Business*

☎ 202-265-1600; www.hilton.com; 2015 Massachusetts Ave NW; weekend s/d from $145/165, weekday from $175/195; Metro: Dupont Circle

Diplomatic visitors favor this luxurious yet reasonably priced hotel, set amid the stately mansions on Embassy Row. Although it is big (193 rooms, 11 floors), it blends modestly into its elegant surroundings. Its rooms have niceties like two phones (one in the bathroom), and there's a rooftop pool, outdoor bar and underground parking (although the Metro is nearby). Staff speak six languages.

HOTEL HELIX Map pp258-60 *Boutique*

☎ 202-462-9001, 866-508-0658; www.hotelhelix.com; 1430 Rhode Island Ave NW; r from $119; Metro: McPherson Sq

'Is it Pop Art or is it DC's most fashionable hotel?' is the question posed – in all seriousness – by Kimpton Group's first DC hotel. From the pink neon lights and sliding doors at the entrance, to the sign in the gym commanding 'Burn, baby, burn,' to the orange, Barbie-doll throw pillows decorating the rooms, this place is playful and kitschy. Specialty rooms include 'Bunk' (that's right, bunk beds) and the more enticing 'Zone,' which features lounge seating and a loaded entertainment center.

HOTEL MADERA Map pp258-60 *Boutique*

☎ 202-296-7600, 800-368-5691; www.hotelmadera .com; 1310 New Hampshire Ave NW; weekend/weekday from $99/169; Metro: Dupont Circle

Cozy yet cosmopolitan, this boutique hotel is one of five that Kimpton has opened in DC in recent years. Besides the usual amenities, guests can enjoy satin and terry bathrobes and freshly brewed Starbucks coffee. The restaurant downstairs, **Firefly** (p129), is one of Dupont's hottest spots for dinner or cocktails.

INN AT DUPONT CIRCLE

Map pp258-60 *B&B*

☎ 202-467-6777; www.theinnatdupontcircle.com; 1312 19th St NW; r with bathroom $135-195, without bathroom $85-130, incl breakfast; Metro: Dupont Circle

Once owned by astrologer-to-the-stars Jeanne Dixon, this 19th-century Victorian townhouse is now a friendly and reasonably priced B&B. Rooms have phones, cable TV and fireplaces. The inn's luxuries include a solarium overlooking the garden and a Steinway concert grand piano in the salon. Continental breakfast is included in the price and served in the sunny dining room. A two-night stay is required on weekends.

JEFFERSON HOTEL Map pp258-60 *Business*

☎ 202-347-2200, 800-23-loews; www.loewshotels.com; 1200 16th St NW; r from $249; Metro: Farragut North

This elegant, two-winged 1923 mansion has an ornate porte cochere, beaux-arts architecture, and a luxurious interior full of crystal and velvet. Favored by diplomatic visitors, its 100 antique-furnished rooms have dual-line speaker-phones, CD players, VCRs, computer hookups, faxes and black-marble baths. Despite all the glitz, the staff are friendly and helpful.

JURY'S WASHINGTON

Map pp258-60 *Business*

☎ 202-483-6000; www.jurysdoyle.com; 150 New Hampshire Ave NW; r $125-235; Metro: Dupont Circle

Smack dab in the center of Dupont Circle, this newly renovated hotel features 314 rooms, a fitness center, valet parking and the excellent Dupont Grill. Rooms have all the expected amenities, including dataports.

MANSION ON O STREET Map pp258-60 *B&B*

☎ 202-496-2020; www.omansion.com; 2020 O St NW; r incl breakfast from $250; Metro: Dupont Circle

It doesn't advertise. It doesn't even have a sign or a brochure. But this place has quite a reputation anyway – it's just about the most flamboyant, original B&B around. Housed in a 100-room 1892 mansion (a remnant of the days when Dupont was a millionaires' neighborhood), it is part inn, part gallery/ performance space and part private club. In this latter incarnation, the Mansion has hosted Hollywood celebrities and Chelsea Clinton's sweet-16 party. Its owner, grande dame HH Leonards, has done the place up like a wedding at Castle Dracula: swags of velvet drapery, ornate chandeliers and lampshades, candelabra and concealed doorways. No two rooms, from the Russian Tea Room to the Log Cabin, are alike, and everything from the bedstead to the pictures for sale. This is one of the few inns in the area that offers handicapped-accessible rooms.

PARK HYATT Map pp258-60 *Business*

☎ 202-789-1234, 800-233-1234; www.parkwashing ton.hyatt.com; 1201 24th St NW; r from $199; Metro: Foggy Bottom-GWU

Occupying almost the entire 1200-block of 24th St midway between Dupont Circle and Foggy Bottom, this massive hotel has lots of quiet lounge space and hundreds of luxurious rooms. So crisply fresh that they smell like new cars, the rooms offer every amenity (even TVs in the bathrooms). A full gym and swimming pool are on-site. Downstairs, Melrose is among DC's best hotel restaurants.

RENAISSANCE MAYFLOWER HOTEL

Map pp258-60 *Business*

☎ 202-347-3000; www.renaissancehotels.com; 1127 Connecticut Ave NW; r from $150; Metro: Farragut North

J Edgar Hoover dined here; Richard Nixon resided here; and there are rumors that John F Kennedy sampled the charms of the fairer sex here. Although it's not the exclusive enclave it once was, this hotel is still pretty regal, with lots of frills and marble, and a beautiful grand ballroom. Rooms sport all the comforts; a business center, babysitting, concierge and currency exchange are available. High tea in the loungey hotel restaurant is great.

RITZ-CARLTON Map pp258-60 *Business*

☎ 800-241-3333; www.ritzcarlton.com; 1150 22nd St NW; r incl breakfast from $329; Metro: Farragut North

Defining standards of luxury, DC's first Ritz-Carlton offers its guests 300 spacious rooms with lots of little perks: goose down pillows, marble baths with separate showers, dataports with high-speed Internet access, and portable phones. The hotel allows access to the Sports Club/LA, a huge spa and fitness center. Special weekend packages throw in treats such as weekend rental of a Mercedes-Benz.

ROUGE HOTEL Map pp258-60 *Boutique*
☎ 202-939-6421; www.rougehotel.com; 1315 16th St NW; r from $119; Metro: McPherson Sq

Rouge is perhaps the most playful of Kimpton's new boutique hotels in DC. Appropriately, the decor is definitively red, with bold designs, funky furniture and hip posters decorating the rooms. Specialty rooms include 'Chat Rooms,' with pentium computers and flat-screen monitors, 'Chow Rooms,' with kitchenettes, and 'Chill Rooms,' with Sony Play Stations and DVD players. As funky as the hotel, Bar Rouge attracts a regular stream of locals, especially for its Thursday happy hours.

SWANN HOUSE Map pp258-60 *B&B*
☎ 202-265-4414; www.swannhouse.com; 1808 New Hampshire Ave NW; r incl breakfast $150-295; Metro: Dupont Circle

Set in an exquisite 1883 Romanesque mansion, Swann House has nine plush rooms, all with luxurious private baths, goose-down pillows, plush bathrobes, cable TV/VCR, and high-speed and wireless Internet access. The grandest of them may have a fireplace or a Jacuzzi, too. In any case, you can sit on the brick, deeply set porch and watch the Dupont scene; or retire to the privacy of the back garden with outdoor pool. Afternoon snacks are included. A two-night stay is required on weekends.

TABARD INN Map pp258-60 *Boutique*
☎ 202-785-1277; www.tabardinn.com; 1739 N St NW; s with bathroom $115-190, s without bathroom $80-110, d $15 extra, incl breakfast; Metro: Dupont Circle

Named for the inn in *Canterbury Tales*, this delightful, historic hotel is set in a trio of Victorian-era row houses. Its 40 rooms are furnished with vintage quirks, like iron bedsteads, overstuffed flowery sofas and wingbacked armchairs. Downstairs, its parlor, beautiful courtyard restaurant (p130) and bar are low-ceilinged, filled with funky old furniture, and highly conducive to curling up with a vintage port and the *Sunday Post*. The Wife of Bath never had it so good.

TOPAZ HOTEL Map pp258-60 *Boutique*
☎ 202-393-3000, 800-424-2950; www.topazhotel.com; 1733 N St NW; r from $159; Metro: Dupont Circle

This Kimpton hotel provides a Zen experience for its guests – special features range from the morning power hour serving energy drinks, to complimentary daily horoscopes, to an in-room teapot with herbal teas. Special 'Energy Rooms' feature treadmills, stairmasters or yoga space in the room.

WESTIN EMBASSY ROW
Map pp258-60 *Business*
☎ 202-293-2100, 888-625-5144; www.westin.com; 2100 Massachusetts Ave NW; r from $199; Metro: Dupont Circle

Appropriate to its name and locale, this international-looking hotel has a majestic, flag-draped, Georgian entrance. The hotel's interior decor retains suave touches of the 1920s, when the hotel was built, and the 200 rooms have both lovely old-fashioned elements (cozy down pillows, overstuffed furniture) and modern ones (dataports, cable TV, honor bars).

WINDSOR INN
Map pp258-60 *Family*
☎ 202-667-0300, 800-423-9111; www.windsorembassyinns.com; 1842 16th St NW ; s/d from $89/99; Metro: Dupont Circle

Operated by the same management as the Embassy Inn up the street, this pleasant inn has an art-deco lobby, and original 1920s moldings and floor tiles. Its 46 small but very tastefully decorated rooms have private baths, cable TV and phones. In the European tradition, guests receive continental breakfast and evening snacks and sherries.

Top Five Scandal-Ridden Hotels

For some reason, scandal is drawn to hotels. And not just seedy hotels, but fine upstanding institutions, too. Here are some suggestions if you want to stay where history was made in the worst way.

- **Hay-Adams Hotel** (p192) Ollie North's venue for wooing contributors to illegal contras.
- **One Washington Circle** (p194) Site of Nixon's office after Watergate toppled his presidency.
- **Washington Hilton & Towers** (p201) Site of John Hinckley's attempted murder of Ronald Reagan.
- **Swissôtel Watergate** (p194) Scandal central.
- **Wyndham Washington** (p201) Where Marion Barry muttered his famous last words 'Bitch set me up' after being busted for cocaine.

WYNDHAM WASHINGTON

Map pp258-60 *Business*

☎ 202-429-1700; www.wyndham.com; 1400 M St NW; rack rates around $199; Metro: McPherson Sq

You gotta feel a little sorry for this place near Thomas Circle: in its former incarnation as the Vista Hotel, it's where the FBI busted former Mayor Marion Barry for smoking crack with an ex-girlfriend. It's a perfectly decent business hotel despite that stigma, with high-speed Internet access in its 12 floors of generic rooms.

Kalorama
TAFT BRIDGE INN

Map pp258-60 *B&B*

☎ 202-387-2007; www.taftbridgeinn.com; 2007 Wyoming Ave NW; s with bathroom $119-134, s without bathroom $59-84, d $15 extra, incl breakfast; Metro: Dupont Circle

Named for the bridge that leaps over Rock Creek Park just to the north, this beautiful 19th-century Georgian mansion is an easy walk to Adams-Morgan or Dupont Circle. The inn has a paneled drawing room, classy antiques, six fireplaces and a garden. Parking and laundry are on the premises.

WASHINGTON HILTON & TOWERS

Map pp258-60 *Business*

☎ 202-483-3000; www.hilton.com; 1919 Connecticut Ave NW; weekend s/d from $145/165, weekday from $175/195; Metro: Dupont Circle

This 1960s-style semicircular structure is a giant hotel with all the amenities you would expect from a Hilton. It is famed as the site of John Hinckley's assassination attempt on President Ronald Reagan, on March 30, 1981. Hoping to impress the actress Jodie Foster, the disturbed young man (now housed at St Elizabeth's mental hospital in southeast DC) shot Reagan, his press secretary and an FBI agent near the T St NW entrance. The hotel has since constructed a big protective entryway.

Cheap Sleeps
BRAXTON HOTEL

Map pp258-60 *Family*

☎ 202-232-7800; www.braxtonhotel.com; 1440 Rhode Island Ave NW; s/d $50/70; Metro: McPherson Sq

Located between downtown and Dupont Circle proper, this somewhat rough-around-the-edges 62-room joint offers funky furnishings, free coffee and donuts, and good rates. Some of the rooms are done up in 'themes' (antiques, Victorian etc).

This is a neighborhood on the edge; be aware of your surroundings and don't hesitate to take a cab if it helps you to feel more comfortable.

BRICKSKELLER INN

Map pp258-60 *Guesthouse*

☎ 202-293-1885; brickskl@aol.com; 1523 22nd St NW; s/d without bathroom $54/73, with bathroom $73/92; Metro: Dupont Circle

Located above the famous saloon by the same name (p152), which carries over 1000 brands of beer from all over the world, the Brickskeller Inn is a convenient place to retire after imbibing. Rooms are basic but clean. They all have TVs and telephones, plus there are coin-operated laundry facilities on the 2nd floor.

DAVIS HOUSE

Map pp258-60 *Guesthouse*

☎ 202-232-3196; fax 202-232-3197; 1822 R St NW; dm/s $40/50; Metro: Dupont Circle

This 11-bed guesthouse operated by the American Friends Service Committee (the Quakers) is in a row house on a quiet residential block. It's open to international visitors, AFSC staff and people 'working on peace and justice projects' (if you work or volunteer for an NGO, this means you). Same-day requests from other travelers may be honored, depending on room availability.

All rooms share a bath, and no alcohol or smoking are allowed on the premises. There is a common area with a TV, a small kitchen with microwave and fridge, and wireless Internet access.

There is no staff on duty after 10pm, so you must check in before 9:30pm.

INTERNATIONAL STUDENT HOUSE

Map pp258-60 *Long-term*

☎ 202-387-6445; www.ishdc.org; 1825 R St NW; dm incl breakfast & dinner from $750 per month; Metro: Dupont Circle

This spectacular mansion houses a vibrantly multicultural residence for 100 guests. Residents sign up for at least three or four months of an in-depth experience in international living, but many stay for a year or even longer. Americans as well as international visitors are welcome; most guests are students or interns. Rates include 13 meals weekly (higher rates for single rooms, private baths, parking etc).

Shared facilities include a laundry, a large-screen TV with cable and DVD player, a computer lab with high-speed Internet access, a gorgeous library with Tudor accents, plus a lovely walled courtyard.

ADAMS-MORGAN

This colorful neighborhood offers its temporary residents an endless array of nightlife options, including restaurants and bars, music and dancing.

That the is primarily residential means that accommodations are all B&Bs and they are set on quiet tree-lined streets with friendly neighbors.

The disadvantage is the lack of public transport – it's a 15-minute walk to the nearest Metro.

ADAM'S INN
Map p261   *B&B*

☎ 202-745-3600, 800-578-6807; www.adamsinn.com; 1744 Lanier Place NW; s with/without bathroom $85/75, d $10 extra, incl breakfast; Metro: Woodley Park-Zoo/Adams Morgan

The owner of this place (and yes, his name really is Adam) converted two adjacent townhouses and a carriage house on a shady residential street into an inviting and homey guesthouse.

The 25 walk-up rooms are comfortably furnished.

The pleasant common areas include a nice garden patio with picnic table, a living room with a TV, a computer room with free high-speed Internet access, and laundry and kitchen facilities.

Cheap Sleeps
KALORAMA GUEST HOUSE
Map p261   *B&B*

☎ 202-667-6369; 1854 Mintwood Place NW; s with bathroom $65-95, without bathroom $45-70, d $5 extra, incl breakfast; Metro: Woodley Park-Zoo/Adams Morgan

This Victorian townhouse is a couple of blocks west of 18th St and was among Washington's first B&Bs. Its 31 rooms have Oriental rugs, down comforters and turn-of-the-century art.

The friendly atmosphere encourages a devoted band of return guests. Continental breakfast and an afternoon sherry are served in the parlor.

WASHINGTON INTERNATIONAL BACKPACKERS
Map p261   *Hostel*

☎ 202-667-7681, 800-567-4150; www.washington dchostel.com; 2451 18th St NW; dm/s incl breakfast $22/55; Metro: Woodley Park-Zoo/Adams Morgan

Young travelers who want to be right in the midst of 18th St's swarming entertainment strip choose this no-frills hostel.

The walk-up building is worn around the edges, but the bathrooms are clean and the dorm rooms are certainly comfortable enough.

Each of five rooms has bunk beds sleeping six to eight people. The hostel also features a common room with a large-screen TV, Internet access for $1 for 10 minutes and beat-up kitchen facilities. Limited parking is available also.

Arrange in advance for free pick-up from the train or bus station; you just can't beat that.

UPPER NORTHWEST DC

You will find the accommodations options in Upper Northwest DC are clustered around Woodley Park. This area offers easy access to transport. There are also many restaurants, as well as some good nightlife, in the immediate vicinity.

WOODLEY PARK GUEST HOUSE
Map pp262-3   *B&B*

☎ 202-667-0218, 866-667-0218; www.woodley parkguesthouse.com; 2647 Woodley Rd NW; r with bathroom $120-175, without bathroom $65-100, incl breakfast; Metro: Woodley Park-Zoo/Adams Morgan

This elegant, 1920s-era home was completely refurbished in 2001, resulting in a beautiful, historic B&B.

Seventeen sunny rooms have antique furniture, telephones and central air-con.

The very wide and welcoming front porch is a wonderful place to sit out a hot summer afternoon.

There is also parking available at a cost of $10 per night.

Cheap Sleeps

KALORAMA GUEST HOUSE AT WOODLEY PARK
Map pp262-3   *B&B*

☎ 202-328-0860; 2700 Cathedral Ave NW; r with bathroom $65-90, without bathroom $45-70, d $5 extra, incl breakfast; Metro: Woodley Park-Zoo/Adams Morgan
This sister to the **Kalorama Guest House** (p202) in Adams-Morgan is a cozy 1910 Victorian row house with 19 antique-furnished rooms. Additional facilities are in another property down the street. In winter guests are served sherry in the evenings; in summer fresh lemonade is poured throughout the day. Laundry and kitchen facilities are on-site.

ARLINGTON & ALEXANDRIA
A comfortable bed in Virginia costs less than one in DC. Loads of chain hotels are clustered around Ballston, Crystal City and National Airport. Pick one near a Metro and it's almost as convenient as staying in the city.

Old Town Alexandria offers a trade-off: Metro is not in the immediate vicinity and prices are higher, but the charming neighborhood makes it worth it. Virginia room tax is about 10% .

Arlington

DAYS INN CRYSTAL CITY   *Family*
☎ 703-920-8600; www.daysinn.com; 2000 Jefferson Davis Hwy; r incl breakfast from $120; Metro: Crystal City
Just a mile from Ronald Reagan Washington National Airport, Days Inn is an affordable option if you need to be near the airport. Traditionally decorated rooms are very spacious and comfortable. Hotel facilities include a fitness center and outdoor swimming pool, as well as free parking.

KEY BRIDGE MARRIOTT
Map pp256-7   *Business*

☎ 703-524-6400; www.marriott.com; 1401 Lee Highway; r from $109; Metro: Rosslyn
Located on the banks of the Potomac, this place is almost as good as staying right in Georgetown – the difference is you are closer to Metro and you can enjoy a lovely view of the university campus from your room. Georgetown is a 20-minute walk across the Francis Scott Key Bridge. The immediate area around the hotel is a bit sterile, but you can't beat the easy access to the George Washington Memorial Parkway and public transportation.

Changing of the Guard, Tomb of the Unknowns, Arlington National Cemetery (p97)

RITZ-CARLTON PENTAGON CITY
Business

☎ 703-415-5000; www.ritz-carlton.com; 1250 S Hayes St; weekend/weekday $140/220; Metro: Pentagon City

Staying at the Ritz in Pentagon City is almost better than staying in DC proper, because the rooms allow you to look out your window and enjoy fabulous views of the city, which you certainly can't do if you are in the middle of it. You will also appreciate cordless phones, plush terry bathrobes and comfy feather beds. The state-of-the-art fitness facility includes a heated lap pool, steam room and sauna and massage therapy.

Alexandria
HOLIDAY INN SELECT OLD TOWN
Map p265   *Family*

☎ 703-549-6080; www.holiday-inn.com; 480 King St; weekend/weekday $99/119; Old Town shuttle from King St Metro

The reliable, universal standards of Holiday Inn do not disappoint here, at the most affordable option in Old Town Alexandria. Enjoy an indoor and outdoor pool and a nice fitness facility with a Jacuzzi. All rooms feature high-speed Internet access and some have a balcony overlooking a lovely central courtyard. Pets and kids are welcome!

MORRISON HOUSE Map p265   *Boutique*

☎ 703-838-8000; www.morrisonhouse.com; 116 S Alfred St; weekend/weekday $150/250; Old Town shuttle from King St Metro

In the heart of Old Town Alexandria, Morrison House captures the neighborhood's charm in its Georgian-style building, marble baths and the Federal-style reproduction furniture.

This boutique hotel offers the service and amenities of a luxury hotel: terry bathrobes and high-speed Internet access come in every room. Rooms are beautifully decorated, especially the elegant library, where afternoon tea is served.

The kicker here is the service of a butler to cater to your every whim, any time of day or night. The hotel houses the **Elysium Dining Room** (p137).

Cheap Sleeps
ALEXANDRIA TRAVEL LODGE
Map p265   *Motel*

☎ 703-836-5100; 702 N Washington St, Alexandria; r $49-89; Old Town shuttle from King St Metro

This motel – on a busy section of Washington St – is about a mile north of Old Town's historic district. It is a good bet for budget travelers who have their own car; parking is free. Basic clean rooms have TVs, telephones and full bathrooms. Amenities are otherwise limited, but you can't beat the price.

Excursions

Excursions

Charming historic towns, forested mountain paths and wide sandy beaches are all just a stone's throw from Washington DC. Get out of the city to escape the heat of the summer, to enjoy the spectacular fall foliage or to delve more deeply into the nation's history.

HISTORIC SITES

The outskirts of DC have no shortage of historic sites in the near vicinity. George Washington's magnificent estate at **Mount Vernon** (p207) is an easy half-day trip out of the city, as is **Manassas** (p218), the site of the first major Civil War battle. The quaint colonial town of **Leesburg** (p220) is one of the oldest settlements in the area. The towns on the **Chesapeake** (p212) – such as Annapolis and St Michaels – preserve their maritime history with harbors that have been bustling for hundreds of years and old mansions overlooking the bay.

NATURE

Your choice here will be determined by the time you have available. If you can only spare a few hours, **Great Falls** (p217) is a wonderful waterside getaway, less than 20 miles northwest of the city. But if you have a day or more, head west to the wonderful forested hills of **Shenandoah National Park** (p210).

BEACHES

Nothing relieves the hellish heat and humidity of DC summers like a trip to the beach. Fortunately, the Atlantic coast of Virginia, Maryland and Delaware offers a wide variety of options. **Assateague Island** (p215) is the most pristine, protected by the National Park Service and void of any development. It is accessible from two towns that are complete opposites in character: quiet **Chincoteague** (p214) in the south and party town **Ocean City** (p214) in the north. Delaware's beach resorts fall somewhere in the middle of this spectrum. **Rehoboth** (p215) and **Dewey** (p215) are fun family towns with a lively bar and club scene and a built-up beach. The protected **Delaware Seashore State Park** (p215) is nearby. The tiny town of **Lewes** (p216) is more demure, with a historic center and a lovely beach at **Cape Henlopen State Park** (p216).

MOUNT VERNON

A visit to George Washington's Virginia home, **Mount Vernon**, is an easy escape from the city – one that the president himself enjoyed. It's also a journey through history:

Mount Vernon (left)

the country estate of this quintessential country gentleman has been meticulously restored and affords a glimpse of rural gentility as it was when Washington lived here. Situated on the Potomac banks, the 19-room mansion displays George and Martha's colonial tastes, while the outbuildings and slave quarters show what was needed for the functioning of the estate. George and Martha are both buried here, as requested by the first president in his will.

In the town of Mount Vernon, **Woodlawn Plantation** features two very different houses that are both splendid examples of their architectural times. The plantation home itself once belonged to Eleanor 'Nelly' Custis, granddaughter of Martha Washington, and her husband, Major Lawrence Lewis, George Washington's nephew. The house contains period antiques and a stunning rose garden.

Also on the grounds, architect Frank Lloyd Wright's **Pope-Leighey House** is a 1940s middle-class 'Usonian' dwelling of cypress, brick and glass. Originally intended as low-cost housing for the middle class, Wright's Usonian dwellings featured aesthetically elegant designs yet used durable, inexpensive materials. It was moved to Woodlawn in 1964 from Falls Church to rescue it from destruction. Furnished with Wright pieces, the house is utilitarian in structure, but quite beautiful.

Southwest of Mount Vernon, on a bend in the Potomac River, is the 1775 brick mansion **Gunston Hall** that belonged to statesman and contemporary of George Washington George Mason. Mason penned the lines 'all men are by nature equally free and independent, and have certain inherent rights' – words adapted by Thomas Jefferson for the Declaration of Independence. Dating from 1755, the mansion is an architectural masterpiece, with elegantly carved wooden interiors and meticulously kept formal gardens.

Transportation

Distance from Washington DC Mount Vernon 18 miles; Woodlawn Plantation 18 miles; Gunston Hall 23 miles.

Direction South.

Travel Time 30 minutes.

Car Drive south on the George Washington Memorial Parkway to Mount Vernon. At the traffic circle at Mount Vernon, head south on Rte 235. Woodlawn is at the intersection of Rte 235 with Rte 1. To reach Gunston Hall, turn left on Rte 1 and left on Gunston Road (Rte 242).

Metro Take a Yellow Line to Huntington, then board **Fairfax Connector** (☎ 703-339-7200) bus No 101 to Mount Vernon.

Boat The cruise ship **Potomac Spirit** (☎ 866-211-3811; www.cruisetomountvernon.com; Metro: Waterfront) departs for Mount Vernon from Pier 4, at 6th & Water Sts SW.

Bicycle From the Key Bridge or Arlington Cemetery, take the George Washington Memorial Parkway trail south.

Sights & Information

Gunston Hall (☎ 703-550-9220; www.gunstonhall.org; 10709 Gunston Rd, Mason Neck, Virginia; adult/child $5/1.50; ☯ 9:30am-5pm)

Mount Vernon (☎ 703-780-2000; www.mount vernon.org; 3200 George Washington Memorial Parkway; adult/child $11/5, audio tour $4; ☯ 9am-4pm Nov-Feb, 9am-5pm Mar, Sep & Oct, 8am-5pm Apr-Aug)

Pope-Leighey House (www.nationaltrust.org/national _trust_sites/pope_leighey.html; 9000 Richmond Hwy, Mt Vernon; Woodlawn combo pass adult/child $13/5; ☯ 10am-5pm Mar-Dec)

Woodlawn Plantation (☎ 703-780-4000; www .woodlawn1805.org; 9000 Richmond Hwy, Mount Vernon; adult/child $7.50/3; ☯ 10am-5pm Mar-Dec)

Eating

Mount Vernon Inn (☎ 703-780-0011; 3200 George Washington Memorial Parkway; lunch $10, dinner $16-24; ☯ lunch & dinner Mon-Sat) A colonial-style restaurant on the grounds of Mount Vernon serving traditional lunches and candle-lit dinners. The ubiquitous food court is in the visitors center.

Sleeping

Comfort Inn Gunston Corner (☎ 703-643-3100; www.cigunston.com; 8180 Silverbrook Rd, Lorton, Virginia; r with continental breakfast from $115) A comfortable suburban hotel with an outdoor pool and exercise facility; provides convenient shuttle to Metro. Lorton is about 5 miles southeast of Mount Vernon (from Rte1 turn right on Lorton Rd and right on Silverbrook Rd).

BALTIMORE

Baltimore's glory has always been rooted in seafaring. Today, the signs are everywhere. The Inner Harbor – the city's heart – displays a collection of traditional sailing vessels ranging in size from the 200-year-old battle frigate USS Constellation to the turn-of-the-century oystering skipjack *Minnie V*. Three other vessels docked at Pier 3 are open for exploration as a part of the Baltimore Maritime Museum.

The National Aquarium in Baltimore put the city on the map as a tourist destination when it opened in 1981. Stretching seven storeys high over two piers, its tanks house more than 10,000 marine animals, including sharks, rays and porpoises, plus dolphins in the Marine Mammal Pavilion.

The Inner Harbor's tourist center is dominated by Harborplace, two complexes with restaurants and shops. More interesting is the World Trade Center, behind the complex on the north shore. Designed by IM Pei, it is the world's tallest pentagonal structure; check out the view from the 27th floor. There are a bunch of other museums around here, but the most distinctive is the American Visionary Art Museum, on the south side of the harbor. This avant-garde gallery showcases the raw genius of 'outsider' artists: broken mirror collages, a maniacally embroidered last will, a giant model ship constructed from toothpicks...you get the idea.

Baltimore boasts two top stops for kids, both within a few blocks of the Inner Harbor. The Maryland Science Center sits at the harbor's southeast corner. The excellent rotating exhibits and IMAX films are the highlight. Two blocks north, Port Discovery is a converted fish market which has a play house, laboratory, TV studio and even Pharoah's tomb. Wear your kids out here.

The Orioles' baseball park, Camden Yards, occupies an entire city block west of the Inner Harbor. It was the first 'retro' ball park which reconciled Major League Baseball's need for more space with fans' nostalgia. Painted baseballs on the sidewalk lead two blocks northwest to the birthplace of a baseball legend; it's now the Babe Ruth Museum.

Four blocks north of Camden Yards is Lexington Market. A city market has thrived on this site since 1782. More than 140 merchants hawk everything from homemade kielbasa to Korean barbecue. Around the corner, Edgar Allan Poe is buried in Westminster Cemetery. If you are here around his birthday, January 19, you may see roses and cognac decorating the gravesite.

Not to be confused with George Washington's estate in Virginia, Baltimore's district of Mount Vernon is 1 mile north up Charles St, centered around the Washington Monument (designed by Robert Mills of *the* Washington Monument – you'll note the resemblance) at Mount Vernon Square. Baltimore's most venerable cultural institutions are clustered around this square. The Peabody Conservatory of Music, at the southeast corner, is the oldest classical music school in the country, boasting alums such as pianist Leon Fleisher and composer Dominick Argento. Walters Art Museum, across the street, is a collection of ancient, medieval, Islamic, Renaissance, Asian and contemporary art. This gallery is a gem, so don't overdose on art at DC's National Gallery.

The city grows more residential north of North Ave and you will probably want to drive or take the Metro. This is where you will find John Hopkins University, an acclaimed institution for medicine, international relations and publishing. On weekdays, free tours leave from Garland House on campus. Adjacent to the campus, the Baltimore Museum of Art – the city's modern art museum – houses Maryland's largest collection of art.

Fells Point is a colorful waterfront community that sits east of the Inner Harbor on the north bank of the river. The Fells brothers from Lancaster, England, settled here in the 1700s, making it one of the oldest maritime communities in the country. If you are interested in history, check out the Fells Point Maritime Museum, which opened in 2003. Along the cobblestone streets, you can see the rising tide of gentrification, and its accompanying antique shops, record stores and restaurants. The clubs and bars here are the center of a rowdy nightlife scene.

Transportation

Distance from Washington DC 45 miles.

Direction North.

Travel Time 45 to 60 minutes.

Car Take I-95 or I-295 (Baltimore-Washington Parkway) north to Russell St, which terminates west of the Inner Harbor. Or take I-95 north to I-395, which spills out downtown as Howard St. Beware of this drive during rush hour.

Train Both Amtrak (p225) and the Maryland Rail Commuter (MARC; p225) travel between Washington DC's Union Station and Baltimore's Penn Station. MARC is cheaper but it runs only on weekdays. Bus Nos 3 and 11 travel up Charles St past Penn Station at 1515 N Charles St.

Sights & Information

American Visionary Art Museum (☎ 410-244-1900; www.avam.org; 800 Key Hwy; adult $9, senior, student & child $6; ⏰ 10am-5pm Tue-Sun)

Babe Ruth Museum (☎ 410-727-1539; www.baberuth museum.com; 216 Emory St; adult/senior/child $6/4/3; ⏰ 10am-5pm Apr-Oct, to 7pm on Orioles' game days, 10am-4pm Nov-Mar)

Baltimore Maritime Museum (☎ 410-396-3453; www.ba ltomaritimemuseum.org; 802 S Caroline St; adult/senior/child $7/6/4; ⏰ 10am-5pm Sun-Thu, 10am-6pm Fri & Sat)

Baltimore Museum of Art (☎ 410-396-7100; www.artbma.org; 10 Art Museum Dr; adult/senior/child $7/5/free; ⏰ 11am-5pm Wed-Fri, 11am-6pm Sat & Sun)

Camden Yards (☎ 410-685-9800, 888-848-BIRD; www.theorioles.com; 333 W Camden St, Baltimore; tickets from $20; ⏰ box office 10am-5pm Mon-Sat, noon-5pm Sun)

Fells Point Maritime Museum (☎ 410-732-0278; www.mdhs.org; 1724 Thames St; adult/child $4/3; ⏰ 10am-5pm Thu-Mon)

Johns Hopkins University (☎ 410-516-8171; www.johnshopkins.edu; Garland Hall, N Charles St; ⏰ Mon-Fri)

Maryland Science Center (☎ 410-685-5225; www.mdsci.org; 601 Light St; ⏰ 10am-5pm Tue-Fri, 10am-6pm Sat, noon-5pm Sun; adult/senior/child $12/11/8, IMAX $7.50)

National Aquarium in Baltimore (☎ 410-576-3800; www.aqua.org; Piers 3-4, 501 E Pratt St; adult/senior/child $15.50/12.50/7.50; ⏰ 10am-7pm Sat-Thu, 10am-10pm Fri Sep-Jun; 9am-8pm Sun-Thu, 9am-10pm Fri & Sat Jul-Aug; enter 2hr before closure)

Peabody Conservatory of Music (☎ 410-659-8124; www.peabody.jhu.edu; Mount Vernon Square)

Port Discovery (☎ 410-727-8120; www.portdiscovery.org; 35 Market Place; adult/senior/child $11/10/8.50; ⏰ 9:30am-4:30pm Tue-Fri, 10am-5pm Sat, noon-5pm Sun)

USS Constellation (☎ 410-539-1719; www.constellation.org; Pier 1, 301 E Pratt St; adult/senior/child $6.50/5/3.50; ⏰ 10am-5:30pm Apr-Oct, 10am-4:30pm Nov-Mar)

Walters Art Museum (☎ 410-547-9000; www.thewalters.org; 600 N Charles St; adult $8, senior $6, student & young adult under 25 $5, child free; ⏰ 10am-5pm Tue-Sun)

Washington Monument (☎ 410-396-0929; 2600 Madison Ave)

World Trade Center (☎ 410-837-8439; www.baltimore .to/TopOfWorld; 401 E Pratt St; admission $4; ⏰ 10am-5:30pm, later in summer)

Eating

Bertha's (☎ 410-327-0426; 734 S Broadway; mussels $9, meals from $12; ⏰ 11:30am-11pm Sun-Thu, 11:30am-midnight Fri & Sat) A Baltimore institution famous for bloodies, mussels, and live blues and jazz. You'll spot 'Eat Bertha's Mussels' bumper stickers around town.

Brewer's Art (☎ 410-547-6925; 1106 N Charles St; mains $15-25; ⏰ 5:30-10pm) Contemporary setting and cuisine. The highlight of Baltimore's 'restaurant row.'

Harborplace (☎ 410-332-4191, 800-HARBOR1; www.harborplace.com; cnr Pratt & Light Sts; ⏰ 10am-9pm Mon-Sat, 11am-7pm Sun) Two pavilions contain a giant food court, and many popular national and local chain restaurants. Some bars and restaurants stay open later. Prices range from inexpensive fast-food to fancy sit-down fare.

Joy America Cafe (☎ 410-244-6500; 800 Key Hwy; lunch $10-20, dinner $30-50; ⏰ 11am-10pm Tue-Sat, 11am-4pm Sun brunch) The food version of the American Visionary Art Museum: radical. Feed the soul with organic ingredients and gorgeous views.

Sleeping

Admiral Fell Inn (☎ 410-522-7377, 800-292-4667; www.admiralfell.com; 888 S Broadway; r $150-200) An old Fells Point sailors' hotel converted into a lovely inn with Federal-style furniture and four-poster beds.

Harbor Court Hotel (☎ 410-234-0550; 550 Light St; r from $199) The city's premier hotel, featuring heavenly harbor views.

HI Baltimore (☎ 410-576-8880; 17 W Mulberry St; dm $25) A newly renovated hostel that's casual and comfortable.

Mount Vernon Hotel (☎ 410-727-2000; www .bichotels.com; 24 W Franklin St; r from $119) Comfortable, utilitarian rooms in a central location. Free shuttle to the harbor.

SHENANDOAH NATIONAL PARK

The backbone of the Shenandoah National Park is the Blue Ridge Mountains, ancient granite and metamorphic formations that are more than one billion years old. The park itself is almost 70 years old, founded in 1935 as a retreat for East Coast urban populations. It is an accessible day-trip destination from DC, but stay longer if you can. The 500 miles of hiking trails, 75 scenic overlooks, 30 fishing streams, seven picnic areas and four campgrounds are sure to keep you entertained.

Skyline Dr is the breathtaking road that follows the main ridge of the Blue Ridge Mountains and winds 105 miles through the center of the park. It begins in Front Royal near the western end of I-66, and ends in the southern part of the range near Rockfish Gap near I-64. Mile markers at the side of the road provide a reference.

Your first stop should be the Dickey Ridge Visitor Center at Mile 4.6, close to the northern end of Skyline Dr, or at Byrd Visitor Center at Mile 50. Both places have exhibits on flora and fauna, as well as maps and information about hiking trails and activities. Miles and miles of blazed trails wander through the park. Some choices for hiking include:

Compton Peak Mile 10.4, 2.4 miles, easy to moderate.

Traces Mile 22.2, 1.7 miles, easy.

Overall Run Mile 22.2, 6 miles, moderate.

White Oak Canyon Mile 42.6, 4.6 miles, strenuous.

Hawksbill Mountain Summit Mile 46.7, 2.1 miles, moderate. This is the park's highest peak.

Horseback riding is allowed on designated trails: pick up your pony at **Skyland Stables**, near Mile 41.7. Cycling is allowed on Skyline Dr only – not off-road. Backcountry camping is allowed but requires a permit, which you can pick up at the visitors centers.

The town of **Front Royal**, at the northern end of Skyline Dr, is a convenient jumping-off point for the park. It's a good place to pack your picnic before heading into the wilderness. If you have some free time here, visit the **Oasis Winery**, known internationally for its sparkling wines. The town is also home to the **Skyline Caverns**, whose interiors are decked with unusual anthodites, or 'cave flowers.' Unlike stalactites and stalagmites, these spiky nodes defy gravity and grow in all directions, one inch every 7000 years.

The small town of **Luray** sits snug between Massanutten Mountain, in George Washington National Forest, and Shenandoah National Park. The eastern US's largest and most popular caves, **Luray Caverns**, are 9 miles west of here on Rte 211.

Transportation

Distance from Washington DC Front Royal 70 miles; Luray 90 miles.

Direction West.

Travel Time 90 minutes to the northern entrance at Front Royal.

Car From Washington DC, take I-66 west to Rte 340. Front Royal is 3 miles south; Luray is 27 miles south.

Sights & Information

Byrd Visitor Center (☎ 540-999-3283; Skyline Dr, Mile 50; ⏱ 9am-5pm Apr-Nov)

Dickey Ridge Visitor Center (☎ 540-635-3566; Skyline Dr, Mile 4.6; ⏱ 9am-5pm Apr-Nov)

Luray Caverns (☎ 540-743-6551; www.luray caverns.com; Rte 211; adult/senior/child $17/15/8; ⏱ 9am-7pm Jun-Aug, 9am-6pm Sep-Nov & Apr-May, 9am-4pm Mon-Fri Dec-Mar)

Oasis Winery (☎ 540-635-7627; www.oasiswine.com; 14141 Hume Rd, off Rte 635 near Front Royal; wine tasting from $5; ⏱ 10am-5pm)

Shenandoah National Park (☎ 540-999-3500; www.nps.gov/shen; 3655 US 211 E, Luray; 7-day entry car $10, walker & cyclist $5)

Skyland Stables (☎ 540-999-2210; guided group rides per hr $22; ⏱ 9am-5pm May-Oct)

Skyline Caverns (⏱ 800-296-4545; www.skyline caverns.com; entrance to Skyline Dr; adult/child $14/7; ⏱ 9am-6:30pm Jun-Aug, 9am-4pm Nov-Mar, 9am-5pm Mon-Fri, 9am-6pm Sat & Sun Sep-Oct & Apr-May)

Eating

Elkwallow Wayside (☎ 540-999-2253; Skyline Dr, Mile 24.1; ⏱ Apr-Oct) Camp store with supplies and ice.

Fox Diner (☎ 540-635-3325; 20 South St, Front Royal) Nothing fancy, just honest, old-fashioned cookin'.

Panorama (☎ 540-999-2265; Skyline Dr, Mile 31.5; sandwiches from $5, mains from $10; ⏱ 9am-5:30pm Apr-Nov) Traditional Virginia country fare and hearty sandwiches.

Parkhurst Restaurant (☎ 540-743-6009; Rte 211W, west of Luray Caverns; sandwiches $5-6, mains $8-15; ⏱ 11:30am-9pm Sun-Thu, 11:30am-10pm Fri & Sat) American continental fare served on a veranda with great views.

Sleeping

Lewis Mountain Campground (☎ 800-365-CAMP; www.nps.gov/shen; Skyline Dr, Mile 57.6; campsite $16; ☯ Apr-Oct) A park-service campground with a store, laundry and showers. Lewis Mountain has several suitably rustic cabins that feature private baths in which you can rejuvenate your weary body after a hard day's hiking.

Potomac Appalachian Trail Club Cabins (☎ 703-242-0693; www.patc.net; weekday/weekend $18/28) Six cabins with bunk beds, water and stoves in beautiful backcountry areas; reservations mandatory.

Skyland Lodge (☎ 540-743-5108, 800-999-4714; Skyline Dr, Mile 41.7; cabins $80-150; ☯ Mar-Dec) Rustic cabins with magnificent views.

CHESAPEAKE BAY

The coves and waterways of the Chesapeake Bay are a wonderful destination for sailors or seafood lovers. A day trip to Annapolis is the easiest way to get a dose of these treats and enjoy the town's colonial charm. But if you have the extra time, the Eastern Shore is also delightful: you will find ancestral farms, working waterways and small towns to explore by bike or boat.

The capital of Maryland, and a national landmark, Annapolis has one of the largest concentrations of 18th-century buildings in the country. And although it is the seat of the state bureaucracy, no modern structures mar the skyline or the narrow brick

> ## Transportation
>
> **Distance from Washington DC** Annapolis 35 miles; Easton 73 miles; St Michaels 79 miles; Oxford 79 miles.
>
> **Direction** East.
>
> **Travel Time** Annapolis 50 minutes; Easton, St Michaels & Oxford 90 minutes.
>
> **Car** Rte 50 east goes straight into downtown Annapolis. To Easton, continue east over the Chesapeake Bay Bridge and stay on Rte 50 (east) to Rte 33 west.

streets. Home of the **US Naval Academy** since 1845, Annapolis Harbor and its connecting tidal creeks shelter dozens of marinas where thousands of cruising and racing sailboats tie up, earning the city the title 'Sailing Capital' in addition to state capital.

The lovely Navy Campus is northwest of the Annapolis historic district; enter through Gate 1 (at the intersection of King George, East and Randall Sts) to the **US Naval Academy Armel Leftwich Visitor Center**, which features a film, some exhibits and guided tours. Preble Hall contains the **US Naval Academy Museum** with lots of artifacts, including remnants of the famed battleship USS *Maine*.

Annapolis' lively harbor, City Dock, is the center of its nightlife and – obviously – its nautical life. There are many opportunities to experience it firsthand. Take one of the regularly scheduled cruises that leave from City Dock, or sign up for a sailing class or rental from **Annapolis Sailing School** or **Womanship**. Note the **Kunta Kinte–Alex Haley Memorial**, which marks the spot where the enslaved African arrived in the USA, as told by Alex Haley's novel *Roots*.

The heart of Annapolis is the **Maryland State House**, a dignified domed building that looks the part. Built in 1792, the building served as the first capitol of the fledgling United States and as a meeting place for the Continental Congress in 1783–84. The period artwork and furnishings are worth a peek around; guided tours are also available.

The collection of historic homes and buildings clustered on Cornhill and Fleet Sts between the State House and the harbor is extraordinary. Guided walking and bus tours abound, or you can pick up a free brochure at the **Annapolis & Anne Arundel County Conference & Visitors Bureau**. Some of the highlights that are open to the public include the jewel **Hammond Harwood House** and the **William Paca House & Garden**.

On the Eastern Shore of the Chesapeake Bay, Easton is known more as a gateway to the nearby town of St Michaels, but it is also the commercial and cultural center of surrounding Talbot County. Travelers will discover a town with an 18th-century center that has all the tradition and charm of Annapolis. Stop by the **Talbot County Chamber of Commerce** for information about the Eastern Shore.

The **Historical Society of Talbot County** runs a local history museum in its 19th-century headquarters and offers guided tours of three historic houses. Other old buildings that are open to the public include the 1794 **Talbot County Courthouse** and the 1682 **Third Haven Meeting House**. The **Academy Art Museum** houses a good collection of 19th- and 20th-century art in an 1820s schoolhouse.

Bay Hundred Peninsula thrusts into the Chesapeake near Easton. Along the shores lie the sweeping manors and productive fishing ports that have typified Chesapeake life for three centuries. The highlight is St Michaels, a colonial town with red-brick Georgian buildings, flowering gardens and historic watercraft tied at the wharf. It is a popular tourist spot; the harbor is crowded with visiting yachts. It also retains traces of its not-so-distant maritime past, when many citizens earned a living harvesting the bay's oysters in winter and blue crabs in summer.

Overlooking the harbor from Navy Point, the 1879 Hooper Strait octagonal lighthouse has become the image most people associate with Chesapeake Bay. It is the focal point for the Chesapeake Bay Maritime Museum, a collection of historic buildings that surround the lighthouse on the 18-acre grounds.

St Michaels is packed with shops and galleries, and a few historic houses. But the real reason to come here is to explore the maze of coves by boat, or to cycle around and admire the stately manor houses. Rent bikes and boats at St Michaels Harbour Inn & Marina or St Michaels Marina.

Travelers come to Oxford to ride the village's historic Oxford-Bellevue Ferry, which has been operating since 1683. The car ferry crosses the Tred Avon River from Oxford to Bellevue in 10 minutes; from Bellevue you can drive or cycle 7 miles to St Michaels. There is always a cooling breeze and a lovely view of the pastoral peace surrounding Oxford.

Sights & Information

Academy Art Museum (☎ 410-822-2787; www.art -academy.org; 106 South St, Easton; admission free; ⏰ 10am-4pm Mon-Sat, to 9pm Wed)

Annapolis & Anne Arundel County Conference & Visitors Bureau (☎ 410-263-9591; 26 West St, Annapolis; ⏰ 9am-5pm)

Annapolis Sailing School (☎ 410-267-7205; www.anna polissailing.com; 601 6th St, Annapolis)

Chesapeake Bay Maritime Museum (☎ 410-745-2916; www.cbmm.org; St Michaels; adult/senior/child $9/8/4; ⏰ 9am-4pm Nov-Feb, 9am-5pm Oct & Mar-May, 9am-6pm Jun-Sep)

Hammond Harwood House (☎ 410-263-4683; www.hammondharwoodhouse.org; 19 Maryland Ave, Annapolis; adult/student/child $6/5.50/4; ⏰ noon-5pm Wed-Sun Apr-Oct)

Historical Society of Talbot County (☎ 410-822-0773; www.hstc.org; 25 S Washington St; admission free; ⏰ 10am-4pm Mon-Sat)

Maryland State House (☎ 410-974-3400; 91 State Circle, Annapolis; admission free; ⏰ 9am-5pm Mon-Fri, 10am-4pm Sat & Sun, tours 11am & 3pm)

Oxford-Bellevue Ferry (☎ 410-745-9023; www.oxford bellevueferry.com; Oxford; car/bicycle/passenger $6/2.50/1; ⏰ 7am-dusk Mon-Fri, 9am-dusk Sat & Sun, closed Dec-Feb)

St Michaels Marina (☎ 410-745-2400; www.stmichaels marina.com; 305 Mulberry St, St Michaels; bike rental per hr/day $4/16; ⏰ May-Oct)

Talbot County Chamber of Commerce (☎ 410-822-4653; www.talbotchamber.org; 210 Marlboro Rd, Easton; ⏰ 8:30am-5pm Mon-Fri)

Talbot County Courthouse (☎ 410-822-2401; 11 N Washington St, Easton; ⏰ 9am-5pm Mon-Fri)

Third Haven Meeting House (☎ 410-822-0293; 405 S Washington St, Easton; admission free; ⏰ 9am-5pm)

US Naval Academy Armel Leftwich Visitor Center (☎ 410-263-6933; www.usna.edu; tours adult/senior/ student $6.50/5.50/4.50; ⏰ 9am-5pm Mar-Dec, 9am-4pm Jan & Feb; tours 10am-3pm Mon-Sat, 12:30-3pm Sun)

US Naval Academy Museum (☎ 410-293-2108; www.usna.edu/Museum; 118 Maryland Ave, Annapolis; admission free; ⏰ 9am-5pm Mon-Sat, 11am-5pm Sun)

Detour: Blackwater National Wildlife Refuge

This 17,000-acre refuge, 20 miles south of Easton, contains tidal marshes protected for migrating waterfowl. It has large populations of bald eagles, snow geese, peregrine falcons, blue herons, ospreys and 20 species of duck. Mid-October to mid-March is prime bird-watching time. You may also spot woodland creatures, like red foxes, fox squirrels and white-tailed deer.

A 5-mile nature drive cuts through the refuge. This is also a great spot for bikes and kayakers to explore: paddling maps are available at the Blackwater Refuge Visitor Center (☎ 410-228-2677; www.friendsofblackwater.org; 2145 Key Wallace Dr, Cambridge; car $3, walker & cyclist $1; ⏰ 8am-4pm Mon-Fri, 9am-5pm Sat & Sun) Take Rte 50 south to Cambridge, then Rte 16 south to State Rd 335. Take a left at Key Wallace Dr.

William Paca House & Garden (☎ 410-267-7619; www.annapolis.org; 186 Prince George St, Annapolis; house or garden only adult/senior/child $5/4/3, combo $8/7/5; ⏱ 10am-5pm Mon-Sat, noon-5pm Sun Apr-Dec, 10am-4pm Sat, noon-4pm Sun Jan-Mar)

Womanship (☎ 410-267-6661; www.womanship.com; 137 Conduit St, Annapolis; 2-day courses $495; ⏱ Apr-Oct)

Eating

Bistro St Michaels (☎ 410-745-9111; 403 S Talbot St, St Michaels; meals from $30; ⏱ 5:30-9pm, reservations required) Exquisite French food and wine in a glamorous clapboard house.

Carpenter St Saloon (☎ 410-745-5111; 113 S Talbot St, St Michaels; mains $10-16; ⏱ 11:30am-9pm) Atmospheric corner bar for oysters and beers, with an airy dining room for families next door.

Chick & Ruth's Delly (☎ 410-268-5665; 165 Main St, Annapolis; meals $5-10, dinners $8-14; ⏱ 6:30am-10pm Sun-Thu, 6:30am-11:30pm Fri & Sat) A second-generation Annapolis institution serving up burgers, milkshakes, crab cakes and breakfast goodies all with a smile.

Hunter's Tavern (☎ 410-822-1300; 101 E Dover St, Easton; breakfast & lunch $12-16, dinners $30; ⏱ breakfast, lunch & dinner) A comfortable restaurant inside Tidewater Inn serving civilized breakfast and lunch and fancy dinners.

Riordan's Saloon (☎ 410-263-5449; 26 Market Space, Annapolis; sandwiches $7-10, dinners $15-20; ⏱ 11am-midnight Sun-Thu, 11am-1am Fri & Sat) Steamed shrimp and microbrews or bloodies and brunch overlooking the lively Annapolis City Dock.

Sleeping

Historic Inns of Annapolis (☎ 410-263-2641; www .annapolisinns.com; 58 State Circle, Annapolis; r from $150) Three historic properties with period furnishings and modern conveniences.

Kemp House Inn (☎ 410-745-2243; www.kemphouse inn.com; 412 S Talbot St, St Michaels; r from $120) Fine 1807 Georgian house with period furnishings and working fireplaces. Robert E Lee spent two nights here.

O'Callaghan Hotel (☎ 410-263-7700; www .ocallaghanhotels-us.com; 174 West St, Annapolis; r from $100) Classic decor and friendly service characterize this Irish hotel.

St Michaels Harbour Inn & Marina (☎ 410-745-9110; www.harbourinn.com; 101 N Harbor Rd, St Michaels; r from $200) Deluxe waterfront hotel overlooking the harbor. Bike rental per hr/day $5/20; canoes & kayaks per hr/day $10/35.

Tidewater Inn (☎ 410-822-1300, 800-237-8775; 101 E Dover St, Easton; r from $160) Queen Ann replica with modern rooms and traditional mahogany furniture.

ATLANTIC COAST

From Virginia through Maryland and up to Delaware, the Atlantic coast is a string of protected marshland and preserved beaches, interspersed with resort towns ranging from charming to cheesy. Chincoteague, Ocean City, Rehoboth and Lewes all offer a most welcome – even necessary – respite from the sometimes unbearable heat and humidity of Washington summers. These places are all too far for a day trip from DC; you will want the weekend to get your fill of boogie boarding and all-you-can-eat crabs.

With no contest, the loveliest of the group is Chincoteague, Virginia. It's also the furthest from DC. The small beach town (population 1600) sits across an inlet from Assateague Island, which contains Chincoteague National Wildlife Refuge. Famous from the 1940s novel *Misty of Chincoteague*, the island is still home to wild ponies, but they are not really that wild. In July they are herded across the channel in an annual celebratory festival.

Transportation

Distance from Washington DC Chincoteague 160 miles; Ocean City 130 miles; Rehoboth, Dewey and Lewes 115 miles.

Direction East.

Travel Time Four hours to Chincoteague; three hours to Ocean City, Rehoboth and Lewes.

Car Take Rte 50 south to Rte 13 in Salisbury, Maryland. To Chincoteague, take Rte 13 south to Rte 175, about 5 miles past Pocomoke City, Maryland. Travel east on Rte 175 to Chincoteague Island, then east on Maddox Blvd. To reach Ocean City, stay on Rte 50, which leads right to the inlet. For Rehoboth and Lewes, take Rte 50 to Rte 404 east. To Rehoboth, go south on Rte 1; to Lewes, head east on Rte 9.

Boat The Cape May–Lewes ferry (☎ 800-643-3779) travels year-round between Lewes and Cape May, the southern tip of the New Jersey shore. The ferry takes 70 minutes to transport cars and bikes across the open mouth of the Delaware Bay. On weekends, make reservations in advance.

Detour: Assateague Island

Assateague Island is among the most pristine, picture-perfect spots on the mid-Atlantic coast. As an undeveloped barrier island, it provides a sharp contrast to the overdeveloped beach resorts that dominate the coast. Besides its natural appeal, the island is home to a legendary herd of wild ponies, whose dramatic silhouettes race across the dunes.

The protected national seashore is managed largely by the National Park Service; the southern end of the island is Chincoteague National Wildlife Refuge. A bridge accesses the northern portion of the island, but roads do not go further. To drive from the northern end near Ocean City to the southern end at Chincoteague requires a circuitous inland detour.

The island is a sanctuary where you can get away from the crowds of Ocean City and swim, bike, hike, fish canoe, kayak or camp, with nothing but the sound of the surf and the whir of the wind as your companions. From Ocean City, drive south on Rte 611 to the **Barrier Island Visitor Center** (☎ 410-641-1441; Rte 11 near Verrazzano Bridge; bike/car $3/10; 🕒 9am-5pm). Flat, paved pathways along the island are ideal for biking; the protected marshland shores make for adventurous canoeing; conditions are ideal for swimming, hiking and bird-watching. Rent bikes and boats at the recreation outpost beyond the Bayside Campground.

Besides miles of pristine, sandy beaches, the refuge contains marshland that attracts migrating waterfowl – a bird-watchers paradise. Paved trails and roads provide various tours for walkers, cyclists and drivers to try to spot birds and ponies and other wildlife. Cycling or kayaking is definitely the way to explore this place. Rent the gear at the **Piney Island Country Store** or **Tidewater Expeditions**. In town, there is not much to keep you occupied in case of rain. Only the **Oyster & Maritime Museum** has exhibits on the history of the area, marine life and seafood.

Over the state border, Ocean City is Maryland's mammoth Atlantic shore beach resort. For most of its length it's barely three blocks wide, yet it sprawls southward from the Delaware border along 10 miles of barrier beach lined with side-by-side hotels and motels. It's a Coppertone-scented town of bikini contests, waterslides, saltwater taffy, airbrushed T-shirts, go-carts and mini golf. Pick up information on all this fun at the **Ocean City Convention & Visitors Bureau**.

The town originated at the southern tip of the Strand, now called 'the Inlet', which retains a tiny hint of Victorian flavor. Here, a 2½-mile boardwalk provides a pedestrian promenade that is the heart of the Ocean City experience. Across the Inlet is Assateague Island.

Further north up Rte 1, the **Delaware Seashore State Park** is a 10-mile long, half-mile wide peninsula with a long, straight, clean beach. Stop at the park office to pick up information about pontoon boat tours, hiking trails and guarded swimming areas. The **Indian River Inlet Marina** is west of the park office – this is where you can charter fishing boats.

Rehoboth and Dewey are Delaware's most popular resorts. They are a sort-of happy medium between family-friendly Chincoteague and kid-crazy Ocean City. Beach houses trimmed in clapboard and cedar shingles sit among tree-lined streets and picturesque lagoons. Modern oceanfront resort motels and hotels break the spell as you get closer to the waterfront. The commercial strip along Rehoboth Ave has something of a honky-tonk feel; but compared to Ocean City, it's small enough to retain some charm. The clientele is a genial mix of white families and a sizable gay community. The **Rehoboth Chamber of Commerce & Visitors Center** is just across the canal bridge in the restored 1879 railway station.

Eight miles north of Rehoboth, the tiny town of Lewes is an often overlooked waterside retreat for travelers. The town is quaint,

Seagull Century

For 15 years Salisbury University has sponsored a nationally acclaimed bicycle event (www.seagull century.org) that attracts thousands of participants to ride for 100 miles along the coast of the Eastern Shore. Every October, cyclists ride from Salisbury, Maryland (west of Ocean City) south to Milburn Landing on the Pocomoke River, then to Assateague Island for fun and refueling before returning to Salisbury. A shorter 63-mile race also takes place on the same day.

with a small but inviting historic center. Stop in at the 1730 Fisher-Martin house, home of the **Lewes Chamber of Commerce & Visitors Bureau**, to pick up a walking-tour map. Next door, the **Zwaanendael Museum** has some exhibits on sunken treasures and period household items. At the northwest end of town, the **Lewes Historical Complex** encompasses seven 17th- and 18th-century buildings that are now open for tours.

Lewes has quite a decent city beach, but the seashore is even more pleasant at **Cape Henlopen State Park**. Formerly part of the WWII defense system, the park now has a reclaimed feel. Still, the shore is just about deserted, save the local fishermen and some families enjoying the water.

Sights & Information

Cape Henlopen State Park (☎ 302-645-6852; www.destateparks.com; 42 Cape Henlopen Dr, Lewes, Delaware; in-state cars $2.50, out-of-state cars $5; ☺ park dawn-dusk, visitors center 8am-5pm)

Chincoteague National Wildlife Refuge (☎ 757-336-6122; http://chinco.fws.gov; Chincoteague, Virginia; 1-week car pass $10, walker & cyclist free; ☺ 5am-10pm May-Oct, 6am-6pm Dec-Mar, 6am-8pm Apr & Nov)

Delaware Seashore State Park Office (☎ 302-227-2800; www.destateparks.com; Rte 1, south of Dewey, Delaware; car Jun-Oct & weekends $5; ☺ 8am-4:30pm)

Indian River Inlet Marina (☎ 302-227-3071; www.irimarina.com; Rte 1, north of Indian River Inlet Bridge, Delaware)

Lewes Chamber of Commerce & Visitors Bureau (☎ 302-645-8074; www.leweschamber.com; 120 Kings Hwy, Lewes, Delaware; ☺ 10am-4pm Mon-Fri, 10am-2pm Sat Jun-Aug)

Lewes Historical Complex (☎ 302-645-7670; www.historiclewes.org; Shipcarpenter Sq & 3rd St, Lewes, Delaware; admission $6; ☺ 10am-4pm Tue-Fri, 10am-1pm Sat May-Oct)

Ocean City Convention & Visitors Bureau (☎ 410-289-8181, 800-626-2326; www.ococean.com; 40th St & Coastal Hwy, Convention Center, Ocean City, Maryland; ☺ 9am-5pm Mon-Fri)

Oyster & Maritime Museum (☎ 757-336-6117; www.chincoteague.com/omm; 7125 Maddox Blvd, Chincoteague; adult $4, senior & child $2; ☺ 10am-5pm Jun-Aug, 10am-5pm Sat & Sun April, May, Sep-Oct, closed Nov-March)

Piney Island Country Store (☎ 757-336-5511; 785 Maddox Blvd, Chincoteague, Virginia)

Rehoboth Chamber of Commerce & Visitors Center (☎ 302-227-2233, 800-441-1329; www.beach-fun.com; 501 Rehoboth Ave, Rehoboth, Delaware; ☺ 9am-5pm Mon-Fri year-round; 9am-2pm Sat, 9am-1pm Sun summer)

Tidewater Expeditions (☎ 757-336-3159; 7729 East Side Dr, Chincoteague, Virginia)

Zwaanendael Museum (☎ 302-645-1148; www.destatemuseums.org/zwa; Kings Hwy & Savannah Rd, Lewes, Delaware; admission free; ☺ 10am-4:30pm Tue-Sat, 1:30-4:30pm Sun)

Eating

Dogfish Head Brewing & Eats (☎ 302-226-2739; 320 Rehoboth Ave, Rehoboth, Delaware; pizzas $12, mains $16-20; 4-11pm Mon-Thu, 4pm-1am Fri, noon-1am Sat, noon-11pm Sun) A popular, family-friendly microbrewery and restaurant with a great menu of pizza and main meals.

La Rosa Negra (☎ 302-645-1980; 128 2nd St, Lewes, Delaware; meals $30; ☺ noon-9pm Mon-Fri, 6-9pm Sat & Sun) A romantic Italian bistro that gets rave reviews from locals.

Seacrets (☎ 410-524-4900; 49th St, Ocean City, Maryland; meals about $20; ☺ 11am-10pm, light fare until 1am) Friendly people, kitschy pirate decor and good Jamaican food.

Steamers (☎ 757-336-6236; 6251 Maddox Blvd, Chincoteague, Virginia; ☺ noon-10pm Apr-Oct, 5-10pm Thu-Sat Nov-Mar) A fun family place – get messy with all-you-can-eat crabs.

Sleeping

Assateague Inn (☎ 757-336-3738; www.assateague-inn.com; Maddox Blvd & Chicken City Rd, Chincoteague, Virginia; r from $85) Reasonable rooms with balconies overlooking the saltwater marsh.

Dunes Manor Hotel (☎ 410-289-1100; www.dunesmanor.com; 28th St & Baltimore Ave, Ocean City, Maryland; r from $145) A huge high-rise with a touch of class and nice ocean views.

Inn at Canal Square (☎ 302-644-3377; www.theinnatcanalsquare.com; 122 Market St, Lewes, Delaware; r from $150) A new inn with a traditional country feel.

Rehoboth Guest House (☎ 302-227-4117; www.guesthse.com/reho; 40 Maryland Ave, Rehoboth, Delaware; r $80-150) Gay-owned beach house with a friendly clientele and a beachy feel.

GREAT FALLS

Fourteen miles upriver from DC's George-town, where the central Piedmont meets the coastal plain, the normally placid Potomac cascades 77ft down a series of beautiful, treacherous rapids known as Great Falls. The Chesapeake & Ohio (C&O) Canal was constructed to allow barges to bypass the falls. Today, there are parks on both sides of the river providing glorious views of the falls, as well as hiking, cycling and picnicking spots. (The entry fee is good for three days at both parks.) The Maryland side hooks up to Georgetown via the C&O Canal Towpath (p74), which is an excellent route for a cyc-ling trip (it's not paved).

On the Virginia side, the falls lie in the

Transportation

Distance from Washington DC 14 miles.

Direction North.

Travel time 20 minutes.

Car To reach the C&O National Historic Park on the Maryland side, take Canal Rd out of Georgetown, then MacArthur Blvd to its end. For Great Falls National Park in Virginia, from I-495 take exit 13 to Georgetown Pike. Drive 4 miles to Old Dominion Dr and turn right to enter the park.

Bike Pick up the C&O canal path anywhere in Georgetown and head north.

800-acre **Great Falls National Park**, in the northern part of the George Washington Memorial Park-way in McLean. Several miles of trails wind through the woods and along the falls. In 1785, George Washington's Patowmack Company built a canal here to circumvent the falls – a 0.75-mile stretch of it remains, and you can explore what's left on foot. You can also hike among the ruins of Matildaville, a trading town that died in the 1820s as canal business declined.

On the Maryland side, the falls are part of **C&O Canal National Historical Park**, the entrance of which is in the sprawling, wealthy suburb of Potomac. **Great Falls Tavern**, built in 1828, holds the park visitors center, which features exhibits on how the canal locks work. The Clipper, a mule-drawn barge, cruises the canal, departing from here several times a day.

From the tavern, a half-mile walk down the towpath and across a series of bridges to **Olmstead Island** leads to the falls overlook, which offers a beautiful view of rugged rock and roaring rapids. (The whitewater is dangerous, so keep kids close.) For serious scramblers, the 2-mile **Billy Goat Trail** traverses mountainous rock crags, and the towpath provides an easy loop back. Other easy loop trails lead through the woods past the remains of gold-mine diggings, prospector's trenches and overgrown Civil War earthworks.

Three miles further up the river, **Swains Lock** was operated by the Swain family for generations. Jesse Swain was lock-tender from 1907 until the lock closed in 1924. Today, his grandson Fred runs Swains Boathouse, which rents bicycles, canoes, kayaks and boats. He also sells fishing tackle and bait, and oversees a hiker/cyclist campground for towpath through-travelers.

Sights & Information

Great Falls National Park (Virginia) (☎ 703-285-2966; www.nps.gov/gwmp/grfa; car/walker $5/3; ☺ park 7am-dusk, visitors center 10am-5pm Jun-Aug, 10am-4pm Sep-May)

Great Falls Tavern (C&O Canal National Park Great Falls Visitor Center) (☎ 301-767-3714; www.nps.gov/choh; 11710 MacArthur Blvd, Potomac, Maryland; car $5, walker & cyclist $3, barge ride adult/senior/child $8/6/5; ☺ 9am-5pm)

Swains Boathouse (☎ 301-299-9006; canoes & kayaks per hr/day $8.50/20; bike rental per hr/day $5.50/12.75; ☺ 10am-6pm May-Sep, 10am-4pm Fri-Sun Oct-Nov & Apr)

Eating

L'Auberge Chez Francois (☎ 703-759-3800; 332 Springvale Rd, Great Falls, Virginia; dinner $50 ☺ 5:30-9:30pm Tue-Sat,

5:30-8pm Sun, reservations required) One of the Washington area's best restaurants. French-Alsation cuisine is served.

Old Angler's Inn (☎ 301-365-2425; 10801 MacArthur Blvd, Maryland; dinner $40-50; ☺ noon-2:30pm & 6-9:30pm, reservations recommended) This hidden gem in the southern tip of the park has been feeding hungry hikers since 1860.

Detour

Twenty miles upriver from Great Falls, **White's Ferry** (☎ 301-349-5200; 24801 Whites Ferry Rd, Dickerson, Maryland; cars one way/round-trip $3/5, bikes 50c; ☺ 5am-11pm) is the last of the many ferries that once plied the Potomac. It's a nice way to hop from the Maryland to the Virginia shore, particularly if you're headed for historic Leesburg, which is just 4 miles west of here.

Excursions – Great Falls

MANASSAS

A visit to the **Manassas National Battlefield Park** is required for enthusiastic historians and Civil War buffs. The battles that took place at Manassas (known as Bull Run in the north) were not the most significant, but the grassy hills tell a dramatic tale of two unexpected Confederate victories. Manassas I, the first major battle of the war, shocked soldiers and spectators alike by its bloody outcome. See the boxed text 'The Battles of Manassas (1861 & 1862)' (opposite). Start at the visitors center, which has a small exhibit and an excellent film about the battles. You can also pick up a pamphlet, which outlines several walking and driving tours around the points of interest in the battlefields. In August, reenactments of the two Civil War battles are staged.

Transportation

Distance from Washington DC 26 miles.

Direction West.

Travel Time 40 minutes.

Car Take Rte 66 to Rte 234 exit 47: the battlefield is half a mile north; the town of Manassas is 5 miles south.

Train A commuter service runs between Washington DC's Union Station and downtown Manassas on weekdays. Unfortunately, once in Manassas there is no way to reach the battlefield without a car.

The town of Manassas lies 5 miles south of the battlefield along Rte 234. Don't be fooled by the heavily trafficked, strip-mall lined highway: the old center of town is a quaint area with antique shops and galleries, and a keen sense of history. The **Manassas Railroad Depot**, built in 1914, also houses the visitors center. Across the tracks, the **Manassas Museum** emphasizes Civil War history, but also displays photographs, artifacts and videos about the community. The **Center for the Arts of Greater Manassas** is a spacious, light-filled gallery housed in a reconverted candy factory.

Other Civil War sights are in the area. The **Ben Lomond Manor House** is famous for its use as a hospital for Union and Confederate soldiers during the war. **Signal Hill** was an integral Confederate observation post during the Civil War (and you'll understand why when you see the view it provides). Signal Hill directly contributed to the Confederate victory at the first Battle of Bull Run.

Manassas National Battlefield Park (right)

Sights & Information

Ben Lomond Manor House (☎ 703-367-7872; www
.benlomondmanorhouse.org; 10311 Sudley Manor Dr;
☯ 10am-5pm Sat)

Center for the Arts of Greater Manassas
(☎ 703-330-ARTS; www.center-for-the-arts.com;
9419 Battle St; admission by donation;
☯ 10am-4pm)

Manassas Museum (☎ 703-368-1873; www
.manassasmuseum.org; 9101 Prince William St; adult/child
$3/2; ☯ 10am-5pm Tue-Sun)

Manassas National Battlefield Park (☎ 703-361-1339;
www.nps.gov/mana; 12521 Lee Hwy; adult/child $2/free,
film $3; ☯ 8:30am-5pm, tours 11:15am, 12:15pm,
2:15pm Jun-Aug)

Manassas Railroad Depot (Visitor Center ☎ 703-361-
6599; 9431 West Street; ☯ 9am-5pm)

Eating

City Square Cafe (☎ 703-369-6022; 9428 Battle St; lunch
$10, dinner $20; ☯ lunch & dinner) A casual European
café with a patio overlooking the train depot.

Philadelphia Tavern (☎ 703-393-1776; 9413 Main St;
dishes around $8; ☯ 11:30am-10pm, to midnight Fri &
Sat) Cheesesteaks and other Phillie specialties.

Victorian Tea Room (☎ 703-393-8327; 9413 Battle St;
sandwiches from $6; ☯ 6am-5pm Mon-Fri, 10am-5pm
Sat) Fancy teas, coffees and sandwiches.

Sleeping

Bennett House (☎ 703-368-6121; www.virginia
-bennetthouse.com; 9252 Bennett Dr; r $85-125) A genteel
Victorian inn with full Virginia-style country breakfast.

Old Towne Inn (☎ 703-368-9191; 9403 Main St; r from
$60) A motel in the center of town, rumored to be haunted.

The Battles of Manassas (1861 & 1862)

Not long after the first shots were fired at Fort Sumter, South Carolina, on April 12, 1861, sizable armies of both Union
and Confederate troops began to gather around the capitals of Richmond and Washington, DC.

The first significant battle of the Civil War occurred after Confederate soldiers, commanded by PGT Beauregard,
camped near the rail junction of Manassas, perilously close to the national capital. The battle that Northerners hoped
would end the war, Manassas I (Bull Run), started with an air of ebullience. Under orders from Abraham Lincoln,
Brigadier General Irvin McDowell roused his 32,000 poorly trained troops on the afternoon of July 16 and marched to
Centreville, 20 miles west of DC. McDowell's men skirmished and scouted near Bull Run, gathering scanty intelligence,
and on July 21, the general committed two divisions, including cavalry and artillery, against the Confederate lines.

McDowell's first assault on the right flank was checked by Stonewall Jackson's soldiers and driven back. Then, what
was meant to be an organized retreat turned into a rout. The Union troops knew tactical drilling techniques well enough,
but they had not been taught the essentials of withdrawal under fire.

On the supposedly 'safe' side of Bull Run, there had been a macabre picnic in progress, with civilians from Washington DC, coming down to witness the fray. As the soldiers fled in panic, they intermingled with this now-befuddled
crowd of onlookers, and there was a melee, especially when a strategic bridge across Cub Run collapsed. When the
counting ended, the Confederates, who incurred about 2000 casualties as opposed to McDowell's 3000, could claim
victory. Both groups were so ill trained at this early stage of the war, however, that any advantage could not be
followed up.

More than a year later, the war returned to Manassas. Following McClellan's Peninsula Campaign and the Seven
Days Battles, Union troops had withdrawn to the safety of DC, and many of McClellan's soldiers were handed over to a
new commander John Pope. By the time Pope was ordered to move against Richmond, Robert E Lee was in command
of the Confederates.

Pope advanced south toward the Rappahannock River, and Lee advanced north to confront Pope's troops before they
could be reinforced by McClellan. Lee brilliantly split his force and consigned an attack on Pope's supply base at Manassas
to Stonewall Jackson's men. Jackson's force came up against a numerically inferior force commanded by Nathaniel Banks
at Cedar Mountain, and, after a seesawing battle, the Union troops were forced back with heavy losses.

Pope's main body came up the next day, and Manassas II (Bull Run) commenced on August 29, with Pope making
heavy but futile attacks on Jackson's troops, who were in defense behind the bed of an unfinished railroad.

The following day, Lee unexpectedly arrived in force with the 30,000-strong force of James Longstreet, which in a
devastating flank assault on the Union's left (combined with Jackson's attacks on the other flank) caused a repeat of
Manassas I, with the Northerners fleeing back across Bull Run to the security of Washington DC. At this stage, almost
all of Virginia had been returned to the hands of the Confederates.

Pope lost his job when it was revealed that he had lost about a quarter of his force of 70,000 (the remainder of which
were then incorporated into the Army of tne Potomac), while Lee had lost only 10,000 of his 60,000.

LEESBURG

One of Northern Virginia's oldest towns, Leesburg has colonial-era buildings, antique shops and nearby plantations. The town has a rich military and political history, which is palpable on its quaint streets. Leesburg sits along the **Washington & Old Dominion Trail** (p98), and makes an excellent cycling destination.

The pleasure of Leesburg is wandering its streets, poking into antique shops and galleries, and soaking up the small-town atmosphere. For historical sights, start at the **Loudoun Museum**, which narrates the history of northern Virginia from Native American times to present. It's of interest to non-Virginian visitors because of its attention to the Civil War and slavery. This is also the starting place for **First Friday Gallery Walks**, which occur every month from 6pm to 9pm, and other walking tours.

Transportation

Distance from Washington DC 35 miles.

Direction Northwest.

Travel Time 40 minutes.

Car Take I-495 or Rte 66 to the Dulles Toll Rd exit (Rte 267). When it turns into the Dulles Greenway, continue 13 miles to the end. Exit left and take the first right exit to Leesburg Business. Follow King St to Loudon St, the center of historic Leesburg. Morven Park is west of Leesburg off Rte 7 (Market St). Turn north onto Fairview St, go 1 mile to the dead end and turn left on Old Waterford Rd. Oatlands is located off Rte 267 at exit 1A, then take the second right on South Warrenton.

Bike Pick up the Washington & Old Dominion Trail just outside the East Falls Church Metro in Arlington and head west.

Located 1 mile outside Leesburg, **Morven Park** is a 1500-acre historic property that was once the home of Virginia Governor Westmoreland Davis. The Greek Revival mansion, with its manicured boxwood gardens, resembles a transplanted White House, and its antique carriage museum includes more than 100 horse-drawn vehicles.

Six miles south of Leesburg, **Oatlands Plantation** was established in 1803 by a great-grandson of Robert 'King' Carter, a wealthy pre-Revolutionary planter. The carefully restored Greek Revival mansion is surrounded by four acres of formal gardens and connecting terraces.

Detour: Tarara Vineyard

Virginia vineyards have gained some degree of attention in recent years, and Leesburg is one place to check them out. Ten miles north of the historic center, nestled in alongside the Potomac, is the **Tarara Vineyard** (☎ 703-771-7100; www.tarara.com; 13648 Tarara Lane, Leesburg; 🕙 11am-5pm). The 475-acre farm produces a wide variety of delicious reds, whites and blushes. The winery, located in a 6000 sq ft cave, is open year-round for tastings; there is also a romantic B&B here. Head north from Leesburg on Rte 15 to Lucketts and turn right on Rte 662.

Sights & Information

Leesburg Tourist Office (☎ 703-777-2420; www.leesburgva.org; 108-D South St, Market Station; 🕙 9am-5pm)

Loudoun Museum (☎ 703-777-7427; www.loudoun museum.org; 16 Loudoun St; admission free, guided city tours adult $4, senior & student $2; 🕙 10am-5pm Mon-Sat, 1-5pm Sun)

Morven Park (☎ 703-777-2414; www.morven park.org; 17263 Southern Planter Lane; adult $7, senior & student $6, child $1; 🕙 11am-4pm Fri-Mon)

Oatlands Plantation (☎ 703-777-3174; 20850 Oatlands Plantation Lane; adult $10, senior & student $9, child $7; 🕙 10am-5pm Mon-Sat, 1-5pm Sun Apr-Dec)

Eating

Lightfoot (☎ 703-771-2233; 11 N King St; lunch from $20, dinner from $30; 🕙 11:30-9pm, to 10pm Fri & Sat) A progressive American bistro with an à la carte seasonal menu.

Tuscarora Mill (☎ 703-771-9300; 203 Harrison St; lunch $15; 🕙 lunch) Hunker down for a hearty lunch in a restored 19th-century mill.

Sleeping

Laurel Brigade Inn (☎ 703-777-1010; 20 W Market St; d $75-100) Founded in 1766, this bargain features lovely gardens and a pleasant restaurant.

Norris House Inn (☎ 703-777-1806; www.norrishouse.com; 108 Loudoun St SW; d $115-150) A renovated 1760 red brick colonial; tea is served in the lovely Stone House Tearoom. The rate is for weekends; week rates are cheaper.

Directory

Directory

TRANSPORTATION
AIR
Airlines
Most major airlines offer service to DC. Here's a nonexhaustive list of those with toll-free telephone numbers (free within the US).

Air Canada	☎ 888-247-2262
Air France	☎ 800-237-2747
Air New Zealand	☎ 800-262-1234
All Nippon Airways	☎ 800-235-9262
American Airlines	☎ 800-433-7300
British Airways	☎ 800-247-9297
Canadian Airlines	☎ 800-426-7000
Continental Airlines	☎ 800-525-0280
Delta Air Lines (& shuttle)	☎ 800-221-1212
Ethiopian Airlines	☎ 877-389-6753
KLM Royal Dutch Airlines	☎ 800-374-7747
Korean Air	☎ 800-438-5000
Lufthansa	☎ 800-645-3880
Mexicana	☎ 800-531-7921
Northwest Airlines	☎ 800-225-2525
Qantas Airways	☎ 800-227-4500
Sabena	☎ 800-955-2000
Southwest Airlines	☎ 800-435-9792
Spanair	☎ 888-545-5757
TACA	☎ 800-535-8780
TWA	☎ 800-221-2000
United Airlines	☎ 800-241-6522
US Airways (& shuttle)	☎ 800-428-4322
Virgin Atlantic	☎ 800-862-8621

Airports
Three major airports serve DC.

Ronald Reagan Washington National Airport (Map pp244-5; ☎ 703-417-8000; www.metwashairports.com), across the river in Arlington, Virginia, handles domestic service only, plus some flights to Canada. After a huge renovation a few years back, National was renamed for the former chief executive, and now contains two fancy terminals (B and C) of shops and restaurants, in addition to the original Terminal A. It is easily accessible by Metro (Yellow or Blue Line).

Washington Dulles International Airport (Map p206; ☎ 703-572-2700; www.metwashairpor

ts.com), designed by Eero Saarinen, looms like a space-age castle in the Virginia suburbs 26 miles west of DC. Take I-66 west to the Dulles Toll Rd. Both domestic and international flights (to Asia, Europe, South America, the Middle East and Africa) depart from here. Dulles is not on a Metro line, although **Washington Flyer** (☎ 888-927-4359; www.washfly.com; 6am-11pm Mon-Fri, 8am-11pm Sat & Sun; round-trip/one way $14/8) operates a shuttle from West Falls Church Metro station.

Baltimore-Washington International Airport (Map p206; BWI; ☎ 800-435-9294; www.bwiairport.com) is 30 miles, or about 45 minutes' drive, northeast of DC in Maryland. Get onto the Baltimore-Washington Parkway via New York Ave NE, follow the parkway until you see the I-195/BWI exit. Often you will find that cheaper fares are available to/from BWI than to either National or Dulles; so despite its geographic inconvenience, this is a handy airport for those on a budget. Both Maryland Rail Commuter (MARC; weekends only) and Amtrak trains travel between DC's Union Station and a terminal near BWI.

If you don't feel like schlepping your bags yourself, **SuperShuttle** (☎ 800-258-3826; www.supershuttle.com; 5:30am-12:30am; National/Dulles $12/22) provides door-to-door service to/from the airports in a shared van.

BICYCLE
Cycling is one of the best ways to get around DC (see Sports, Health & Fitness, p168). Here are some options for rental:

Better Bikes Inc (☎ 202-293-2080; per hr $25) Delivers and picks up bikes anywhere in the DC area.

Big Wheel Bikes (Map pp256-7; ☎ 202-337-0254; 1034 33rd St NW; per hr/day $10/25; Metro: Rosslyn) In Georgetown, just up the hill from the end of the Capital Crescent Trail.

Bike the Sites (Map pp246-8; ☎ 202-842-BIKE; 1100 Pennsylvania Ave, Old Post Office Pavilion; per 3hr/day $21/45; Metro: Federal Triangle) Weekly rentals also available.

Blazing Saddles (Map pp246-8; ☎ 202-544-0055; 445 11th St NW; Metro: Metro Center) Provides maps of favorite biking routes.

City Bikes (Map pp261; ☎ 202-265-1564; 2501 Champlain St; per hr/day $10/25; Metro: Columbia Heights) In Adams Morgan, look for the mural of cycling cows above the shop.

Thompson Boat Center (Map pp256-7; ☎ 202-333-9543; 2900 Virginia Ave; bikes per hr $4, per day $8-25; Metro: Foggy Bottom-GWU) Easy access to Rock Creek Park and the Capital Crescent Trail. As well as hiring out all types of watercraft and offering rowing classes (p170), Thompson Boat Center rents bikes.

In recent years, Metro has taken new measures to encourage bicycle commuting. Riders can take their bikes free of charge on trains, except during rush hour (7am to 10am and 4pm to 7pm Monday to Friday) and on busy holidays, like July 4. Bikes are not permitted to use the center door of trains or the escalator. All buses are now equipped with bike racks so riders can transport their bikes by bus, too.

BUS

DC's bus system (technically called 'Metrobus') is operated by the Washington Metropolitan Transit Authority, or Metro. It provides a clean and efficient bus service throughout the city and to outlying suburbs. Stops are marked by red, white and blue signposts. The fare is $1.10 ($2 on express routes), or 25¢ with a Metrorail transfer. Kids under five ride free. Automatic fare machines accept paper dollars, but you must have exact change. Useful bus routes include:

30, 32, 34, 36, Wisconsin Ave Runs from Friendship Heights down Wisconsin Ave (through Georgetown) to Foggy Bottom-GWU.

98 (The Link) Traverses Adams Morgan from Woodley Park-Zoo to U Street-Cardozo Metro stations.

L2, 18th St NW Connects Woodley Park-Zoo to Foggy Bottom-GWU via Adams Morgan.

D2, P St NW Connects Georgetown to Dupont Circle.

Intercity bus service in the US is cheap, but it sure isn't pleasant – although it's useful if you're on a tight budget.

The main bus company is **Greyhound** (Map pp252-3; fares & schedules ☎ 800-229-9424; customer service ☎ 402-330-8552; www.greyhound.com; 1005 1st St NE), which provides nationwide service.

Peter Pan Trailways (☎ 800-343-9999), which travels to northeastern US, uses a terminal just opposite Greyhound's. This run-down

neighborhood is deserted after dark, and the nearest Metro station is several blocks south (via 1st St NE) at Union Station. Cabs are usually available at the bus station, and you should use one; don't walk across town from the bus station at night.

CAR & MOTORCYCLE
Driving

Many visitors are surprised to learn that DC has some of the nation's worst traffic congestion. As of 2000, it was second only to Los Angeles. The worst bottlenecks are in the suburbs, where the Capital Beltway (I-495) meets interstates: Maryland's I-270 and I-95, and Virginia's I-66 and I-95. Avoid the Beltway in early-morning and late-afternoon rush hours (about 6am to 9am and 3pm to 6pm). Clogged rush-hour streets in DC include the main access arteries from the suburbs: Massachusetts, Wisconsin, Connecticut and Georgia Aves NW, among others.

Certain lanes of some major traffic arteries (such as Connecticut Ave NW) change direction during rush hour, and some two-way streets become one way. Signs indicate hours of these changes, so keep your eyes peeled. Except where otherwise posted, the speed limit on DC surface streets is 25mph (15mph in alleys and school zones). You must wear your seat belt and restrain kids under three years in child-safety seats.

For emergency road service and towing, members can call the **American Automobile Association** (☎ 800-222-4357). It has a branch, **AAA travel agency** (Map pp246-8; ☎ 202-942-2050; 1440 New York Ave NW, Suite No 200; ☯ 9am-4.30pm Mon-Fri), near the White House.

Parking

Finding street parking is difficult in popular neighborhoods (Georgetown and Adams-Morgan are particularly heinous), but it's reasonably easy in less-congested districts. Note that residential areas often have a two-hour limit on street parking. This limit is enforced, even if it is not metered (parking police monitor the comings and goings of cars by chalking their tires). You must park at least 3ft from other cars, 5ft from private driveways and alleys, 10ft from fire hydrants, and 25ft from the corner of one-way streets. You can leave a car on the street for only 72 hours before moving it. Parking garages in the city normally cost about $6 an hour or $25 a day.

Rental

All the major car-rental agencies and many small local ones are represented, especially at the airports. Many big agencies maintain offices downtown and at Union Station. Airport rates are often better than those at downtown offices. Car-rental rates do fluctuate radically, but weekly rates are often the best deal. An economy-sized car typically costs $120 to $150 per week. Expect to pay more during peak visitor times, such as the Cherry Blossom Festival, and when big conventions and political demonstrations are in town. Add 5.75% sales tax in DC (up to 8% at the airports).

Basic liability insurance, required by US law, is generally included in the rental price, but check the contract carefully. You can also purchase Loss/Damage Waiver (LDW) insurance, usually about $8 to $12 per day. Your personal auto-insurance policy may also cover car-rental insurance (if so, bring along a photocopy of your policy). Most rates include unlimited mileage: if a rate seems cheap, it may be because you'll get a mileage charge. Return the car with a full tank of gas. Booking well in advance of your visit usually yields the best rate.

Unfortunately for young drivers, most major agencies in DC won't rent to anyone under 25. Some local companies rent to drivers over 21 who have a major credit card, but their rates generally aren't competitive. Agencies in DC include the following:

Alamo (☎ 800-327-9633, 703-260-0182; Dulles airport)

Avis (Map pp258-60; ☎ 800-331-1212, 202-467-6585; 1722 M St NW); **National airport** (☎ 703-419-5815); **Dulles airport** (☎ 703-661-3505)

Budget (Map pp250-1; ☎ 800-527-0700, 202-289-5373; Union Station); **National airport** (☎ 703-920-3360)

Dollar National airport (☎ 800-800-4000, 703-519-8700); **Dulles airport** (☎ 703-661-6630)

Enterprise (Map pp246-8; ☎ 800-325-8007, 202-393-0900; 1029 Vermont Ave NW); **National airport** (☎ 703-553-7744); **Dulles airport** (☎ 703-661-8800)

Hertz (Map pp246-8; ☎ 800-654-3131, 202-628-6174; 901 11th St NW); **National airport** (☎ 703-979-6300); **Dulles airport** (☎ 703-471-6020)

National (Map pp250-1; ☎ 800-328-4567, 202-842-7454; Union Station); **National airport** (☎ 202-783-1590); **Dulles airport** (☎ 703-471-5278)

Thrifty (Map pp246-8; ☎ 800-367-2277, 202-783-0400; 1001 12th St NW); **National airport** (☎ 703-658-2200); **Dulles airport** (☎ 703-481-3599)

METRO

DC's sleek modern subway network is the Metrorail, commonly called **Metro** (☎ 202-637-7000; www.wmata.com;   ⏰5:30am-midnight Mon-Thu, 5:30am-3am Fri, 7am-3am Sat, 7am-midnight Sun; fares from $1.20). It is managed by DC, Maryland, Virginia and the federal government. Thanks to ample federal funding, its trains and stations are well marked, well maintained, well lit, climate controlled, reasonably priced, decently staffed, reliable and safe. Parking is available at certain outlying stations.

To ride Metro, buy a computerized farecard from the self-service machines inside the station entrance. The minimum fare is $1.20, although it increases for longer distances and during rush hour. The posted station-to-station chart provides exact fares for each route. You must use the farecard to enter *and* exit station turnstiles. Upon exit, the turnstile deducts the fare and returns the card. If the value of the card is insufficient, you need to use an 'Add-fare' machine to add money. Other machines inside the gates dispense free bus transfers that enable you to pay just 25¢ on connecting bus routes.

A variety of passes are available, including a one-day pass ($6) or a weekly pass ($30). Special passes are available from the **Sales & Information office** (Metro Center station, 12th & F Sts NW), from the website (www.wmata.com), and from Safeway and Giant grocery stores.

The Metro is still growing and changing; new stations are under construction and station names are changing. At the time of research the new New York Ave station was under construction on the Red Line, and the U Street-Cardozo station on the Green Line had changed its name to U St/African-American Civil War Memorial/Cardozo. In this book, and because not many locals will actually be using such a cumbersome name, we'll stick with the old appellation of U Street-Cardozo.

TAXI

Taxicabs are plentiful in central DC; hail them with a wave of the hand. **Diamond** (☎ 202-387-6200), **Yellow** (☎ 202-544-1212) and **Capitol** (☎ 202-546-2400) are three major companies. The fare structure works on a complicated zone system rather than by the traditional metered system. DC consists of eight concentric zones (zone maps are posted in cabs), and rates are determined by how many zones you cross, the number of passengers and time of day (there's a $1 rush-hour surcharge). You pay a base fare of $5 to travel within one zone. Each additional zone costs $1.50. Each additional passenger costs $1.50. More fees are added for extra services (large bags, ordering a cab by phone, traveling during snow emergencies). Taxis in the Virginia and Maryland suburbs use the usual metering method. Taxi drivers are usually tipped about 10%.

TRAIN

In addition to Metro, two commuter train systems serve downtown DC from the Maryland and Virginia suburbs. Remember they're *commuter* lines: most trains run weekdays only, with the most regular service during rush hour.

Maryland Rail Commuter (MARC; ☎ 800-325-7245; www.mtamaryland.com; ☺ 5am-minight Mon-Fri) is a 40-station, 187-mile system connecting DC, the northern Maryland suburbs, Baltimore and eastern West Virginia. It has three lines, one of which stops at BWI airport. A fare from Baltimore to DC would cost about $6.50. The MARC train's only DC stop is Union Station.

From downtown DC, **Virginia Railway Express** (VRE; ☎ 703-684-1001, 800-RIDE-VRE; www.vre.org) serves northern Virginia's suburbs with lines to Manassas (stops include Fairfax and Alexandria) and Fredericksburg (stops include Quantico, Franconia/Springfield and Crystal City). VRE has only two stops in DC itself: Union Station and L'Enfant Plaza.

The center of train travel to/from DC is the magnificent, beaux-arts **Union Station** (Map pp250-1; ☎ 202-371-9441; www.unionstation dc.com; 50 Massachusetts Ave NE; Metro: Union Station). It is the flagship terminal of the national train company, **Amtrak** (☎ 800-872-7245; www.amtrak.com), which is located on the ground floor.

Most trains departing Union Station are bound for other East Coast destinations. The station is the southern terminus of the northeast rail corridor, which stops at Baltimore, Philadelphia, New York, New Haven (Connecticut), Boston and intermediate points. There is usually at least one departure per hour throughout the day. Regular (unreserved) trains are cheapest, but pokey. Express Metroliners (reserved) to New York are faster; fastest of all are the new super-expensive Acela trains that zing to New York and on to Boston at speeds in excess of 150mph.

Trains also depart for Virginia destinations (Richmond, Williamsburg, Virginia Beach), and southern destinations, including Florida, New Orleans, Montréal and Amtrak's national hub, Chicago, where you can connect to Midwest- and West Coast-bound trains. MARC and VRE commuter trains connect Union Station to Virginia and Maryland.

Fares vary according to type of seating (coach seats or sleeping compartments) and season. Amtrak also offers a variety of all-inclusive holiday tour packages and rail passes, including a 30-day USA Rail Pass for unlimited coach-class East Coast travel for $240/225 in high/low season.

PRACTICALITIES

ACCOMMODATIONS

Accommodations options are listed in the Sleeping chapter according to neighborhood. They are in alphabetical order, with 'Cheap Sleeps' (rooms under $85 a night) listed at the end. Accommodations prices fluctuate widely according to season and availability. Peak seasons are spring (April to June) and autumn (September to October). Hotels that cater mainly to business and government travelers drop their prices significantly – by as much as 25% – on weekends. The best rates are usually available by reserving on the Internet or through a booking agent. Many small Bed & Breakfast options do not advertise or book rooms *except* through a booking agent. See Sleeping (p191) for more information on web-based hotel deals. Check-in/check-out time is normally 2pm/11am. Many places will allow early check-in as long as the room is available, or will provide temporary luggage storage if it is not.

Booking Services

Bed & Breakfast Accommodations Ltd (☎ 413-582-9888, 877-893-3233; www.bnbaccom.com) Specializing in private-home B&Bs and long-term accommodations in the Washington DC area.

Capitol Reservations (☎ 800-847-4832; www.capitol reservations.com)

Washington DC Accommodations (☎ 703-875-8711; www.dchotels.com)

BUSINESS

Most offices and government agencies are open 9am to 5pm Monday to Friday. Most shops are open 10am to 7pm Monday to Saturday, noon to 5pm Sunday. Smaller shops may be closed

Sunday or Monday or both. Restaurants are usually open 11:30am to 2:30pm for lunch and 5:30pm to 10pm for dinner Monday to Friday. They tend to stay open later (until 11pm or midnight) on Friday and Saturday nights. Bars are open until 1am or 2am during the week and 3am on weekends. Banks, schools and offices are closed on all public holidays; most shops, museums and restaurants stay open on public holidays, except July 4, Thanksgiving, Christmas and New Year's Day.

CHILDREN

Washington may be the best big city in the US to travel with children: all the major museums are oriented (in part or in total) toward kids; the monuments and historical sites are child-friendly; and there's plenty of parkland and green space where kids can romp. Furthermore, a vacation to Washington is usually educational; best of all, most attractions here are absolutely free.

The *Washington Post* weekend section, published each Friday, features 'Saturday's Child,' which details upcoming family- and kid-oriented activities, exhibits and cultural events. See also the great 'Our Kids' website (www.our-kids.com) for event listings and local kid-related news. Helpful books include *Going Places with Children in Washington DC* by Pamela McDermott and *Travel with Children* published by Lonely Planet. See also the boxed text 'For Children' (p46).

Baby-sitting

Many hotels offer baby-sitting services on site. If your lodge does not have a relationship with a childcare provider, a reputable organization is **Mothers' Aides** (☎ 703-250-0700, 800-526-2669; www.mothersaides.com), which will send a caregiver to a hotel for a minimum of four hours. Rates generally run $14 per hour for one or two kids, $16 to $18 for more.

CLIMATE

The best time to visit DC is spring (April to May) or autumn (September to October). Summer is a busy tourist season, but weather can be extremely hot and humid, especially in July and August. Plan your travel for the cooler mornings and late afternoons (advance planning can also reduce your time in line); aim to be inside in air-conditioning during the midday heat; carry water; and wear hats, sunblock and loose, light clothing. Winters are generally mild, with tem-

peratures hovering around freezing. The city has been known to shut down due to snow storms, especially in January. For weather conditions and forecasts, go to www.washingtonpost.com and click on 'Weather.'

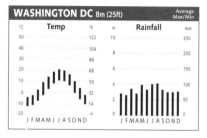

CUSTOMS

Everyone entering the US is required to fill out a customs declaration form. Visitors over 21 can bring in 200 cigarettes and 1L of alcohol. US citizens are allowed a $400 duty-free exemption; non-US citizens are allowed $100. Strict rules apply to fruit, flowers, meats and animals. There's no limit on the amount of cash, traveler's checks etc that you can bring in, but you must declare any amount over $10,000.

DISABLED TRAVELERS

DC is an excellent destination for disabled visitors. Most museums and major sights are wheelchair accessible, as are most large hotels and restaurants. The **Smithsonian** (☎ 202-357-2700, TTY ☎ 202-357-1729) and many other museums arrange special tours for people with visual, auditory or other impairments.

All Metro trains and most buses are wheelchair accessible. All Metro stations have elevators, and guide dogs are allowed on trains and buses. Disabled people who can't use public transit can use **MetroAccess** (☎ 301-562-5361), a door-to-door transport provider. Many large hotels have suites for disabled guests, but call the hotel itself – not the chain's 800 number – to check before you reserve. Larger car-rental agencies offer hand-controlled models at no extra charge. All major airlines, Greyhound buses and Amtrak trains allow service animals on board and frequently sell two-for-one packages if you need an attendant to accompany you.

Out of doors, hindrances to wheelchair users include buckled brick sidewalks in the historic blocks of Georgetown and Capitol Hill, but sidewalks in most other parts of DC are in good shape and have dropped curbs. Unfortunately, only a handful of crosswalks, mostly near the Mall, have audible crossing signals.

The **Washington DC Convention & Visitors Association** (Map pp246-8; ☎ 202-789-7000; www .washington.org; 901 7th St NW; Metro: Gallery Pl-Chinatown) provides a fact sheet with details regarding accessibility at local attractions, lodgings and restaurants.

Hearing-impaired visitors should check out **Gallaudet University** (p69) in northeast DC, which hosts lectures and cultural events especially for the deaf.

ELECTRICITY

Electric current in the USA is 110-115V, 60Hz AC. Outlets may accept flat two-prong or three-prong grounded plugs. Adapters are readily available at drugstores and anywhere that sells hardware.

EMBASSIES

Nearly every country in the world has an embassy in DC, making this one of the US's most vibrant multinational cities. The handy Electronic Embassy (www.embassy.org) offers links to all DC embassy homepages. The hours listed represent the visa office.

Australia (Map pp258-9; ☎ 202-797-3000; 1601 Massachusetts Ave NW; ☺ 8:30am-2:30pm; Metro: Dupont Circle)

Canada (Map pp246-8; ☎ 202-682-1740; 501 Pennsylvania Ave NW; ☺ 9am-12pm; Metro: Archives-Navy Memorial)

China (Map pp258-9; ☎ 202-328-2500; 2300 Connecticut Ave NW; Metro: Woodley Park-Zoo/Adams Morgan; **visa office** Map pp262-3; ☎ 202-338-6688; 2201 Wisconsin Ave NW, Suite 110; ☺ 10am-12:30pm & 1-3pm; Metrobus No 30, 32, 34 or 36 from Tenleytown station)

France (Map pp256-7; ☎ 202-944-6000; 4101 Reservoir Rd NW; ☺ 8:45am-12:45pm; Metrobus D6 from K St NW downtown)

Germany (Map pp256-7; ☎ 202-298-4000; 4645 Reservoir Rd NW; ☺ 8:30-11:30 am; Metrobus D6)

India (Map pp258-60; ☎ 202-939-7000; 2107 Massachusetts Ave NW; **visa office** 2536 Massachusetts Ave NW; ☺ 9:30am-12:30 pm; Metro: Dupont Circle)

Ireland (Map pp258-60; ☎ 202-462-3939; 2234 Massachusetts Ave NW; ☺ 9am-1pm & 2-4pm; Metro: Dupont Circle)

Israel (Map pp262-3; ☎ 202-364-5500; 3514 International Drive NW; ☺ 9:30am-1pm; Metro: Van Ness-UDC)

Japan (Map pp258-60; ☎ 202-238-6700; 2520 Massachusetts Ave NW; ☺ 10am-noon & 2-4pm; Metro: Dupont Circle)

Mexico (Map pp246-8; ☎ 202-728-1600; 1911 Pennsylvania Ave NW; ☺ 8am-1pm; Metro: Farragut West)

Netherlands (Map pp262-3; ☎ 202-244-5300; 4200 Linnean Ave NW; ☺ 10am-noon; Metro: Van Ness-UDC)

New Zealand (Map pp262-3; ☎ 202-328-4800; 37 Observatory Circle; ☺ 9am-5pm; Metrobus N6 from Farragut Square downtown)

Russia (Map pp262-3; ☎ 202-298-5700; 2650 Wisconsin Ave NW; **visa office** 2641 Tunlaw Rd NW, behind main office; ☺ 9am to 12:15pm; Metrobus No 30, 32, 34 or 36)

South Africa (Map pp262-3; ☎ 202-232-4400; 3051 Massachusetts Ave NW; ☺ 9am-12:30pm; Metrobus N6)

Spain (Map pp246-8; ☎ 202-452-0100; 2375 Pennsylvania Ave NW; ☺ 9am-12:30pm; Metro: Foggy Bottom-GWU)

UK (☎ 202-588-6500; 3100 Massachusetts Ave NW, around corner from visa office; **visa office** Map pp262-3; 19 Observatory Circle NW; ☺ 8-11:30am; Metrobus N6)

EMERGENCY

ambulance/police/fire	☎ 911
DC Rape Crisis Center	☎ 202-333-7273
Poison Control	☎ 202-362-3867
Travelers' Aid Society	☎ 202-546-3120

GAY & LESBIAN TRAVELERS

Home to more than 30 national gay and lesbian organizations and more than 300 social, athletic, religious and political support groups, DC is one of the most gay-friendly cities in the US. The community is most visible in the Dupont Circle and Capitol Hill neighborhoods, where there are many gay-friendly businesses, including the landmark bookstore **Lambda Rising** (p182). The *Washington Blade* (www.washingtonblade.com), the gay and lesbian weekly newspaper, offers coverage of politics, information about community resources, and lots and lots of nightlife and meeting-place listings. Other good sources include the *WOMO* (www.womo.com), a monthly publication with information about a slew of women's organizations in the Washington area, from the DC Lesbian Avengers to Older, Wiser Lesbians (OWLS). You can also check out the Washington DC Convention & Visitors Association's free *Gay &*

Lesbian Guide to Washington DC, available at the organization's website (www.washington.org).

AIDS Hotline (☎ 800-342-2437) 24-hour help line.

Bi Women's Cultural Alliance (☎ 202-828-3065) Organizes casual get-togethers for lesbians and bisexual women.

Gay and Lesbian Hotline (☎ 202-833-3234) Phone counseling; referrals.

Whitman-Walker Clinic (Map pp258-60; ☎ 202-797-3500; www.wwc.org; 1407 S St NW; Metro: U Street-Cardozo) General health care and HIV/AIDS care.

Women in the Life (Map pp258-60; ☎ 202-483-9818; www.womeninthelife.com; 1611 Connecticut Ave NW; Metro: Dupont Circle) An advocacy group for lesbians of color. Sponsors a variety of events during the summer.

HOLIDAYS

Much of Washington DC shuts down over Christmas and New Year, but other holidays are bustling. The busiest times are in the spring, especially during the **Cherry Blossom Festival** (p72) and Easter week; early summer and the week of Independence Day; and Thanksgiving weekend. At these times, expect museums to be packed and prices to be high. Alternatively, during the month of August, and from mid-December to mid-January when Congress is not in session, crowds disappear and bargains abound. For a listing of public holidays, see p9.

INTERNET ACCESS

For travelers without a computer, the cheapest place to access the Internet is at any branch of the DC public library. Fifteen-minute-limit terminals are available free to the public. If you wish to use the Internet for longer than 15 minutes, you must sign up for a user's card, which is also free and allows access to computers at any DC public library:

Cleveland Park Branch (Map pp262-3; ☎ 202-282-3080; 3310 Connecticut Ave at Macomb St NW; Metro: Cleveland Park)

Martin Luther King Jr Memorial Library (Map pp246-8; ☎ 202-727-1126; 901 G St NW; Metro: Metro Center)

Tenley-Friendship Branch (Map pp262-3; ☎ 202-282-3090; 4450 Wisconsin Ave at Albemarle St NW; Metro: Tenleytown)

West End Branch (Map pp258-60; ☎ 202-724-8707; 1101 24th St at L St NW; Metro: Foggy Bottom-GWU)

Other commercial ventures that offer Internet access include:

Atomic Grounds (Map p264; ☎ 703-524-2157; 1555 Wilson Blvd, Arlington; Metro: Rosslyn)

CyberStop Café (Map pp258-60; ☎ 202-234-2470; 1513 17th St NW; Metro: Dupont Circle)

Kinko's Georgetown (Map pp256-7; ☎ 202-965-1414; 3329 M St NW; Metro: Rosslyn)

Kinko's White House Area (Map pp246-8; ☎ 202-466-3777; 1612 K St NW; Metro: Farragut North)

Kramerbooks & Afterwords Café (Map pp258-60; ☎ 202-387-1400; 1517 Connecticut Ave NW; Metro: Dupont Circle)

LEGAL MATTERS

You must be 21 to buy or drink alcohol in DC. Club and bar bouncers are generally picky about seeing photo ID for proof of age, especially in university districts like Georgetown. Stiff fines, jail time and loss of your driver's license are the usual penalties for driving while intoxicated.

If you are arrested you have the right to remain silent and the right to a lawyer. There is no legal reason to speak to a police officer if you don't want to, but never walk away from an officer until given permission. If you're arrested, you are legally allowed one phone call. If you don't have a lawyer or a relative to help you, call your embassy. The police will give you the phone number upon request.

MAPS

Lonely Planet's *Washington DC* street map is a laminated pocket-size guide that shows all major DC attractions. ADC's *Washington DC* street atlas is a folio-size book that shows all city streets in detail. The best place to buy maps is the **ABC Map & Travel Center** (Map p246-8; ☎ 202-628-2608; 1636 I St NW; Metro: Farragut West), a wee downtown storefront packed with everything from DC activity guides to bus-route maps to huge foldout sheet maps of DC.

MEASUREMENTS

Like the rest of the country, DC is afraid of the metric system and uses the US measurement system instead. Distances are in feet, yards and miles; weights are in ounces and pounds. There's a conversion chart inside the front cover of this book.

MEDICAL SERVICES

Washington DC has no unexpected health dangers and excellent medical facilities; the only real concern is that a collision with the US medical system might injure your wallet.

Directory – Practicalities

Remember to buy health insurance before you travel. Recommended medical facilities include:

DC General Hospital (Map pp250-1; ☎ 202-675-5000; 199 Massachusetts Ave SE; Metro: Stadium-Armory) Most noninsured emergency patients are brought here.

George Washington University Hospital (Map pp246-8; ☎ 202-994-1000; 901 23rd St NW; Metro: Foggy Bottom-GWU) Serves many State Department types.

Institute of International Medicine (Map pp246-8; ☎ 202-715-5100; 2151 K St NW, Suite 600; Metro: Foggy Bottom-GWU) Offers immunizations and health advice for travelers going anywhere on the planet.

MONEY

Most DC businesses accept cash, credit and/or debit cards and traveler's checks; for security and convenience, it is useful to have all three. A credit card may be required for renting a car or making reservations at some hotels.

ATMs

Most banks have 24-hour ATMs affiliated with various networks, including Exchange, Accel, Plus and Cirrus. If you use a credit card, however, you probably will be charged a small fee and incur interest on the withdrawal until you pay it back. Furthermore, if you use an ATM that doesn't belong to your own bank, you'll be charged $1.50 per withdrawal.

Changing Money

Although the airports have exchange bureaus, better rates can usually be obtained at banks in the city.

American Express (Map p258-60; ☎ 202-457-1300; 1150 Connecticut Ave NW; Metro: Farragut North)

Thomas Cook (Map pp246-8; ☎ 800-287-7362; 1800 K St NW; Metro: Farragut West)

Credit Cards

Carry copies of your credit card numbers separately from the cards. If you lose a card or it's stolen, contact the company. Following are the main companies' toll-free numbers:

American Express	☎ 800-528-4800
Diners Club	☎ 800-234-6377
Discover	☎ 800-347-2683
MasterCard	☎ 800-826-2181
Visa	☎ 800-336-8472

Currency & Exchange Rates

The only currency accepted in DC is the US dollar ($), consisting of 100 cents (¢). Coins are the penny (1¢), nickel (5¢), dime (10¢), quarter (25¢), half-dollar and dollar (the new, gold-colored 'Sacajawea' coin). Keep a stash of quarters for use in vending machines, parking meters and laundromats. US bills can confuse the foreign visitor – they're all the same color and size – and exist in denominations of $1, $2 (rare), $5, $10, $20 (the only bills dispensed by ATMs), $50 and $100. There is a handy currency converter site at www.oanda.com.

Traveler's Checks

Traveler's checks are generally as good as cash in the US. Their major advantage is that they are replaceable if stolen. American Express and Thomas Cook (see office locations under Changing Money, left) have efficient replacement policies. A record of the check numbers is vital should you need to replace them – note them carefully and keep the record separate from the checks themselves. Buy checks in US dollars and in large denominations to avoid excessive service fees.

NEWSPAPERS & MAGAZINES

The *Washington Post* (www.washingtonpost.com) is among the nation's top newspapers. Its competitor is the conservative and less-respected *Washington Times*. The *Washington Afro-American* is the city's black newspaper. The *Washington City Paper* (www.washingtoncitypaper.com) is an alternative weekly, distributed free throughout the city. It scrutinizes DC politics and has great entertainment coverage. *On Tap* is another freebie, providing the scoop on local watering holes. Most DC neighborhoods have their own papers, such as the *Georgetown Independent* and the *Hill Rag*. *The Washingtonian* is a gossipy lifestyle magazine. The *Smithsonian* has articles about the institution – an enjoyable, less slick *National Geographic*.

PHARMACIES

The most prominent pharmacy chain is CVS, with locations all around the city. These convenient branches are open 24 hours:

CVS Dupont Circle (Map pp258-60; ☎ 202-833-5704; 6-7 Dupont Circle; Metro: Dupont Circle)

CVS Thomas Circle (Map pp258-60; ☎ 202-737-3962; 1199 Vermont Ave NW; Metro: McPherson Sq)

POST

The most convenient post offices are located in the **Old Post Office Pavilion** (Map pp246-8) and the **National Postal Museum** (Map pp250-1). Branch post offices (☎ 800-275-8777) are found throughout the city.

The **main post office** (Map pp252-3; ☎ 202-635-5300; 900 Brentwood Rd NE; ☹ 8am-6pm Mon-Fri, 7:30am-4pm Sat; Metro: Rhode Island Ave) is where you will receive poste restante. Items should be addressed to you c/o General Delivery, Main Post Office, 900 Brentwood Rd NE, Washington DC 20066, with 'Hold for Arrival' written on the exterior. Mail is usually held for 10 days; a picture ID is required for pick-up. **American Express** (p229), **Thomas Cook** (p229) and **Mailboxes, Etc** (Map pp258-60; ☎ 202-986-4900; 17th & M Sts NW; Metro: Farragut North) all provide mail services for their customers.

Priority & express mail service (www.usps.com) is available. You can buy stamps at post offices and ATMs around the city. If you have the correct postage, you can drop mail into any blue street mailbox. If your items require packaging, you might call on a local packaging service, such as Mailboxes, Etc, which provides shipping services and sells packaging materials.

Item	Postal Rates
1st-class mail within the USA	37¢ for letters up to 1oz, 22¢ each additional ounce
postcards within USA	20¢
letters to Canada and Mexico	60c per ½oz
international airmail rates	80¢ per ½oz letter, 70¢ per postcard

RADIO

National Public Radio programs and classical music are on WETA-FM 90.9; more NPR and talk shows are on WAMU-FM 88.5. Alternative plays on WHFS-FM 99.1, and album-oriented dinosaur rock is on the menu at WWDC-FM 101.1. News junkies like WTOP-FM 107.7 for round-the-clock local and national political coverage. Radioheads will enjoy tours of DC-based **National Public Radio** (p55).

SAFETY

Washington DC has a reputation for violent crimes: in 2002, 262 murders brought the rate to 46 in 100,000, the highest in the country for a city this size. (At the time of writing, the city was headed for a 23% increase.) For better or for worse, the violence is very localized, and visitors do not need to worry too much about being victims themselves. Dupont Circle, Adams-Morgan, Georgetown, Foggy Bottom and most of downtown are quite safe.

Visitors should be cautious in particularly poverty-stricken areas: all of Anacostia, southeast and northeast DC east of about 15th Sts SE and NE; and the southeastern waterfront near the Navy Yard. These areas have attractions of their own, but use extra caution when visiting them. You should take a cab if you visit at night. Other normally safe districts may have some dodgy areas on their fringes. If you visit at night, be very aware around Shaw, especially east of 13th St NW, and in Adams-Morgan east of Columbia Rd and 16th St.

TAXES

Some tax is charged on nearly everything you buy in the USA. It may be included in the price or added onto advertised prices. When inquiring about lodging rates, always ask whether taxes are included. Unless otherwise stated, prices given in this book don't include taxes. Airport departure taxes ($6 for foreign-bound passengers) are usually included in the price of tickets bought in the US, but they may not be included with tickets bought abroad. A US$6.50 North American Free Trade Agreement tax is charged to foreigners entering the US from abroad. Both fees are essentially 'hidden' taxes added to the purchase price of your ticket.

Tax	%
DC sales tax	5.75
DC restaurants, bars, rental cars, liquor tax	10
DC room tax	14.5 (plus an additional $1.50 per night surcharge)
Maryland sales tax	5
Maryland room tax	10
Virginia sales tax	4.5
Virginia restaurant/bar tax	8
Virginia room tax	10

TELEPHONE

Pay phones are generally coin-operated and cost 35¢ to make a local call. Prepaid phone cards are sold at newsstands and pharmacies around town. Fax services are available (but expensive) at **Kinko's** (p228), **Mailboxes, Etc** (above) and many upscale hotel business centers. When calling DC from abroad, first dial the

US country code (1). To place an international call from DC, dial ☎ 011 + country code + area code (dropping the leading 0) + number.

Useful Numbers

DC area code	☎ 202
Directory assistance for toll-free numbers	☎ 800-555-1212
Directory assistance outside DC	☎ 1 + area code + 555-1212
Directory assistance within DC	☎ 411
International operator	☎ 00
Maryland suburbs area code	☎ 301
Operator	☎ 0
Toll-free prefixes	☎ 800 or 888
US country code	☎ 1
Virginia suburbs area code	☎ 703 or ☎ 571

TELEVISION

All of the national networks are represented on the DC dial: NBC is on Channel 4, Fox on Channel 5, ABC on Channel 7 and CBS on Channel 9. Each of these channels has its own Sunday morning political talk show based in Washington and focusing on national events: *Meet the Press* on NBC; *Face the Nation* on CBS; *This Week* on ABC. The federally supported Public Broadcasting System, based in DC, is on WETA Channel 26. C-SPAN broadcasts live from the floor of Congress (aired in offices and bars across Capitol Hill).

TIME

DC is on Eastern Standard Time, five hours behind Greenwich Mean Time. Daylight Saving Time is observed between April and October. When it's noon in DC, it's 5pm in London, 6am the next day in Sydney and 8am the next day in Auckland.

TIPPING

Gratuities are not optional in the US. Waitstaff, hotel-room attendants, valet parkers and bellhops receive the minimum wage or less and depend on tips for their livelihoods. Service has to be pretty dreadful before you should consider *not* tipping. In restaurants tipping 15% of the total bill is the accepted minimum. If service is good, 20% is a decent average tip, while it is appropriate to tip more if service is exceptional. Hotel-room attendants should get $1 per guest per day, eg $10 for two people who have stayed five days. Tip taxi drivers about 10% of your fare.

Airport baggage handlers get about $1 per bag. Hairdressers usually get tips, too (20%), as do coat-check staff ($1).

TOURIST INFORMATION

Washington DC operates several information centers in the city to help travelers arrange accommodation and develop itineraries.

DC Chamber of Commerce Visitor Information Center (Map pp246-8; 202-328-4748; www.dcchamber.org; 1300 Pennsylvania Ave NW, Ronald Reagan Bldg; ☼ 8am-6pm Mon-Sat; Metro: Federal Triangle) Offers tours, maps, lodging brochures and events listings, and sells film, tickets and souvenirs.

International Visitors Information Service (☎ 703-572-2536; International Arrivals Bldg, Dulles airport; ☼ 6:30am-10:30pm) Free brochures, maps and information.

NPS Ellipse Visitor Pavilion (Map pp246-8) Situated at the northeast corner of the Ellipse, south of the White House.

NPS Information Office (Map pp246-8; ☎ 202-208-4747, Dial-a-Park vv ☎ 202-619-7275; Interior Department, C St NW; 9am-3pm Mon-Fri) Supplies pamphlets on most NPS-managed DC sites and US national parks.

Smithsonian Visitors Center (Map pp246-8; ☎ 202-357-2700, TTY 357-1729; www.smithsonian.org; 1000 Jefferson Dr SW, Smithsonian Institution Bldg – The Castle; ☼ 9am-4pm Mon-Sat; Metro: Smithsonian) Everything you ever wanted to know about the museum programs.

Washington DC Convention & Visitors Association (Map pp246-8; ☎ 202-789-7000; www.washington.org; 901 7th St, 4th floor; Metro: Gallery Pl-Chinatown; ☼ 9am-5pm Mon-Fri; Metro: Metro Center) Distributes information on lodgings, restaurants and attractions by mail, or you can pick them up at its office.

Other useful websites include:

www.culturaltourismdc.org An extensive calendar of events, tours and information.

www.dc.gov The website of the local government.

www.dcmusicnet.com An extensive database of Washington DC area bands.

www.dcpages.com Information and links on everything from A-arts to Z-zoos.

www.dcregistry.com Extensive listings and links to DC-area businesses.

TRAVEL AGENTS

Two convenient agencies specializing in low-budget and student-oriented travel are **STA Travel** (Map pp256-7; ☎ 202-337-6464, www.statravel.com; 3301 M St NW, Georgetown) and **American Youth Hostel Travel Center**

(Map pp246-8; ☎ 202-737-2333, 800-909-4776; 1009 11th St NW; ☺ 10am-7pm Mon-Sat) downtown on the 1st floor of the Hostelling International–Washington, D.C. hostel. They help find airfare discounts and sell Eurail passes; the Travel Center hosts travel seminars, and maintains a small library and bookstore as well.

On-line travel agencies and bid-for-tickets Internet sites often offer the best deals on airfares (or at least a basis for comparison, if you prefer to deal with a human travel agent). Check out:

www.cheaptickets.com

www.expedia.com

www.priceline.com

VISAS

With the exception of Canadians, who need only proper proof of Canadian citizenship, all foreign visitors to the USA must have a valid passport, and most must also have a US visa. Check current regulations with the US embassy in your home country before you depart. Keep photocopies of these documents, too; if stolen, they'll be easier to replace. Your passport should be valid for at least six months longer than your intended stay in the USA. Documents of financial stability and/or guarantees from a US resident are sometimes required, particularly for visitors from Third World countries.

The reciprocal Visa Waiver Pilot Program allows citizens of certain countries to enter the USA for stays of 90 days or less without a visa. They must have a nonrefundable round-trip ticket and a passport valid for six months past their scheduled departure date. Currently, these countries are Andorra, Austria, Australia, Belgium, Brunei, Denmark, Finland, France, Germany, Iceland, Ireland, Italy, Japan, Liechtenstein, Luxembourg, Monaco, the Netherlands, New Zealand, Norway, Portugal, San Marino, Singapore, Slovenia, Spain, Sweden, Switzerland and the UK. For an updated list, see www.uscis.gov. Other travelers must obtain a visa from a US consulate or embassy. Contact your local US consulate for requirements, or see Lonely Planet's website at www.lonelyplanet.com.

Visa Extensions

Tourist visitors are usually granted a six-month stay on first arrival. If you try to extend that time, immigration authorities' first assumption is that you're working illegally – so hang on to evidence that shows you've been a model tourist (like receipts to demonstrate that you've spent money in the USA or ticket stubs to show that you've traveled extensively). You must apply for an extension *before* the six months have expired. Visitors admitted under the Visa Waiver Pilot Program cannot apply for extensions. To extend your stay, you must file Form I-539, obtained from the **Bureau of Citizenship & Immigration Service** (☎ 800-870-3676; www .uscis.gov; Washington District Office, 4420 N Fairfax Dr, Arlington, Virginia 22203; ☺ 8am-2: 30pm Mon-Fri; Metro: Ballston).

WOMEN TRAVELERS

Washington is a safe and fascinating destination for women travelers: innumerable monuments and historic sites remember women's key roles in the nation and the city, including the **National Museum of Women in the Arts** (p55), the **Women in Military Service for America Memorial** (p97), the **Mary McLeod Bethune Council House** (p91).

Women traveling alone might appreciate the all-woman hostel **Thompson-Markward Hall** (p195) on Capitol Hill. Other useful organizations include:

Columbia Hospital for Women (Map pp246-8; ☎ 202-293-6500; 2425 L St NW; Metro: Foggy Bottom-GWU) Provides a range of health-care services.

Lammas (Map pp258-60; ☎ 202-775-8218; 1607 17th St NW; Metro: Dupont Circle) The city woman's bookstore: a place to find out about women-oriented groups and events.

Planned Parenthood (Map pp258-60; ☎ 202-347-8512; 1108 16th St NW; Metro: Farragut North) Offers obstetric, gynecological and counseling services.

Washington Women Outdoors (☎ 301-864-3070; www.washingtonwomenoutdoors.org; 19450 Caravan Dr, Germantown, Maryland 20874) About 30 miles northwest of DC. A full calendar of hikes, climbs and biking trips that are a great way to befriend local women.

WORK

Foreign visitors are not legally allowed to work in the USA without the appropriate working visa. But US citizens, especially young ones, flock here in summer to take up internships on Capitol Hill, at federal agencies and in think tanks. If you want an internship, it's important to start looking early – the fall of the preceding year is a good time to start. Find your congressional representatives' office addresses via the **Capitol switchboard** (☎ 202-224-3121).

Behind the Scenes

THE LONELY PLANET STORY

The story begins with a classic travel adventure: Tony and Maureen Wheeler's 1972 journey across Europe and Asia to Australia. There was no useful information about the overland trail then, so Tony and Maureen published the first Lonely Planet guidebook to meet a growing need.

From a kitchen table, Lonely Planet has grown to become the largest independent travel publisher in the world, with offices in Melbourne (Australia), Oakland (USA), London (UK) and Paris (France).

Today Lonely Planet guidebooks cover the globe. There is an ever-growing list of books and information in a variety of media. Some things haven't changed. The main aim is still to make it possible for adventurous travellers to get out there – to explore and better understand the world.

At Lonely Planet we believe travelers can make a positive contribution to the countries they visit – if they respect their host communities and spend their money wisely.

THIS BOOK

The 1st edition of *Washington DC* was written by Laura Harger, and it formed the basis for this edition, which was updated and written by Mara Vorhees. Mark H Furstenberg contributed the 'State of the Kitchen' boxed text. This edition was commissioned in Lonely Planet's Oakland office and produced by:

Commissioning Editors Jay Cooke, with assistance from Valerie Sinzdak
Cooordinating Editor Julia Taylor
Editor Jackey Coyle
Proofer Kristin Odijk
Managing Cartographer Alison Lyall
Coordinating Cartographers Amanda Sierp, Simon Tillema
Cartographer Chris Tsismetzis
Layout Designers Sonya Brooke, Dianne Zammit, Tamsin Wilson, Katherine Marsh, Adam Bextream
Cover Designer Nic Lehman
Series Designer Nic Lehman
Series Design Concept Nic Lehman & Andrew Weatherill
Mapping Development Paul Piaia
Series Development Team Jenny Blake, Anna Bolger, Fiona Christie, Kate Cody, Erin Corrigan, Janine Eberle, Simone Egger, James Ellis, Nadine Fogale, Roz Hopkins, Dave Mc-Clymont, Leonie Mugavin, Rachel Peart, Ed Pickard, Michele Posner, Howard Ralley, Dani Valent
Regional Publishing Manager Maria Donohoe
Series Publishing Manager Gabrielle Green
Project Manager Huw Fowles
Thanks to Glenn Beanland, Kerryn Burgess, Dan Caleo, Ryan Evans, Gabrielle Green, Adriana Mammarella, Vivek Wagle, Gerard Walker

Cover photographs Thomas Jefferson Memorial, Peter Gridley/Getty Images (top); Abraham Lincoln Memorial, Richard Cummins/Lonely Planet Images (bottom); Library of Congress, Dan Herrick/Lonely Planet Images (back).

Internal photographs by Dan Herrick/Lonely Planet Images except for the following: p146 (#4) Bill Bachmann/Lonely Planet Images; p2 (#2) Rob Blakers/Lonely Planet Images; p2 (#3), p84 (#2), p85 (#1), p86 (#1), p86 (#3), p146 (#1) Richard Cummins/Lonely Planet Images; p218 Lee Foster/Lonely Planet Images; p2 (#4), p87 (#2), p146 (#2) Rick Gerharter/Lonely Planet Images; p146 (#3) Dennis Johnson/Lonely Planet Images; p85 (#2) Kevin Levesque/Lonely Planet Images; p207 John Neubauer/Lonely Planet Images; p87 (#1) Peter Ptschelinzew/Lonely Planet Images. All images are the copyright of the photographers unless otherwise indicated. Many of the images in this guide are available for licensing from Lonely Planet Images: www.lonelyplanetimages.com.

ACKNOWLEDGEMENTS

Many thanks to Washington Metropolitan Area Transit Authority (WMATA) for the use of their Metro map.

THANKS
MARA VORHEES

I will never be able to show the extent of my gratitude to Linda and Michael Moodie for the hospitality and generosity they have poured on me over the years. It was a joy to spend time back at the homestead on Kentbury Dr. At LP, I am grateful to Gabrielle Green for the chance to work on this book; to Jay Cooke for his guidance and patience; and to Laura Harger for her efforts on the 1st edition. Contributions from Mark Furstenberg of the BreadLine and Warren Brown of CakeLove are appreciated. Many friends added their two cents to this book: Susannah Gardiner provided excellent referrals for contributors; Jason Gluck was my primary restaurant recommender and co-reviewer; Tim O'Brien was the Arlington expert; and Bob Post (whose name seems to appear in every book I write) offered insights on Dupont

Circle and gay DC. Additional thanks to Caroline Chebli, Victoria Curtis, Karen Jacobs, Alex Leal, Rosalind Mackenzie, Shirl Smith, Matuś Sulek and Luc Vaillancourt. My inspiration, of course, is Jerry Easter and our shared memories of the city where we met.

OUR READERS

Many thanks to the travelers who used the last edition and wrote to us with helpful hints, useful advice and interesting anecdotes. Your names follow:

Helen Battleson, Lesli Bell, Anne-trime Benjaminsen, Jo Ann Berlin, Andrzej Blachowicz, Leah Bloomfield, John Borg, Michael Borger, Christian Bosselmann, Clare Braithwaite, Peter Braithwaite, Marianne Busch, Michael Campilia, Amelie Cherlin, James Collier, Adam Crain, Jeri Dansky, Mark Davey, Nuala Ui Dhuill, Tony Dragon, Mary Duffy, Denise Evangelista, Annette Ferguson, Margo Freistadt, Erith French, Ross Geraghty, Yvonne Green, Deb Grupenhoff, Murray Hassan, Lisa Hatle, Annette Hilton, Krisztian Hincz, Mindy Hohman, Pat Holbrook, Pat and Brian Holbrook, Kelly Holmes, Leo Hornak, Louise Joergensen, Leah Kaplan, Mirjam Knapp, Michael La Place, Zippy Larson, Yuli Law, Carl Long, Marc Lutz, John Lynch, Janna Marks, Erik Marr, James Marshall, Rob McMeekin, Deb Moore-Marchant, Dominique Morrow, Ron Myers, Robin Nahum, Allan Parker, Linda C Perry, Tony and Jill Porco, Wade Price, Thomas Reiser, Thomas J Reiser, M Riphagen, David Roland, Norman Sadler, Carol Schwartz, Elizabeth Sercombe, Kerri Shimshock, John Sietsema, Adam Simmons, Peter Smith, Sandy Smith, Jennie So, Christopher Springate, Carl Sprute, Ian C Story, Katie Sweetman, Joshua Taylor Barnes, Jettie van Caenegem, Rob van den Brand, Joan Walsh, Dr Peter Wehmeier, Linda Wilson, Laura Winton, John Witten, Cathy Wright, Alex Young and Andrew Young.

SEND US YOUR FEEDBACK

We love to hear from travelers – your comments keep us on our toes and help make our books better. Our well-traveled team reads every word on what you loved or loathed about this book. Although we cannot reply individually to postal submissions, we always guarantee that your feedback goes straight to the appropriate authors, in time for the next edition. Each person who sends us information is thanked in the next edition – and the most useful submissions are rewarded with a free book.

To send us your updates – and find out about LP events, newsletters and travel news – visit our award-winning website: www.lonelyplanet.com.

Note: We may edit, reproduce and incorporate your comments in Lonely Planet products such as guide-books, websites and digital products, so let us know if you don't want your comments reproduced or your name acknowledged. For a copy of our privacy policy visit www.lonelyplanet.con./privacy.

Index

See also separate indexes for Eating (p241), Shopping (p241) and Sleeping (p242).
Abbreviations: MD – Maryland, VA – Virginia, DE – Delaware.

A

Academy Art Museum (MD) 212, 213
accommodations 189-204, 225, see also Sleeping index
  booking services 190, 191, 225
  costs 17, 190
Adams-Morgan 79-82, **89**, **110**, **261**
  accommodations 202
  clubbing 164
  drinking 153, **89**, **141**
  festivals 11
  food 132-3
  shopping 184-5
  tours 109-10
Adams Building 64-5
Adams Morgan Festival 11, 79
Adas Israel Synagogue 52
African Americans 5, 12
  history 66, 75
  literature 24-5
  music 26-7
  neighborhoods 80-91, 111-12
  population 12
African American Civil War Memorial 82, **112**
African American Civil War Museum 111, 34
African American Heritage Park (VA) 99
AIA 59, 161
AIDS Hotline 228
AIDS Memorial Quilt 19
Air 56, 161
air travel 222
Albert Einstein Planetarium 49
Albert Einstein statue 59
Alexandria (VA) 43, 96, 97, 99-100, 108-9, **265**
  accommodations 203, 204
  drinking 154-5
  food 136-8
  shopping 187-8
Alexandria Archaeology Museum (VA) 99
ambulance services 227
American Automobile Association 223
American Express 229
American Institute of Architects 59

American Red Cross Museum 57, 114
American Visionary Art Museum (MD) 209, 210
Anacostia Museum 47, 66
  shopping at 178
Anderson, Marian 39, 45
Anderson House 78, 102
Andre Chreky Salon 172
Annapolis Sailing School (MD) 212, 213
Antietam 36
Anton Gallery 24
Ape 163
Apollo 11 49
aquariums 54, 209, 210
architecture 22-3
area codes 231
Arena Stage 28, 155
Arlington (VA) 96-9, **264**
  accommodations 203-4
  drinking 154-5
  food 136
Arlington House (VA) 97, 108
Arlington National Cemetery (VA) 5, 97, **88**
Aroma Company 153
Arthur M Sackler Gallery 47
  shopping at 174
arts 21-30
Arts & Industries Building 48
Arts of Peace 108
art galleries 23-4, 78, see also individual entries
  eating at 117-18
  shopping at 176-81, 187-8
  tours 177
Art Museum of the Americas 60
Asian Stories in America (VA) 28, 156
Assateague Island (MD) 207, 215
Athenaeum (VA) 99
Atlantic Coast 214-16
Atlantic Kayak 170
Atomic Grounds 228
Aveda Georgetown 172
Awakening 70
Aztec Gardens 60, 114

B

B'nai B'rith Klutznick Museum 76-7
Babe Ruth Museum (MD) 209, 210

baby-sitting 226
Backyard Band 160
Baltimore-Washington International Airport 222
Baltimore (MD) 209-10, **146**
Baltimore Maritime Museum (MD) 210
Baltimore Museum of Art (MD) 209, 210
Banana Café & Piano Bar 150
Barron's 27
Barry, Marion 16, 18, 32, 39, 40, 200, 201
Bartholdi Fountain 50
baseball 15, 167-8
Basilica of the National Shrine of the Immaculate Conception 68, **68**
Basin Street Lounge (VA) 137, 159
basketball 14-15, 167
Battery Kemble 94
Battery Kemble Park 92
Battleground National Cemetery 92
Bead Museum 52
Beall Mansion 106
Bed & Breakfast Accommodations Ltd 225
Beltway bandits 16, 96
Ben Lomond Manor House (VA) 218, 219
Bethune, Mary McCleod 91, 112, 232
Better Bikes Inc 222
bicycle travel, see cycling
Big Hunt 151
Big Wheel Bikes 222
Bike the Sites 43, 169, 222
Bilbo Baggins (VA) 154
Billy Goat Trail (MD) 217
Bill of Rights 54
Birchmere (VA) 159
bird-watching 213, 215
Bi Women's Cultural Alliance 228
Blackwater National Wildlife Refuge (MD) 213
Black Cat 8, 26, 159
Black Fashion Museum 82, 112
Black Heat 160
Black History Month 9
Black History Resource Cente (VA) 99

blading 170
Blaine Mansion 102
Blair House 57
Blazing Saddles 222
Blues Alley 159
Blue Room 164
boat travel
  canoeing 170, 214, 215
  cruises 43-4
  ferry travel 213, 214
  kayaking 170, 214, 215, 217
  paddleboating 71
  sailing 170, 212, 213, 214
Bohemian Caverns 26, 27, 81, 112, 159, **142**, **159**
Bonsai & Penjing Museum 69
Bonus Army 19
books 24-6, 27, 30, 32
Bossa 159-60
Bottom Line 149
Bradlee, Benjamin 15, 106
Bravo Bravo 162
Brickskeller Inn 152
Brookland & Northeast DC 8, 67-9, **252-3**
  accommodations 196
  clubbing 162
  food 124-5
Brown, Warren 13, 131, **83**
Buffalo Billiards 152
Bukom Café 110, 160
Bureau of Citizenship & Immigration Service 232
bus travel 44, 223
business hours 116, 174, 225-6
Butlers Cigar Bar 149

C

C&O Canal 37, 42, 45, 73, 217
C&O Canal National Historical Park (MD) 217
C&O Canal Towpath 168, 171, **143**, **168**
Café des Artistes 58, 113, 114
Café Saint-Ex 154
Camden Yards (MD) 209, 210
camping 211, 212
canoeing 170, 214, 215
Cape Henlopen State Park (DE) 207, 216
Capital Children's Museum 46, 68

235

Index

SLEEPING

Index

MAP LEGEND

ROUTES

Freeway	One-Way Street
Primary Road	Mall/Steps
Secondary Road	Tunnel
Tertiary Road	Walking Tour
Lane	Walking Trail
	Walking Path

TRANSPORT

Metro	Rail

HYDROGRAPHY

River, Creek	Water
Swamp	

BOUNDARIES

State, Provincial

AREA FEATURES

Airport	Cemetery, Christian
Area of Interest	Forest
Building, Featured	Land
Building, Information	Mall
Building, Other	Park
Building, Transport	Sports
Campus	

POPULATION

✪ CAPITAL (NATIONAL)	◉ CAPITAL (STATE)
● Large City	● Medium City
○ Small City	○ Town, Village

SYMBOLS

Sights/Activities	Eating	Information
Beach	Eating	Bank, ATM
Castle, Fortress	**Drinking**	Embassy/Consulate
Christian	Drinking	Hospital, Medical
Islamic	**Entertainment**	Information
Jewish	Entertainment	Internet Facilities
Monument	**Shopping**	Parking Area
Museum, Gallery	Shopping	Police Station
Point of Interest	**Sleeping**	Post Office, GPO
Ruin	Sleeping	Telephone
Skiing	**Transport**	**Geographic**
Swimming Pool	Airport, Airfield	Lookout
Zoo, Bird Sanctuary	Bus Station	National Park

Map Section

MARYLAND

BETHESDA

Bradley Blvd

Old Georgetown Rd

355

See Upper Northwest DC Map (pp262-3)

410

Wilson La

188

191

East-West Hwy

CHEVY CHASE

190

Wisconsin Ave

Western Ave NW

UPPER NORTHWEST DC

MacArthur Blvd NW

River Rd

Massachusetts Ave

Military Rd NW

Rock Creek Park

Capital Beltway

George Washington Memorial Parkway

Clara Barton Parkway

MacArthur Blvd

Fort Reno Park

University of DC

Georgetown Pike

193

American University

US Navy Security Station

See Adams-Morgan Map (p261)

123

To Wolf Trap Filene Center (6mi), Washington Dulles International Airport (8mi)

Massachusetts Ave NW

National Zoological Park

309

Old Dominion Dr

Canal Rd

Fletcher's Boathouse

Mt Vernon College

Whitehaven Park

US Naval Observatory

Kalorama

Dulles Toll Rd

Dumbarton Oaks Park

To Tysons Corner & Fairfax Sq (1.2mi)

GEORGETOWN

Georgetown University

Leesburg Pike

VIRGINIA

Lee Hwy

M St NW

Theodore Roosevelt Island

Foggy Bottom

To Nissan Pavilion (30mi)

Custis Memorial Parkway

29

See Georgetown Map (pp256-7)

Broad St W

Washington Blvd

N Fairfax Dr

Wilson Blvd

50

Broad St E

Fort Myer

Arlington National Cemetery

120

Columbia Gardens Cemetery

S Glebe Rd

50

Arlington Blvd

244

See Arlington Map (p264)

Pentagon City

1

Ronald Reagan Washington National Airport

Washington & Old Dominion Trail (Start)

395

King St

To Potomac Mills (18.6mi)

See Alexandria Map (p265)

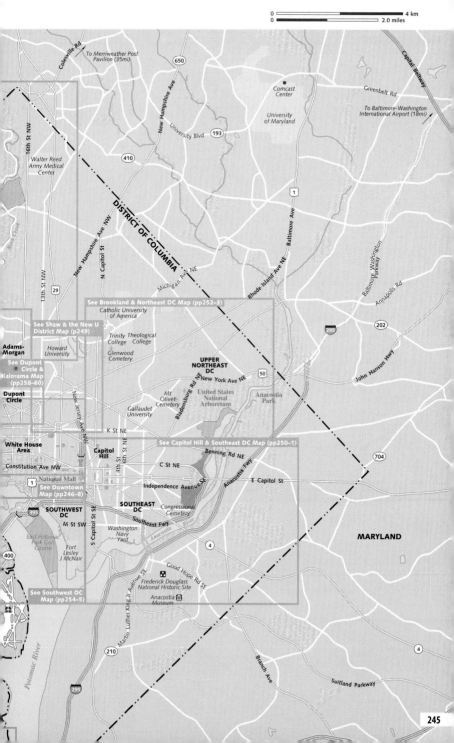

0 [========================] 4 km
0 [========================] 2.0 miles

Colesville Rd
To Merriweather Post
Pavilion (35mi)
650
Comcast
Center
Greenbelt Rd
University
of Maryland
16th St NW
University Blvd
193
To Baltimore-Washington
International Airport (18mi)
Walter Reed
Army Medical
Center
410
New Hampshire Ave
1
DISTRICT OF COLUMBIA
New Hampshire Ave NW
N Capitol St
13th St NW
Baltimore Ave
Baltimore-Washington Parkway
Michigan Ave NE
Rhode Island Ave NE
Annapolis Rd
29
See Brookland & Northeast DC Map (pp252-3)
Catholic University
of America
See Shaw & the New U
District Map (p249)
Trinity Theological
College College
295
202
Adams-
Morgan
Howard
University
Glenwood
Cemetery
UPPER
NORTHEAST
DC
John Hanson Hwy
See Dupont
Circle &
Kalorama Map
(pp258-60)
New York Ave NE
50
Dupont
Circle
Mt
Olivet
Cemetery
United States
National
Arboretum
Anacostia
Park
Gallaudet
University
Bladensburg Rd NE
New Jersey Ave NE
K St NE
White House
Area
Capitol
Hill
Benning Rd NE
704
Constitution Ave NW
4th St
6th St NE
C St NE
Anacostia Fwy
1
See Downtown
Map (pp246-8)
Independence Avenue SE
E Capitol St
SOUTHEAST
DC
395
SOUTHWEST
DC
Congressional
Cemetery
MARYLAND
S Capitol St SE
M St SW
Southeast Fwy
East Potomac
Park Golf
Course
Fort
Lesley
J McNair
Washington
Navy Yard
Anacostia River
400
4
See Southwest DC
Map (pp254-5)
Good Hope Rd SE
Martin Luther King Jr Avenue SE
Frederick Douglass
National Historic Site
Anacostia
Museum
Potomac River
210
4
295
Branch Ave
Suitland Parkway

Church St NW **E**

15th St NW

Vermont Ave NW

Logan Circle (pp258–60)

Rhode Island **F** Ave NW

10th St NW

9th St NW

8th St NW

P St NW

Marion St NW

6th St NW

G

Q St NW

Franklin St NW

4th St NW

3rd St NW

Bates St NW

H

Kirby St NW

P St NW

1

Massachusetts Ave NE

Thomas Circle

116 Green Ct NW

160

156

Massachusetts Ave NE

11th St NW

M St NW

N St NW

L St NW

Kennedy Playground

O St NW

New Convention Center

M Mt Vernon Sq/7th St-Convention Center

5th St NW

New York Ave NW

New Jersey Ave NW

2

See Dupont Circle & Kalorama Map (pp258–60)

See Brookland & Northeast DC Map (pp252–3)

164 85 145 K St NW

133 89 McPherson Square

Franklin Square

166 148 147

Mt Vernon Square 13

53

K St NW

M McPherson Sq

152 I St NW

Zei Al NW

H St NW

165

52

Former Washington Convention Center

181 134 139 97 14 27 108 88 109

CHINATOWN

H St NW

2nd St NW

H St NW

See Shaw & the New U District Map (p249)

Massachusetts Ave NW

Treasury Annex

167 168

30

12th St NW

13th St NW

135 Metro Center

36

110

95

Gallery Pl-Chinatown

122

G St NW

42

4th St NW

3rd St NW

G St NW

3

70 100 102 136

125 132

DOWNTOWN

124 48

151

45 Judiciary Sq

North Central Fwy

1st St NW

99 153 162 123 129 113

F St NW

61 120

10th St NW

9th St NW

128 31

86 176 137

E St NW

Judiciary Square

46

4

177 182

Pennsylvania Ave NW

Department of Commerce Building

64 171 118 Federal Triangle

149 163

107

40

Interstate Commerce Commission

59

11th St NW

22

104

90 126 131 142 83 80 141

56 111

24

7th St NW

8th St NW

Indiana Ave NW

84

169 John Marshall Park

Department of Labor

C St NW

Pennsylvania Ave NW

5

15th St NW

14th St NW

41 Archives-Navy Memorial

Constitution Ave NW

49 50

74

Madison Dr NW

54 44

National Mall

7th St NW

121

43

Constitution Ave NW

Madison Dr NW

See Capitol Hill & Southeast DC Map (pp250–1)

14th St SW

Smithsonian

M Jefferson Dr SW

179 12 29

26 6 21 47 7 28 39

51

Smithsonian

Jefferson Dr SW

71

Independence Ave SW

6

Raoul Wallenberg Pl

SOUTHWEST DC

C St SW

National Bureau of Engraving and Printing

13th St SW

Department of Agriculture

12th St SW

Forrestal Building

US Postal Service

Department of Energy

L'Enfant Promenade

L'Enfant Plaza

D St SW

FAA Building

Hancock Park

9th St SW

7th St SW

M L'Enfant Plaza

Virginia Ave SW

School St SW

Maryland Ave SW

Department of Health & Human Services

6th St SW

4th St SW

3rd St SW

C St SW

D St SW

E St SW

M Federal Center SW

2nd St SW

Washington Ave SW

247

SHAW & THE NEW U DISTRICT

SIGHTS & ACTIVITIES	(pp41–100)
African American Civil War	
Memorial	1 B3
African American Civil War	
Museum	2 A3
Black Fashion Museum	3 B3
Founders' Library	4 B2
Howard University	5 C3
John Wesley AME Zion Church	6 A4
Mary McLeod Bethune Council	
House	7 A5
Moorland-Spingarn Research Center	8 B3

EATING	(pp115–38)
Ben's Chili Bowl	9 A3
Florida Avenue Grill	10 A3
Hamburger Mary's	11 A5
Islander Caribbean	12 A3
Kaffa House	13 A3

DRINKING	(pp149–55)
Café St-Ex	14 A4
King Pin	15 B3
Polly's Cafe	16 A3
Titan	17 A4

ENTERTAINMENT	(pp147–64)
2:K:9	18 B3
9:30 Club	19 B3
Black Cat	20 A4
Bohemian Caverns	21 A3
Lincoln Theatre	22 A3
Republic Gardens	23 A3
Source Theatre Company	24 A4
Velvet Lounge	25 B3

SHOPPING	(pp173–88)
Go Mama Go!	(see 28)
Home Rule	(see 28)
Mad T Musicbox	26 A3
Pulp	(see 28)
Shop Pop	(see 28)
Up Against the Wall	27 B3
Vastu	28 A4

INFORMATION	
Children's National Medical	
Center	29 D2
Howard University Hospital	30 B3
Howard University Welcome	
Center	31 B4

To Childers Hall & Howard
University Gallery of Art (0.06mi)

See Upper Northwest DC Map (pp262–3)

SHAW & THE
NEW U DISTRICT

See Downtown Map (pp146–8)

See Brookland & Northeast DC Map (pp252–3)

See Dupont Circle & Kalorama Map (p258–60)

249

400 m
0.2 miles

CAPITOL HILL & SOUTHEAST DC

A   **B**   **C**   **D**

H St NW
G St NW
Capitol St
Union Station
I St NE
E St NE
9th St NE
Florida Ave NE
17th St NE

Massachusetts Ave NE
7th St NE
G St NE
H St NE
Benning Rd NE

52
19
30
28
46
Linden Pl NE
13th St
Elliot St
Gales St NE

1
3rd St NW
2nd St NW
42
59
31
2nd St
3rd St NE
Morris Pl NE
F St NE
8th St NE
Maryland Ave NE
Emerald St NE

57
E St NW
Acker St
11th St NE
12th St
D St NE
14th St NE
15th St
16th St
17th St

Union Station Plaza
Lexington Pl NE
E St NE
E St NE
North Carolina Ave NE
Constitution Ave NE

C St NW
Louisiana Ave
Delaware Ave NE
36
44
29
Stanton Park
D St NE
10th St
C St NE
14th Pl NE

Russell Senate Office Building
61
54
6th St
A St NE
15
8
18
6
A St SE

26
Constitution Ave NE
24
25
E Capitol St
Independence Ave SE
Massachusetts Ave SE

2
3rd St NW
5
27
10
4
2
Capitol Plaza
See Inset
4th St SE
5th St SE
North Carolina Ave SE
21
Tennessee Ave NE
North Carolina Ave

United States Botanic Garden
Rayburn House Office Building
13
Cannon House Office Building
14
3
7
38
Independence Ave SE
17th St SE
Stadium-Armory

Federal Center SW
47
C St SE
South Carolina Ave SE
Kentucky Ave SE
D St SE
18th St

Washington Ave SW
Capitol South
D St SE
37
45
South Carolina Ave SE
Potomac Ave
Congressional Cemetery

3
G St SW
Folger Park
58
Eastern Market
48
Potomac Ave
G St SE
H St SE

Lansburgh Park
3rd St SW
S Capitol St
New Jersey Ave SE
Virginia Ave SE
Marion Park
Garfield Park
22
F St SE
2nd St SE
47
39
32
11
51
16
9th St SE
11th St SE
12th St SE
13th St SE
E St SE
SOUTHEAST DC
15th St SE

I St SW
50
K St SE
L St SE
Southeast Fwy
I St SE
K St SE
L St SE

M St SW
Van St SE
Half St SE
Cushing Pl SE
1st St SE
2nd Pl SE
3rd St SE
M St SW

4
1st St SW
Navy Yard
N St SE
Washington Navy Yard
Tingey St SE
Patterson Ave SE
Paulding St SE
Isaac Hull Ave SE
Parsons Ave SE
10th St SE
Water St SE
Anacostia River

O St SW
O St SE
20
17

P St SW
P St SE
N Pl SE
Wells Memorial Bridge
Anacostia River Park

Q St SW
Potomac Ave
R St SW
Potomac Ave SW

Fort Lesley J McNair
Half St SW
S St SW
Ridge Pl SE
18th St SE

5
V St SW
Buzzard Point
Robbins Rd SW
Brookley St SW
Howard Rd SE
Anacostia Fwy
W St SE
14th St SE
15th St SE
17th St SE
U St SE
U Pl SE
Fendall St

Defense Blvd
Shannon Pl SE
Talbert St SE
Anacostia
Morris Rd SE
High St SE
9
Galen St SE
16th St SE

6
Anacostia Naval Station
S Capitol St
Martin Luther King Jr Ave SE
1

John Phillip Sousa Bridge

250

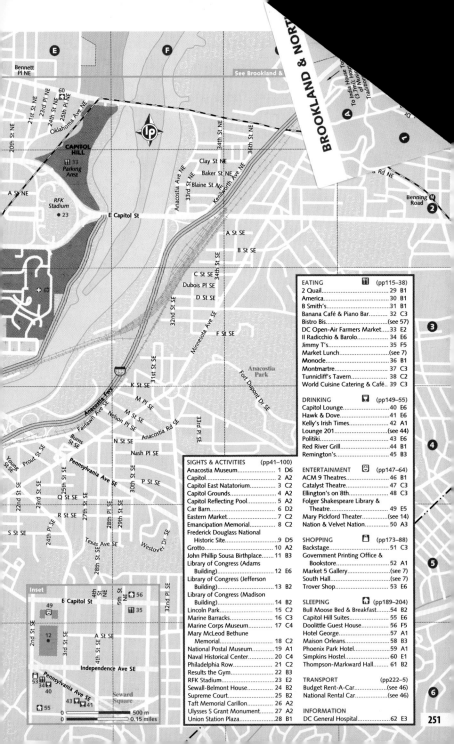

Bennett
Pl NE

21st St NE
23rd St NE
24th St NE
25th St NE
60
Oklahoma Ave NE

20th St NE

CAPITOL
HILL

🏛 33
Parking
Area

RFK
Stadium
● 23

A St NE

E Capitol St

34th St NE
36th St NE

Clay St NE

Baker St NE
Blaine St NE

Anacostia Ave NE
33rd St NE
Kenilworth Ave NE
North Ave NE

Benning
Road M

2

Rd NE

A St SE

B St SE

C St SE

Dubois Pl SE

D St SE

34th St SE

32nd St SE

Minnesota Ave SE

F St SE

Anacostia
Park

Anacostia Fwy

31st St SE

K St SE

Fort Dupont Dr SE

M Pl SE

M St SE

Nelson Pl SE

Fairlawn Ave SE

Anacostia Rd SE

33rd St SE

N St SE

Burns St SE

Nash Pl SE

Young St SE
Prout St SE

Pennsylvania Ave SE

22nd St SE
23rd St SE
24th St SE
25th St SE
27th St SE
28th St SE
29th St SE
30th St SE

Q St SE
P St SE

Texas Ave SE

Westover Dr SE

S St SE

28th Pl SE

3

4

5

6

Inset

E Capitol St

4th St
5th St

🏨 56

🏛 35

49

12

3rd St
4th St

A St SE

32nd St NE

Independence Ave SE

2nd St SE
3rd St

Pennsylvania Ave SE

53 34
40

43 41

Seward
Square

🏨 55

0 ————— 500 m
0 ————— 0.15 miles

251

To Adams
Memorial
(0.6mi)

B

Scale Gate Rd NE

Harwood Rd

9

Catholic
University
of America

John McCormack Rd

10th St NE

C

Ritchie Pl NE

13

Quincy St NE

Perry St NE

16

Otis St NE

Newton St NE

D

5

Franciscan
Monastary

Fort
Bunker
Hill Park

To Adams
Memorial
(4.3mi)

Arnold... Hos... NW

1

Brookland-CUA

12

Bunker Hill Rd NE

18th St NE

Michigan Ave NE

Monroe St NE

Brookland

11

12th St NE

13th St NE

14th St NE

15th St NE

16th St NE

17th St NE

Theological
College

4th St NE

7th St NE

8th St NE

9th St NE

14

10th St NE

Kearney St NE

Jackson St NE

Irving St NE

Hamlin St NE

Girard St NE

2

1st St NW

Trinity
College

Michigan Ave NW

McMillan
Park

Franklin St NE

Glenwood
Cemetery

Evarts St NE

Edgewood St NE

Evarts St NE

Douglas St NW

Douglas St NE

Douglas St NE

3

Channing St NW

Channing St NE

Saratoga Ave NE

Bryant St NW

Bryant St NE

Brentwood Rd NE

13th Pl NE

Downing St NE

14th St NE

Adams St NW

Adams St NE

Lincoln Rd NE

W St NW

St
Marys

Rhode Island Ave NE

M Rhode
Island
Ave

W St NE

W Pl NE

Flagler Pl NW

V St NW

V St NE

5th St NE

U St NW

1

Summit Pl NE

3rd St NE

4th St NE

18

T St NW

T St NE

6th St NE

4

Seaton Pl NW

2nd St NE

S St NE

15

Okie St NE

Kendall St NE

Fenwick St NE

West Virginia Ave NE

S St NW

Randolph Pl NW

R St NW

R St NE

Capitol Ave NE

Mt
Olivet
Cemetery

Q St NW

Quincy Pl NE

Q St NE

Bates St NW

Florida Ave NE

Eckington Pl NE

New York Ave NE

Brentwood Parkway

Gallaudet
University

Mount Olivet Rd NE

5

1st St NW

P St NW

P St NE

50

O St NW

O St NE

Neal Pl NE

Brentwood
Park

Lincoln Cir W

Switzer Drive NE

Simms Pl NE

Raum St NE

Meigs Pl NE

N St NW

N St NE

6

Holbrook Tce NE

Queen St NE

Patterson St
NE

M St NW

M St NE

5th St NE

M St NE

L Pl
NW

Pierce St NE

Abbey Pl NE

Owen Pl NE

Montello Ave NE

Oates St NE

Lewis St NE

L St NW

L St NE

L St NE

Neal St NE

Trinidad Ave NE

Morse St NE

Orren St NE

Staples St NE

Holbrook St NE

16th St NE

17

Fenton St NE

Callan St NE

Florida Ave NE

K St NW

K St NE

K St NE

Parker
St NE

17th St NE

6

1st St NW

N Capitol St

I St NE

2nd St

3

3rd St

4th St

I St NE

H St NE

5th St

6th St NE

7th St

8th St

9th St

10th St

11th St

12th St

13th St

H St NW

G Pl NE

Union Station **M**

G St NE

G St NW

G St NE

Union
Station

Benning Rd NE

See Shaw & the New U District Map (p249)

See Downtown Map (pp246-8)

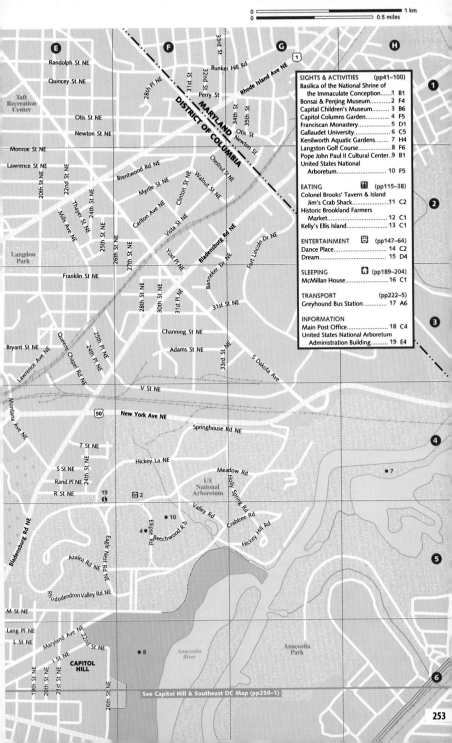

0 — 1 km
0 — 0.5 miles

SIGHTS & ACTIVITIES (pp41–100)
Basilica of the National Shrine of the Immaculate Conception......1 B1
Bonsai & Penjing Museum...........2 F4
Capital Children's Museum.........3 B6
Capitol Columns Garden............4 F5
Franciscan Monastery................5 D1
Gallaudet University....................6 C5
Kenilworth Aquatic Gardens.......7 H4
Langston Golf Course.................8 F6
Pope John Paul II Cultural Center..9 B1
United States National Arboretum...........................10 F5

EATING (pp115–38)
Colonel Brooks' Tavern & Island Jim's Crab Shack....................11 C2
Historic Brookland Farmers Market...............................12 C1
Kelly's Ellis Island....................13 C1

ENTERTAINMENT (pp147–64)
Dance Place............................14 C2
Dream....................................15 D4

SLEEPING (pp189–204)
McMillan House........................16 C1

TRANSPORT (pp222–5)
Greyhound Bus Station..............17 A6

INFORMATION
Main Post Office........................18 C4
United States National Arboretum Administration Building.........19 E4

See Capitol Hill & Southeast DC Map (pp250–1)

SOUTHWEST DC

Marshall Dr

L'Enfant Dr

Schley Dr

Memorial Ave

Eisenhower Dr

Halsey Dr

Mc Clellan Dr

Grant Dr

York Dr

Marshall Dr

Arlington
National
Cemetery

Nimitz Dr

Bradley Dr

Macarthur Dr

Arnold Dr

Patton Dr

Dewey Dr

Fort
Myer

Army Navy Dr

S Nash St

S Arlington Ridg Rd

S Hayes St

Boundary Dr

George Washington Memorial Parkway

Jefferson Davis Hwy

Washington Blvd

Lady Bird
Johnson
Park

Arlington
Cemetery

Arlington
Memorial
Bridge

Lincoln
Memorial

Reflecting Pool

Daniel French Dr SW

Independence Ave SW

W Basin Dr SW

Ohio Dr SW

Potomac River

FDR
Memorial
Park

Tidal
Basin

Inlet
Bridge

Rochambeau
Memorial
Bridge

Defense Department
(The Pentagon)

Pentagon

Boundary Dr

Old Jefferson Davis Hwy

S Ball St

12th St S

Crystal Dr

14th Rd S

George Washington Memorial Parkway

Defense Department
(The Pentagon)

Crystal
City

Pentagon City

See Downtown Map (pp246–8)

See Arlington Map (p264)

254

0 _____ 1 km
0 _____ 0.5 miles

E

F

National Mall

Madison Dr NW

CAPITOL HILL & SOUTHEAST D

H

US Capitol

Capitol Plaza

1

The Castle

Smithsonian

Freer Gallery of Art

Arts and Industries Building

Hirshhorn Museum

Jefferson Dr SW

4th St SW

National Air and Space Museum

US Botanic Garden

North Central Fwy

Raoul Wallenberg Pl

14th St SW

15

9

US Department of Agriculture

12th St SW

US Postal Service

Forrestal Building

Department of Energy

9th St SW

FAA Building

Independence Ave SE

Maryland Ave SE

Department of Health & Human Services

Washington Ave SW

1st St SW

Rayburn House Office Building

C St SE

D St SE

13th St SW

Hancock Park

Virginia Ave

C St SW

Federal Center SW

10

L'Enfant Promenade

L'Enfant Plaza

24

L'Enfant Plaza

D St SW

School St SW

2nd St

M

Outlet Bridge

E St SW

Dwight D Eisenhower Fwy

Southeast Fwy

2

12

20

Benjamin Banneker Park

7th St SW

G St SW

H St SW

Southeastern University

I St SW

6th St SW

3rd St SE

Lansburgh Park

I St SE

Water St SW

21

Maine Ave SW

K St SW

L St SW

S Capitol St SE

P

P

2

East Potomac Park

Buckeye Dr SW

23

22

16

SOUTHWEST DC

Delaware Ave SW

Canal St SW

Howison Pl SW

N St SE

19

M St SW

Waterfront-SEU

3

11

7

18

4th St SW

N St SW

Washington Channel

Ohio Dr SW

17

Waterside Park

14

O St SW

East Potomac Park Golf Course

3

P St SW

A St

3rd Ave

B St

Q St SW

Potomac Ave SW

R St SW

South Capitol St

Potomac Ave SE

4

Fort Lesley J McNair

5th Ave

4th Ave

4

2nd Ave

1st St SW

2nd St SW

S St SW

Half St SW

T St SW

1st Ave

C St

V St SW

D St

Buzzard Point

Anacostia River

5

Gravelly Point

Greenleaf Point

Robbins Rd SW

Defense Blvd

DISTRICT OF COLUMBIA

VIRGINIA

Ohio Dr SW

1

Hains Point

Anacostia Naval Station

6

See Capitol Hill & Southeast DC Map (p250–1)

GEORGETOWN

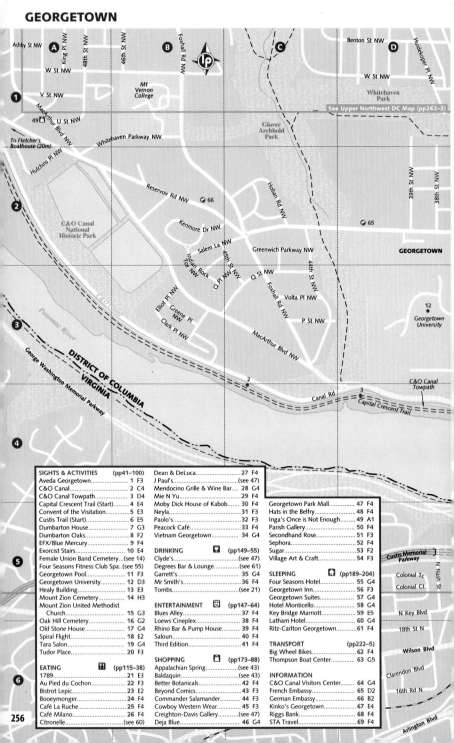

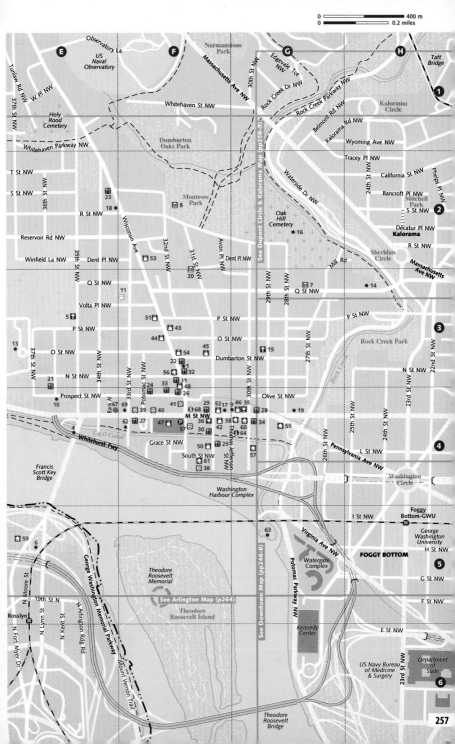

DUPONT CIRCLE & KALORAMA

Edgevale Tce NW

Benton Pl NW

Rock Creek Dr NW

Rock Creek

Rock Creek Parkway NW

Rock Creek Park

Kalorama Circle

Belmont Rd NW

Kalorama Rd NW

Taft Bridge

Connecticut Ave NW

Kalorama Park

20th St NW

19th St NW

See Adams-Morgan Map (p261)

Kalorama

123

See Georgetown Map (pp256-7)

114

Wyoming Ave NW

10

129

Tracey Pl NW

24th St NW

California St NW

Leroy Pl NW

116

Phelps Pl NW

Montrose Park

Waterside Dr NW

Massachusetts Ave NW (Embassy Row)

Bancroft Pl NW

Mitchell Park

Dupont Circle

89
48
S St NW

23
19

28
30

Oak Hill Cemetery

Decatur Pl NW

20
80
93
79

GEORGETOWN

R St NW

41

1
5
8
65

Sheridan Circle

77

Mill Rd

6
Hillyer NW
Ct

Hillyer Pl NW

84

29th St NW

28th St NW

128
127

12
52
94

135

88

Q St NW

54

16
117

101

83

See Downtown map (pp246-8)

20th St NW

14

26th St NW

P St NW

Dumbarton Oaks Park

49
P St NW
40

42
92

21st St NW

125

64
Twining Ct NW

44
35

Hopkins St NW

Church St NW

O St NW

108

Dumbarton St NW

27th St NW

Rock Creek

N St NW

Newport Rd NW

103
9
Sunderland Pl NW

New Hampshire Avenue NW

Dupont Circle

Olive St NW

25th St NW

24th St NW

23rd St NW

N St NW

Ward Pl NW

7

109

M St NW

100

27

33

M St NW

111

West End

32

29th St NW

26th St NW

Pennsylvania Ave NW

132
L St NW

21st St NW

20th St NW

22nd St NW

DUPONT CIRCLE & KALORAMA

ADAMS-MORGAN

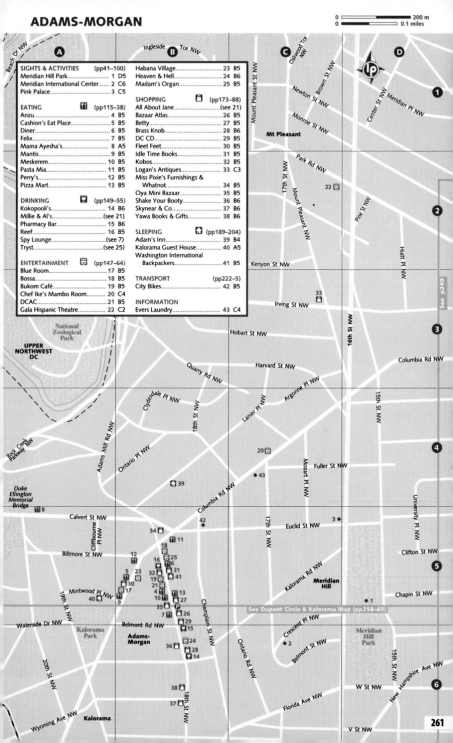

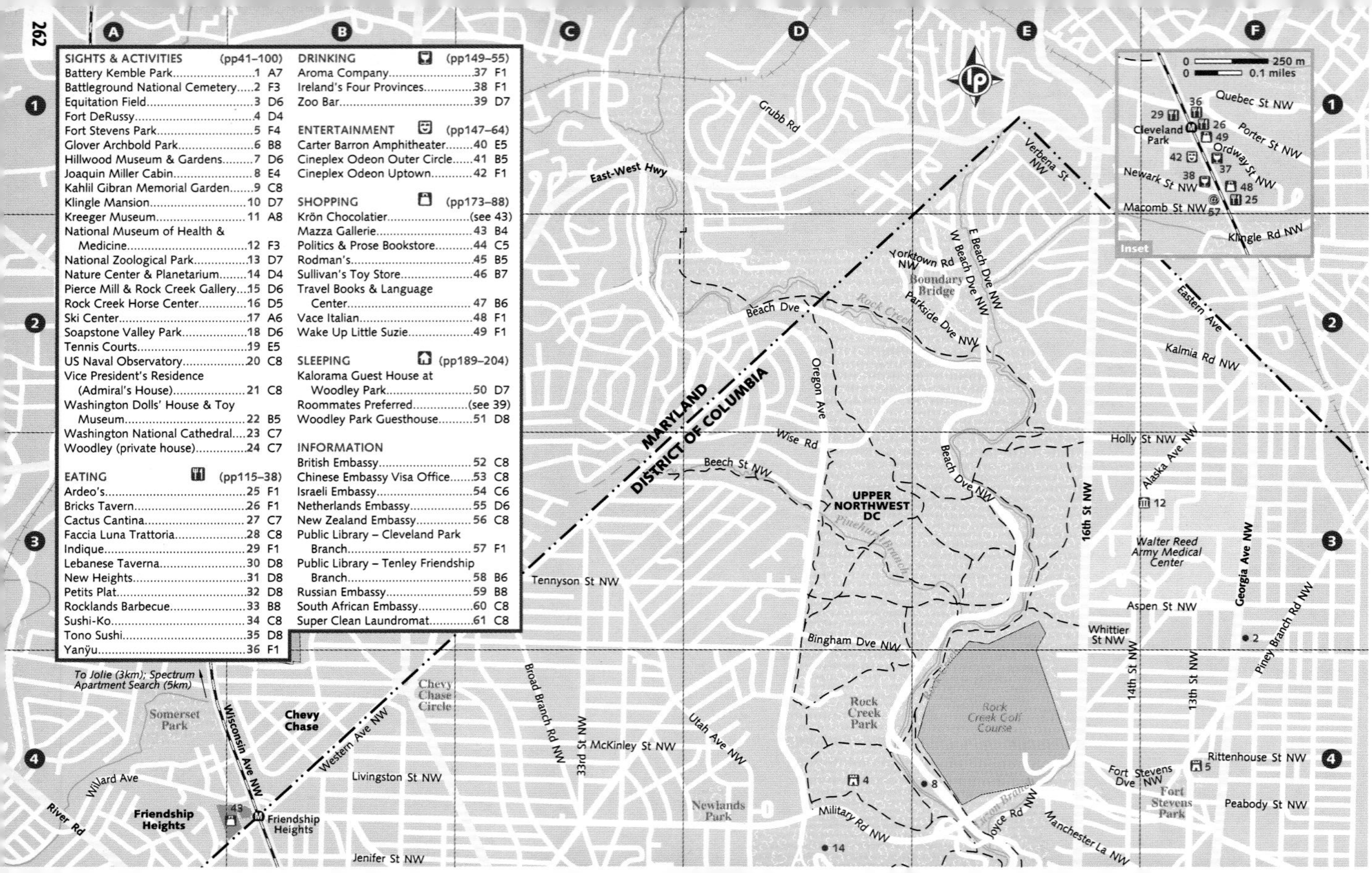

SIGHTS & ACTIVITIES (pp41–100)
Battery Kemble Park.....................1 A7
Battleground National Cemetery....2 F3
Equitation Field..............................3 D6
Fort DeRussy.................................4 D4
Fort Stevens Park...........................5 F4
Glover Archbold Park......................6 B8
Hillwood Museum & Gardens..........7 D6
Joaquin Miller Cabin.......................8 E4
Kahlil Gibran Memorial Garden.......9 C8
Kingle Mansion.............................10 D7
Kreeger Museum...........................11 A8
National Museum of Health &
    Medicine.................................12 F3
National Zoological Park................13 D7
Nature Center & Planetarium.........14 D4
Pierce Mill & Rock Creek Gallery....15 D6
Rock Creek Horse Center...............16 D5
Ski Center....................................17 A6
Soapstone Valley Park...................18 D6
Tennis Courts...............................19 E5
US Naval Observatory....................20 C8
Vice President's Residence
    (Admiral's House).....................21 C8
Washington Dolls' House & Toy
    Museum..................................22 B5
Washington National Cathedral......23 C7
Woodley (private house)................24 C7

EATING [icon] (pp115–38)
Ardeo's.......................................25 F1
Bricks Tavern...............................26 F1
Cactus Cantina.............................27 C7
Faccia Luna Trattoria....................28 C8
Indique..29 F1
Lebanese Taverna........................30 D8
New Heights.................................31 D8
Petits Plat....................................32 B8
Rocklands Barbecue.....................33 B8
Sushi-Ko......................................34 C8
Tono Sushi...................................35 D8
Yanyu...36 F1

DRINKING [icon] (pp149–55)
Aroma Company............................37 F1
Ireland's Four Provinces................38 F1
Zoo Bar..39 D7

ENTERTAINMENT [icon] (pp147–64)
Carter Barron Amphitheater...........40 E5
Cineplex Odeon Outer Circle.........41 B5
Cineplex Odeon Uptown................42 F1

SHOPPING [icon] (pp173–88)
Krön Chocolatier.......................(see 43)
Mazza Gallerie............................43 B4
Politics & Prose Bookstore............44 C5
Rodman's....................................45 B5
Sullivan's Toy Store......................46 B7
Travel Books & Language
    Center....................................47 B6
Vace Italian.................................48 F1
Wake Up Little Suzie....................49 F1

SLEEPING [icon] (pp189–204)
Kalorama Guest House at
    Woodley Park...........................50 D7
Roommates Preferred..............(see 39)
Woodley Park Guesthouse............51 D8

INFORMATION
British Embassy.............................52 C8
Chinese Embassy Visa Office.........53 C8
Israeli Embassy.............................54 C6
Netherlands Embassy....................55 D6
New Zealand Embassy...................56 C8
Public Library – Cleveland Park
    Branch....................................57 F1
Public Library – Tenley Friendship
    Branch....................................58 B6
Russian Embassy..........................59 B8
South African Embassy.................60 C8
Super Clean Laundromat..............61 C8

Inset labels:
Quebec St NW
Porter St NW
Ordway St NW
Newark St NW
Macomb St NW
Cleveland Park
Kingle Rd NW

Map area labels:
Rock Creek Golf Course
Rock Creek Park
Rock Creek Park
UPPER NORTHWEST DC
Walter Reed Army Medical Center
Fort Stevens Park
Georgia Ave NW
Piney Branch Rd NW
Eastern Ave
Kalmia Rd NW
Holly St NW
Alaska Ave NW
Aspen St NW
Whittier St NW
16th St NW
14th St NW
13th St NW
Manchester La NW
Rittenhouse St NW
Peabody St NW
Verbena St NW
E Beach Dve NW
W Beach Dve NW
Boundary Bridge
Parkside Dve NW
Yorktown Rd NW
Beach Dve NW
Beach Dve
Oregon Ave
Wise Rd
Bingham Dve NW
Joyce Rd NW
Military Rd NW
Grubb Rd
East–West Hwy
MARYLAND
DISTRICT OF COLUMBIA
Tennyson St NW
Broad Branch Rd NW
33rd St NW
McKinley St NW
Utah Ave NW
Newlands Park
Chevy Chase Circle
Livingston St NW
Jenifer St NW
Western Ave NW
Chevy Chase
Friendship Heights
Wisconsin Ave NW
Somerset Park
Friendship Heights
Willard Ave
River Rd
To Jolla (3km); Spectrum
Apartment Search (5km)

Scale:
250 m
0.1 miles

Kennedy St NW

New Hampshire Ave NW

⑤

⑥

Georgia Ave-
Pentworth

Princeton Pl NW

Kansas Ave NW

Kenyon St NW

Irving St NW

4th St NW

McMillan
Reservoir

Howard
University

6th St NW

⑧

See Shaw & the New U District Map (p249)

⑦

Georgia Ave NW

Sherman Ave NW

Girard St NW

Fairmont St NW

Euclid St NW

Bannaker
Recreation
Center

10th St NW

11th St NW

Spring Rd NW

Columbia
Heights

14th St NW

Clifton St NW

9th St NW

Georgia Ave NW

8th St NW

7th St NW

U Street-Cardozo

19 ●

Morrow Dve
NW

⑥

Arkansas Ave NW

14th St NW

13th St NW

17th St NW

Meridan
Pl NW

Hiatt Pl
NW

16th St NW

15th St NW

Fuller St NW

U St NW

40 🅿

Colorado Ave NW

Blagden Ave NW

Piney Branch Pkwy NW

Monroe St NW

Mount Pleasant St NW

Meridian
Hill Park

V St NW

Piney
Creek
Park

Monroe St NW

Park Rd NW

Lamont St NW

Kilbourne
Pl NW

Hobart St NW

Lanier Pl NW

Adams Mill Rd NW

Quarry Rd NW

Columbia Rd NW

Meridian
Hill

See Adams-Morgan Map (p261)

3 ●

Clover Rd NW

Beach Dve NW

W Beach Dve NW

Rock Creek

Adams-
Morgan

Kalorama
Park

16 ●●

Grant Rd NW

Broad Branch

7 🏛

15 ●

10 ●

Olmsted Walk

13 🏛

Hawthorne St NW

Duke Ellington
Memorial
Bridge

30

35

Woodley
Park-
Zoo/Adams
Morgan

31 🏛

32

51

39 ●

50

Woodley
Park

McGill Tce

Woodland Dve NW

20th St NW

Ellington Bridge

Kalorama
Circle

Rock Creek Pkwy NW

Sangamore Branch

55

18 ●

Tilden St NW

Melvin C
Hazen Park

Cleveland
Park

Klingle Rd

24 ●

Cleveland Ave NW

Normanstone
Park

21 ●

9

52

60

56

Whitehaven St NW

29th St NW

28th St NW

27th St NW

Brandywine St NW

30th St NW

Linnean
Playground

Van Ness-
UDC

Upton St NW

Piney Branch Pkwy NW

See Inset

Rock Cr

Linnean Ave NW

Sonapstone Valley Park

University
of
DC

International
Pl NW

54 ●

Klingle Rd

Fulton St NW

Whitehaven Pkwy NW

53

Davenport St NW

32nd St NW

30th St NW

International
Dr NW

34th St NW

Cleveland
Park

Macomb St NW

Lowell St NW

Woodley Rd NW

Wisconsin Ave NW

Edmunds
St NW

US
Naval
Observatory

Observatory Cir

26 ●

34

37th St NW

28

61

33

Connecticut Ave NW

Rodman St NW

Quebec St NW

36th St NW

23 🏛

Davis
St NW

Nebraska Ave NW

36th St NW

38th St NW

Reno Rd
NW

44 🅿

Yuma St NW

Warren St NW

Wisconsin Ave NW

46 🅿

Newark St NW

27

39th St NW

Idaho Ave NW

Massachusetts Ave NW

Calvert St NW

59 🅿

Tunlaw Rd NW

Benton St NW

GEORGETOWN

Harrison St NW

Garrison St NW

Fort Dve
NW

Fort Reno
Park

38th St NW

41 🅿

58 🅿

47

Tenleytown-AU

Tenleytown

US Navy
Security
Station

Ward
Circle

American
University

US Navy
Security
Station

Massachusetts Ave NW

42nd St NW

43rd St NW

River Rd NW

45 🅿

22 🏛

Fessenden St NW

44th St NW

Wesley
Circle

Nebraska Ave NW

45th St NW

Cathedral Ave NW

42nd St NW

43rd St NW

Wesley
Heights
Park

Glover
Archbold
Park

6 ●

Whitehaven
Park

Wisconsin Ave NW

37th St NW

53

See Georgetown Map (p267-7)

Albemarle St NW

Fort Dve
NW

46th St NW

47th St NW

48th St NW

49th St NW

American
University

Tilden St NW

Upton St NW

17 ●

Rodman St NW

Loughboro Rd NW

Battery
Kemble
Park

Nebraska Ave NW

44th St NW

45th St NW

Garfield St NW

11 🏛

Foxhall

King Pl NW

48th St NW

49th St NW

W St NW

1 ●

⑤

⑥

⑦

⑧

263

0 —————— 400 m
0 —————— 0.2 miles

FOGGY BOTTOM

New York Ave NW

20th St NW   E St NW

Rawlins Park

C St NW

Constitution Ave NW

Vietnam Veterans Memorial

23rd St NW

Virginia Ave NW

US Navy Bureau of Medicine & Surgery

Independence Ave SW

W Basin Dr SW

Ohio Dr SW

Tidal Basin

Rochambeau Memorial Bridge

To Ritz-Carlton Pentagon City (0.3mi); Pentagon City (0.6mi); Doubletree Crystal City (1.2mi); Crystal City (1.3mi); Alexandria (6mi)

To Gravelly Point (1.6mi) & Ronald Reagan National Airport (2mi)

Pentagon

Potomac Parkway NW

Potomac River

Arlington Memorial Bridge

George Washington Memorial Parkway

Boundary Dr

Lady Bird Johnson Park

Washington Blvd

Army Navy Dr

Theodore Roosevelt Memorial

Theodore Roosevelt Island

To Francis Scott Key Bridge (0.4mi); Key Bridge Marriott (0.06mi)

Mount Vernon Trail

DISTRICT OF COLUMBIA
VIRGINIA

George Washington Memorial Parkway

Memorial Parkway

Jefferson Davis Hwy

Arlington Cemetery

Halsey Dr

York Dr

Marshall Dr

Macarthur Dr

Bradley Dr

Patton Dr

Pershing Dr

N Arlington Ridge Rd

N Kent St

N Lynn St

Rosslyn

N Key Blvd

N Fort Myer Dr

12th St N

N Nash St

N Meade St

Marshall Dr

Old & Weitzel Dr

L'Enfant Dr

Lincoln Dr

Schley Dr

Roosevelt Dr

Sherman Drive

Mc Clellan Dr

Eisenhower Dr

Arlington National Cemetery

Grant Dr

Clayton Dr

Jessup Dr

Southgate Rd

Washington Blvd

Fort Myer

N Quinn St

Clarendon Blvd

Wilson Blvd

16th St N

Arlington Blvd

Westmoreland Ave

Jackson Ave

Fort Myer

McNair Rd

Meigs Dr

Farrar Dr

Wilson Dr

Memorial Dr

McPherson Dr

Porter Dr

Sheridan Ave

Ord Dr

Gun Dr

Court House

N Rhodes St

N Rolfe St

N Troy St

N Courthouse Rd

Forrest Cir

Court House

N 18th St

N Adams St

Lee Hwy

N Edgewood St

N Fillmore St

N Garfield St

Clarendon

N Hudson St

Clarendon Blvd

N Barton St

N Cleveland St

N Danville St

N Daniel St

9th St N

N Pershing Dr

4th St N

N Bryan St

N Filmore St

N Wayne St

Arlington Blvd

To Ballston (1.5mi); Bureau of Citizenship & Immigration Service (1.5mi)

Washington Blvd

To Ski Chalet of Arlington (2mi)

Curtis Memorial Parkway

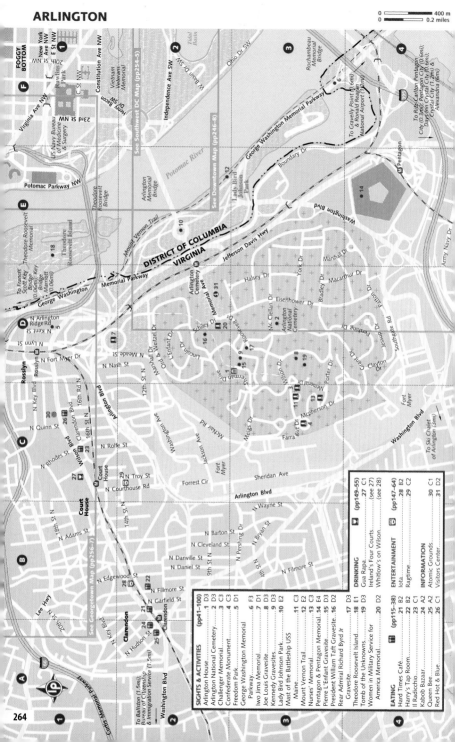